FLASH® MX 2004
at Your Fingertips

Get In, Get Out, Get Exactly What You Need

SHAM BHANGAL AND JEN DEHAAN

SYBEX®

San Francisco • London

Associate Publisher: Dan Brodnitz

Acquisitions Editor: Mariann Barsolo

Developmental Editor: Pete Gaughan

Production Editor: Dennis Fitzgerald

Technical Editors: Marlene Spector, Denise Tyler

Copyeditor: Sally Englefried

Compositor: Maureen Forys, Happenstance Type-O-Rama

Proofreaders: Laurie O'Connell, Amy Rasmussen, Nancy Riddiough

Indexer: Ted Laux

Book Designer: Franz Baumhackl

Cover Designer: Daniel Ziegler

Cover Illustrator/Photographer: Daniel Ziegler

Library of Congress Card Number: 2003115577

ISBN: 0-7821-4291-5

The artwork throughout the pages of this book was used with the permission of the following:

Anna Augul; anna@quikanddirty.com, www.quikanddirty.com

Stephen Bliss; www.stephenbliss.com

Jason Chesebrough; www.studiocmd.com

James Chew; www.chewman.net

Jonathan Clark; www.jonathan-clark.com/afterlife

Peter Lacalamita; www.magneticstudio.com

Peter O'Dwyer; www.sixsidia.com; www.zachgold.com

Adam Phillips; www.biteycastle.com

Ari Sideman; vhost.oddcast.com

Manufactured in the United States of America

10 9 8 7 6 5 4 3 2 1

Dear Reader,

Thank you for choosing *Flash MX 2004 at Your Fingertips*. This book is part of a new wave of Sybex graphics books, all written by outstanding authors—artists and teachers who really know their stuff and have a clear vision of the audience they're writing for. It's also part of our growing library of truly unique web and animation books.

Founded in 1976, Sybex is the oldest independent computer book publisher. More than twenty-five years later, we're committed to producing a full line of consistently exceptional graphics books. With each title, we're working hard to set a new standard for the industry. From the paper we print on, to the writers and photographers we work with, our goal is to bring you the best graphics books available.

I hope you see all that is reflected in these pages. I'd be very interested to hear your comments and get your feedback on how we're doing. To let us know what you think about this, or any other Sybex book, please visit us at www.sybex.com. Once there, go to the product page, click on Submit a Review, and fill out the questionnaire. Your input is greatly appreciated.

Please also visit www.sybex.com to learn more about the rest of our growing graphics line.

Best regards,

Dan Brodnitz
Associate Publisher
Sybex Inc.

To Mum and Dad: you always have the time, even when I don't.
—Sham Bhangal
To Rod Roddy for many years of colorful entertainment.
—Jen deHaan

Acknowledgments

Jen and Sham both send their thanks to:

- Mariann Barsolo, for putting up with our rambling phone conversations and moving ahead with our oh so vague book ideas.
- Pete Gaughan, for making this the book it is and for preventing Sham from overrunning on many of his sections (a favorite weakness of his!) and Jen's over-the-top attempts at humor (you're not so funny, deHaan).
- Dennis Fitzgerald, for being the calmest production guy going.
- Dan Brodnitz, for publishing this book.
- Denise Tyler and Marlene Spector, for reviewing it all.
- Sally Engelfried, for dealing with our tendency to become rather excitable when writing about Flash and fixing Sham's British and Jen's Canadian spelling.
- Maureen Forys, for converting all the cryptic design notes into a thing of beauty.

From Sham Bhangal

Thanks to everyone around me who has put up with the late hours and "I can't, I'm busy" messages over the course of this book, especially Karen, who has had to put up with not only this book, but the last 20 or so of them.

Also, thanks to Carole McClendon over at Waterside Productions for helping me to decide what is in my best interest (and stopping my worst habit: saying "yes" to everything and then doing it for nothing!)

Big thanks go out to the Flash MX 2004 beta gang, many of whom answered all the usual Sham Bhangal silly questions without flinching (they must be getting used to it). Special thanks to Bradley Kaldahl, Shane Rebenschied, Adam Bell, and Duncan McAlester for helping me track down and shooting a particularly reluctant panther…

From Jen deHaan

First and foremost, thanks to my brother Jason, who was the only one to talk to me at 3 A.M. I would like to thank all things made of caffeine. From Wake-Ups to Starbucks, you are all wonderful and are much appreciated assistance in whatever form you arrive in.

Mr. Nate Weiss is a friendly and attractive fellow, and I believe he also enjoys late-night beverages on the other side of the continent while writing ingenious books on similar topics. Nate was a great buddy on certain legendary e-mail lists, making them a much more interesting and entertaining.

I thank all the Macromedians who placated our ways with professionalism. Thanks Lucian, Nivesh, Gary, Brad, and Erik—I hope I served my duty well.

Thank you to agent Carole McClendon. And thanks to Jess, Nanny, Mom, Dad, and the cats for keeping things in perspective: it's only Flash. I'd like to thank anyone who can read and particularly those of you who purchase this book.

About the Authors

Sham Bhangal has been writing about New Media for years and has been involved in over 15 books including *New Masters of Flash* and *Foundation Flash*. He has considerable working experience with web motion graphics, 2D and 3D digital design, and HTML web design. He lives in West Yorkshire, England, with his partner Karen.

Jen deHaan is a Calgary-based Flash "deseloper" (designer/developer) who has been involved in 15 books (so far), primarily on Macromedia products, and is entering the wonderful world of video tutorials with VTC. While not developing, she pickles her liver in caffeinated beverages and teaches web design at the local university. deHaan skippers sites such as www.flash-mx.com and www.flashmx2004.com; you can find her personal portfolio and rants at www.ejepo.com; and she one day plans to begin and finish www.deseloper.com. She is the manager of the Calgary Flash Users Group and thus can promote things for other people's financial gain. She enjoys rainbows, unicorns, walks on the beach, and her iPod, and she hopes that one day a reader will buy her a G5.

Contents

CHAPTER 14 Working with Extensions and Commands 265

SCRIPTING

TASKS

273

CHAPTER 15 Working with Basic Scripts 275

CHAPTER 16 Working with Variables and Objects 293

CHAPTER 17 Code Structures 309

TESTING AND PUBLISHING TASKS

WHAT'S NEW

497

Introduction

Macromedia Flash started out as an application called SmartSketch. It was hoped this vector-based drawing program would result in a new, keyboard-free type of computer: the pen computer. Advances in computing followed a different direction, though. The earliest precursor of Flash to make waves was not SmartSketch but a vector animation system for the Web called FutureSplash.

In the mid 1990s, FutureSplash was being used by Disney to create animated features on the Web. This product came to the attention of Macromedia through Disney (because Disney was also using Macromedia Shockwave) and, in November 1996, a new product was born: Macromedia Flash 1.

Flash 2 soon followed with sound and nonvector images. Flash 3 was the first version that is recognizable as the Flash you see today: a timeline-based animation system backed up with a basic coding language that allows interactivity. Flash 3 had fewer than 15 code commands, but it was the start of what would become a fully fledged language in Flash 4 and 5: ActionScript.

Flash MX ("Flash 6") gave the Flash developer more options to create large applications based on Flash using a more structured version of Action-Script, plus it included components (prewired interface elements) that could quickly create compelling front ends for websites, software, or "rich Internet applications."

This trend continues in Flash MX 2004, and now Flash is essentially a two-tiered system. On the one hand, you have the ability to create interactive Web content that incorporates animation, video, and sound using minimal code. On the other end of the scale, Flash allows you to use ActionScript to produce interactive sites that act as front ends to server-based Web (or offline) applications.

In addition to the extreme flexibility of the Flash development platform for the developer, ubiquity has made Flash the number one multimedia content delivery system for the Web. Well over 95 percent of web users have a version of Flash Player installed, which means (unlike other web-multimedia delivery methods) those users will be able to view your site without having to download anything else.

If you want to present the user with a rich interactive web experience, you need to use Macromedia Flash.

Who Should Read This Book?

If you are reading this, you are probably standing in a bookstore or a library, surrounded by dozens of other books about Flash MX 2004 and trying to select the one that will best suit your needs. If you are looking for a complete resource for Flash, one that will help you learn new skills and improve existing ones, you have chosen the right book.

When you're faced with a particular job, would you like to be able to quickly find out how to accomplish just that task? Would you like to know the shortcuts and secrets that help you work faster and better in Flash? If you are a designer from a nonweb field who wants a book to guide you through learning Flash, then this is one you need.

This is also the book for you if you're a developer who knows Flash but requires a quick reference to find a particular and specific task quickly, or to polish up your knowledge of the new features in Flash MX 2004.

The concept behind writing *Flash MX 2004 at Your Fingertips* was to give Flash users a well-organized, comprehensive, and visual resource. Regardless of your skill level, this book provides immediate access to the program.

Beginning If you are new to Flash, use this book to get acquainted with the Flash interface and get step-by-step instructions in fundamental tasks so you can get right to work on your first few sites.

Intermediate After you master the basic Flash skills, you can use this book to discover shortcuts and more efficient ways of finishing routine tasks. You can use it as a springboard to specialize your skills for particular uses such as sound and video, advanced interactivity (games and user interfaces), and web applications.

Advanced Flash has undergone a lot of changes in the last few years and staying ahead of the curve is never easy. This book is a comprehensive reference manual, with thorough cross-referencing to help you find the detailed information you need to stay up-to-date and pick up a few tricks and tips.

How This Book Is Organized: A Task-Based Reference

When you're working in Flash, you're trying to *do* something. That's why *Flash MX 2004 at Your Fingertips* is organized around the many tasks you perform and breaks these down to explain the various ways to perform them.

Flash Workspace Chapters 1–6 introduce you to the Flash MX 2004 interface and detail all the different parts you will be using. Here is general information about menus, tools, panels, and preferences, with references to where in the book you can find more information on using them.

Authoring Tasks Chapters 7–14 provide the skills that every Flash user needs to master the core Flash content creation tools and techniques. From setting up the Stage to building your graphics and creating your animations, it's all here.

Scripting Tasks Chapters 15–25 deal with the specific issues involved in adding more advanced features to your content through the use of Action-Script. As well as allowing you to extend the features of your site with scripting, this section also gives you the fundamental information required to help you learn ActionScript and Flash MX 2004 components.

Testing and Publishing Tasks Chapters 26 and 27 teach you specific skills needed to properly test your content for correct operation and finally, how to deploy it to the Web.

What's New The last part of the book lays out the new features and functions in Flash MX 2004 and the changes from previous versions of the program and points you to the specific book section where you can read about each feature that's listed.

A Book for All Users

This book includes information about all of the most recent features in Flash MX 2004 and Flash MX 2004 Professional; where features or functions differ significantly in previous versions, we've noted that. In addition, you can use this book with any of the popular operating systems on which Flash is available:

Windows Flash runs on all versions of Windows 98 SE, Windows 2000 (Service Pack 3), and Windows XP, and it works the same in most versions, although the appearance of certain interface objects (such as the title bar) varies from version to version. Most Windows screenshots in this book were taken using the Windows XP theme and the Silver color scheme.

Mac OS X Flash runs in Mac OS X starting with version 10.2.6. If you are using version 10.2.6, it's recommended that you upgrade to version 10.3 (Panther), which offers a significant speed boost.

We've illustrated the book with screens from both Windows and Mac operating systems.

Remember to install the Flash MX 2004 updater for both editions of Flash, which fixes several bugs and issues from the original release. You need to install this updater only if you installed Flash in November 2003 or earlier; otherwise, the fixes are already included in your installation. The updater is available as a free download from

```
http://www.macromedia.com/support/flash/
downloads.html
```

Do *not* uninstall Flash prior to installing the updater; the updater installs over the top of the program.

Flash MX 2004 at Your Fingertips also supplies keyboard shortcuts using both operating systems' conventions. In the margins, you'll see both the Windows and Macintosh versions on separate lines, in that order. In text, we've run them together a bit but still provide you with both: Command+Option/ Ctrl+Alt means the Command and Option keys on a Mac, the Ctrl and Alt keys in Windows.

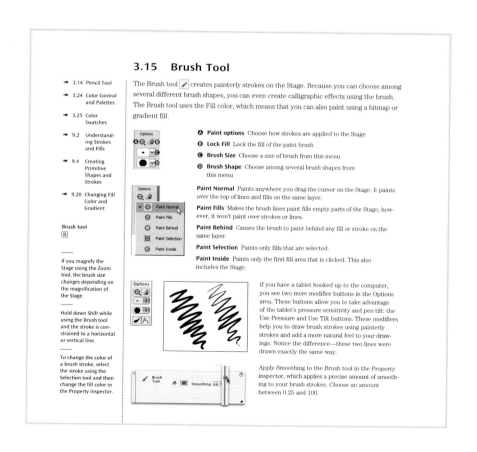

3.15   Brush Tool

→ 3.14 Pencil Tool

→ 3.24 Color Control and Palettes

→ 3.25 Color Swatches

→ 9.2 Understanding Strokes and Fills

→ 9.4 Creating Primitive Shapes and Strokes

→ 9.20 Changing Fill Color and Gradient

Brush tool
B

If you magnify the Stage using the Zoom tool, the brush size changes depending on the magnification of the Stage.

Hold down Shift while using the Brush tool and the stroke is constrained to a horizontal or vertical line.

To change the color of a brush stroke, select the stroke using the Selection tool and then change the fill color in the Property inspector.

The Brush tool creates painterly strokes on the Stage. Because you can choose among several different brush shapes, you can even create calligraphic effects using the brush. The Brush tool uses the Fill color, which means that you can also paint using a bitmap or gradient fill.

A Paint options Choose how strokes are applied to the Stage

B Lock Fill Lock the fill of the paint brush

C Brush Size Choose a size of brush from this menu

D Brush Shape Choose among several brush shapes from this menu

Paint Normal Paints anywhere you drag the cursor on the Stage. It paints over the top of lines and fills on the same layer.

Paint Fills Makes the brush lines paint fills empty parts of the Stage; however, it won't paint over strokes or lines.

Paint Behind Causes the brush to paint behind any fill or stroke on the same layer.

Paint Selection Paints only fills that are selected.

Paint Inside Paints only the first fill area that is clicked. This also includes the Stage.

If you have a tablet hooked up to the computer, you see two more modifier buttons in the Options area. These buttons allow you to take advantage of the tablet's pressure sensitivity and pen tilt: the Use Pressure and Use Tilt buttons. These modifiers help you to draw brush strokes using painterly strokes and add a more natural feel to your drawings. Notice the difference—these two lines were drawn exactly the same way.

Apply Smoothing to the Brush tool in the Property inspector, which applies a precise amount of smoothing to your brush strokes. Choose an amount between 0.25 and 100.

Using This Book

Each section in this book is organized around the idea of letting you quickly scan the information to see if a page has what you need or sending you to another section in the book to look for related information. Rather than burying cross-references and keyboard shortcuts in the text, we placed these in their own column, along with general tips and warnings relevant to the topic at hand.

In addition, this book makes extensive use of lettered "callout" labels on the figures to help you identify the various parts of the Flash MX 2004 interface and how they work. These are generally integrated with step-by-step instructions or bulleted lists, which refer to particular dialogs or palettes, with the callouts explaining how to set the various options.

Numbered section head Each new section in a chapter starts at the top of a page and is numbered for quick reference.

Quick cross-references Each topic points you to other sections that relate to the subject or offer alternative or more detailed information.

Keyboard shortcuts Keyboard commands relevant to the section's subject are provided.

Tips Additional notes and warnings about the task or tool presented in the section are included.

Callouts Hundreds of images in the book provide detailed labeling to eliminate the guesswork of figuring out how the Flash interface works.

Sidebars You'll find additional information that can be applied to the tasks presented in the chapter.

Flash MX 2004 at Your Fingertips on the Web

Sybex strives to keep you supplied with the latest tools and information you need for your work. Please check our website at www.sybex.com for additional content and updates that supplement this book. Enter the book's ISBN—4291—in the Search box (or type **flash** and **fingertips**) and click Go to get to the book's update page.

Sham and Jen are always happy to answer any questions that you have about the content included in this book. E-mail them with your questions at:

Sham Bhangal
sham@futuremedia.org.uk
www.futuremedia.org.uk

Jen deHaan
fingertips@flash-mx.com
www.ejepo.com

Additionally, you can bring all of your Flash questions to Jen's Flash MX 2004 forums at www.flashmx2004.com/forums. There's even a special forum set up for this book.

FLASH WORKSPACE

CHAPTER 1

Interface Overview

WHEN YOU OPEN FLASH for the first time, you will most likely see a central white drawing area ("the Stage") surrounded by all sorts of panels and buttons. It may seem a little daunting, but Flash has only four main areas: the Stage, Timeline, toolbars, and panels.

Flash is available in Windows and Macintosh flavors. The only real major difference between these is that Windows supports dockable panels; otherwise, getting to know Flash in Windows is the same as getting to know it on the Macintosh.

In this chapter, we introduce the main areas of the Flash interface, looking at how the interface works in general.

1.1 Overview: Creating Flash Animation

Although there are different ways of making your "consecutive Stage views" look different (you can either use Timeline animation or move things around between frames using ActionScript, Flash's coding language), the principle remains the same: a playhead that moves quickly through a succession of frames, each associated with a slightly different Stage. When viewed over time, this process causes animation.

For those coming to Flash from an HTML or Photoshop background, the Flash interface can seem a little alien. The reason for this is that web design and Photoshop have a *print-based* mindset. Flash follows a very different *animation-based* mindset. Let's see how the interface works to create animation.

Start Flash and select the default user interface (Window > Panel Sets > Default Layout). In the middle of the screen is the Stage. This is currently a blank white rectangle; an empty Stage. The content that you add here is what the user sees when you put your Flash site onto the Web. At the top of the screen is the *Timeline*.

Think of the Timeline as a *film reel*, each rectangle corresponding to one frame in your movie. Above frame 1 is a pink rectangle, the *playhead*. The playhead always sits above the current frame, and during movie playback, it will move forward through the Timeline, left to right.

So how does that cause animation? Well, for each frame in the Timeline, you will have a different corresponding Stage view as the animated content moves slightly per frame. Assume your Stage looks as shown in the top image for frames 1–10; as the playhead moves between these frames, the dot will appear to move from left to right, causing animation, as seen in the bottom image.

1.2 Overview: Testing Flash Content

When you create your animations in the Flash authoring environment, you are creating the *source* file, the FLA. The file that the user will see is a compiled version of the FLA, the SWF file. The compiled SWF content can only be viewed via the Flash Player and *not* in the authoring environment. To compile and view the final compiled SWF content, you need to move from the authoring environment into the *test environment* window (Ctrl-/⌘-Enter).

At the bottom of the Test window is the Stage area. At the top is a graph, the Bandwidth Profiler, which tells you something about how big (in file size) your animation will be, how long it will take to load into the user's browser, and whether it will play over the Web as intended. To the right you will (by default) see the Projects panel if you are using Flash MX Professional 2004.

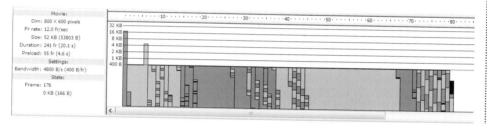

Here is a bandwidth profile for an 80+ frame animation. The frame number is listed along the top, and the bar graph shows the bandwidth each frame needs to play on time. As you can see, frame 1 requires about 16K to be loaded within one frame (about ¹⁄₁₂ of a second, assuming the default frame rate) to play on time. A 56K modem would give you (worst case) around 400 bytes a second, and anything above the 400 B line on the profiler would result in the frame content not loading in time, causing a pause.

You can see this happening in real time if you press Ctrl-/⌘-Enter a second time. The movie will start again, this time simulating what would happen on the Web. A green band appears signifying the number of frames that has loaded into the browser, and the pointer (shown at frame 21) shows the position of the playhead. As long as the next frame is always loaded (i.e., painted green) before the playhead gets to it, the Flash movie will play without any delays caused by low bandwidth. This process of starting to play a timeline before it is fully loaded is called *streaming content*. The opposite process (waiting until everything is loaded before starting) is called *preloading content*.

➡ 26.1 Using the Test Environment

➡ 26.4 Using the Debugger Panel

Test Movie
⌘ Enter

⌘ Enter

———

When testing your Flash productions, you should *always* test content destined for the Web via the browser every so often: Although the Flash test environment is good, it cannot model all the quirks of the browser, which is what all users will be using to view your Flash web content.

———

When you use the test environment, a Shockwave for Flash (.swf) and (if your Flash also contains ActionScript) a Shockwave diagnostic (.swd) file are created. The SWF is a compiled and compressed version of the FLA file and is what the browser needs to display your Flash content. The SWD file contains diagnostic information created by the test environment. It is kept separate from the SWF file for security reasons (the SWD is used to debug ActionScript and contains a full uncompiled listing of your code, so it could be used to steal your scripts and uncover any security measures you are using). In most cases, you can delete the SWD after testing.

1.3   Overview: Publishing Flash Content

➡ 27   Publishing
        and Deploy-
        ing Flash
        Content

Publish
[Ctrl] [F12]
[Shift] [F12]

———

When uploading con-
tent to the server, you
need to upload the
HTML and SWF files,
and not the FLA. If you
see an unexpected
empty white stage
when you view the
HTML file, it is usually
because the browser
is not finding the SWF
file; make sure you
have uploaded the cor-
rect file and put it in
the correct place.

———

FTP functions are built-
in to Internet Explorer
6.x and higher, and it
seems to be one of the
easiest options for
uploading Flash con-
tent to your server.

Once you have a working animation together, you need to deploy it onto the Web. For this
you need an HTML file (.html) and a Shockwave for Flash file (.swf). Although some
browsers can view the Flash SWF file directly, for maximum compatibility, you will usually use an HTML file that references the SWF file. To create these two files you need to
select File > Publish Settings.

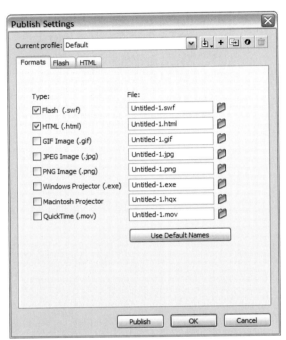

The Formats tab allows you to select the output formats. Usually, you only need to select
the first two, Flash (SWF) and HTML. Clicking the Publish button (top-right corner)
creates the HTML and SWF files. To see the final Flash presentation in a browser, select
File > Publish Preview > Default (HTML) or File > Publish Preview > HTML.

To actually deploy your content onto the Web, the easiest option is to use a modern browser
with built-in FTP (file transfer protocol) abilities, and this includes current versions of Internet Explorer. Simply enter the name of your FTP (e.g., ftp://myUserID@mydomain.com/)
as the web address and drag and drop the HTML and SWF files into the browser window
to upload.

1.4   Windows Authoring Interface

The Windows interface incorporates a system of dockable panels, something that is not available on the Macintosh.

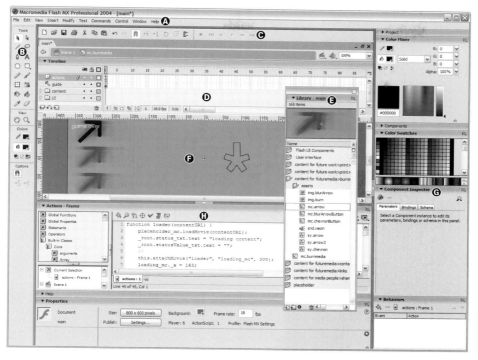

➡ 1.6 Working with Panels (Windows)

Although the recommended minimum screen resolution is 1024×768, most designers use something considerably higher; 1280×1024 is a realistic minimum for the purposes of efficiency. Flash was initially designed as an operating system for a pen- or tablet-based computer, and it does seem to work best when combined with a pen or tablet, particularly when using the drawing tools.

The toolbars do not appear by default, but they are extremely useful. To make them appear, select Window > Toolbars and check Main, Status, and Controller in the submenu that appears.

ⓐ Menu bar Click any of the menu headings to open the corresponding drop-down menus.

ⓑ Tools panel Click these icons to select tools and tool options. The tools are used to create vector-based graphics and text. Flash can also handle bitmaps, but these have to be imported into the environment; they cannot be created within Flash.

ⓒ Toolbars Provide a quick way of accessing common functions. Although the toolbars do not appear in the default configuration, you are strongly recommended to have them showing.

ⓓ Timeline Used to create sequences of animation frames, or to attach frame-based scripts.

ⓔ Library panel One of the most used panels. Used to organize and store assets, including Flash graphic symbols, video, sound, and bitmaps.

ⓕ Stage The viewable area of the final Flash movie. Assets are also created on the Stage before being moved to the Library panel (E).

ⓖ Side docked panel area The default area that most panels will first appear.

ⓗ Lower docked panel area The default area that the Actions and Help panels and the Property inspector will appear.

1.5   Windows Test Interface

**Simulate download
(toggle)**
[Ctrl] [Enter]
[⌘] [Enter]

**Test movie (from
authoring enviroment)**
[Ctrl] [Enter]
[⌘] [Enter]

**Toggle bandwidth
profiler**
[Ctrl] [B]

Toggle Output window
[F2]

**Toggle Debugger
window**
[Shift] [F4]

Exit test mode
[Ctrl] [F4]
[⌘] [F4]

To make the toolbars
appear, select Win-
dow > Toolbars and
check Main, Status, and
Controller in the sub-
menu that appears.

Although somewhat hidden when you first start Flash, the test environment is integral to the Flash production workflow. It is used to run Flash content via the Flash Player and to investigate the bandwidth profile of the movie under test. It is also used via the debugger and output windows to test ActionScript.

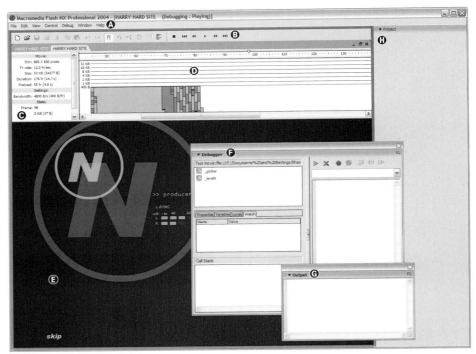

Ⓐ Menu bar Click any of the menu headings to open the corresponding drop-down menus.

Ⓑ Toolbars Provide a quick way of accessing common functions. Although the toolbars do not appear in the default configuration, you are strongly recommended to have them showing.

Ⓒ Bandwidth Profiler; info Provides basic information regarding the movie under test.

Ⓓ Bandwidth Profiler; graph Provides per-frame bandwidth information for the movie under test.

Ⓔ Stage The viewable area of the final Flash movie. The Stage will be shown rendered and animated in real time via the Flash Player.

Ⓕ Debugger Debugs scripts via a number of features, including the ability to watch or change variables in real time, as well as code breakpoints.

Ⓖ Output window Allows scripts to output information to the test environment via the Action-Script `trace()` action. Trace actions are usually (by default) ignored outside the test environment (i.e., when you deploy the Flash presentation online, view it on a browser or via the standalone Flash Player). In the test environment, the output window will appear whenever a trace action is encountered.

Ⓗ Docking area The Projects panel will appear to the right of the test environment for Flash MX 2004 Professional.

1.6   Working with Panels (Windows)

Flash for Windows uses a system of dockable panels. Although they look different, they all have the same basic features.

Ⓐ Drag this icon to dock or undock the panel to the sides, top, or bottom of the screen or to another panel.

Ⓑ Click the arrow icon or title text to toggle maximized or minimized views of the panel.

Ⓒ Drag this bar to move the panel without docking.

Ⓓ Click this button to close the panel. (To close a docked panel, click the panel menu icon and select Close Panel.)

Ⓔ Click this icon to access the panel menu.

➠ 5   Panels

Toggle all panels on/off
`Tab`

———

You can also minimize, maximize, or close a panel by right-clicking the panel title area and selecting from the contextual menu. This menu also allows you to select Help on the current panel.

———

You can open and close all panels via the Window menu.

Docked, maximized

Docked, minimized

Undocked, minimized

Continues

FLASH WORKSPACE

AUTHORING TASKS

SCRIPTING TASKS

TESTING AND PUBLISHING TASKS

WHAT'S NEW

1.6 Working with Panels (Windows) *(continued)*

➡ 2.11 Window
      Menu

Note that the Timeline
and toolbar are also
panels, although there
is usually little reason to
dock them away from
their default positions.
A useful trick is to tem-
porarily minimize the
Timeline panel when
you are using the Stage,
thus giving you a bigger
view of the Stage.

Most panels will remem-
ber where they were
last closed and reappear
in the same position if
you reopen them.

Although you can dock
to any of the four edges
of the screen, there is
usually no reason to
dock panels far from
their default positions.

To undock a panel, click-drag the knurled area on its title bar ⦙⦙ and drop it outside the
docking area. To redock it, simply do the reverse.

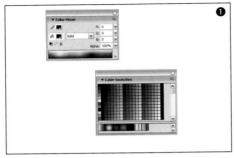
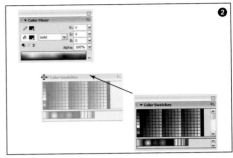
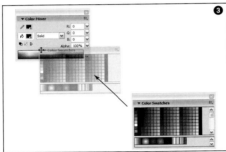
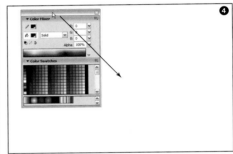

In addition to docking panels to the sides of the screen, you can also dock panels into floating
groups. Click-drag a panel by the knurled area (1) until it is over the panel you want to dock to
(2, 3). The target panel will also inherit a bold outline when this happens. Release, and the dropped
panel will dock onto the target panel. You can move the panel group by using the window's drag bar
at the top of the groups (4).

INTERFACE DIFFERENCES BETWEEN "STANDARD" AND PROFESSIONAL

The following differences are apparent between the interfaces of the two versions of
Flash: Flash MX Professional 2004 contains a full-screen ActionScript editor, a slide-
based editing environment, and the Projects panel. It also contains more file options in
the File > New (and Start panel) options and more default components in the
Components panel (not all of which work with Flash MX 2004).

1.7   Mac OS X Authoring Interface

The OS X authoring interface does not support the docking system used by Windows versions, but it is otherwise identical, and all the major interface areas (Tools panel, menus, Timeline, Stage) are in the same relative positions as the PC version.

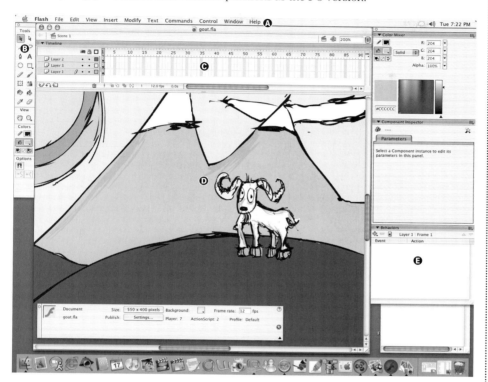

➡ 1.9   Working with Panels (Mac)

Although the recommended minimum screen resolution is 1024×768, most designers use something considerably higher; 1280×1024 is a realistic minimum for the purposes of efficiency. Flash was initially designed as an operating system for a pen- or tablet-based computer, and it does seem to work best when combined with a pen or tablet, particularly when using the drawing tools.

The toolbars do not appear by default, but they are extremely useful. To make them appear, select Window > Toolbars and check Main, Status, and Controller in the submenu that appears. They are not shown in the image, which is the default appearance.

ⓐ Menu bar Click any of the menu headings to open the corresponding drop-down menus.

ⓑ Tools panel Click these icons to select tools and tool options. The tools are used to create vector-based graphics and text. Flash can also handle bitmaps, but these have to be imported into the environment; they cannot be created within Flash.

ⓒ Timeline Used to create sequences of animation frames or to attach frame-based scripts.

ⓓ Stage The viewable area of the final Flash movie. Assets are also created on the Stage, before being moved to the Library panel (E).

ⓔ Panels Mac panels are always floating and undocked given that there is no docking system in the Mac version.

1.8   Mac OS X Test Interface

**Simulate download
(toggle)**
⌘ Enter

**Test movie
(from authoring
environment)**
⌘ Enter

**Toggle Bandwidth
Profiler**
⌘ B

Toggle Output window
F2

**Toggle Debugger
window**
Shift F4

Exit test mode
⌘ F4

To make the toolbars
appear, select Win-
dow > Toolbars and
check Main, Status, and
Controller in the sub-
menu that appears.

The Mac test environment is substantially the same as the Windows-based version but
without docking panels. The interface is again substantially the same, with all major portions in the same place.

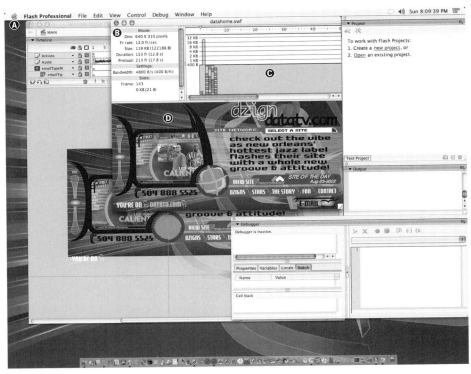

Ⓐ Menu bar Click any of the menu headings to open the corresponding drop-down menus.

Ⓑ Bandwidth Profiler; info Provides basic information regarding the movie under test.

Ⓒ Bandwidth Profiler; graph Provides per-frame bandwidth information for the movie under test.

Ⓓ Stage The viewable area of the final Flash movie. The Stage will be shown rendered and animated
in real time via the Flash Player.

1.9   Working with Panels (Mac)

Mac panels are much simpler than their Windows-based cousins: they don't have the docking features, although you can maximize or minimize them. To maximize or minimize the panel, click the panel's top bar.

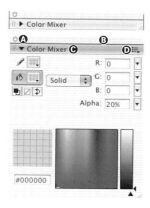

A Click the title to close the panel.

B Drag this bar to move the panel.

C Click the arrow icon or title text to toggle minimized (top) or maximized (bottom) views of the panel.

D Click this icon to access the panel menu.

➠ 5   Panels

➠ 2.9   Window Menu

Toggle all panels on or off

[Tab]

―――

You can also minimize, maximize, or close a panel by ⌘-clicking the panel title area and selecting from the contextual menu. This menu also allows you to select Help on the current panel.

―――

You can open and close all panels via the Window menu.

―――

Note that the Timeline and toolbar are also panels, although there is usually little reason to dock them away from their default positions. A useful trick is to temporarily minimize the Timeline panel when you are using the Stage, thus allowing you a bigger view of the Stage.

―――

Most panels will remember where they were last closed and reappear in the same position if you reopen them.

FLASH WORKSPACE

AUTHORING TASKS

SCRIPTING TASKS

TESTING AND PUBLISHING TASKS

WHAT'S NEW

1.10   Interface Objects

➡ 3.3   Controller
        Toolbar

The menu icon will disappear when you minimize a panel because the panel is will be deemed to be inactive.

The Minimum/Maximum feature (which switches between two levels of information detail or window views) should not be confused with Maximized and Minimized panels (which totally open and close the panel).

In many cases, sliders limit the maximum and minimum values you can manually enter. Their values are *not* always the absolute ranges; you can usually go further if you make the same changes through ActionScript, allowing you to *overdrive* a value for some interesting effects. This occurs particularly for the Sound and Color objects, where you can create phase reversed or distorted sound (through volume overdrive or underdrive) and create some cool color filtering effects (through overdriven color transitions).

Flash has common controls that are spread across the interface. These each work in a standard way, so if you understand how an instance of one works, you will probably understand it the next time you see the same thing for a different control. It works both ways however, because some controls are a little subtle, and if you miss them the first time, you will probably always miss them. It's a good thing there are reference books!

Text labels next to a text field, check box, or other input device can be clicked to activate the input area. For example, clicking the text here will toggle the check box in the same way clicking the check box directly would. This is useful for those with high resolution screens, or if you use laptops with those inaccurate and small mouse touchpad areas—accuracy is no longer a problem!

Tooltips are little bits of help text that show up if you hover over a control or button long enough. When you do, a yellow text rectangle will appear. If you don't see tooltips, select Edit > Preferences > General tab and check Show Tooltips.

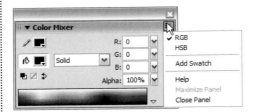

Panel menu icon For standard panels, the menu icon is 🗾. The menu is accessed through a different icon on the Timeline 🗂.

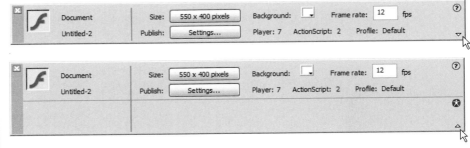

Some panels have an arrow icon at the bottom right, which makes the panel show its maximum or minimum information or resizes between a minimum open (with scrollbars) and maximum open (no scrollbars required—panel opens to show all content) size. It is particularly used on the Property inspector, the Color Mixer, and the Components panel.

1.10 Interface Objects *(continued)*

Nonstandard User Interface Elements

As with most applications, Flash uses many standard user interface elements, including check boxes, radio and standard buttons, text input fields, and drop-down menus. Assuming all Flash designers are familiar with common interface elements, this section lists the nonstandard ones, or those that sometimes appear with a nonstandard appearance.

Slider or "value spinner" Where a slider is next to a value, the value will update as you move the slider up or down the scale. Where the value controls something else (such as the thickness of a line), the "something else" will not update until the slider closes. You can also type a value directly into the value field and bypass the slider altogether (this is useful for entering exact values).

Tree Flash content is internally structured in a hierarchy rather like the file structure of your hard drive (which contains folders within folders and paths such as `c:/myFolder/myfile`). Rather than folders, Flash uses *timelines* to form its hierarchy, and instead of files, you have content on the Timeline. Whenever Flash needs to show you this structure, it uses a hierarchical tree with collapsible branches. To open a branch, click the + at the bottom of a branch, and to close it, click the –.

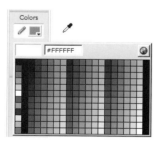

Color picker The Tools panel, Property inspector, and Color Mixer panel make extensive use of color pickers. You will know when a color picker is available when you see a little down-arrow at the bottom right of a color. Clicking such a color will cause the Color Mixer to appear and the cursor to change into the Eyedropper tool. By default, the swatch that appears will consist of the web-safe palette. You can also select a color by entering its HTML hexadecimal number (# followed by a six-digit hexadecimal number) or by using the eyedropper to select a color (either from the swatch or by clicking any pixel within the Flash application window). Clicking the icon at the top-right of the color picker ⊙ allows you to use the operating system color window instead.

The tree is also used for other things, such as to hide detailed information until you elect to see it by opening a particular tree branch. You do this in the Keyboard Shortcuts window (Edit > Keyboard Shortcuts) and when viewing certain types of object in the debugger (such as arrays).

You cannot select a gradient with the color picker from the Stage (although you can from the color picker swatch); it will always return the value of the pixel currently under the eyedropper tip when you are using color picker's eyedropper on the Stage. To select a gradient from the Stage as your color, you must use the Eyedropper tool on the Tools panel.

Continues ●

AUTHORING TASKS

SCRIPTING TASKS

TESTING AND PUBLISHING TASKS

WHAT'S NEW

Unlike Adobe Photoshop, Flash doesn't allow you to zoom in or out with the color picker open to select the target color pixel accurately. In Flash, you must make sure you have zoomed into the target pixel (if you will be using the eyedropper on a Stage pixel) *before* you open the color picker.

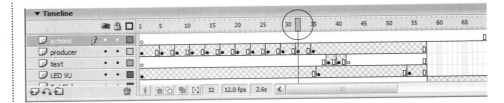

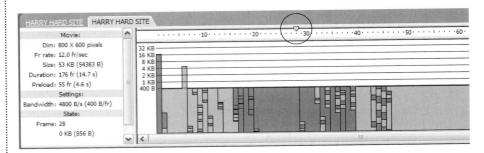

Playheads are used only on multimedia applications, including video editing and animation applications, and they always point to the current frame being played or edited. The playhead appears in two forms, depending whether you are in the authoring (top) or test environment (bottom). In both cases, the playhead runs along a numbered track as the movie progresses (the numbers being the frame numbers). To move to a specific frame, click the number track. You can also drag the playhead by click-dragging it to a new frame.

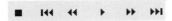

Controller You can use the video controls provided by the Controller toolbar (make it appear via Window > Toolbars Controller if you don't see it). This allows you to make more complex changes to the playhead position.

MOVING BETWEEN THE AUTHORING AND EDITING ENVIRONMENT

You do not have to close the test environment to get back to the authoring environment because both exist in separate windows. You can instead minimize or reduce the size of the test environment window and leave it running. Many professional designers use a dual display and have the two separate windows on separate screens, which is especially useful when debugging.

CHAPTER 2

Menus

MENUS ARE USED IN FLASH for a variety of actions, although in many cases you can also perform the same action more efficiently via a panel; where this occurs, this chapter will provide appropriate cross indexing. Flash also has two sets of menus: one for the authoring environment and another for the test environment. This chapter will look closely at all the menus available.

2.1 Menu Overview

Enter test mode
`Ctrl` `Enter`

Enter authoring mode
`Ctrl` `F4`

Some menus and menu items appear in both the authoring and test environments but are only relevant to the former. Where this occurs, the text in this book points it out.

Menus are context sensitive, so if an option is not relevant to the current situation, it will appear grayed out.

The menus also include the keyboard shortcuts for many options. Using the menus is a good way of learning the shortcuts!

As with many other applications, you can use the menus without a mouse by pressing Alt followed by the underlined letter for your option. For example, you can select File > New by typing Alt+F+N. The F will open the File menu, and the N will select New.

Flash has 10 menus when you are in the authoring environment (the environment you are in when you start Flash) and 7 in the test environment. Flash menu options and functions can be grouped into the following types:

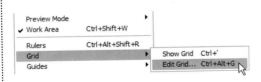

Submenu A menu option with an arrow at the end of it will open a submenu consisting of additional and related options that you can select.

Command A menu item may be an instruction for the Flash environment to do something immediately, that is, a command.

Dialog A menu item with an ellipsis opens up a pop-up dialog window.

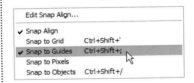

On/Off Toggle Some menu items allow you to turn a feature on or off. The state of the feature is signified by the appearance of a check next to the option. Note that you can usually have more than one adjacent checkbox checked. This is in contrast to 'mutually exclusive options' as noted below.

Mutually Exclusive Options The View menu has a cluster of options that are mutually exclusive, in that you can only select one of them at a time. It is *very* easy to mistake this group for On/Off toggles (many people do, and wonder why reselecting doesn't toggle the options!). The secret is to look at the marker; it's a dot, not a check.

Be careful, because the View > Download Settings submenu (and a few other places in the test environment) has a similar set of mutually exclusive options that use checks rather than the dot...so it's easy to get confused! You can tell if a check is part of a mutually exclusive group, because selecting it twice will *not* toggle it.

The menu bars for the different operating systems have the same general appearance, although the chrome (areas of the interface) may have differing cosmetic appearances. The menus for the authoring (left) and test (right) environments are shown here.

2.2   File Menu

The File menu allows you to handle all content that is used or created by the Flash environment. It contains all options for starting a new FLA file or opening an existing one. It also contains all the options for importing and exporting assets, as well as setting up publishing settings and printing.

➡ 7.1   Starting a
        New Movie

➡ 27.1 Understanding
        the Files Cre-
        ated by Flash

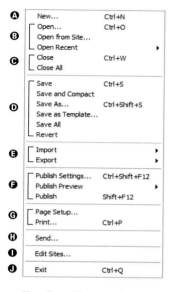

Ⓐ Opens the New Document window, allowing you to select from all the general document types and document templates available. The options available will be different for Flash and Flash Professional. In particular, Flash 2004 has only one general document type (Flash Document), and Flash Professional has several.

Ⓑ Open options allow you to open a file (from top to bottom) either by using the standard file browser window, from your list of defined sites, or from a list of the ten most recently opened files.

Ⓒ The Close options allow you to either close the currently open file or close all currently open files. Flash will prompt you if you try to close any file that contains unsaved changes.

Ⓓ The Save option saves the current file. Save And Compact does the same thing but clears out any unused data still in the file (usually things you have deleted since the last Save And Compact). Save As Template makes your current file appear when the New option is selected for future new files. Save All saves all currently opened files. Flash may prompt you to enter a name for any file you have not yet saved at least once. Revert allows you to go back to the last saved version of the current file.

Ⓔ Allows you to import/export assets to/from the current file. These options may be different or partially present for certain Flash file types that do not support the full range of Flash assets (such as ActionScript files, which don't support *any* assets because they don't contain a library).

Ⓕ Allows you to set publishing options, preview the published movie in one of a number of formats, or publish the movie without preview. The latter two options will create Flash output files (such as SWFs) in the same folder as the original source file (such as the FLA).

Ⓖ Page Setup allows you to set up page options for printing; Print allows you to select/set up the printer and print the current Stage.

Ⓗ Opens a new blank e-mail using your default e-mail application and attaches the current source file (such as a FLA) to it.

Ⓘ Opens the Edit Sites window, allowing you to edit and manage the files associated with a full site.

Ⓙ Closes Flash. If you have any open files with unsaved edits, Flash will prompt you to save before closing.

New
[Ctrl] [N]
[⌘] [N]

Open
[Ctrl] [O]

Close Window
[Ctrl] [W]

Save
[Ctrl] [S]

Save And Compact
[Ctrl] [Shift] [S]

Publish settings
[Ctrl] [Shift] [F12]

Publish
[Shift] [F12]

Print
[Ctrl] [P]

Exit
[Ctrl] [Q]

Be wary of using Save if you are editing files from previous versions of Flash because the files will no longer be editable by legacy versions of the Flash editing environment (the file format of legacy files will be updated to the latest version during the save, and some versions of the Flash environment (such as Flash 5) don't warn you of this).

2.3   Edit Menu

Cut frames
Ctrl Alt X

Copy frames
Ctrl Alt C

Paste frames
Ctrl Alt V

Clear frames
Alt Backspace

Select all frames
Ctrl Alt A

Some users find it quicker to use the copy and paste options by right-clicking/Control-clicking a selection or single Stage element and selecting the options from the pop-up contextual menu (this depends on whether you work primarily with the mouse or with the keyboard). A similar feature is also available for frame-based copy and paste options.

The Edit menu contains options to edit primitive graphics and symbols and the Timeline. It also contains options to configure the Flash environment. The menu described in this section appears in the authoring environment. When in the test environment, the Edit menu is not relevant and much of it disappears or is grayed out (you cannot edit in the test environment). You *can* use the Preferences and Keyboard Shortcuts options in test mode, although there is no special reason you would want to do this.

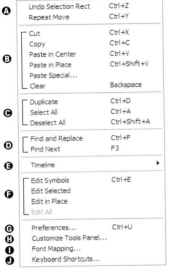

A Undo or Repeat the last operation. Both will be followed by some text describing the operation they will affect.

B This section allows normal clipboard cut/paste operations. Cut and Copy allow cut (delete from Stage, copy to clipboard) and copy (leave on Stage, copy to clipboard) operations to the clipboard; Paste In Center and Paste In Place allow you to paste the current clipboard contents to either the center of the Stage or in the same position as the original. Paste Special allows you to paste from the clip-board in one of several formats (such as text from Microsoft Word), which will vary to suit the clipboard contents. Clear deletes the current selection without altering the clipboard.

C These options give you quick options for editing or creating a Stage selection. Duplicate duplicates the current selection (the selection will be copied to the Stage with a slight offset to the original) without affecting the clipboard, Select All will select all Stage contents, and Deselect All will unselect any current selection.

D Find and Replace brings up a window that allows you to search and replace text strings in the current document. Find Next will perform the search again, starting from the last found string.

E Opens a submenu that allows cut-paste operations with frames. Frame-based cut-paste does not use the operating system clipboard, although the available options are similar to normal cut-paste.

F Edit Symbols allows you to edit the currently selected Symbol. Edit Selected: edit the currently selected group. Edit In Place edits the currently selected symbol in Stage view, with all noneditable content appearing dimmed. Edit All returns from any current edit mode to the current main timeline. Note that you can usually edit symbols and groups much more quickly by double-clicking them from the Library (Edit Symbol) or on the Stage (Edit In Place) or by double-clicking any blank area of the Stage (Edit All).

G Opens the Preferences window, allowing you to set preferences for the Flash environment.

H Opens the Customize Toolbar window, allowing you to specify which standard and user-defined (via third-party JSAPI code) tools you want to see on the Tools panel.

I Allows you to change the font mapping (font substitution) if you open a FLA that requires fonts not available on your current machine. Font mapping will take place only if the required font is not available; if the font later becomes available, the font mapping is ignored (this allows you to take work home without having to change the fonts around between the home and office machines).

J Opens the Keyboard Shortcuts window, allowing you to change keyboard shortcuts (typically so they are more like other applications you are familiar with; otherwise it may be better to leave them as is).

2.4   View Menu

This section covers the two View menus available in Flash: one for the authoring environment and another for the test environment.

Authoring Environment View Menu

Ⓐ Opens a submenu allowing you to navigate between scenes if your FLA contains them; otherwise this option will be grayed out. The same options are presented better in the Scene panel.

Ⓑ Zooms into or out of the Stage by 100 percent.

Ⓒ Opens a submenu containing standard zoom settings. This submenu can also be reached directly elsewhere (e.g., as a drop-down at the bottom-right of the Timeline panel).

Ⓓ Opens a submenu allowing you to select a number of Stage rendering options. Selecting Outlines is the fastest but least detailed; Full is the most detailed but may cause sluggishness on slower machines. This submenu relates to the authoring environment only—it has no effect on the exported SWF.

Ⓔ Toggles between a work area (free space around the Stage) and no work area (Stage stays in the top left corner). The latter view has few advantages and is a legacy view mode from previous versions of the Flash environment; you are unlikely to ever need it.

Ⓕ Toggles between showing or hiding rulers. You can alter the units of measurement from the Document Properties dialog (right-click/Control-click on a blank area of the Stage and select Document Properties or select Modify > Document).

Ⓖ Opens submenus to allow you to work with the Stage grid and guides.

Ⓗ Opens a submenu that allows you to edit the snapping grid or change what is snapped to. You can choose to Snap Align (snap to nearest 15 degrees), Snap To Grid (snap to nearest grid line/intersection), Snap To Pixels, or Snap To Objects (snap to the nearest symbol or primitive).

Ⓘ Toggles between showing or hiding the rectangular envelope that surrounds Symbols and Groups.

Ⓙ Toggles between showing or hiding shape hints associated with shape tween animations (see Chapter 5 for a discussion of shape tweens and shape hints). To add shape hints, select Modify > Shape > Add Shape Hint.

➠ 7.10 Using Rulers, Guides, Grids, and Snaps

➠ 26.1 Using the Test Environment

100 percent magnification
[Ctrl] [1]

Toggle show grid
[Ctrl] [']

Toggle snap to grid
[Ctrl] [Shift] [#]

Toggle show guides
[Ctrl] [;]

Toggle lock guides
[Ctrl] [Alt] [;]

➠ 26.2 Using the
      Bandwidth
      Profiler

Toggle snap to guides
`Ctrl` `Shift` `'`

Toggle snap to objects
`Ctrl` `Shift` `/`

**Toggle show
shape hints**
`Ctrl` `Alt` `H`

Flash Player menu

**Right-click Stage of a
running SWF**

**Control-click Stage of a
running SWF**

Test Environment View Menu

The options not appearing in the authoring environment are:

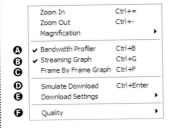

A Toggles between viewing or hiding the Bandwidth Profiler.

B Toggles between restarting the movie with simulated streaming or no streaming.

C Toggles to set the Bandwidth Profiler to show either a streaming graph or a frame by frame graph. A streaming graph simulates what would happen online, where frames are loaded as fast as they can be downloaded. A frame by frame graph shows what would happen if frames were loaded instantaneously when they were needed; although it is not true to life, it allows you to identify your most bandwidth-heavy frames.

D Toggles between simulated web conditions and instantaneous download. For simulated web conditions, it will simulate the performance of your SWF based on specified download rates. For instantaneous download, the SWF will play with no download delays. The simulate option only simulates web conditions for the file under test. If your site or application loads runtime assets, these will always load *immediately* and will not be addressed by the simulation.

E Opens a submenu allowing you to set the download rate. The presets allow you to quickly simulate most common download rates seen on the web.

F Opens a submenu that allows you to set the quality that the Flash Player will use. This submenu is the same as the Quality menu on the default Flash Player contextual menu.

2.5   Insert Menu

The Insert menu allows you to insert (create) new symbols into the library, add timeline effects to the Timeline, or add scenes. All options except timeline effects are better selected from other parts of the interface, so this menu is not often used (and it has reduced in size in Flash 2004 to reflect this).

Ⓐ Opens the Create New Symbol dialog, allowing you to create a new movie clip, button, or graphic symbol. This option is rarely used; the New Symbol option in the Library panel's drop-down menu is usually better placed for efficient workflow.

Ⓑ Opens a submenu allowing you to add timeline elements. The right-click/Control-click context menus of the Timeline panel are more popularly used.

Ⓒ Opens a submenu showing all installed timeline effects and allowing you to add one.

Ⓓ Adds a new Scene. This option doesn't allow you to rename or re-order scenes, so the Scene panel is more often used instead.

New symbol
Ctrl F8

Add frame
F5

Add keyframe
F6

_____

Although you can add effects using Insert > Timeline Effects, the options to delete effects are in the Modify menu.

USING PANEL MENUS

All panels also have a menu associated with them, accessed via the icon seen at the top right corner of all panels. These are discussed in later chapters that actually use the available options during standard workflows.

2.6   Modify Menu

The Modify menu is used to create or modify graphics and symbols. It can also be used to alter the global document values (Stage size, frame rate, background color) and the attributes of layers within the document. Many of the Modify menu options are usually grayed out and only become available when you select something the option can actually work with. For example, the Swap Bitmap and Trace Bitmap options only become available when you select a bitmap.

Add shape hint
[Ctrl] [Shift] [H]

Rotate 90° CW
[Ctrl] [Shift] [9]

Rotate 90° CCW
[Ctrl] [Shift] [7]

Remove transform
[Ctrl] [Shift] [Z]

Many of the commonly used options available in the Modify menu can be accessed much more quickly with context sensitive menus (right-click/Control-click on the thing you want to modify).

After using Trace Bitmap, it is usually standard practice to follow with Optimize on the result. This reduces the file size and redraw time of the resulting vector graphic.

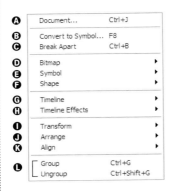

Ⓐ Opens the Document Properties dialog for the current file, which allows you to set Stage dimensions, frame rate, background color and ruler units.

Ⓑ Opens the Convert To Symbol dialog, allowing you to convert the current Stage selection into a movie clip, button, or graphic symbol.

Ⓒ Breaks apart the current Stage selection.

Ⓓ Opens a submenu allowing you to swap or trace the currently selected bitmap on the Stage.

Ⓔ Opens a submenu allowing you to create a duplicate library symbol of the currently selected Stage symbol or swap it for another symbol.

Ⓕ Opens a submenu of options allowing you to modify shapes (i.e., strokes and fills), including optimizations, conversion of strokes to fills, and editing fills. Also contains options for working with shape hints.

Ⓖ Opens a submenu allowing you to modify layers and frames.

Ⓗ Allows you to edit or remove timeline effects previously added via the Insert menu.

Ⓘ Gives you many of the same options available via the Free Transform tool in the Tools panel and also contains some useful preset transformations, such as rotate by 90 degrees, flip horizontal/vertical, and the option to remove all previous transformations.

Ⓙ Opens a submenu allowing you to change the depth of symbols and shapes on the Stage.

Ⓚ Opens a submenu allowing you to arrange groups of symbols or shapes on the Stage. The same options are available in the much more user friendly Align panel (Window > Align, or select the ⊞ icon from the main toolbar).

Ⓛ Makes a group from the current selection or removes the grouping of an existing group. Ungrouping does not delete any Stage graphics.

2.7 Text Menu

The Text menu provides control of text formatting. This menu is very rarely (if ever) used by most designers, given that there are more efficient ways of formatting text via the Properties panel.

A Opens a submenu containing all fonts available to Flash, allowing you to select one when using the Text tool on the toolbar.

B Opens a submenu of font sizes

C Opens a submenu of font styles.

D Opens a submenu of available text alignments.

E Opens a submenu allowing you to alter the tracking between letters in the current text selection. The options in this submenu become available for static text only.

F Allows you to choose whether the current text field can show scrollable content. This option is only available for Dynamic and Input text fields.

G Check Spelling allows you to check the spelling of all text in your document; Flash will check text fields in the order they appear in the Movie Explorer panel. Spelling Setup allows you to select the dictionaries to use and rules to apply during the spell check.

➧ 20.2 Understanding Text in Flash

➧ 20.7 Working with Static Text

➧ 20.9 Creating Dynamic Text Fields

The Text menu is somewhat superceded by the Properties panel, which provides all the same formatting controls in a more visual and efficient interface. Only spell-checking is not available from this panel.

Font options are also available from the Property Inspector whenever you use the text Tool.

USING CONTEXT MENUS

Most main menu options are available from Right-click/⌘-click context menus and the Property Inspector, plus keyboard shortcuts. You will hardly ever use certain menus because of this, particularly Control and Text.

2.8   Commands Menu

➠ 5.15 History Panel

➠ 14.5 Installing and
          Uninstalling
          Commands
          and Behaviors

You can create your
own basic commands
by selecting a number
of steps in the History
panel and then select-
ing Save As Command
from the panel's menu.

More advanced com-
mands (and even
new tools) can be writ-
ten using Flash Java-
Script and Flash MX
Professional.

The Commands menu allows you to manage and run commands using Flash's JSAPI. The JSAPI allows you to create commands and tools for use in the authoring environment and is based around a dialect of JavaScript called Flash JavaScript.

Ⓐ Manage Saved Commands...
Ⓑ Get More Commands...
Ⓒ Run Command...

Ⓓ Detect Accessibility

Ⓐ Opens a dialog allowing you to manage (rename and delete) installed JSAPI commands.

Ⓑ Links to a web page that allows you to download additional JSAPI commands.

Ⓒ Allows you to run commands not currently installed by finding them via a file browser. The file browser will be set to filter on Flash JavaScript (JSFL) files.

Ⓓ The menu items from this point onward are a list of installed commands.

2.9   Control Menu

There are two separate versions of this menu for the authoring and test environments. The authoring environment Control menu allows you to control the movement of the playhead and includes toggle options to handle simple scripts and frame-based sound.

The test environment Control menu has the same level of control of the playhead but also contains more complex options for controlling the ActionScript debugging environment when using code breakpoints.

Authoring Environment Control Menu

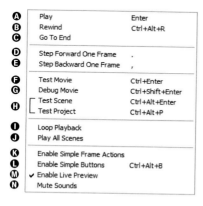

A Plays the Timeline, starting from the current frame. If the Timeline is already playing, this option will change to Stop; the keyboard shortcut (Enter) will remain the same.

B Goes back to the first frame in the current timeline and stops.

C Goes to the last frame in the current timeline and stops.

D Goes forward one frame in the current timeline and stops. It is usually faster to select the next frame from the Timeline.

E Goes back one frame in the current timeline and stops. It is usually faster to select the next frame from the Timeline.

F Opens the test environment using the current FLA.

G Opens the test environment with an active Debugger window, using the current FLA.

H Opens the test environment using the current scene, or opens the project within the browser, displaying the Project Panel's default file first.

I Toggles to loop the current timeline (restarts the Timeline every time the last frame is reached). When this is unselected, the Timeline will stop at the last frame. If the next option (J) is also checked, the Timeline will restart when the last frame of the last scene is reached.

J Toggles to include scenes. This will modify the actions of options A, B, C, D, and E. For example, the rewind option B will go to the first frame of the first scene with this option selected.

K Toggles to run simple timeline control actions (such as `play()` and `stop()`) when playing the Timeline.

L Toggles to respond to simple buttons, allowing interactive inputs to be made by the developer while the Timeline is playing in the authoring environment.

M Toggles to show live preview, a feature associated with components.

N Toggles to mute sound when playing the Timeline. This forces Flash to ignore any sounds attached to frames (more complex ActionScript-based sounds will not play in the authoring environment in any case).

➡ 3.3   The Controller Toolbar

➡ 19.1   Introducing v2 Components

➡ 26.1   Using the Test Environment

➡ 26.2   Using the Bandwidth Profiler

➡ 26.5   Using the Debugger Window

The test environment does not address scenes because scenes only exist in the authoring environment as a feature to make development easier. In the test environment, scene information is discarded and one long timeline (consisting of all the scenes in order, with no breaks) is shown.

Test Environment Control Menu

The following options are unique to the test environment:

To get to the test environment, choose Control > Test Movie.

Most of the options in this menu can be accessed more quickly via the Controller toolbar (Window > Toolbars > Controller) or the Debugger panel. (Enter the test environment with the Debug Movie option from the authoring environment Control menu to make this active.)

The Disable Keyboard Shortcuts menu option is used to test forms or other content that needs to respond to keyboard shortcuts (such as the Tab key). Not disabling keyboard shortcuts would mean that the Flash environment would instead "steal" the keypresses, and the SWF under test would appear to be ignoring them.

Ⓐ Compiles all files defined for the current project. The Associated Project Panel is only available in Professional.

Ⓑ The first two options set or clear a breakpoint at the line the cursor is currently at (or the last line executed if no line is selected by the cursor) when you are troubleshooting a script using breakpoints. The third clears all breakpoints in the current test.

Ⓒ Continues to the next breakpoint.

Ⓓ Ignores all further debugging. You can do the same thing more quickly by closing the debugger.

Ⓔ Executes the current line of code. If it is a line such as function or a loop, you will single step through every line caused to be executed by that line. If the block is a function, the debugger will single step through every line of the function. If it is a loop, the debugger will run through the code line by line for every iteration.

Ⓕ Executes the current line of code. If it is a line in a function call or loop, the debug will execute the whole call (for a function) or current loop, and pause at the start of the next line (for a function call) or iteration (for a loop).

Ⓖ Executes all further lines in the current script and continues to the next breakpoint. This is an easy way to exit out of long loops and other repetitive code.

Ⓗ Forces the test environment to ignore all Flash-specific keyboard shortcuts.

2.10 Debug Menu

The Debug menu appears in the test environment only. It allows you to display a list of all objects (movie clips, buttons, and ActionScript objects) or variables in the Output panel.

Ⓐ
Ⓑ

List Objects	Ctrl+L
List Variables	Ctrl+Alt+V

Ⓐ Sends a list of all movie clips, buttons, and text fields for the current frame.

Ⓑ Lists all variables that exist in the current frame. "Variables" refers to all nongraphic objects (i.e., all ActionScript objects except movie clips and buttons), including events, functions, and built-in and user-defined class instances.

➥ 16.1 Understanding Variables

➥ 16.9 Using Flash Classes

➥ 16.9 Using Flash Objects

Although somewhat superceded by the debugger when used to output diagnostic information with the options in the Debug menu, one advantage of the Output panel is that you can print the information contained in it for offline review.

The two output listings will be swamped by the objects and variables used by components if your movie contains them. It is better to initially debug long scripts in files that do not contain components if you expect the debugging process to be nontrivial, and only add the components once your scripts are working well.

2.11 Window Menu

The Window menu is used to navigate between open document windows, as well as to view and close panels. There are two versions of the Window menu, one for the authoring environment and a smaller one for the test environment.

The Toggle Output Panel option is not usually used because in most cases it appears automatically when required (i.e., when there is an error in your code or you request any outputs from the interface or through scripts). It is also easy to close via the window itself (click the window's ✕).

When tiling or cascading windows, you can have a mixture of windows in authoring and test environments. This can be useful if you have a very large monitor or a multiple monitor setup; you can debug/test and edit your Flash content simultaneously.

To return to the normal document view (one document viewed in full-screen) after selecting tiling or cascading, simply maximize your chosen window so that it fills the available workspace.

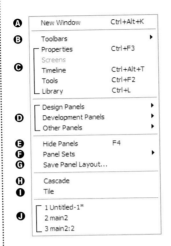

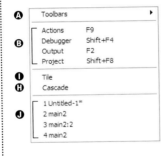

Ⓐ Opens a new window on the current document, allowing you to view content on more than one frame at the same time or to open different views on the same Stage content.

Ⓑ Opens a submenu allowing you to view or hide the Main, Status (a one-line status area that appears at the bottom of the Flash environment), and Controller toolbars.

Ⓒ Toggles to show or hide the primary panels in the Flash environment.

Ⓓ Opens submenus (sorted by function) that allow you to toggle all subsidiary panels in the Flash environment.

Ⓔ Toggles to show or hide all panels except the Timeline.

Ⓕ Allows you to set panel positions and visibility to predefined configurations.

Ⓖ Allows you to add the current panel positions and visibility to the list shown in the previous option.

Ⓗ Places all open windows in a stack.

Ⓘ Places all open windows in a tile pattern.

Ⓙ Lists the last few opened files.

FLASH MX 2004 MENU RE-ORGANIZATION

The flash 2004 menus have been re-organized since Flash MX, and this is most noticeable in the Insert and Modify panels. In 2004, use the Insert Panel to *create* things, and the Modify panel to *change them.*

2.12   Help Menu

The Help menu provides help, documentation, tutorials and links to Flash resources.

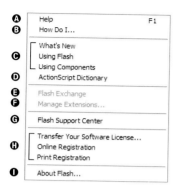

Ⓐ Opens the Help panel at the Help tab.

Ⓑ Opens the Help panel at the How Do I tab.

Ⓒ Opens a number of core help titles in the Help panel.

Ⓓ Opens links to the sample files in the Help menu.ß

Ⓔ Opens an online link to the Macromedia Flash exchange, where you will find additional free and paid-for components.

Ⓕ Opens the Manager window; this option becomes available when you install the Macromedia Extensions Manager (available free from the Macromedia site; you need this to install new components).

Ⓖ Opens an online link to the Flash Support center, which provides technical information and help resources.

Ⓗ Allows you to manage your Flash software license and registration.

Ⓘ Opens a window that includes the application version and software revision.

Using Flash
F1

2.13   Contextual Menus

Right-clicking/Control-clicking many of the following areas will bring up a context-sensitive menu. These are a handy alternative to the main menus.

Right-Clicking/Control-clicking on the area behind the file tabs (top of the timeline panel) is the same as Right-Clicking/Control-clicking on the current tab.

Not mentioned here is the menu that will appear if you Right-Click/Control-click on the Flash application title bar. The contents of this menu are controlled by the Operating system.

HOTSPOT	RESULTING CONTEXTUAL MENU
Blank Stage area	Includes clipboard operations, selection, ruler/guides/snap options, and Document Properties.
Symbol or group on the Stage	Includes all edit options available for the current symbol/group except color effects and changing the instance name (which appear on the Properties inspector).
Text field	Includes all options available for the current text field. This is a smaller subset of the Symbol context menu, but this also includes spell checking.
Primitive on the Stage	Includes all options available for a primitive except Optimize, which you can access via Modify > Shape > Optimize.
Frame or frame selection	Includes all edit and modify options for the current frame selection.
Top pane (symbol thumbnail) of the Library panel	Allows you to alter the way the thumbnail is rendered.
Symbol or other asset (sound files, etc.) in Library	Gives you all edit, modify, and export/update options available for the currently selected asset.
Within the Output panel	Allows you to perform clipboard operations and text searches with a selection or the entire contents of the panel.
On a running movie in test mode	Opens the normal Flash Player context menu.
On a tab at the top of the Timeline panel	Includes a number of common file operations.

CHAPTER 3

Toolbars and Tools

HOW YOU SET UP YOUR AUTHORING ENVIRONMENT, including arranging the toolbars, depends a great deal on how you tend to create Flash documents and what you develop. A notable improvement in Flash is you can use Document Tabs (like Dreamweaver). This is a considerable improvement in the usability of the authoring environment. The Tools panel includes a wide arrange of brushes, selection tools, and modifiers that help you design and construct your documents.

3.1   Toolbars Overview

There are no toolbars
available for the Mac
environment because
of how the Mac OS is
designed. Therefore,
Mac users can only
open the Controller
(which is like a floating
panel) and the edit bar.
Mac users have to use
menus or keyboard
shortcuts instead.

Toolbars are button sets on the Flash user interface and act as an alternative to menu selections or keyboard commands. Some Flash users do not display the toolbars within the user interface to maximize their screen real estate. Most Flash users display the edit bar because it is extremely useful when navigating around a Flash application.

The toolbars are not open by default. To open them, choose Window > Toolbars and then one of two or three options from the menu. If the option is checked, the toolbar is already open in the authoring environment.

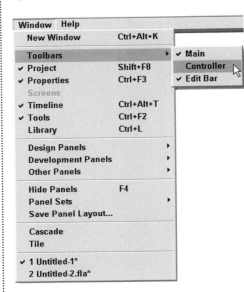

Main The main toolbar at the top of the authoring environment (Windows only).

Controller A set of buttons that control the playback of a Flash animation.

Edit Bar Contains links, drop-down menus, and zooming capabilities that help you navigate through the Flash document.

3.2 Main Toolbar

Choosing Window > Toolbars > Main in Windows opens the Main toolbar at the top of the authoring environment, directly under the application menus. The Main toolbar has a lot of useful buttons that help speed up Flash development.

You can undock the Main toolbar in the Windows environment: just click within the tool-bar area and drag it anywhere in the authoring environment. You can redock the toolbar on the sides, bottom, or top of the authoring environment.

A **New** Create a new document.

B **Open** Open a saved document.

C **Save** Save the current document.

D **Print** Print the current document.

E **Cut** Cut selected object from the document and place it on the clipboard.

F **Copy** Copy a section from the Stage onto the clipboard.

G **Paste** Paste a selection on the Stage.

H **Undo** Undo the last command.

I **Redo** Redo the last deleted command.

J **Snap To Objects** Snap to objects and the grid.

K **Smooth** Smooth a line on the Stage.

L **Straighten** Straighten a line on the Stage.

M **Rotate and Skew** Rotate and/or skew an object on the Stage.

N **Scale** Scale an object on the Stage.

O **Align Panel** Open or close the panel.

If you try to dock the Main toolbar to the bottom of the authoring environment, you might find that it docks next to the Property inspector and Help panels (if they are docked beneath the Stage). This is unlikely to be a desirable location for the toolbar because it wastes a lot of screen real estate. If you move the toolbar directly beneath and slightly to the right of these panels, it should properly dock at the bottom of the authoring environment.

→ 2.2 File Menu

→ 2.3 Edit Menu

→ 5.6 Transform Panel

New
Ctrl N
⌘ N

Open
Ctrl O
⌘ O

Save
Ctrl S
⌘ S

Print
Ctrl P
⌘ P

Undo
Ctrl Z
⌘ Z

Redo
Ctrl Y
⌘ Y

Snap To Objects
Ctrl Shift /
⌘ Shift /

Toggle Transform panel
Ctrl T
⌘ T

In Flash MX 2004, you can no longer dock the Main toolbar directly beneath the Tools panel. Instead the panel docks to the left of the Tools panel, which is a greater waste of screen real estate and similar to docking it to the right of the authoring environment.

Some buttons might appear grayed out. In order to use these buttons, you must have an object selected on the Stage.

3.3   Controller Toolbar

➡ 2.9   Control Menu

Play
[Enter]
[Return]

Rewind
[Ctrl] [Alt] [R]
[⌘] [Option] [R]

**Step forward
one frame**
[.] or [>]

**Step backward
one frame**
[,] or [<]

In Flash MX 2004, unfortunately you cannot dock the Controller toolbar directly beneath the Tools panel. Instead, the panel docks to the left of the Tools panel, which is quite a waste of screen real estate.

Like the Main toolbar, you can dock the Controller toolbar to the right of panels you might have docked beneath the Stage (such as the Property inspector). Doing so wastes a lot of screen, so you probably won't ever find yourself docking the Controller in this location.

The Controller toolbar can be opened by choosing Window > Toolbars > Controller. The toolbar opens as a floating window. You can dock it by grabbing the window and dragging it to the top, left, or right of the authoring environment.

If you have animation or multiple frames in your FLA, these buttons can be used to navigate along the Timeline. If you do not have multiple pages then these buttons are grayed out, or *dimmed*.

Ⓐ Stop Stop an animation that is playing.

Ⓑ Rewind Move the playhead to the first frame.

Ⓒ Step Back One Frame Move the playhead back one frame.

Ⓓ Play Play the animation.

Ⓔ Step Forward One Frame Move the playhead forward one frame.

Ⓕ Go To End Move the playhead to the last frame in the animation.

If you try to dock the Controller toolbar to the bottom of the authoring environment, you might find that it docks next to the Property inspector and Help panels (if they are docked beneath the Stage). This is unlikely to be a desirable location for the toolbar. If you move the Controller beneath and slightly to the right of these panels, it should properly dock beneath the panels.

3.4   Edit Bar

You can open and close the edit bar by choosing Window > Toolbars > Edit Bar. The edit bar helps you change your Stage view and navigate to or within object instances on the Stage; whatever you select in the edit bar opens for editing. You can move the edit bar above and below the Timeline by pressing Shift+Alt (or Shift+⌘ on the Mac) and then double-clicking anywhere on the edit bar.

Ⓐ Back Navigate one element left on the edit bar.

Ⓑ Name of the current Scene.

Ⓒ Name of the instance being edited.

Ⓓ Edit Scene Choose a Scene to edit.

Ⓔ Edit Symbol Choose a symbol to edit.

Ⓕ Choose a Stage magnification from the drop-down menu:

Fit In Window Update the size of the Stage depending on the size of the window area (frame) containing it. The Stage changes size if you open and close panels or resize the authoring environment.

Show Frame Maximize the Stage in the frame.

Show All Provide a close-up of the objects on the Stage, maximized to the frame surrounding the Stage.

25% to 800% Display Stage contents at the chosen percentage.

CUSTOMIZING THE TOOLS PANEL

Look for third-party tools to add to the Tools panel. The Tools panel can be customized, so you can add many tools to the authoring environment that are made by Flash developers. Tools might include custom shapes such as stars or useful symbols such as arrows. When you add new tools to the Tools panel, you can opt to create drop-down menus that open from any of the tools. How you organize custom tools is up to you.

⟶ 3.23 Zoom Tool

100%
[Ctrl] [1]
[⌘] [1]

Fit In Window
[Ctrl] [2]
[⌘] [2]

Show All
[Ctrl] [3]
[⌘] [3]

Move edit bar
[Shift] [Alt]
double-click
[⌘] [Shift]
double-click

The edit bar used to be called the Information bar in Flash MX.

The edit bar changes to a darker gray color when you are editing an object on the Stage. This helps you remember you are editing an instance of a movie clip or button instead of something on the main Stage.

The edit bar is most useful when you are working with many nested elements in an object instance. Whatever you select in the edit bar opens for editing.

You can choose any percentage between 8% and 2000% as a Stage view. Simply enter a number into the text field in the edit bar.

3.5   Tools Overview

Zoom in/out toggle
[Option]
[Alt]

───

The Selection tool is also unofficially referred to as the Arrow tool.

The Tools panel contains many modifiable tools used to draw, illustrate, select, erase, and move the Stage. Open the Tools panel by selecting Window > Tools. Each tool can be chosen using a hotkey, listed here in parentheses.

Some tools can be modified to increase their use. After selecting a tool in the Tools section, look in the Options area for more buttons. You can also change settings for a selected tool in the Property inspector. Select a tool and open the Property inspector (Window > Properties). Check for other ways to modify the tool to best suit what you need to use it for.

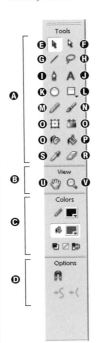

Ⓐ Tools These tools help you create, select, and manipulate text and graphics on the Stage.

Ⓑ View Use these tools for panning over the Stage or zooming.

Ⓒ Colors Select stroke and fill colors or gradients in this area.

Ⓓ Options This context-sensitive area of the Tools panel changes depending on what tool you have selected. Many tools have various options (modifiers) available, and they are selected from this area.

Ⓔ Selection tool (V)

Ⓕ Subselection tool (A)

Ⓖ Line tool

Ⓗ Lasso tool

Ⓘ Pen tool

Ⓙ Text tool

Ⓚ Oval tool

Ⓛ Rectangle tool

Ⓜ Pencil tool

Ⓝ Brush tool

Ⓞ Free Transform tool

Ⓟ Fill Transform tool

Ⓠ Ink Bottle tool

Ⓡ Paint Bucket tool

Ⓢ Eyedropper tool

Ⓣ Eraser tool

Ⓤ Hand tool (spacebar)

Ⓥ Zoom tool

If there is a down arrow next to a tool graphic, it means a menu of additional tools opens. Click and hold on a tool button, and a drop-down menu opens.

3.6 Selection (Arrow) Tool

The Selection tool ![] selects and moves objects on the Stage or edits their size and shape. You can lengthen or reshape lines, or select a fill and modify it. This multifunctional tool is also called the Arrow tool.

Smooth ![] Select a stroke and click this button to make it smoother.

Straighten ![] Select a stroke and click this button to make it more angled.

Snap To Objects ![] Selected objects will snap to other objects that are close when they are moved around the Stage.

When you use the Selection tool to move things around the Stage, outlines and guides help you place the graphic in a new position.

Selection Tool Cursors

CURSOR	USE
	Select fills using the Selection tool. When a fill is selected, a crosshatch pattern covers the selected area.
	You can select symbols such as movie clip or text instances on the Stage. This graphic symbol is selected and can be moved to a new location. You can tell it is selected because you can see its registration point and bounding box. You can also select raw (or *primitive*) graphics on the Stage and move them.
	When you move a graphic symbol, you see an outline that helps you reposition the instance. New dashed guidelines help you place it in relation to other elements on the Stage.

➡ 3.7 Subselection Tool

➡ 3.8 Line Tool

➡ 3.14 Pencil Tool

Select all content
⌘ Ⓐ
Ctrl Ⓐ

Deselect all content
⌘ Shift Ⓐ

———

To select a fill and its stroke outline, double-click the fill. To only select the fill, click the fill once.

———

Double-click a line to select all lines connected to it.

AUTHORING TASKS

SCRIPTING TASKS

TESTING AND PUBLISHING TASKS

WHAT'S NEW

Continues ●

3.6   Selection (Arrow) Tool *(continued)*

➥ 3.15 Brush Tool

➥ 9.2 Understand-
     ing Strokes
     and Fills

Selection tool
⌐V⌐

Duplicate selection
⌐Ctrl⌐+**Drag**
⌐⌘⌐+**Drag**

———

To make multiple selec-
tions, hold down the
Shift key when clicking
objects or primitive
graphics.

For precise placement,
select an object using
the Selection tool, and
then use the keyboard's
arrow keys to move it
around the Stage.

The Selection tool can also modify primitive graphics and shapes. Line ends can be dragged to resize the line and snap it to other objects. Lines and strokes can be curved if the mouse is positioned in the middle of the line segment. To select all content within a rectangular area, click and drag the Selection tool on the Stage. You see a rectangle marquee, and everything within it is selected. If you have symbols within that area, the entire bounding box of that object must be within the marquee to select it.

The Selection tool is used at the end of a line to reshape it.
Use the Selection tool at the corner of a square to change its size and shape.

The Selection tool is used in the middle of a line to create a new curve. Because this is a brush stroke, the fill color fills the curve. A pencil stroke does not fill in this area.

3.7 Subselection Tool

Use the Subselection tool ⌨ to select and modify vector points in illustrations created using the Pen tool, or lines using the Line tool. Using the Subselection tool is a lot like editing line segments and vector points using the Pen tool. It selects and then adds or modifies curves, angles, and placement of vector shapes and lines. You can even use this tool to select other lines made using the brush or pencil. Now these lines display vector points that are modifiable using the Subselection tool.

Use the Subselection tool to edit the slope or curve of curved vector lines, the length and angle of straight lines, or the position of these lines and shapes. A white box means the mouse is over a vector point, and a black box means the cursor is near a line segment.

➠ 3.6   Selection Tool

➠ 3.8   Line Tool

➠ 3.10 Pen Tool

➠ 3.14 Pencil Tool

➠ 3.15 Brush Tool

Subselection tool

[A]

―――

Use the Subselection tool to edit brush and pencil strokes and shapes. When you select the shapes, you see vector points you can move. You also see tangent handles that you can manipulate to reshape the graphic.

3.8   Line Tool

Select Line tool
[N]

————

You can change line attributes in the Property inspector or the Custom Stroke style dialog. You can also change the stroke using the Color Mixer panel.

————

If you double-click a shape with several joined line segments, it selects all of the joined line segments. If you single-click, it selects only the segment that was clicked.

————

A hairline is a one pixel wide line and always remains one pixel wide no matter what the movie's magnification is. Even at 800 percent zoom, the line appears to be one pixel wide.

Use the Line tool ✎ to create straight lines from any starting point (the initial click on the Stage.) Simply click on the Stage, drag to where you want the line to end, and then release the mouse to create a line.

When the Line tool is selected, the Property inspector contains several settings that you can change depending on the appearance you want the line to have. Change a line's stroke color, width, and style using the Property inspector. If you click on the Custom button, you can further customize the stroke style.

The Property inspector allows you to change the stroke's appearance. You can change the color and thickness and apply a number of basic styles to the line. Click the Custom button to open the Stroke Style dialog.

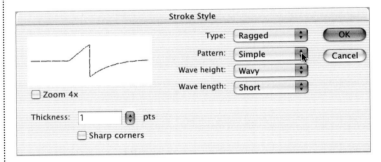

The Stroke Style dialog allows you to customize line styles. Notice that there is a Sharp corners option available here.

Create shapes using the Line tool by joining several lines together. Make sure the ends snap together (Snap to Objects must be turned on) if you need to fill the shape using the Paint Bucket tool. You can tell that a line is snapping to the grid or another object when a larger circle icon is visible at the cursor. If you want to change the line style, select the line using the Selection tool, and then change the line style in the Property inspector.

Several lines can create a shape. When you are drawing, moving, or modifying the line and the cursor is not near a line to snap to, the circle under the crosshair is small. If the circle is large, it means the line closes the shape if the mouse is released. This means you can fill the shape using the Paint Bucket tool.

3.9　Lasso Tool

The Lasso tool selects objects on the Stage. You can draw a freehand line around an object to select it, use a polygon lasso, or use the magic wand to select objects. You can even use a combination of the freehand or straight-edge modes of the lasso.

If you are using the Polygon mode, simply click points around the object, and straight lines are created to connect each point. Double-click to close the selection area. If you are using the default lasso mode, release the mouse button to finish making a selection.

➥ 3.6　Selection (Arrow) Tool

➥ 8.3　Editing a Stage Selection

Toggle Normal and Polygon mode
[Option] click
[Alt] click

Lasso tool
[L]

If you are selecting a symbol instead of a primitive graphic, you need to make sure the selection encompasses the entire bounding box of the object or it will not all be selected.

The default setting is to select objects using a freehand Lasso. You can also select the Polygon mode that allows you to create straight lines for selection by clicking various points on the Stage.

Use the Magic Wand to select areas of pixels in bitmap images or areas of color in a primitive graphic. How it selects these pixels depends on Threshold (tolerance) settings. The Magic Wand identifies and selects the same color so you can modify or delete pixels.

Ⓐ Magic Wand　Selects a color range of pixels in bitmap or primitive graphics.

Ⓑ Magic Wand Properties　Click to open the Magic Wand Settings dialog, shown below.

Ⓒ Polygon Mode　Sets the lasso to Polygon mode, so you can make selections by clicking points on the Stage.

Threshold　A higher number means a greater range of similar colors are selected. A lower number selects a smaller range of colors (or a single color).

Pixels　Selects only the area of pixels.

Rough　Makes the selected area very rectangular in nature.

Normal　Slightly rounds the selected area (although not as much as smooth).

Smooth　Rounds the corners of the selection.

3.10   Pen Tool

Pen tool
P

——

Select the Snap to Objects button before trying to make closed, filled shapes using the Pen tool. If you don't, you have to have master precision in order to click right on the corner to close the shape.

You can edit lines and curves made using the pen using the Pen tool itself or the Subselection tool.

——

You don't have to use the Pen tool if you want to manipulate vector points. You can create illustrations using the pencil and brush, and then use the Subselection tool to view and modify vector points.

The Pen tool ⟨pen⟩ creates straight or curved vector lines and shapes. The pen creates line segments, which can then be manipulated. These segments can have the slope, curve, angle, or length changed using the Pen tool or the Subselection tool. There are no options available for the Pen tool, although you can modify stroke and fill settings using the Property inspector.

Specify a stroke and fill color and style for the Pen tool using the Property inspector. You see the fill color only if you create closed shapes.

1 Select the Pen tool and click on the Stage to create the first point, and then click in a second location. A segment is drawn between those two points.

2 Click a third location on the Stage and hold down the mouse button and drag. You see a curve instead of a straight line joining the second and third points.

3 Move the cursor to the first point you created to join the lines together and create a shape. Watch for a small circle to appear next to the cursor and the final point and then click. The shape closes, and the center of the shape fills with the designated fill color.

Pen Cursors

CURSOR	USE
⟨pen⟩₀	This cursor appears when the tool is near or on the first point you placed on the Stage. When you click, it closes and fills the shape.
⟨pen⟩×	You see this cursor when there is no line segment or point to manipulate (the cursor is over the empty Stage). When it moves close to points or segments, the cursor changes.
⟨pen⟩–	This cursor deletes the vector point it is hovering over.
⟨pen⟩+	This cursor adds a vector point to the line segment it is hovering over.
⟨pen⟩↰	If you click the vector point with this cursor, it changes into a right angle.
⟨arrow⟩□	When you hold down the Ctrl key, the cursor looks like this when it is over a point.
⟨arrow⟩	When you hold down the Ctrl key, the cursor looks like this when it is over a segment.

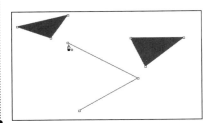

A shape is created using the Pen tool. It is automatically filled using the current Fill settings after the shape is closed. Make sure you have Snap to Objects button selected before creating closed shapes using the Pen tool.

3.11   Text Tool

You can create three different kinds of text in Flash: static, dynamic, and input text. The Text tool is one of the ways you can add any of these three kinds of text to a movie.

The Property inspector is a very important area for making modifications to text. You are able to select the type of text you intend to create and a font from the drop-down menu. Select the Text tool and then open the Property inspector.

Static text   Text rendered in a movie that does not change dynamically. The font does not have to be embedded or on a user's system. It displays similar to a graphic on the Stage.

Dynamic text   Text can be changed or updated dynamically or loaded into a Dynamic text field.

Input text   This creates a text field that users can type into at runtime. These are particularly useful in forms.

Ⓐ Font and Font Size   Specify a font for the text field from a drop-down list (this is a list of fonts installed on your computer system) and the font size in points.

Ⓑ Character Spacing and Character Position   Adjust the spacing between each character and set the character position to Normal, Subscript, or Superscript.

Ⓒ Line Type   Set the line type of a Dynamic or Input text field to Single Line, Multiline, or Multiline No Wrap. Input text fields allow you to also set the line type to Password.

Ⓓ URL Link   Enter a URL into this field to create a link from the selected text field.

Ⓔ Selectable   Make text selectable on the Stage at runtime.

Ⓕ Render Text As HTML   Add basic HTML formatting to text entered into Dynamic text fields.

Ⓖ Show Border Around Text   Show a border around the text and add a background. The default color is white, but this can be changed using ActionScript.

Ⓗ Text (fill) Color   Set the text color.

Ⓘ Var   Enter a variable to be associated with Dynamic or Input text fields.

Ⓙ Toggle Bold and Italic   Set selected characters to boldface or italics.

Ⓚ Alias Text   Optimize selected characters. This makes small fonts clearer and easier to read when they don't appear to be anti-aliased.

Ⓛ Text Orientation   Change the text direction. Only static text can take advantage of being set to vertical.

Ⓜ Text Justification   Justify text left, right, or center or fully justify.

Ⓝ Format and Character   Set line indentation, spacing, and left and right margins; and embed font outlines.

➡ 15.4 Adding an Instance Name

➡ 20.9 Creating Dynamic Text Fields

Text tool

Ⓣ

To have a fixed-width text field snap back to expanding with text, double-click the handle.

Use the circle or square handle to resize a text field.

To warp, distort, or apply gradients to text you must break the text and characters apart using Modify > Break Apart.

If you are using small fonts, make sure to click the Alias text button in the Property inspector to optimize the fonts for easy readability.

_sans, _serif, and _typewriter are three device fonts included with Flash (equivalent to Arial, Times Roman, and Courier, respectively). If you select one of these fonts, the movie uses the system font on the end user's computer that is closest to the font you specify. The font is not embedded (decreasing SWF file size); however, some results are unpredictable.

Continues ●

You can use simple HTML 1.0 formatting within text to create links, change color, or boldface text. Make sure you have the Render Text As HTML button enabled in the Property inspector.

You can set your default text orientation to vertical in the Editing tab of the Preferences dialog.

To change the settings of a text field (including font), either select the text itself or the entire object using the Selection tool, and change settings in the Property inspector.

Remember to enter an instance name instead of entering a value into the Var field, whenever possible. Refer to Scripting Tasks for more information.

You can create scrolling text by creating more text in a field than is displayed within its bounds. Do this by holding down Shift while double-clicking its handle or choosing Text > Scrollable. Now you can type more text into the field than is displayed.

- Create a text field with a fixed width by clicking on the Stage and dragging a box of a certain dimension. You see a square on the right-hand side of a fixed-width text field.

- Create a text field with an expanding width by clicking on the Stage and beginning to type. The field expands while you type. You see a circle on the right-hand side of an expanding text field.

- When you double-click or create a text field, Dynamic text fields have a square or circle in the lower right-hand corner of the field. Input text fields always have a square in this corner of the field.

- A Static text field always displays with a square or circle in the upper right-hand corner when it's being typed into, depending on whether it is expanding or set to a predetermined fixed width.

This chapter is brought to you by the number 7 and the letter K.

A text field is created on the Stage. You can tell by the position of the square on the left-hand side that it is a fixed-width Static text field.

3.12   Oval Tool

The Oval tool 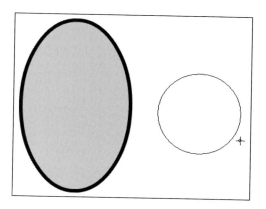 draws circles and ovals on the Stage. Create an oval by clicking the Stage and dragging diagonally to the opposite corner of the shape. Hold down the Shift key while clicking and dragging the cursor to create a perfect circle.

There are no options associated with the Oval tool. However, you can use the Property inspector to choose a fill and stroke color and style. You can specify this before creating the oval, or select the fill and outline after it is created using the Selection tool and then make modifications.

A perfect circle is created by holding Shift while clicking and dragging the mouse cursor. A hairline cursor allows you to create shapes with precision.

➡ 3.13 Rectangle Tool

➡ 3.19 Paint Bucket Tool

➡ 3.24 Color Control and Palettes

➡ 9.2 Understanding Strokes and Fills

➡ 9.4 Creating Primitive Shapes and Strokes

Oval tool
O

Create perfect circle
Shift drag

Click the No Color button to create a rectangle or square without a stroke outline.

3.13　Rectangle Tool

Rectangle tool
Ⓡ

**Create sides of
equal length**
Shift drag

You can change the
shape of any square or
rectangle using the
Selection tool. Simply
hover near an unse-
lected corner or seg-
ment and adjust the
shape as necessary.

The Rectangle tool ▢ draws squares and rectangles on the Stage. You create a rectangle by clicking on the Stage and dragging diagonally to the opposite corner of the shape. You are able to set stroke and fill properties using the Property inspector.

There is one option available for the Rectangle tool. Round the corners of a rectangle by using one of the options called Round Rectangle Radius. Click this button in the Options area before creating the rectangle. After entering a value (measured in points), click OK and create a rectangle on the Stage.

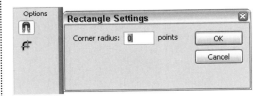

You can change how round the corners of the rectangle are. Use higher numbers to round the corners more, and the rectangle becomes increasingly like a circle.

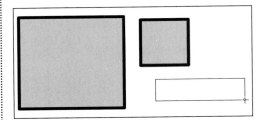

Rectangles or squares can be created using the Rectangle tool. Set fill and stroke prop- erties in the Property inspector. The cursor looks like a crosshair, which allows for pre- cise positioning.

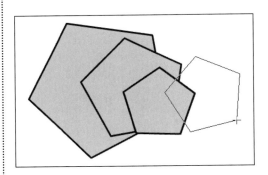

Select the PolyStar tool by clicking and holding the Rectangle tool in the Tools panel. This tool is used in exactly the same way as the Rectangle tool, but the resulting shape is five-sided. Click and drag the Stage to create the shape, and move the cursor up and down or side to side to rotate the shape. Release the mouse button when you are finished.

3.14 Pencil Tool

Use the Pencil tool to create freeform lines and drawings. You can use a simple solid line or a number of line styles to create unique illustrations.

The Property inspector allows you to change line style of the Pencil tool.

There are several different drawing options in the Options section of the Tools panel. These options give you varying degrees of control over the strokes you make on the Stage. The sensitivity of how much Flash "helps" you draw is controlled in the Editing tab of the Preferences dialog (Edit > Preferences). If you hold down Shift while using the Pencil tool, it is constrained to horizontal and vertical lines.

Straighten Use this option if you are trying to draw regular shapes (circles, rectangles, triangles) and want Flash to "correct" them when rendering the shape on the Stage.

Smooth Use this option if you want Flash to smooth only jagged strokes on the Stage.

Ink Use this option if you do not want Flash to change your strokes at all.

Left, Straighten; center, Smooth; right, Ink. The three line style options change how your drawings are rendered on the Stage. The Straighten option helps you draw regular shapes, such as circles and triangles.

Remember that Flash anti-aliases your drawings by default. The strokes look slightly different than when you actively draw using the Ink option, since even the Ink edges are smoothed or blurred to create a soft edge.

➡ 3.6 Selection (Arrow) Tool

➡ 9.4 Creating Primitive Shapes and Strokes

Pencil tool
Y

You can change drawing preferences in the Editing tab of the Preferences dialog (Edit > Preferences). The settings in these preferences change the sensitivity of the pencil modifier options.

To change the style of a line already drawn on the Stage, select the line using the Selection tool and then change the style in the Property inspector.

To make a pencil stroke more angled or smooth, select the stroke using the Selection tool and then click the Smooth or Straighten buttons within the Options section of the Tools panel.

When the pencil stroke is selected, use Modify > Shape > Optimize to simplify the lines you draw using the Pencil tool. This command reduces the file size of the SWF when you publish the movie.

Only use special strokes when absolutely necessary. Any stroke other than a normal solid stroke is processor intensive at runtime.

3.15   Brush Tool

Brush tool

B

If you magnify the
Stage using the Zoom
tool, the brush size
changes depending on
the magnification of
the Stage.

Hold down Shift while
using the Brush tool
and the stroke is con-
strained to a horizontal
or vertical line.

To change the color of
a brush stroke, select
the stroke using the
Selection tool and then
change the fill color in
the Property inspector.

The Brush tool creates painterly strokes on the Stage. Because you can choose among several different brush shapes, you can even create calligraphic effects using the brush. The Brush tool uses the Fill color, which means that you can also paint using a bitmap or gradient fill.

Ⓐ Paint options Choose how strokes are applied to the Stage

Ⓑ Lock Fill Lock the fill of the paint brush

Ⓒ Brush Size Choose a size of brush from this menu

Ⓓ Brush Shape Choose among several brush shapes from this menu

Paint Normal Paints anywhere you drag the cursor on the Stage. It paints over the top of lines and fills on the same layer.

Paint Fills Makes the brush lines paint fills empty parts of the Stage; how-ever, it won't paint over strokes or lines.

Paint Behind Causes the brush to paint behind any fill or stroke on the same layer.

Paint Selection Paints only fills that are selected.

Paint Inside Paints only the first fill area that is clicked. This also includes the Stage.

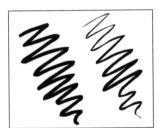

If you have a tablet hooked up to the computer, you see two more modifier buttons in the Options area. These buttons allow you to take advantage of the tablet's pressure sensitivity and pen tilt: the Use Pressure and Use Tilt buttons. These modifiers help you to draw brush strokes using painterly strokes and add a more natural feel to your draw-ings. Notice the difference—these two lines were drawn exactly the same way.

Apply Smoothing to the Brush tool in the Property inspector, which applies a precise amount of smooth-ing to your brush strokes. Choose an amount between 0.25 and 100.

3.16   Free Transform Tool

The Free Transform tool ⊞ allows you to rotate, skew, distort, and resize a selected object or primitive graphic on the Stage. When selected, a bounding box appears around the item with several handles used to control the size and rotation of the shape.

When the cursor is near the bounding box or a handle, several different cursors appear, as shown in the following table.

Ⓐ **Rotate and Skew** Rotate an object around the center point or opposite corner, and skew the object horizontally or vertically.

Ⓑ **Scale** Only scale the object using the Free Transform tool.

Ⓒ **Distort** Modify and taper objects so you can add a sense of perspective to graphics.

Ⓓ **Envelope** Warp and distort selected objects. Use the bounding box handles and tangent handles to distort objects.

Free Transform Tool Cursors

CURSOR	USE
↺	Appears when you hover over corner points and rotates the object around the registration point. You can move the center registration point to change how the object rotates.
↔	Skews the object when you hover over an object's bounding box side. You can skew horizontally or vertically, on all four sides of the bounding box.
⤡	Scales the object horizontally and vertically, while maintaining the same proportions, if you press the Shift key. You find this cursor when hovering over the handles at each corner. Resize the object horizontally or vertically using handles between the four corners.
⬥	Moves the object to a different location on the Stage.
▷	You see this cursor when you use the Distort or Envelope modifiers. Use this cursor to move the handles and edit the object.
▶	This is how the cursor appears when it is not near a handle or the bounding box.
▷	Press Shift when using the Distort option, and you see this cursor. This allows you to taper the object evenly on the opposite side, vertically or horizontally.

When you select an object on the Stage using the Free Transform tool, a bounding box and handles appear.

Distort allows you to distort and taper an object. You can distort several objects at once by selecting a group and then clicking the Distort option.

Envelope gives you the most control over transforming an object. Drag the handle points around the object's bounding box, and then move tangent handles to warp the object.

➡ 3.6   Selection (Arrow) Tool

➡ 5.4   Info Panel

➡ 5.6   Transform Panel

➡ 9.1   Basics of Primitives

➡ 9.7   Conforming Primitives to Curves with the Envelope Tool

Free Transform tool
Ⓠ

Press Shift while Scaling using a corner handle. This allows you to Scale while maintaining the object's proportions.

———

You can only use the Distort and Envelope options on primitive graphics. These modifiers do not work on symbols, bitmaps or video objects. To distort a bitmap, select Modify > Break Apart first.

———

Press Shift when you rotate objects, and they rotate in 45 degree increments.

———

Press the Alt key (Option key on the Mac) when rotating objects to rotate around the corner that is directly opposite of the selected handle, or skew in the opposite direction.

———

You can modify more than one object within a single envelope. Select both objects, and then click the Envelope option.

51

3.17   Fill Transform Tool

Fill Transform tool

F

___

You can use the Fill
Transform tool to cre-
ate interesting lighting
effects. These effects
can help add a sense of
depth or 3D to your
Flash movies.

The Fill Transform tool 🖼 is useful for editing different kinds of gradients or bitmap fills. The kind of gradient applied to a shape affects how you edit it using this tool. If you apply a radial gradient, you see different handles and a different bounding box for editing than if you are editing a linear gradient.

To use the Fill Transform tool, select the tool and then click an object that has a gradient fill. Notice how several handles appear along with either a circle, square, or pair of lines to bound the area.

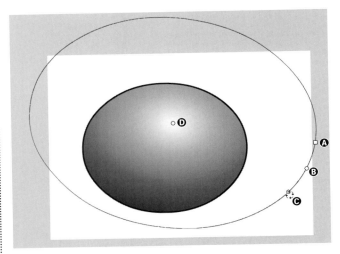

Ⓐ **Size** Drag this handle to change the gradient's size.

Ⓑ **Radius** Drag this handle to change the radius of the gradient.

Ⓒ **Rotation** Drag this handle to rotate the gradient.

Ⓓ **Center point** Drag this handle to change the gradient's center point.

3.18 Ink Bottle Tool

Use the Ink Bottle tool  to change the thickness, style, and color of a primitive stroke. The tool can also create a new stroke around a shape or drawing. Click a primitive graphic using the Ink Bottle, and a stroke is added around the perimeter using the current stroke properties.

The Property inspector is used to change the stroke that is applied to a graphic using the Ink Bottle tool.

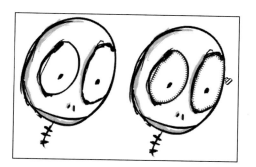

A graphic can have a stroke added to it with the Ink Bottle. If there is already a stroke around the graphic, the Ink Bottle can change the stroke to a new style or color.

➡ 3.20 Eyedropper Tool

➡ 3.24 Color Control and Palettes

➡ 9.2 Understanding Strokes and Fills

Ink Bottle tool
S

You can sample a stroke using the Eyedropper tool, and it automatically changes into an Ink Bottle. The style that you just selected is automatically applied to the Ink Bottle.

3.19 Paint Bucket Tool

Paint Bucket tool
K

You can even fill an object with a bitmap image. Just break apart a bitmap (Modify > Break Apart) and select it using the Eyedropper tool. It will then be sampled as the Fill. Then you can click on the Stage using the Paint Bucket tool as usual, and it will be filled with the bitmap.

Keep in mind that even though you may choose Fill Large Gaps, the gap cannot be too large. The gap must be a relatively small space between two line ends in your drawing.

The Paint Bucket tool  fills an object with a color, bitmap, or gradient. Colors can be selected using the eyedropper or color controls in the Tools panel or any palette in Flash with color swatches.

Don't Close Gaps Select this option if you have parts of your drawings that should not be filled when using the Paint Bucket. Any gaps in your outline are not closed, and the object you click within does not fill.

Close Small Gaps Fills drawings even if there are small gaps in the lines. Flash estimates how the shape should be filled, although no additional lines are added to the shape.

Close Medium Gaps Fills drawings with moderate gaps and approximates the missing areas.

Close Large Gaps Fills drawings, despite large gaps in the shape outline. Flash compensates for the missing area.

You can select many different fill options using the drop-down menu. The second button is to Lock Fill, which is typically used to apply a gradient or bitmap fill to several selected objects on the Stage at once. This text has a gradient fill applied across all selected letters using Lock Fill.

Replace a color using the Paint Bucket tool.

3.20 Eyedropper Tool

The Eyedropper tool  selects fill, stroke, and bitmap samples on the Stage. Using this tool you can sample the style, width, and color of a stroke. Then you can apply this style to any other stroke on the stage. When you sample color or stroke attributes using the Eyedropper tool they become the current style or color. When you hover over and click a stroke, the tool samples the stroke properties. When you hover over and click a fill, the tool samples the fill properties.

Hover the Eyedropper tool over a fill and it changes into a Paint Bucket tool. Then you can apply the color to a new fill area. If you hover over a stroke, it samples that stroke style and changes into the Ink Bottle so you can apply it to other strokes on the Stage.

➡ 3.18 Ink Bottle Tool

➡ 3.19 Paint Bucket Tool

➡ 9.2 Understanding Strokes and Fills

Eyedropper tool
[I]

You can sample a bitmap by hovering over and clicking it, as long as it has Modify > Break Apart applied to it.

You cannot sample symbols. You can only sample primitive objects on the Stage or broken apart bitmaps.

ADDING COMMANDS TO THE ENVIRONMENT

Custom commands can be added to the Flash authoring environment. There aren't any Commands included when Flash is installed: you have to create or download your own. Commands can do many useful things, such as set up the workspace. For example, a command could set up the Timeline, library, and layers just the way you want them to be set up. Commands are written from a language called JSFL, or Flash JavaScript. If you use Flash Professional, you can create new JSFL files when you choose File > New.

3.21 Eraser Tool

➥ 8.3 Editing
a Stage
Selection

Eraser tool

You can remove primi-
tive strokes and fills by
selecting them using
the Selection tool and
pressing Backspace or
Delete.

———

To remove a text,
graphic, or movie clip
symbol instance from
the Stage, select the
object using the Selec-
tion tool and press
Backspace or Delete.

The Eraser tool 🖉 erases lines and fills. Use the Options menu to choose from several different ways to remove content from the Stage.

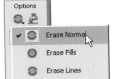

Ⓐ Erase Options Allows you to use the eraser in several different ways. See the next section for details.

Ⓑ Faucet Acts more like a vacuum than a faucet: it completely removes color from a fill or stroke.

Ⓒ Eraser Shape Use this menu to select a particular size and shape for the eraser.

Erase Normal Erases all lines and fills.

Erase Fills Erases fills only without erasing the stroke.

Erase Lines Erases only lines and strokes while leaving fills intact.

Erase Selected Fills Erases only the fill that is selected beforehand. Nothing else is erased outside of that selection.

Erase Inside Erases only the first fill color that is clicked. Nothing other than that fill is erased.

Erase Normal erases all of the fill and lines in a graphic.

3.22   Hand Tool

The Hand tool  pans the Stage left, right, up, and down. All you need to do is click and hold and then drag the mouse. This is particularly useful when the content you are working on extends farther than the viewable frame area.

When your FLA is zoomed way in so you can add detail, you might need to use the Hand tool to move the Stage around.

➡ 1.4   Windows
         Authoring
         Interface

➡ 3.23 Zoom Tool

Hand tool
⌑ H

Hand tool on the fly
⌑ Spacebar

You can automatically use the Hand tool by pressing the spacebar. This changes the cursor into a hand, and then you only have to click and drag to move the Stage around.

3.23   Zoom Tool

The Zoom tool zooms in and out from the Stage 🔍. This allows you to edit objects on the Stage in great detail (by zooming in), or view all of the items on or around the Stage at once (by zooming out). There are two options for the Zoom tool: Enlarge zooms in, and Reduce zooms out.

Use the Enlarge modifier (left) to zoom in, and the Reduce modifier (right) to zoom out. Select the modifier and then click the Stage to change your magnification level.

➡ 2.4   View Menu

➡ 3.4   Edit Bar

➡ 3.22 Hand Tool

➡ 5.4   Info Panel

Zoom tool
M or Z

Zoom In
⌘ =
Ctrl =

Zoom Out
⌘ −
Ctrl −

100% zoom
⌘ 1
Ctrl 1

Fit In Window
⌘ 2
Ctrl 2

Show All
⌘ 3
Ctrl 3

Toggle zooming in/out
Option
Alt

―――

You can also choose magnification in a drop-down menu on the edit bar.

―――

You can zoom all the way from 8% to 2000%. This allows you to get a very close up view of the Stage or to view your FLA file like a thumbnail.

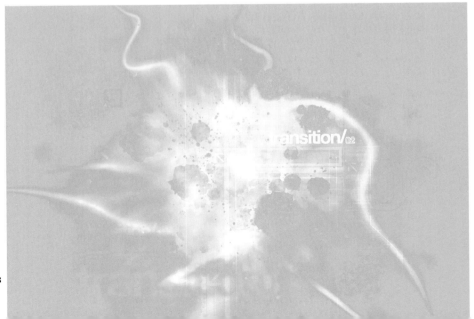

3.24   Color Control and Palettes

Stroke and fill colors are chosen in the Colors part of the Tools panel. When you click and hold either the stroke or fill color, a color pop-up window opens where you can choose any one of a number of swatches. You can also press buttons to restore default black and white colors, set the fill to none, or swap current fill and stroke colors. Fill color can also be set to a bitmap using the Eyedropper tool or gradients. Gradients can be customized using the Color Mixer panel.

A **Stroke Color** Displays the current stroke (line) color.

B **Fill Color** Displays the current fill color.

C **Black and White** Changes the current stroke and fill colors to black and white (default colors).

D **No Color** Select the stroke or fill and then click this button, which sets either one to no fill. This is only available when you are creating new shapes.

E **Swap Colors** Swaps the current stroke and fill colors.

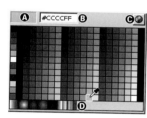

A **Current Color** Displays the currently selected color.

B **Hex Value** Shows you the current hex value for the current color. You can also type a value into this field to choose a hex color manually.

C **Color** Opens the Color dialog, which allows you to access system colors.

D **Gradient swatches** This area allows you to select default color swatches for a fill.

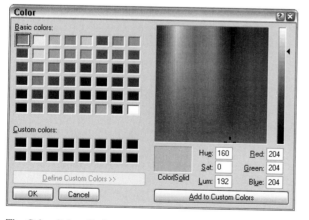

The Color dialog displays system colors. Use this panel to add custom colors to your swatch. You can choose colors using RGB and HSL values. You can open this panel by pressing Alt and double-clicking anywhere a Color picker opens.

➨ 3.6   Selection (Arrow) Tool

➨ 5.2   Color Mixer Panel

➨ 5.3   Color Swatches Panel

➨ 9.2   Understanding Strokes and Fills

➨ 9.3   Understanding Color and Gradients

Add Custom colors to the Color dialog by choosing a color and then clicking the Add To Custom Colors button. It will be added to your custom color swatches.

If you are using the Colors section of the Tools panel to change a stroke or fill of an existing primitive graphic, it must be selected beforehand using the Selection tool.

FLASH WORKSPACE

AUTHORING TASKS

SCRIPTING TASKS

TESTING AND PUBLISHING TASKS

WHAT'S NEW

3.25 Color Swatches

You can change the default palette that opens with each Flash document. Choose Save As Default from the Color Swatches panel menu to do this.

Some artists find it much easier to work with a palette when it is organized by hue. To reorganize your color palette by hue, select Sort By Color from the Color Swatches panel menu. Select Web 216 again to return to the default palette.

Colors can be changed in the Color Swatches panel, the color area of the Tools panel, or the Property inspector.

You can use a set of default swatches (palettes) in Flash MX or create your own swatches to work with. Open the Color Swatches menu by selecting Window > Design Panels > Color Swatches. A swatch applies fill and stroke colors for objects on the Stage. Objects can be filled using a solid color, gradient, or bitmap. You can import, export, modify, and delete color swatches using the Color Swatches panel. The default swatch palette is 216 Web Safe colors. Colors can be added to this by using the Color Mixer panel.

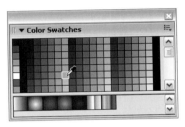

Select a Swatch (a colored square) using an Eyedropper cursor. The panel's menu is in the upper right-hand corner. Gradients are available for fills only.

You can duplicate a swatch by selecting one in this panel and selecting Duplicate Swatch from the Color Swatches panel Options menu. If you want to delete the color from the swatch palette, choose Delete Swatch from the Options menu.

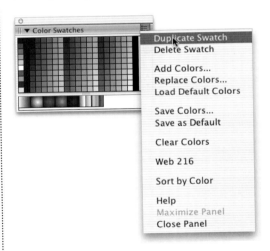

The Color Swatches menu allows you to open and customize color palettes. You can transfer the swatch between other programs such as Fireworks and Photoshop. You can save your custom palette by selecting Save Colors.

CHAPTER 4

Timelines and Screens

THE TIMELINE IS THE way Flash represents animation, and it is crucial to understanding how Flash works. Understanding the Timeline allows you to efficiently create both tween and scripted animation; it is the starting point to creating motion graphics. This chapter describes the Timeline panel; later chapters (mostly in the "Authoring Tasks" part of the book) tell you how to use it. To understand the techniques required to use the timeline for traditional animation, including working with frames, refer mainly to Chapter 10.

As well as timeline-based content, Flash MX Professional allows you to create page-based content using screens, which are introduced at the end of this chapter.

To understand the techniques required to use the timeline for scripted animation (and the associated skill scripted multimedia handling) refer to the "Scripting Tasks" section of this book.

- 4.1 **Timeline overview**
- 4.2 **Layer options**
- 4.3 **Timeline options**
- 4.4 **Timeline menus and modes**
- 4.5 **Screens**
- 4.6 **Slides and forms**

4.1 Timeline Overview

Toggle Timeline panel

Ctrl Alt T
⌘ Option T

———

The Edit Scene icon (rather confusingly) has controls only for jumping around the scenes. To actually edit the scene order or add/delete scenes, you need to use the Scene panel (Window > Scene).

The Timeline panel is split into several major sections:

Ⓐ These controls navigate between embedded timelines.

Ⓑ The main part of the Timeline panel contains the Timeline itself, which is made up of frames.

Ⓒ This cluster of icons is mainly concerned with onion skinning and Edit In Place. (These controls are not actually part of the Timeline panel but are mentioned here because they are so closely associated with it.)

Ⓓ Displays basic information about the Timeline and playhead. This shows the frame number, the frame rate, and the elapsed time since the start of the current timeline and moment the playhead will reach the selected frame. Double-clicking anywhere in this area brings up the Document Properties dialog.

Ⓔ These miscellaneous controls are concerned with scenes, the library, and Stage magnification. The only one related to the Timeline is the first, the Edit Scene icon, which allows you to move between scenes in your timeline. Clicking a scene takes you to the first frame in that scene.

Ⓕ This area is concerned with layers.

SUPPORT FOR SCREENS

Flash MX 2004 Standard does not support screens, and you will not see the options to open screen-based FLAs in this version. Also, screens are a Flash Player 7 feature only; they will not work in previous versions of Flash Player.

4.2   Layer Options

When traditional animators create cartoons, they use a system of transparent cels onto which the frames of the animation are painted. A cel is a transparent sheet consisting of a small portion of the animation. For example, an animation of a face would include a cel of the face oval and separate cels over the top of it containing the eyes, nose, and mouth, respectively. This allows each major part of the animation to be painted separately; you don't have to keep redrawing the whole face if the only movement is that the eyes are blinking. The advantage of this is that you can add separate and smaller animations by laying various cels on top of others, rather than having to redraw everything in every frame.

The Flash Timeline uses a system that is functionally identical to the cel-based system called *layers*. These are stacked on the Timeline in the same way cels are stacked on top of each other, and for the same reason; it allows you to separate your animation into separate parts.

Ⓐ   Layer name   To change the name, click it. The name will change to a text entry box, allowing you to enter a new name.

Ⓑ   Edit status   Indicates whether the current layer contents are editable 🖉 or uneditable 🔒. In most cases, the reason a layer is uneditable is that it is locked.

Ⓒ   Show/Hide   Controls layer visibility. To set all layers invisible, click this eye icon. To set the visibility of an individual layer, click the icon to the right of the layer title and in the column under the eye and it will toggle between show • and hide ✖. Here, all layers are visible except mainTitle.

Ⓓ   Lock/Unlock   Toggles between locked 🔒 and unlocked •. A locked layer's Stage contents cannot be edited or modified. Here, all layers are unlocked except the one named status. By locking/unlocking content you can create complex selections, or preserve the contents of layers you no longer wish to edit.

Ⓔ   Draw mode   Toggles between a normal and outline draw modes. Outline mode lets you see through the layer content to layers below it while still retaining cues about where the layer content is. Here, the two layers whose names begin with *guide* are set to show outlines.

The color of the outlines drawn in outlines mode will be the same as the layer color. The layer color is the color of the square in the draw mode column. You can change this color via the Layer Properties dialog, which can be accessed from the Timeline by double-clicking the square.

➡ 10.20 Adding Layers

➡ 10.21 Setting Layer Properties and Layer Types

➡ 10.25 Creating and Using Masks and Masked Layers

———

Layers are discarded and converted to *depths* in the final SWF file; layers don't exist in the final Flash presentation.

———

When you hide a layer, it can no longer be selected or edited, so you effectively lock it as well.

———

Many designers tend to lock all layers on a completed timeline to prevent accidental editing.

———

Setting all layers to outline draw mode makes for faster screen redraws.

———

The layer options can also be accessed from a context menu; right-click/~Control-click the layer title bar.

———

Motion tweens work on only one symbol at a time, and shape tweens may give odd results if you use more than one separate shape. It therefore makes sense to have only one symbol or graphic on each layer at a time.

4.3   Timeline Options

———

The path shown by the Path Explorer should not be confused with an ActionScript dot path or dot notation; the former refers to symbol library names, and the latter refers to instance names.

———

The contents of tween frames contain nothing as far as Edit Multiple Frames is concerned. To move a tween, make sure that the brackets enclose the start and end keyframes.

———

Onion skinning can cause sluggish Stage redraws because you are asking Flash to redraw much more information. On slower machines, consider keeping the onion skin range low, or use Onion Skin Outlines (which is generally much faster in terms of screen redraws).

Timelines are hierarchical in Flash (i.e., you can have timelines within timelines), much as file folders on your operating system are. The hierarchy is defined by a *path,* and to work with nested timelines, you have to be able to navigate forward and backward along the path. This is done via the Path Explorer. You will see it above and to the left of the Timeline panel.

To move forward along the path, double-click a symbol on the Stage. This will open the symbol (the process is called Edit In Place). To move back one level along the path, click the Back button (the arrow at the far left of the Path Explorer). To move back to a specific level, click any part of the path that is underlined.

The cluster of icons to the bottom left of the Timeline are useful when editing timeline-based animations:

Ⓐ Center Frame Moves the currently highlighted frame to the center of the panel (only works for timelines that are longer than the Timeline panel, causing a scrollbar to appear).

Ⓑ Onion Skin Toggles onion skinning mode. In onion skin mode, the Start Onion Skin and End Onion Skin markers appear at the top of the Timeline. All frames enclosed by these markers will be used in the onion skin. The markers can be dragged via click-dragging.

Ⓒ Onion Skin Outlines Toggles between showing the full symbols and symbol outlines for the onion skin. The outline colors used are the layer colors.

Ⓓ Edit Multiple Frames Allows you to select content within all frames enclosed by the onion skin markers. This is useful when you want to move the contents of a tween in a single operation.

Ⓔ Modify Onion Markers Brings up a menu for quick-editing the behavior of the onion skin markers:

Always Show Onion Markers Displays the markers even when you don't have onion skinning enabled. You usually do this when you are using the markers for Edit In Place but don't want to see onion skinning at the same time.

Anchor Onion Fixes the position of the markers. By default, they will always center themselves around the playhead, but enabling this option is useful when you want the onion skin to stay still while you move around frames within it (typically while you are editing keyframes within the onion skin).

Onion 2, Onion 5, Onion All Moves the onion skin markers to two or five frames on either side of the playhead or to include the entire Timeline. Selecting Onion All is not recommended for long timelines, because it forces Flash to draw all frame content for that timeline, and can result in Flash becoming *very* sluggish.

Onion skin markers

Full symbols in onion skin mode (left); symbol outlines (right)

4.4   Timeline Menus and Modes

The Timeline panel has three contextual menus to handle layers, frame editing, and time-line view modes.

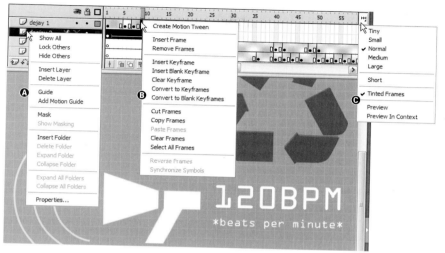

Although there are several timeline view options, only a very few of them are commonly used because the default view is adequate for most purposes. The most used options are those that create smaller frames.

Preview and Preview In Context modes can cause slow timeline redraw, so be wary of using them in long timelines or where there are large amounts of detailed graphics.

Ⓐ   Right-click a layer title bar to bring up the Layer contextual menu.

Ⓑ   Right-click a frame to bring up the Frame contextual menu.

Ⓒ   Right-click the Timeline icon at the top right of the Timeline to bring up the Timeline View contextual menu.

In earlier versions of Flash, Synchronize Symbols (the last option on the Frame menu) should be selected when you have embedded looping timelines of an unequal number of frames. (For example, you could have a main timeline of 10 frames, and on frame 1, have a movie clip myClip of 12 frames. The main timeline will end before myClip, and this can sometimes cause problems.) Occasionally, this may lead to jumps in the animation, caused by one of the timelines completing its loop before the other, and synchronizing the symbols will prevent this. This issue doesn't seem to happen often with the later Flash players (Flash 5+), so you are unlikely to need to do this often.

The Timeline View menu allows you to alter the way frames are rendered. From left to right, the Tiny, Small, Normal, Medium, and Large options alter frame width; Normal is the default.

The Short option allows you to choose between two frame heights and is unselected by default.

Continues

The Timeline panel has three contextual menus to handle layers, frame editing, and timeline view modes.

The Tinted Frames option allows you to select between two ways of displaying frame shading. Frames are tinted (shaded) by default. The Preview option allows you to see thumbnails of keyframe contents. Thumbnails are cropped to exclude empty areas of the Stage; if you don't want what you see to be cropped, select Preview In Context, which shows thumbnails of the entire Stage.

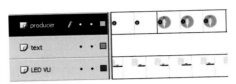   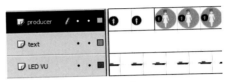

Preview   Preview in Context

Most frame editing options can be more quickly performed via keyboard shortcuts or via icons, which are discussed in Chapter 10.

Script-heavy timelines, or timelines that contain no tween-based animation, tend to make viewing large frames unnecessary. Consider changing to small frame sizes to make more of the Timeline visible.

SUPPORT FOR SCENES

Scenes are now deprecated (although they are retained to maintain backward compatibility), and you should avoid using them. Rather than splitting up a timeline into scenes, consider using layer folders or even screens instead.

4.5　Screens

Rather than being frame-based, screen presentations are based around a hierarchy of page-like containers, and the screen interface changes appearance to reflect this. (Screens are a feature of Flash MX Professional 2004 only.)

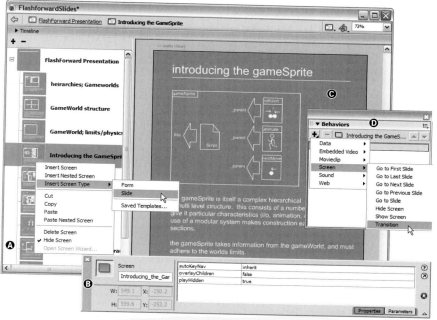

Ⓐ Screen hierarchy To add or delete a screen, press the + and – icons at the top. To change the title of a screen, double-click it and enter a new name. There is also a context menu that allows more complex editing operations.

Ⓑ Property Inspector The Properties and Parameters tabs of this panel allow you to change values that alter the way the screens work. To make changes to a screen, select it in the hierarchy pane (A) *not* the Stage (C). Selecting C will make the Property inspector show properties for the over-all FLA.

Ⓒ Stage area showing the screen You can add all the standard Flash symbols, text and primitives you can in a normal Flash Stage. Note that the Timeline panel is minimized by default.

Ⓓ Behaviors panel You can control the way your screens will work by adding behaviors to them. You can attach a behavior to a screen by selecting the screen in the hierarchy pane, clicking the Behavior panel + button, and then selecting a behavior within the screen options.

➡ 4.6　Slides and Forms

➡ 7.4　Starting a Flash Slide Presentation or Form Application

➡ 10.28　Building Slide Presentations

➡ 10.29　Building Form Applications

➡ 11.2　Understanding Behaviors

Although the Timeline is minimized by default in a screen presentation (given that screens are slide-based rather than frame-based), you will need to open it if your slide content is complicated enough to warrant using layers.

Before starting a screen-based presentation, it is a good idea to plan it out, noting all the major slides and interslide navigation you will need.

When using screens, the Path Explorer will display the screen hierarchy rather than the Timeline hierarchy.

Slides are an alternative way of representing navigation to the Timeline. They should not be confused with symbols; screens do not appear in the library!

4.6 Slides and Forms

Slides are a quick and easy way of creating Microsoft PowerPoint-style presentations.

Forms are an easy way of creating web form pages when you want to either make the next page conditional on what the user enters on the current page, conditionally change the appearance of the current form page.

A FLA that contains screens cannot also contain scenes. When authoring a screen-based FLA, the Edit Scene icon 🎬 will become the Edit Screen icon 🔲.

A screen can be one of two types: a slide or form. (Slides and forms are features of Flash MX Professional 2004 only.)

Slides Used when you want to create a sequential sequence, such as a business presentation. You can move forward and back through the slides in the final presentation (at runtime) by pressing the ← and → keys.

Forms Used when you want to move forward and back in a nonsequential manner, for example, if the page you go to (or the appearance of the current page changes) depends on user interaction.

Although you are able to mix the two types within a single FLA, Flash allows you to choose between Flash Slide Presentation and Flash Form Document when you open a new document. Your choice should be based on whether your FLA will contain mostly slides or mostly forms.

To add a slide or form to a currently open FLA, open the context menu in the Hierarchy pane. Then do one of the following:

■ If you select Insert Screen, a screen will be added after the current insertion point. The screen type will be the default for the FLA you are working with (slide for Flash Slide Presentation, form for Flash Form document).

■ If you want to override the default, select Insert Screen Type, and then select either Form or Slide from the submenu.

It can be difficult to tell whether the current screen is a slide or a form when you have a mixture of both types. The easiest way to tell is to select the screen and check its class in the Property inspector in the Properties tab. The class will be `mx.screens.Slide` for a slide and `mx.screens.Form` for a form. Alternatively, keep the text "slide" or "form" in the screen titles (a much easier option!).

CHAPTER 5

Panels

UNDERSTANDING THE FLASH WORKSPACE has a lot to do with learning what panels have to offer and how they work. Looking at panel functionality is very important if you expect to use the tools in Flash efficiently. Understanding what each feature does helps streamline your workflow and assist you in building your projects more quickly and with fewer mistakes.

5.1   Align Panel

Align panel
Ctrl K
⌘ K

Using the Align/Distribute To Stage button is a quick way to center an object in the absolute center of your Flash movie.

The Align panel (Window **>** Design Panels **>** Align) is used to align and distribute objects on the Stage along a horizontal or vertical axis. The Align panel can also be used to distribute the selected objects so the space between each object is equal based on edges or the axis. Objects can be aligned relative with each other or relative to the Stage.

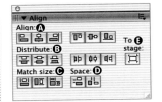

Ⓐ Align Aligns edges or center points of the selected objects. If the Align/Distribute To Stage button is selected, the objects are aligned in relation to the dimensions of the Stage. If the button is not selected, they align to other selected objects.

Ⓑ Distribute Distributes selected objects by the edge or the center points of the object. If the Align/Distribute To Stage button is selected, then the objects are distributed in relation to the dimensions of the Stage. If it isn't, then they align to the other selected objects.

Ⓒ Match Size Resizes all selected objects so that their widths match the widest, tallest, or largest selected object.

Ⓓ Space Rearranges selected objects so they are equal distances from each other, either vertically or horizontally.

Ⓔ Align/Distribute To Stage Aligns and distributes objects relative to the Stage instead of each other.

5.2 Color Mixer Panel

The Color Mixer panel (Window > Design Panels > Color Mixer) is used to create solid fills and gradients using hexadecimal, RSB, or HSB modes. This panel lets you create complex linear or radial gradient fills using between two and eight colors. Choose Linear or Radial from the drop-down menu, and then change or add colors to the gradient definition bar that appears. Change colors by clicking each color pointer and then changing the color in the color control. Add colors to the gradient by clicking beneath the gradient definition bar, and a new color pointer is added.

You can also fill shapes by setting the fill style to Bitmap and choosing an image to fill the object with. Any imported bitmap images are shown in the Color Mixer panel, which you can choose by clicking one of them.

Ⓐ **Stroke color** Opens the color pop-up window where you can select a color for a stroke.

Ⓑ **Fill color** Opens the color pop-up window where you can select a color or gradient for the fill.

Ⓒ **Fill style** Allows you to select between None, Solid, Linear, Radial, or Bitmap.

Ⓓ Sets the current stroke color to black and the current fill color to white.

Ⓔ Sets the current stroke color or fill color to No Color. This button is only available when you are creating a new shape on the Stage.

Ⓕ Swaps the current stroke color with the current fill color.

Ⓖ Allows you to adjust the level of red, green, or blue to the current color selection.

Ⓗ Allows you to adjust the level of alpha in the current color selection.

Ⓘ **Options menu** Allows you to switch between RGB and HSB color modes, as well as to add the active color to the current document's color swatch list.

Ⓙ Allows you to enter a color in hexadecimal format.

Ⓚ **Color control** Allows you to choose a color from the color pop-up window.

Ⓛ **Brightness control** Allows you to control the brightness of the selected color in any color modes.

Ⓜ **Hide/Show Advanced Options** Toggles between an area that shows the Hexadecimal color text field, color space, and brightness slider, and an area that shows only a smaller color bar.

Color Mixer panel

You cannot set the stroke or fill color of an existing object to No Color; instead, you must select the stroke or fill of the object and delete it.

To access your system's default color picker, you can hold down the Alt or Option key and double-click the stroke color or fill color in the Color Mixer panel or Property inspector, or the stroke color or fill color control in the Tools panel.

FLASH WORKSPACE

AUTHORING TASKS

SCRIPTING TASKS

TESTING AND PUBLISHING TASKS

WHAT'S NEW

5.3   Color Swatches Panel

Color Swatches panel

Ctrl F9
⌘ F9

———

To access your system's
default color picker,
you can hold down the
Alt or Option key and
double-click the stroke
color or fill color in
the Color Mixer panel,
Property inspector, or
the stroke color or fill
color in the toolbar.

———

To remove a color
or gradient from the
Color Swatches panel,
hold the Ctrl or Com-
mand key while click-
ing a color with your
mouse. Your mouse
cursor changes to a
pair of scissors indicat-
ing the color will be
removed from the
palette when you click
the swatch. You'll prob-
ably encounter a slight
lag between pressing
and releasing the Ctrl
or Command key and
the cursor changing its
appearance. You might
also have to move your
mouse first.

The Color Swatches panel (Window > Design Panels > Color Swatches) provides easy access to predefined colors and gradients. Flash makes it easy to create custom swatches, duplicate existing swatches, make sure your movie uses the standard 216 web safe color palette, and even share your palettes with other programs such as Macromedia Fireworks or Adobe Photoshop.

Ⓐ Options menu Allows you to duplicate and delete swatches; sort the color palette by hue; use a web safe 216 color palette; and add, replace, or save the color swatches.

Ⓑ Color palette Displays the color swatches in the cur-rent color palette being used.

Ⓒ Gradient bar Displays any gradients that have been added to the current color set.

5.4   Info Panel

You can use the Info panel (Window > Design Panels > Info) to move and resize objects on the Stage, view the current X and Y position of a selected symbol or the mouse, and check the current RGB and alpha values for a selected object. You can choose whether the Info panel displays the X and Y coordinates of the upper left corner of the symbol or whether the panel shows the X and Y coordinates of the symbol's registration point. Toggle between these two values by clicking the center or upper left square on the coordinate grid.

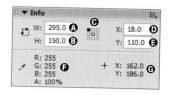

A **Width of instance** Displays the width of the selected object on the Stage.

B **Height of instance** Displays the height of the selected object on the Stage.

C **Coordinate grid** When the top left corner of the square is black (default) the X and Y coordinates in the Info panel and Property inspector display the location of the upper left corner of the selected symbol. If the center square is black, the Info panel and Property inspector shows the coordinates for the registration point.

D **X location of instance** Displays the X coordinate of the upper left corner or registration point of the selected object on the Stage.

E **Y location of instance** Displays the Y coordinate of the upper left corner or registration point of the selected object on the Stage.

F **Color at cursor location** Displays the red, green, blue, and alpha values of the object at the current mouse position (if the object has a solid fill).

G **Cursor location** Displays the current X and Y coordinates of the cursor location on the Stage.

➥ 5.6   Transform Panel

➥ 5.22 Property Inspector

Info panel
[Ctrl] [I]
[⌘] [I]

You can modify the width and height of the selected object on the Stage as well as the X and Y coordinates by changing the values in the Info panel.

From the Info panel, there is no easy way to constrain the aspect ratio when resizing an object on the Stage. If you want to resize the object on the Stage without distorting the dimensions, you should use the Property inspector and make sure the lock icon to the left of the Width and Height text fields is closed.

5.5   Scene Panel

➡ 10.26 Working
     with Scenes

Scene panel
[Shift] [F2]

To bypass the confirma-
tion dialog when delet-
ing a scene, hold down
the Ctrl or Command
key while clicking the
Delete Scene button in
the Scenes panel.

Double-click the scene
names in the list to
rename them.

You cannot use scenes
in a movie that uses
slides, such as a Flash
slide presentation or
Flash form application.

The use of scenes is
generally discouraged
unless they are abso-
lutely needed because
they can cause unpre-
dictable problems with
targeting in Action-
Script after your movie
is published. Therefore,
your code might break
after the file is pub-
lished. Scenes also
sometimes encourage
overlong Flash movies
that must be entirely
downloaded by your
end user.

When you publish a
movie with more than
one scene, the scenes
are arranged into one
long row of frames
when creating the SWF,
based on their order in
the Scenes panel.

If you're working on a Flash document containing more than one scene, you can use the Scene panel (Window > Design Panels > Scene) to manage your different scenes. The Scene panel is where you can add, duplicate, delete, rename, and reorder scenes in your Flash document. This panel is not available when you are working with a Flash slide presentation or a Flash form application because you cannot add scenes when working with either of these kinds of Flash files.

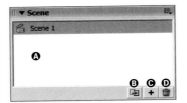

Ⓐ Scenes Lists all the scenes in the current document.

Ⓑ Duplicate scene Makes a copy of the selected scene.

Ⓒ Add scene Adds a new blank scene to the current document.

Ⓓ Delete scene Deletes the selected scene. Flash doesn't allow you to delete all scenes from your Flash docu-ment; you must always have at least one scene.

5.6 Transform Panel

The Transform panel (Window > Design Panels > Transform) can be used to resize, scale, skew, and rotate objects on the Stage. The Transform panel allows you to constrain your transformations so you can maintain the same ratio for your symbol.

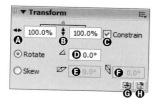

ⓐ Width Scales the width of the selection on the Stage by a given percentage.

ⓑ Height Scales the height of the selection on the Stage by a given percentage.

ⓒ Forces the width and height values above to use the same percentage value for width and height while rescaling the object on the Stage. This means you can retain the aspect ratio while transforming the object.

ⓓ Rotates the object on the Stage by a specified number of degrees.

ⓔ Skews the object on the Stage along its horizontal axis.

ⓕ Skews the object on the Stage along its vertical axis.

ⓖ Copy and apply transformation Duplicates the object on the Stage and applies the transformation to the new object.

ⓗ Reset Resets the values in the Transform panel back to their defaults.

➧ 2.5 Modify Menu

➧ 5.4 Info Panel

➧ 5.22 Property Inspector

Transform panel
Ctrl T
⌘ T

Rotate 90 degrees clockwise
Ctrl Shift 9
⌘ Shift 9

Rotate 90 degrees counterclockwise
Ctrl Shift 7
⌘ Shift 7

Remove transform
Ctrl Shift Z
⌘ Shift Z

———

You can also transform and modify objects on the Stage using the Modify menu. The Modify menu includes a Transform submenu from which you can choose various ways to transform the object.

———

You can restore an instance back to its original shape by resetting the transform, or you can select Modify > Transform > Remove Transform.

5.7 Actions Panel

➡ 6.6 Actions Panel Preferences

➡ 15.5 Entering Code in the Actions Panel

Actions panel
`F9`

Pin script
`Ctrl` `=`
`⌘` `=`

Close script
`Ctrl` `-`
`⌘` `-`

Close all scripts
`Ctrl` `Shift` `-`
`⌘` `Shift` `-`

View line numbers
`Ctrl` `Shift` `L`
`⌘` `Shift` `L`

Word wrap
`Ctrl` `Shift` `W`
`⌘` `Shift` `W`

Preferences
`Ctrl` `U`
`⌘` `U`

———

Turning on line numbers makes debugging any errors you may receive in the Output panel much easier. Flash reports the layer, frame, and line number in the error messages.

———

Pinning scripts can makes it a lot easier to quickly switch between ActionScript snippets.

The Actions panel (Window > Development Panels > Actions) is where you add Action-Script code to frames and objects within your Flash document. The Actions panel is one of the most important panels in Flash, because it is where you add or control code being added to the SWF file. Even if you are adding your code using include files, you still need to tell Flash to compile that code while the SWF is being published.

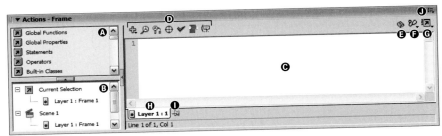

A **Actions toolbox** Provides a full reference to the ActionScript language.

B **Script navigator** Allows you to browse the active Flash document and view any ActionScript that may be bound to a frame or instance.

C **Script pane** Displays any ActionScript for the current selected object or the selected frame.

D **Actions panel toolbar** Includes a group of buttons for using features that help you write and edit ActionScript in the Script pane.

Add A New Item To The Script Adds ActionScript to the Script pane when you select options from a contextual drop-down menu.

Find Searches the current code in the Script pane for a specific series of words or letters

Replace Searches and replaces.

Insert A Target Path Inserts an instance's relative or absolute path

Check Syntax Validates ActionScript.

Auto Format Formats your code.

Show Code Hint Displays code hints when you enter code into the Script pane.

Reference Brings up context-aware help in the Help panel for the selected word.

E **Debug Options** Adds and removes breakpoints from the current ActionScript in the Script pane.

F **View Options pop-up menu** A contextual menu that allows you to view shortcut keys for adding ActionScript to your Flash document, view line numbers in the Script pane, and toggle word wrap.

G **Script tab** Easily cycles through pinned scripts.

H Pins a script to the Script pane so you can easily edit ActionScript code without having to use the Movie Explorer panel or the Script navigator.

I **Options menu** Pin or close scripts, search and replace text, set auto format options, print ActionScript code, check ActionScript syntax, import and export scripts, and set preferences.

5.8 Behaviors Panel

The Behaviors panel (Window > Development Panels > Behaviors) is new to Flash, and the behaviors you add from the panel allow you to add ActionScript to your Flash document without having to write the code yourself. Behaviors can be used to control embedded videos, open URLs, load external movie clips and graphics, load external MP3s into your Flash documents, and add navigation and transitions to slide presentations and form applications. Behaviors add ActionScript either to frames on the Timeline or to objects on the Stage, so you must ensure you have the correct element selected before clicking the Add Behavior button. This menu is context sensitive and only shows behaviors that can be added to a frame or a symbol depending on what is selected.

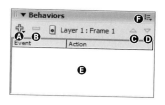

Ⓐ Add Behavior Adds a new behavior to the selected object.

Ⓑ Delete Behavior Removes the selected behavior from the list.

Ⓒ Move Up Moves the selected behavior up in the list.

Ⓓ Move Down Moves the selected behavior down in the list.

Ⓔ Behaviors pane Displays a list of any behaviors attached to the current frame, object, screen, or component.

Ⓕ Options menu Allows you to easily reload the listed behaviors.

➡ 11.2   Understanding Behaviors

➡ 11.11 Adding Movie Clip Control Using Behaviors

➡ 11.15 Adding Video Control Using Behaviors

➡ 11.17 Adding Basic Button Navigation Using Behaviors

➡ 12.4   Changing Stage Symbol Behaviors

➡ 14.5   Installing and Uninstalling Commands and Behaviors

Behaviors panel

Sometimes it is necessary to slightly tweak the code generated by a behavior, although this often means you are unable to edit the behavior using the Behavior Wizard.

Behaviors are aimed at beginners only, and intermediate users and beyond are strongly recommended to write their own ActionScript.

You can easily change the event that triggers a behavior to execute. After adding the behavior, change the value to the event you need under Event in the drop-down menu.

5.9   Components Panel

Components panel
Ctrl F7

—

The new components
included in Flash MX
2004 are known as "V2
UI Components."

—

If you are familiar with
Flash MX components,
you will quickly discover
there is no ScrollBar
component included
with Flash MX 2004. If
you find the component
useful, you can search
for a replacement
online and install it into
Flash using the Exten-
sion Manager. Expect to
find third-party versions
matching the V2 com-
ponent set available
through community
websites.

The Components panel (Window **>** Development Panels **>** Components) is where you see all the installed components available to Flash MX 2004. New components can be down-loaded from the Macromedia Exchange and installed using the Extension Manager. You need the Extension Manager 1.6 or greater to install components into Flash MX 2004. The UI (*User Interface*) components allow you to quickly add working user interface (UI) ele-ments to your FLA files. The components have been completely rewritten for Flash MX 2004, although many of the previous components have returned.

Some of the new components allow you to easily integrate with remote web services and XML documents (Flash MX Professional only). You definitely want to watch how much any of the components add to your SWF file size. Adding five or six components alone can add over 100K to the SWF, depending on which ones you use. If you are adding many components, make sure you frequently check your current file size during development, use a preloader (or ProgressBar component), and dynamically load as much information as possible.

ⓐ **Components pane** Lists all the components currently installed on your system.

ⓑ **Options menu** Allows you to easily reload the Compo-nents pane if any new components have been added or removed from your system.

5.10 Component Inspector Panel

The Component Inspector panel (Window > Development Panels > Component Inspector) allows you to change the properties of a selected component. You can modify certain properties of the component using the Property inspector; however; sometimes there are properties that are only accessible in the Components panel or by using ActionScript.

The Inspector includes three tabs in Flash MX Professional: Parameters, Bindings, and Schema. In Flash MX 2004, only the Parameters tab is available.

Ⓐ Options menu Allows you to easily find help on the currently selected component, add or remove bindings, add properties and fields to the schema tab, or import an XML schema.

Ⓑ Wizards for this component Opens a wizard for using the component.

Ⓒ Parameters tab Lists the editable parameters for the selected component on the Stage.

Ⓓ Bindings tab Allows you to define bindings between components (Flash MX Professional only).

Ⓔ Schema tab Allows you to import an XML schema representing some sample data. This allows Flash to add the proper fields and properties to your schema for you (Flash MX Professional only).

Ⓕ Parameters pane Allows you to modify the parameters for the currently selected component on the Stage.

➡ 5.9 Components Panel

➡ 5.22 Property Inspector

➡ 19 Setting Up and Using Components

➡ 25 Web Services and XML

Component Inspector panel
[Alt] [F7]
[Option] [F7]

———

Remember that while the Component Inspector panel has a full list of parameters to edit for a component, you can also edit the most commonly used parameters from the Property inspector.

———

The Bindings and Schema tabs in the Component Inspector panel are available only in Flash MX Professional.

5.11 Debugger Panel

Debugger panel
Shift F4

Set or remove break-point
Ctrl Shift B
⌘ Shift B

Remove all breakpoints
Ctrl Shift A
⌘ Shift A

Debug movie
Ctrl Shift Enter
⌘ Shift Return

Continue
F10

Stop debugging
F11

———

The Status bar displays whether the debugger is inactive, otherwise gives the URL or path of the file you are currently debugging.

———

When debugging, you can even modify the value of your variables in the Watch list to test your application more fully.

The Debugger panel (Window > Development Panels > Debugger) is an invaluable resource for troubleshooting any bugs that may occur during development. It is commonly used to show variables and their values used in a SWF file. You can watch and track values, and then debug the file.

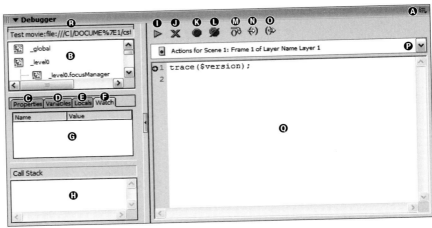

Ⓐ Options menu Allows you to stop debugging, step in, step over, step out of code, add or remove watches, and enable remote debugging.

Ⓑ Display list Displays properties and variables defined in the various levels, scopes, and objects within a movie.

Ⓒ Properties tab Displays the properties of the currently selected item in the Display list.

Ⓓ Variables tab Displays the name and value of any `_global` or Timeline variables in the Flash document.

Ⓔ Locals tab Shows the value of any local variables within a user-defined function.

Ⓕ Watch tab Allows you to track the value of flagged variables.

Ⓖ Watch list Lists all variables that have been flagged as "watched" and displays their current value.

Ⓗ Call Stack pane Shows function calls in a SWF file.

Ⓘ Continue Begins the debugging session and takes you to the next breakpoint.

Ⓙ Stop Debugging Cancels the debugging session but continues playing the SWF.

Ⓚ Toggle Breakpoint Removes an existing breakpoint.

Ⓛ Remove All Breakpoints Removes all existing breakpoints for the current Flash document.

Ⓜ Step Over, Step In, Step Out Steps over a line of code in the debugger, or advances the debugger to or out of a user-defined function.

Ⓝ Jump menu Lists scripts in the current Flash document that you can debug.

Ⓞ Code View Displays the code for the selected frame. Flash doesn't let you modify your Action-Script in this pane; you can only set or clear breakpoints.

5.12 Output Panel

The Output panel (Window > Development Panels > Output) has many uses in Flash. First and foremost it allows you to debug your Flash applications by using the Action-Script trace action. The trace action lets you output the value of a variable to the Output panel, where you can help debug any potential problems that may arise during development. The Output panel appears in the testing environment when values are returned. You can output any number of things to help you construct or debug movies, such as numbers, variables, text blocks, and returned values. Of course, the Output panel also alerts you when you have ActionScript errors in the SWF file and provides hints at how to correct them.

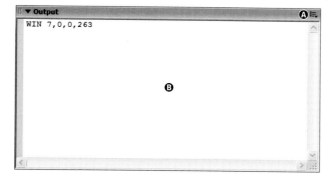

Ⓐ Options menu Allows you to toggle word wrap in the Output panel, clear the existing output, copy the text to the clipboard, search the output for keywords, and save the output to a file

Ⓑ Output pane Displays any syntax or programming error that may have occurred while testing your movie or where your trace actions would appear.

If your ActionScript has errors, the Output panel automatically opens and displays the scene, layer, frame, and line number of the problem code and a small amount of guidance at how to rectify the problem.

➡ 1.3   Publishing Flash Content

➡ 6.11   Publish Settings

➡ 26.4   Debugging with the Output Window

Output panel
`F2`

Copy
`Ctrl` `C`
`⌘` `C`

Find
`Ctrl` `F`
`⌘` `F`

Find again
`F3`

List objects in Output panel
`Ctrl` `L`
`⌘` `L`

List variables in Output panel
`Ctrl` `Alt` `V`
`⌘` `Alt` `V`

If you use the trace action in your Action-Script code, the output is sent to the Output panel while testing the movie in the authoring environment. Trace actions are not shown when the movie is published to the Web or when viewed within the standalone Flash player.

If you use trace actions in your document, you can omit trace actions from being published with the SWF file in your Publish Settings.

5.13   Web Services Panel

Web Services panel

Ctrl Shift F10
⌘ Shift F10

————

The Web Services panel
is only available in
Flash MX Professional.

————

If you are consuming
your own web service, it
might be necessary to
refresh the web service
if you make changes to
the server-side code.
You can refresh the list
of services, along with
their methods, by press-
ing the Refresh Web Ser-
vices button, using the
Web Services Options
menu or by right-click-
ing the Web Service list
and selecting Refresh
Web Services from the
contextual menu.

The Web Services (Window > Development Panels > Web Services) panel is used to define web services that you want to integrate into your Flash document. These can be custom web services that you write yourself, or they can be third-party services found on a site such as www.xmethods.net. Web services allow two different applications (such as a server and a Flash movie) to communicate and send data between them. A series of functions are contained in the web service, which is then accessed by another computer which is then sent XML formatted data.

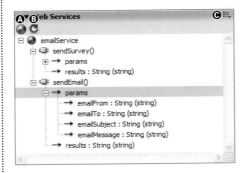

Ⓐ Define Web Services Opens the Define Web Services window.

Ⓑ Refresh Web Services Refreshes the list of currently available web services that are defined in your authoring environment.

Ⓒ Options menu Allows you to define new web services, refresh existing web services, add a method call to your Flash document, or view the WSDL (Web Service Definition Language) for the selected web service.

5.14 Accessibility Panel

Accessibility was introduced in Flash MX (version 6), and since then it has been greatly improved. New additions have been made to Flash accessibility not only in SWF files and components, but also in the Flash authoring environment. The authoring environment is now easier for people with disabilities to use because it allows visually impaired users to use keystroke combinations to open and control various areas of the workspace. The Accessibility panel (Window > Other Panels > Accessibility) allows you to set a tab index number, show or hide instances from a screen reader, and assign names and descriptions to objects or the movie itself.

Using Screens in Flash MX Professional allows you to build applications facilitating keyboard shortcuts as opposed to mouse navigation. Users can navigate using keypresses, which is much friendlier to visually impaired users.

ⓐ Make Object Accessible Makes the selected object accessible to screen readers.

ⓑ Make Child Objects Accessible Makes nested objects visible to the screen reader. Do not check this option if you have a large amount of nested objects, or if reading them would make your SWF very confusing.

ⓒ Name Assigns a name for the object, which is read aloud by screen readers.

ⓓ Description Screen readers read the description you enter into this field.

ⓔ Shortcut You can make the screen reader read a shortcut. This does not assign an actual shortcut to the selected object but is read as the shortcut for the selected object.

ⓕ Tab Index You can set a number in this field that orders the objects when they are tabbed on the Stage. Order the objects from 1.

➡ 12.9 Making Your
        Site Accessible

Accessibility panel
Alt F2
Option F2

The Accessibility panel is context sensitive. This means that it is slightly different depending on what you have selected.

You can enable indexing on child objects as well by using Action-Script. This means you can target instances nested inside a parent instance on the Stage.

If you have many dynamically created movie clips inside a parent clip, you should definitely make sure that child objects are not accessible. This would wreak havoc on a screen reader trying to interpret that data and read it aloud.

If you click the Stage and open the Accessibility panel, make sure that you have Make Movie Accessible selected. You can also enter a description and name for the movie itself.

Screen readers are extremely unpredictable: test your SWFs often with a screen reader.

Compatible screen readers, starting with Flash Player 6, are Window Eyes and JAWS for Windows.

5.15   History Panel

History panel
[Ctrl] [F10]
[⌘] [F10]

Preferences
[Ctrl] [U]
[⌘] [U]

The higher the number of Undo levels in the Preferences, the more resources Flash consumes.

Regularly using File > Save And Compact trims the file's history and results in smaller FLA file sizes.

Using Undo removes items from the History panel.

Be careful when clearing the History panel because you cannot "undo" this command.

The History panel (Window > Other Panels > History) displays a list of steps performed on the current document since the file was created or last opened. By default, Flash MX 2004 shows the last 100 steps; however, this can be changed in Flash's Preferences dialog from anywhere between 2 steps and 9999 levels. Change this value in the Undo levels section of the Preferences dialog, General tab. To erase the document's history, you can save and compact the Flash movie by selecting Save and Compact from the File menu, selecting Clear History from the Options menu, or right-clicking the History Panel and selecting Clear History from the contextual menu.

You can also save individual or a series of steps as a command that can be executed in other documents. This allows you to easily complete repetitive tasks.

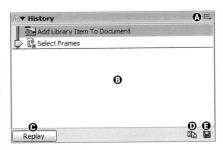

A Options menu Allows you to replay the selected steps, copy steps to the clipboard, save the selected steps as a command, clear the document's history, or change the view settings for the History panel.

B History pane Displays the most recently performed steps in the active document. By default, Flash displays the 100 most recent actions (from oldest to newest), but this value can be changed from 2 to 9999 steps in the Preferences dialog (under Undo levels).

C Replay selected steps Replays the selected steps in the current document.

D Copy selected steps to the clipboard Copies the selected steps to the clipboard so they can be replayed in a different file.

E Save selected steps as a command Saves the selected steps to an external file as a command. This command can be played back in any document at a later time by selecting the command from the Commands menu, or by selecting Commands > Run Command from the menu and selecting the JSFL (Flash JavaScript) file.

5.16   Movie Explorer

The Movie Explorer (Window > Other Panels > Movie Explorer) allows you to quickly and easily find items within your Flash document. By using the Movie Explorer, you can view all the objects within your current Flash document, find them, and locate and view any ActionScript that has been placed within a frame, Timeline, or object.

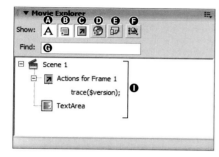

Ⓐ Show Text Toggles whether or not any Static text, Dynamic text, or Input text instances are shown in the Movie Explorer's hierarchical tree.

Ⓑ Show Buttons, Movie Clips and Graphics Toggles whether or not any buttons, movie clips, graphics, or components are shown in the Movie Explorer's hierarchical tree.

Ⓒ Show Action Scripts Toggles whether Action-Script code is visible in the Movie Explorer.

Ⓓ Show Video, Sounds, and Bitmaps Toggles embedded video, sounds, and bitmaps in the Movie Explorer.

Ⓔ Show Frames and Layers Toggles whether frame and layers are shown in the Movie Explorer. When frames and layers are hidden, all the symbols and objects are shown in a list instead of being broken down by frames and layers.

Ⓕ Customize Which Items to Show Brings up the Movie Explorer Settings dialog.

Ⓖ Options menu Allows you to rename and edit symbols, toggle between all scenes and the current scene, copy the text from the Movie Explorer panel to the clipboard, and find the currently selected symbol in the library.

Ⓗ Find element Searches the document for a specific element.

Ⓘ Document Navigation tree Displays a collapsible list of the elements within your Flash document.

➡ 15.13 Managing Scripts with the Movie Explorer

Movie Explorer panel
[Alt] [F3]
[Option] [F3]

Library
[Ctrl] [L] or [F11]
[⌘] [L] or [F11]

You can also use the Script navigator in the Actions panel to view where ActionScript is located in a Flash document.

5.17   Strings Panel

➡ 20.19 Using the
        Strings Panel

Strings panel
Alt F11
Option F11

———

When publishing a
Flash document with
multilanguage content,
Flash automatically
creates all the neces-
sary folders and XML
content for you and
generates the code to
automatically detect
the user's language.

The Strings panel (Window > Other Panels > Strings) allows you to easily create full multilanguage websites and define what languages you want to integrate into an application
you are building. You can enter text for each of the languages you have specified, and the
String panel embeds ActionScript to detect the client computer's default language and
display the language-specific content you specify it to display.

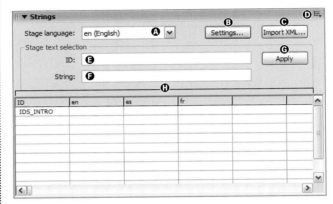

Ⓐ   Select Language for Stage/Test Movie Sets the language for the currently active Flash document.

Ⓑ   Edit Settings Opens the Settings window where you can define which languages you want to integrate with your Flash document and set the default language.

Ⓒ   Import XML File Opens the Import XML window where you can select the language you want to
import strings for.

Ⓓ   Options menu Allows you to edit the settings for the Strings panel.

Ⓔ   String Identifier Sets an identifier (ID) to a text object on the Stage.

Ⓕ   String Displays a text string for the specified ID and current Stage language.

Ⓖ   Apply Applies changes to the String identifier and String.

Ⓗ   Strings pane Displays all the language-specific strings for the current Flash document.

5.18 Common Libraries

The common libraries in Flash MX 2004 include a library of buttons, Classes and Learning interactions. Open common libraries by selecting Window > Other Panels > Common Libraries and then choose Buttons, Classes, or Learning Interactions.

The Buttons library includes over 50 premade buttons that can be added to your Flash applications. The Learning Interactions library has 6 items for common tasks such as drag and drop, fill in the blanks, multiple choice, and true or false. You can also create your own common libraries of symbols which can then be shared among multiple Flash documents.

Common libraries open just like any other library in Flash. They dock to the column of panels to the left of the Stage in Windows and attach to the left column of panels on the Mac. Navigate through the folders to discover some of the included functionality and assets in the libraries that install with Flash.

➡ 13.4 Importing Sound

➡ 18.5 Writing Button Scripts for Flash Movie Navigation

➡ 18.6 Writing Button Scripts for Web Navigation

➡ 19.7 Writing Button Scripts for Interactive Control and Navigation

The PushButton component button in the Buttons library (Component Buttons folder) does not have a down or hover state because it is only there to illustrate parameterization of components.

Common libraries are a great way to quickly build a site without having to make all your assets from scratch.

5.19   Project Panel

Project panel
[Shift] [F8]

———

Be very careful when
removing files from
Flash projects because
there is no confirma-
tion before a file is
removed. If you choose
to remove it, it is imme-
diately removed from
the project.

The Project panel (Window > Project) is new to Flash and is only available in Flash MX
Professional 2004. Projects can be used to group files together and add version control to
your Flash files, which is useful if you have multiple people working on a single project. A
Flash project file has the file extension FLP and is an XML file that contains a list of all the
files contained within the project. If a project is not defined, the Project panel displays
selections that allow you to open an existing project or to create a new one.

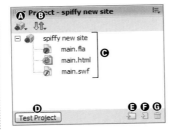

Ⓐ Project Opens a contextual menu that allows you to create
a new project, open an existing project, close the current
project, rename a project or folder, or remove files from a
project.

Ⓑ Version Control Opens a contextual menu that allows you
to check files in and out of the version control system. You
can also refresh the status of the files in the project repository and edit any existing sites you have defined.

Ⓒ Project pane Displays the files associated with the current
project.

Ⓓ Test Project Easily tests the Project's default document,
similar to how the Test Movie command works. If your project does not have a default document defined, a dialog
appears the first time you press the Test Project button
prompting you to select a default document (which can
either be a FLA or HTML document) from a list of files in
your project.

Ⓔ Add Folder to Project Opens the Project Folder dialog
that allows you to create a new folder within your Flash
project.

Ⓕ Add File(s) to Project Opens the Add Files to Project dialog
that allows you to add multiple files to your Flash project.

Ⓖ Remove from Project Removes the currently selected
files or folders from the Flash project.

5.20   Panel Sets

Flash MX 2004 ships with two default panel sets: a set that includes the most common panels and the training panel set, which includes a minimal number of panels. You can choose one of these panel sets by selecting Window > Panel Sets and then choosing either Default Layout or Training Layout.

You can also create your own panel layouts, save them within the Panel Sets menu, and use the panel set whenever you use Flash. Or someone else can create their own panel set on the same computer, and use it when they start up Flash. This is very useful because the panel set a developer uses can be radically different than one a designer uses. To create your own panel set, follow these steps.

1   Create the layout you want to save in Flash by opening the panels you use most often. Maximize the panels you want maximized when you open your custom layout.

2   Choose Window > Save Panel Layout from the main menu.

3   In the Save Panel Layout dialog that opens, type in a name for your panel set and then click OK.

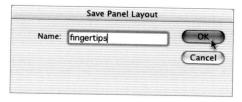

When you are finished, the custom panel set is saved under Panel Sets in the Window menu.

➡ 1.6   Working with Panels

➡ 1.11 Working with Panels (Mac)

➡ 2.9   Window Menu

Hide panel
F4

You can change your custom panel set by overwriting your old panel set. Make the necessary changes to the panel set, and then choose Save Panel Layout from the Window menu. Enter the same name for the panel set and click Save. This overwrites your panel set with the new one.

Pressing F4 hides all the visible panels and let you easily see your Stage and Timeline. Pressing F4 again restores your panels to their previous states.

5.21   Arranging Windows

Often you'll find the default tabbed document layout the easiest to work with when working with multiple Flash documents.

You can organize your windows in three different ways within Flash. The first way is to maximize the open documents and use the Document tabs above the Timeline to switch between open documents (in Windows only). This is the default view.

The other two ways of viewing your open files are by cascading or tiling the open windows, and this works the same way in Windows and Mac. Cascading arranges the open windows so that each window is slightly offset to the bottom right of the previous window. Cascade windows in the Flash workspace by choosing Window > Cascade. Tiling the open windows arranges the documents in a grid. To tile your document windows, choose Window > Tile from the main menu. If you have only two documents currently open, tiling them splits them both vertically so documents appear beside each other and take up 100 percent of the height of the document area. If you tile four documents, you'll see the documents arranged in a 2×2 grid.

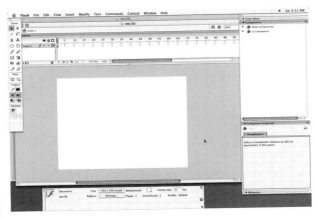

You even have the option to hide all open panels, which gives you the ability to see much more content on the Stage.

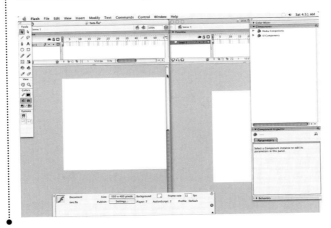

5.22   Property Inspector

The Property inspector (commonly known as a *PI*) is one of the most important and most complex panels in Flash. The Property inspector is context sensitive, so its appearance changes depending on what is selected on the Stage or Timeline. If the Stage is selected, the Property inspector allows you to change the dimensions of the Stage, publish settings, background color, and frame rate of the SWF file. If a component is selected, the PI allows you to change some of the more common settings associated with that particular component, for example, you can set the size of instances and objects on the Stage, assign instance names, set the X and Y coordinates of objects, and do countless other tasks, all depending on the current selection on the Stage.

➡ 5.7   Actions Panel

➡ 5.14   Accessibility Panel

➡ 5.10   Component Inspector panel

➡ 15.11 Working with Properties

ⓐ Instance name Adds or edits an instance name for some selections on the Stage.

ⓑ Size and location Displays X and Y coordinates, and they can be edited. The Width and Height properties are also displayed and can be edited in these text fields.

ⓒ Properties tab Displays what symbol the instance is a copy of and also allows you to change the color tint, alpha, and brightness of some selections.

ⓓ Parameters tab Allows you to change many different component parameters if a component is selected.

ⓔ Help for Property inspector Opens Help content for the panel.

ⓕ Edit ActionScript Edits ActionScript attached to the selected object (or adds new code).

ⓖ Edit Accessibility settings Opens the Accessibility panel so you can change the Accessibility settings such as whether it is made accessible, or add a description.

Properties
Ctrl F3
⌘ F3

Component Inspector panel
Alt F7
Option F7

Document properties
Ctrl J
⌘ J

—

You can open and close the Accessibility panel by clicking the small blue icon in the Property inspector.

—

The type of file you have open and the document's name is displayed in the Property inspector when you have the Stage selected.

—

Expand or collapse the Property inspector by clicking the Expand/Collapse The Information Area button in the lower right corner.

THIRD-PARTY EXTENSIONS

You can find new extensions (including behaviors, components and commands) for download on the Web. Although behaviors are new to Flash MX 2004, you'll probably find many of them already available for download. That's one of the advantages of being part of such a large development community. Start out at the Macromedia Exchange for the extensions (and the Extension Manager if you don't already have it) at www.macromedia .com/cfusion/exchange/. Also try community websites for Flash MX 2004, such as www.flash2004.com.

5.23   Help Panel

➡ 2.10 Help Menu

Help panel
`F1`

Copy
`Ctrl` `C`
`⌘` `C`

___

Don't forget to update the Help panel contents, which is updated regularly, as often as possible. If new updates are not available, Flash doesn't try to download anything. Always keeping your documentation up to date helps ensure you will encounter as few errata as possible in the Help files.

The Help panel has been redesigned in Flash MX 2004 and is now more useful than ever. This panel is broken down into two major tabs. The Help tab provides you with a Getting Started with Flash guide, an ActionScript Reference guide, an ActionScript Dictionary, and a walkthrough of all the documentation associated with the new components for Flash MX. The second tab is the How Do I tab, which walks you through some of the more common tasks of building Flash applications.

There are also two methods of browsing the help documentation, either by clicking through the Table of Contents on the left-hand side and finding the topic you are looking for, or by searching the help files based on a keyword or phrase. You can print the current help page with the click of a button. The final feature of the Help panel is the Update button, which downloads the latest help files from the Internet. Updating your documentation on a regular basis ensures that the documentation has as few bugs and mistakes as possible.

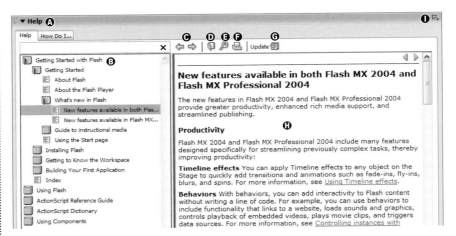

ⓐ **Help tab and How Do I tab**   Contains the main bulk of Flash documentation, tutorials, and reference materials. The How Do I tab contains tutorials on how to use Flash.

ⓑ **Table of Contents pane**   Lists each book of documentation or your search results. Click the X above the Table of Contents to close it.

ⓒ **History back and History forward**   Steps you back and forward through the documentation selections you have read, similar to the back and forward buttons in a web browser.

ⓓ **Table of Contents button**   Opens and closes the Table of Contents.

ⓔ **Search button**   Opens the search feature. Enter keywords and press Enter or Return to initiate the search. If no results are found, you are notified in the Table of Contents pane.

ⓕ **Print button**   Prints the selected documentation.

ⓖ **Update button**   Downloads new help if it is available.

ⓗ **Documentation pane**   Displays the selected documentation. Click the Next and Previous buttons in the documentation to step through documentation entries.

ⓘ **Options menu**   Displays options to Copy and Print from this menu.

Preferences and Printing

CHANGING YOUR PREFERENCES IN Flash MX 2004 is a great way to customize the authoring environment to suit your working style. If you are used to certain hotkey shortcuts in other programs or custom colors for writing code, you can probably make similar settings in Flash. You might have a particular way you tend to draw, so you can change how the pen and brush are controlled. All of these changes are possible by using Flash preference settings.

6.1 Preferences Overview

Open Preferences (Windows only)
[Ctrl] [U]

———

The Font Mapping dialog can also be reached when a FLA is opened with missing fonts. A warning dialog appears and you need to select Choose Substitute.

If you click the Edit menu (Windows) or the Flash menu (Macintosh) and scroll to the items at the end of the list, you find several options that change preferences and settings in Flash. You can change much of the authoring environment's functionality using five tabs found in the Preferences dialog. You can customize keyboard shortcuts, the Tools panel, and the way missing fonts are mapped in three other dialogs launched from the Edit menu.

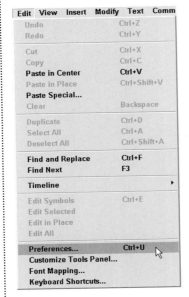

Preferences Opens the Preferences dialog that contains a majority of the authoring environment editing preferences available. Settings can be changed in the General, Editing, Clipboard, Warnings, and ActionScript tabs.

Keyboard Shortcuts Allows you to set new keyboard shortcuts for existing shortcuts and tasks.

Customize Tools Panel Allows you to change what tools are in the Tools panel, as well as their placement.

Font Mapping You can set defaults for how fonts are substituted in your FLA files if you do not have them on your system.

6.2   General Preferences

Choose Edit > Preferences (Windows) or Flash > Preferences (Mac) and click the General tab to change the general preferences in Flash. This tab covers some of the basic settings used to control the Flash interface and authoring. There are a wide range of settings in this tab. One of the most important settings controls how the Timeline functions. Many Flash users prefer "span-based selection," which is how Flash 5 handled Timeline editing: frame selections are made over a span of many frames. In Flash 4, MX, and MX 2004, the Timeline defaults to frame-based selection: selections are made frame by frame.

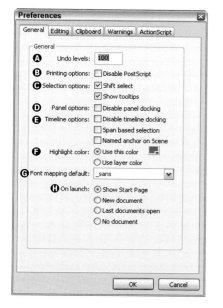

A **Undo Levels** Sets a number between 0 and 9999 for undo/redos.

B **Printing Options** Allows you to disable PostScript when printing from Flash. Windows only.

C **Selection Options** Allows you to enable or disable Shift selecting (clicking additional objects adds to the additional selection) and tooltip highlights in the authoring environment.

D **Panel Options** Allows you to disable panel docking in the authoring environment.

E **Timeline Options** Allows you to set how the Timeline works in the authoring environment. You can also disable panel docking and choose whether you want a named anchor to be set at the beginning of each scene.

F **Highlight Color** Allows you to change the color of the bounding box that appears when you select objects on the Stage. You can choose between a color or use the layer's designated color instead.

G **Font Mapping Default** Allows you to set a default font for mapped missing fonts.

H **On Launch** Sets a default kind of document or documents that open when you start up Flash.

Open Preferences (Windows only)
Ctrl U

———

The higher the number set for levels of undo/redo, the more system memory is used up. Keep this number as low as possible.

———

Span-based selection is Flash 5 style authoring. Frame-based selection is Flash 4/MX style selection and is set as the default.

———

Even though you can set a preference for adding a named anchor at the beginning of each scene, remember that you should avoid using scenes whenever possible. Scenes are rarely necessary.

AUTHORING TASKS

SCRIPTING TASKS

TESTING AND PUBLISHING TASKS

WHAT'S NEW

EXPORTING COMPONENTS

To export components on a different frame rather than the default "first frame," select File > Publish Settings. Click the Settings button on the Flash tab. In the ActionScript Settings dialog that appears, change the Export Frame For Classes frame to something other than frame 1. This allows you to add a progress bar on frame 1.

6.3 Editing Preferences

Choose Edit > Preferences (Windows) or Flash > Preferences (Mac) to access the Preferences dialog, and click on the Editing tab. This tab is where you change preferences for vectors, drawing, and text. The drawing settings largely deal with the level of accuracy required for Flash to render them more accurately as a particular smoothness or shape. How you change these settings greatly depends on how you create drawings or illustrations.

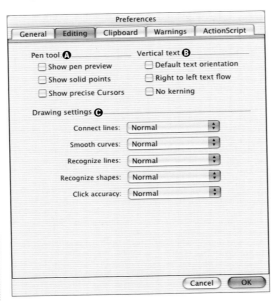

Flash MX Professional has additional settings available for Projects and Input Languages. This allows you to choose whether all project files are closed when you close a project, and whether the files are all saved when you publish. The Input Languages settings allow you to toggle between the kinds of languages you are typing into the FLA.

You don't have to select Show Precise Cursors in the Editing tab. You can also toggle between the pen and crosshair cursors by pressing the Caps Lock key while using the Pen tool.

Ⓐ **Pen Tool** Use these options to set a pen preview (displays a preview of the next line segment in relation to your cursor), solid points (displays selected anchor points as solid and unselected as hollow), and precise cursors (switches between a pen and crosshair cursor for fine tuning your drawings).

Ⓑ **Vertical Text** You can set vertical text as the default direction for all text fields, set text flow from right to left, or set text to no kerning, which is typically used for rendering Asian text.

Ⓒ **Drawing Settings** Allows you to change how lines connect (how close each line is before they snap together), smooth curves (amount of smoothing applied), recognize lines (how straight line is drawn before recognized as straight), recognize shapes (how accurate a shape has to be drawn before recognized), and click accuracy (how close the cursor is to an object before Flash recognizes it).

6.4 Clipboard Preferences

Choose Edit > Preferences (Windows) or Flash > Preferences (Mac) to open the Preferences dialog, and then click the Clipboard tab. This tab is used primarily for image settings. Bitmap settings can be made for copying images to the clipboard. However, gradients are only affected when pasting from Flash to another program. If you are using a Macintosh, images will be referred to as PICT files instead of bitmaps.

A **Color Depth** Allows you to set a color depth for images that are copied to the clipboard.

B **Resolution** Sets the image resolution to Screen (default) or preset values up to 300 dpi. You can also manually enter a value into the text field.

C **Size Limit** Sets a size limit for RAM handling the clipboard content. The value is measured in kilobytes.

D **Quality** Specifies quality of gradients that you copy and paste to a location outside of Flash. It can be set to None, Fast, Normal, or Best values. Windows only.

E **FreeHand Text** If checked, text pasted from FreeHand will remain as editable text. Left unchecked, Flash will paste as text outlines.

➥ 9.3 Understanding Color and Gradients

Open Preferences (Windows only)
Ctrl U

If you are pasting large files (such as those with high resolution), make sure that you set a larger size limit.

When you are pasting gradients within Flash (between FLA files), gradients will always be pasted at the best quality possible.

Remember that the Maintain Text As Blocks option controls only text that is pasted from the clipboard between FreeHand and Flash. It will not control FreeHand when *importing* into Flash. There is a separate option available for this when importing FreeHand documents.

6.5 Warnings Preferences

**Open Preferences
(Windows only)**
Ctrl U

Choose Edit **>** Preferences (Flash **>** Preferences on a Mac) to open the Preferences dialog, and then click the Warnings tab. In this tab, you choose which warnings appear while you are working in Flash. If you do not want to see particular warnings, you may also disable them here by deselecting the check box. This is useful for experienced users who do not want to continue being bombarded with particular warnings they are already aware of on tasks performed on a regular basis.

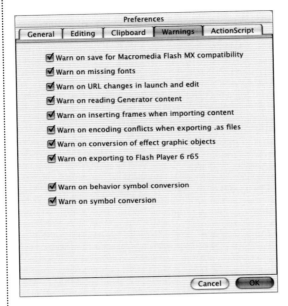

6.6   ActionScript Preferences

Choose Edit > Preferences or Flash > Preferences to open the Preferences dialog, and then click the ActionScript tab. Changing preferences for the Actions panel is quite important if you are used to writing your scripts in a different environment. You might be used to particular text size, indentation, and coloring. The settings that you make here also change the settings for the ActionScript editor (File > New > ActionScript File).

Ⓐ Automatic Indentation If checked, code automatically indents in the Script pane when it is typed in.

Ⓑ Tab Size Sets the amount of code indentation.

Ⓒ Code Hints When checked, this setting turns on code completion for syntax, methods, and events.

Ⓓ Delay Sets the amount of delay before code hints pop up.

Ⓔ Open/Import and Save/Export You can toggle between UTF-8 and normal encoding here. Use UTF-8 for Unicode encoding.

Ⓕ Text Sets the font and font size for code typed into the script pane.

Ⓖ Syntax Coloring Sets the foreground, background, and text colors in the script pane. Different colors can be set for keywords (with, while, on), comments, identifiers (play, stop), and strings.

Ⓗ ActionScript 2.0 Settings Opens the ActionScript Settings dialog.

Ⓘ Reset to Defaults Restores all preferences in the Preferences dialog to default settings.

➠ 6.7 ActionScript Settings Preferences

➠ 15.1 Script Overview

➠ 15.5 Entering Code in the Actions Panel

Open Preferences (Windows only)

———

The preferences you set in this tab change both the Script pane in the Actions panel and the Script window in Flash MX Professional.

———

Sometimes editing syntax coloring can make your code easier to read. The syntax coloring settings are also useful if you are used to a particular color combination in another program. You can change the color coding to a system you are already accustomed to.

6.7 ActionScript Settings Preferences

Choose Edit > Preferences (Windows) or Flash > Preferences (Mac) to open the Preferences dialog, and then click the ActionScript tab. Then click the ActionScript 2.0 Settings button to open the ActionScript Settings dialog, which contains settings for modifying the global class path. This path is used when you compile a SWF or create a component. You can set a frame for exporting classes in this dialog and modify a directory to the class path. In order to remove or move a class listed in the pane, make sure you select it first.

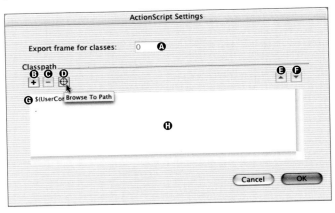

The class path in the ActionScript Settings dialog is initially empty.

The global class path is set using the Action-Script Settings dialog. A local class path that only refers to the current FLA file is set in the Publish Settings dialog.

Ⓐ Export Frame For Classes Sets the export frame for classes.

Ⓑ Add New Path Adds a new class path.

Ⓒ Remove Selected Path Removes a selected path.

Ⓓ Browse To Path Opens a file browser so you can select a particular path.

Ⓔ Move Path Up Moves a class up.

Ⓕ Move Path Down Moves a class down.

Ⓖ Default path.

Ⓗ A new path that has not been set.

6.8 Keyboard Shortcuts Dialog

You can open the Keyboard Shortcuts dialog by choosing Edit > Keyboard Shortcuts in Windows or Flash > Keyboard Shortcuts on a Mac. If you are used to different keyboard shortcuts, this dialog allows you to check out the current shortcut settings and switch them with custom key combinations as necessary. You can also create your own set of keyboard shortcuts.

➡ 2.1   Menu
          Overview

➡ 3.5   Tools
          Overview

Ⓐ Current This drop-down menu tells you what set of shortcuts is being displayed.

Ⓑ Duplicate Set Creates a new set of custom shortcuts.

Ⓒ Rename Set Renames your set of shortcuts.

Ⓓ Delete Set Deletes a set of shortcuts.

Ⓔ Commands This drop-down menu contains groups of commands.

Ⓕ This tree displays the group of commands for the selected menu item above. Click the plus symbol to display more shortcuts in a tree below. When you click a specific command, it will display in the Shortcuts pane.

Ⓖ Description This area gives you a tooltip that tells you what each command does. Highlight any shortcut in the tree above to see a description.

You cannot rename the Macromedia Standard set of shortcuts.

In order to make your own custom shortcuts you have to duplicate the default set called Macromedia Standard. Flash will not allow you to edit these shortcuts.

Ⓗ Add Shortcut Adds a shortcut to the list.

Ⓘ Remove Shortcut Removes a selected shortcut.

Ⓙ Shortcuts are displayed in this pane.

Ⓚ Press Key Displays the keypress combination entered for the selected command.

Ⓛ Change Click this button to assign the shortcut in the Press Key field to the command.

Creating a Keyboard Shortcut

1 Click the Duplicate Set button, and then enter a name into the Duplicate dialog.

2 In the Commands menu, select a subset of shortcuts that includes the ones you want to change.

3 Select a shortcut from the tree. If a shortcut is available, it displays in the Shortcut field below. Select the shortcut and click the Remove Shortcut button.

4 Click the Add Shortcut button to assign the shortcut. Press the keypress combination for the shortcut you want, which will appear in the Press Key field.

5 Click the Change button to assign the shortcut to this command.

6.9   Customize Tools Panel

➡ 3.5   Tools
         Overview

Tools can be added to the Tools panel by installing Flash extensions. Flash developers can create custom tools that are installed into the Flash user interface. Then you can add them to the Tools panel using the Customize Tools Panel command.

If you add more tools to the Fill Transform tool, the down arrow will be very difficult to see because of the graphics of the icon button.

When you mouse over a Tools panel button with a menu, a tooltip tells you which hotkeys can be used.

The Customize Tools Panel dialog is opened by choosing Edit > Customize Tools Panel (Windows) or Flash > Customize Tools Panel (Mac). This dialog allows you to modify the Tools panel in Flash by removing or adding tools. It is possible to add several tools to one single menu, so a drop-down menu spawns when the button is pressed. This dialog is useful when you have downloaded and installed Flash extensions for additional tools that can be used in the Tools panel, or you wish to rearrange the Tools panel. The tools that are available in Flash by default are already available without needing to use this dialog.

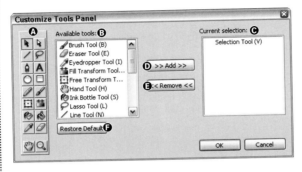

Ⓐ Select a tool from this group of buttons.

Ⓑ **Available Tools** Lists all of the tools that are available to add to the Tools panel.

Ⓒ **Current Selection** Tools in the selected menu button are listed here.

Ⓓ **Add** Adds a selection.

Ⓔ **Remove** Removes a selection.

Ⓕ **Restore Default** Restores defaults.

To customize the Tools Panel:

1 Select a tool icon. This is the tool that you are editing (by adding to, or removing from the Tools panel). This tool is shown as selected in the Current Selection pane.

2 Use the Add and Remove buttons to either add to or remove from the Current selection dialog. A tool must be selected before these buttons will work.

3 If you add multiple selections to one icon, a drop-down menu is created after you close the dialog.

4 After you are finished with editing a Tools panel button, select a new button and repeat the process.

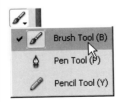

If you add multiple tools to one Tools panel button, a drop-down menu is created.

When you hover a cursor over a tool button, notice the tooltip showing hotkeys (keyboard keypresses) used to select the tool. If you press any key specified in that tooltip, it selects the tool and cycles through the other tools in the drop-down menu.

6.10   Font Mapping

You can open the Font Mapping dialog by choosing Edit **>** Font Mapping (Windows) or Flash **>** Font Mapping (Mac). You can also reach this dialog when you try to open a FLA that contains fonts that are not installed on your computer: if you see the Missing Font Warning when opening the file, click the Choose Substitute button. This button opens the Font Mapping dialog.

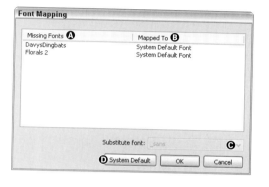

Ⓐ Names of missing fonts are listed in this column.

Ⓑ Name of the substitute font that the missing font will be mapped to.

Ⓒ Select a substitute font from this drop-down menu.

Ⓓ Click to set the substitute font to the System Default font.

➠ 6.1   Preferences Overview

➠ 6.2   General Preferences

➠ 6.5   Warnings Preferences

➠ 6.11   Publish Settings

➠ 20.24 Embedding Font Outlines

➠ 24.4   Creating Font Symbols

➠ 24.11 Using Run-time Shared Libraries

Missing certain fonts is a common issue when you are working with other Flash developers on a team. Using this dialog lets you assign fonts on your system to particular missing fonts.

Mapping a font will not replace the designated font in that FLA document. It simply substitutes that font for the missing one while you are working on it in Flash.

COPY AND PASTE

To copy and paste effectively between Flash and Photoshop, you should make some minor modifications in the Preferences dialog. Choose Edit **>** Preferences and then select the Clipboard tab. Set the Resolution to 300 (the normal value for Photoshop print-based work) and up the maximum size to a value more in keeping with your computer (typically a couple of megabytes).

6.11   Publish Settings

Publish Settings
Ctrl Shift F12
⌘ Shift F12

___

It's recommended to
have a separate Publish
profile per site you are
currently working on.
That way, it is harder
to publish a site with
the wrong settings, or
overwrite the settings
of a previous site when
working on a new one.

Once you have created your Flash source content, you need to compile it to a form that can be viewed outside the Flash environment. This process is called *publishing*. Choose File > Publish Settings to open the Publish Settings dialog.

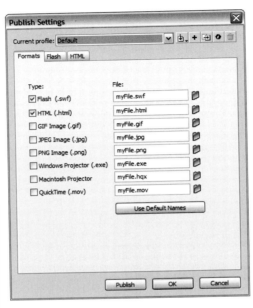

There are three tabs in this dialog by default: Formats, Flash, and HTML. The Formats tab specifies which file types Flash will export. Additional tabs will appear as you select more export options. The most common types of file you will need to export are the following.

- For web content, check Flash (.swf) and HTML (.html). These are the default selections.

- For content to be played by the standalone Flash player, check Flash (.swf). When you double-click the SWF file created, the standalone Flash player will play the file.

- To build a completely standalone desktop application, select either Windows Projector or Macintosh Projector. This will create a single file that contains both the animation information plus the player software needed to view it.

- To publish a bitmap image of the current frame, select either GIF Image (.gif), JPEG Image (.jpg), or PNG Image (.png). The GIF format also gives you the option of saving the whole animation as an animated GIF.

- To publish a QuickTime MOV file that can be displayed in the QuickTime player or edited in video editing and compositing suites, select QuickTime (.mov). You must have Flash 5 Player or earlier selected as your SWF version.

6.11 Publish Settings *(continued)*

To publish to all the selected formats, click the Publish button. The files will be saved in the same place as the source FLA file and with the same name as the FLA (but with different extensions) by default. You can specify new filenames by entering them into the dialog. The most common change you may want to make is to the HTML file; changing it to `index.html` if it will be the first file loaded is a must, because that is the file the browser will look for if no filename is specified in a URL.

Publish Setting Profiles

You can save the current Publish Settings as a profile. To switch between installed profiles, use the Current Profile drop-down menu. Using the buttons at the top of the Publish Settings dialog, you can also:

- Import or export the current profile as an XML file.
- Create a profile.
- Duplicate a profile.
- Rename the current profile.
- Delete the current profile.

→ 27.5 Publishing Bitmap Formats

→ 27.6 Publishing QuickTime Movies

You cannot publish to a sequence of JPEGs or PNGs from the Publish Settings dialog. To do this, you need to use File > Export.

If you are sending source files to a client or third party, don't forget to include the publish profile for the site, otherwise you will almost certainly be getting a call when their published site doesn't work!

RETRO SCRIPT PANE

To change the font used in the Script pane of the Actions panel to what was used in earlier versions of Flash (Flash 5 and earlier), select Edit > Preferences and click the ActionScript tab. Change the font listed in the Text drop-down menu to Lucinda Console.

6.12 Printing and Sending Files

Print dialog

Ctrl P
⌘ P

————

Flash only allows you to print the main Timeline. If you want to print the contents of another Timeline, the best way around is to open a new FLA and copy the Timeline to it.

Flash allows you to take hard copies of the Stage for the main Timeline (but not embedded Timelines).

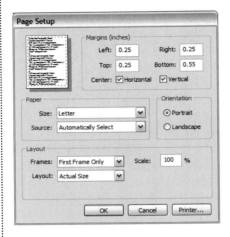

To set up the page for printing, select File > Page Setup. This opens a fairly intuitive and standard printer page setup dialog. The Flash-specific portion of this dialog is in the Layout section.

To set up to print the first frame of your main Timeline, select First Frame Only from the Frames drop-down. You can also select a scaling ratio by entering a value in the Scale field. Note that you cannot print frames other than frame 1 in the same way. If this is what you want to do, a good workaround is to temporarily copy the frame you want to print to frame 1 of a new FLA.

To set up to print all the frames in the main Timeline, select All Frames in the Frames drop-down. This will print each frame, one per page.

You can save time (and paper!) by printing in other layout formats via the Layout drop-down menu. Select Fit On One Page if your frames are bigger than a single page when you use 100% scaling (much better than trying to find the optimum percentage value!). Select Storyboard-Boxes, Storyboard-Grid, or Storyboard-Blank to get alternative formats. You can specify how many frames or rows and the margin between them by entering values in the Frames Across and Frames Margin requesters that will appear when you select story board options.

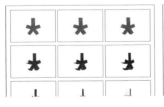  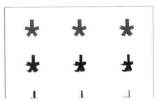

Left to right: Storyboard-Boxes, Storyboard-Grid, and Storyboard-Blank. These images were produced with Frames Across = 3 and Frames Margin = 9 px.

To print all pages in your print run, select File > Print. This will bring up the Print dialog, which allows you to select and configure your printer using the drop-down menu and Properties button, as well as select the print range. When you are finished, click OK.

Selecting File > Send will open a blank new e-mail (using your default e-mail application) with the current FLA as an attachment.

AUTHORING TASKS

FLASH WORKSPACE

AUTHORING TASKS

SCRIPTING TASKS

TESTING AND PUBLISHING TASKS

WHAT'S NEW

CHAPTER 7

Flash File Operations

FLASH IS USED TO open and edit several different kinds of files for authoring. It is used by designers and developers alike to create animations, applications, code files, or as a project organizer used to FTP files to a server. In Flash MX Professional 2004, you can create slide presentations or form applications using screens. There are so many different things Flash can do and several different kinds of file you can create.

- 7.1 **Opening new files**
- 7.2 **The Start page**
- 7.3 **Starting Flash documents**
- 7.4 **Starting Flash slide presentations or form applications**
- 7.5 **Starting ActionScript, Communication, or Flash JavaScript files**
- 7.6 **Starting Flash projects**
- 7.7 **Opening from templates**
- 7.8 **Opening from sites**
- 7.9 **Printing from movies**
- 7.10 **Using rulers, guides, grids, and snap**
- 7.11 **Changing movie properties**
- 7.12 **Saving files or templates**
- 7.13 **Exporting movies**

7.1   Opening New Files

New
[Ctrl] [N]
[⌘] [N]

New Flash document
[Ctrl] [Alt] [N]
[⌘] [Option] [N]

——

If you are using Flash
MX Professional, you
can also open XML,
HTML, and TXT docu-
ments in Flash. They
open in the code editor.

——

You can only open FLA
files in Flash MX 2004,
although Flash MX Pro-
fessional also allows
you to open code and
Flash project files.

The Flash MX 2004 authoring environment handles Flash documents (FLA) files as well as new ActionScript (AS), ActionScript Communication (ASC), Flash JavaScript (JSFL) files, and Flash project (FLP) files. The authoring environment interface might change depending on what kind of file you open or create. Flash does not attempt to replace robust code editors like HomeSite+ or Dreamweaver, although it allows you to avoid round trip editing between Flash and other programs and has many useful features. Organizing all of your files into a sin-gle project is possible using Flash MX Professional. Projects can be directly uploaded to a server and provide version control that is useful when working with members on a team.

Opening an Existing File

You can open existing files that have the following extensions: AS, FLA, FLP, JSFL, SPA, SSK, and SWF. These files might have been created using Flash or other animation or code editors.

1   Choose File > Open and the Open dialog opens where you can browse the hard drive for supported files.

2   Browse for a file and then click to select it. If you only want to browse for a certain kind of file, use the Files Of Type drop-down menu to filter the files shown in the dialog.

3   When you have selected a file, click the Open button. The Open dialog allows you to open supported file formats in Flash.

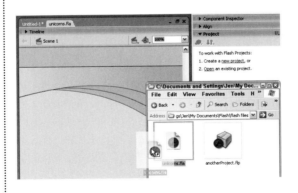

You can also open an existing file by dragging a file icon onto the Flash user interface or by double-clicking the file.

Flash File Types

FORMAT	EXTENSION	USE
ActionScript file	.as	External code that is compiled into a Flash movie
Flash document	.fla	Editable Flash document
Flash project	.flp	Set of files that creates a Flash project; together these files form an application
Flash JavaScript file	.jsfl	Flash JavaScript file
FutureSplash document	.spa	Predecessor of Flash
SmartSketch drawing	.ssk	Predecessor of FutureSplash
Flash movie	.swf	A rendered Flash movie

7.1   Opening New Files *(continued)*

Creating a New Document

To open a new document, select File **>** New from the main menu. The New Document dialog opens where you select one of a number of document types to create. Click a document type, and then click OK to create a new document.

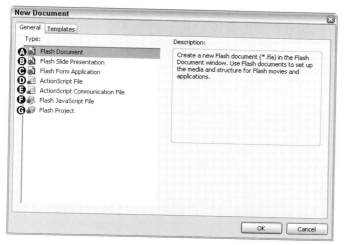

Ⓐ Opens a new Flash document and saves to the FLA file format.

Ⓑ Opens a new Flash document using screens and saves to the FLA file format (Flash MX Professional only).

Ⓒ Opens a new Flash document using screens and saves to the FLA file format (Flash MX Professional only).

Ⓓ Opens a new ActionScript file and saves to the AS file format (Flash MX Professional only).

Ⓔ Opens a new ActionScript Communication file and saves to the ASC file format. These files are for using with the Flash Communication Server (Flash MX Professional only).

Ⓕ Opens a new Flash JavaScript file and saves to the JSFL file format (Flash MX Professional only).

Ⓖ Opens a new Flash project, and saves to the FLP file format (Flash MX Professional only).

➠ 7.6   Starting Flash Projects

➠ 7.13 Exporting Movies

Open
[Ctrl] [O]
[⌘] [O]

Close
[Ctrl] [W]
[⌘] [W]

7.2   The Start Page

You can turn off the
Start page by checking
the Don't Show Again
check box at the bot-
tom of the Start page.
You can enable the
Start page again by
selecting Show Start
Page on the General
tab of the Preferences
dialog.

The Start page is a new feature in Flash MX 2004. The Start page gives you easy access to your most recently used Flash files, a quick way to open brand new documents or a new file from a template, and a link to the Macromedia Exchange so you can access extensions and components. The Start page might be updated by Macromedia from time to time.

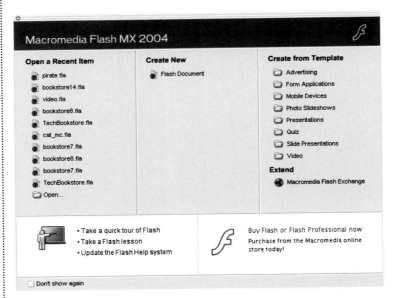

The Start page appears when you open up Flash MX 2004, or when you don't have any documents currently open. You can disable the Start page by going to Edit **>** Preferences and selecting the General tab. Turn off the Start page by changing the value of the On Launch radio controls. Selecting New Document will start up Flash with a new empty document when Flash is opened. Last Documents Open will reopen any documents you had open when you last closed Flash. The final setting, No Document, opens up the Flash environment with a blank workspace and no documents or start panel.

7.3 Starting Flash Documents

To create a new Flash document (FLA file), select File > New and choose Flash Document from the Type list and click OK. Flash opens a new FLA document with the default document settings or the default settings you might have specified earlier. The authoring environment is set up with the most recent panel layout.

You can change the default document settings in the Document Properties dialog, and set them as default so these settings are used for every new FLA you create. You can create a profile that contains a custom set of publish settings, which affects how the FLA document publishes SWF and HTML files.

➡ 5.20 Panel Sets

➡ 6.1 Preferences Overview

➡ 7.11 Changing Movie Properties

➡ 27.2 Choosing Publishing Options

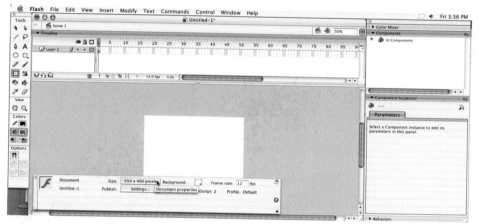

A new Flash document opens with your default settings and panel layout. Click the Size button in the Property inspector to change the documents settings.

New
Ctrl N
⌘ N

New Flash document
Ctrl Alt N
⌘ Option N

Open
Ctrl O
⌘ O

Close
Ctrl W
⌘ W

Preferences
Ctrl U
⌘ U

If you want to bypass the New Document dialog, use the Ctrl+Alt+N shortcut (or Command+Option+N on the Mac), which automatically creates a new Flash document.

You can only open Preferences if a document is already open.

You can make settings so Flash opens with a new document, the last documents that were open, or no document at all.

FINDING FLASH TEMPLATES

Flash templates are available from online sources. Sometimes you can download the templates for free; sometimes you have to pay for them. A good place to start is by searching the Macromedia Exchange for templates at: www.macromedia.com/cfusion/exchange/index.cfm. Otherwise, you might try searching Google for templates to download.

7.4 Starting Flash Slide Presentations or Form Applications

New
Ctrl N
⌘ N

Open
Ctrl O
⌘ O

Close
Ctrl W
⌘ W

———

You cannot use scenes in a Flash document that uses screens.

———

Slide presentations and form applications are just like other FLA documents, except the authoring environment opens with the Screen Outline pane open.

You can create a new slide presentation or form application using Flash MX Professional when you create a new file. These files will save as FLA files; however, the user interface will open and include the Screen Outline pane. When you open a new document, the Screen Outline pane includes one root screen called Presentation or Application and one child screen called Slide 1 or Form 1. The screens are used to construct the entire FLA document, and then you export the document as a SWF (or a projector) as usual.

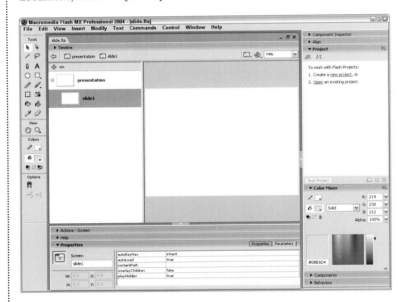

The Flash slide presentation uses screens. If you open a new slide presentation or form application, Flash opens with the Screen Outline pane visible.

If you create a new slide presentation, the Property inspector opens many different parameters you can edit for each screen. The root Presentation screen and all additional screens you create have these editable parameters.

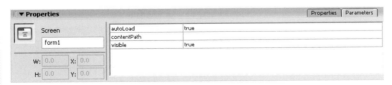

If you create a new form application, the Property inspector opens with these editable parameters. The root Application screen has these parameters, as will each new screen added to the application.

7.5 Starting ActionScript, Communication, or Flash JavaScript Files

The Flash authoring environment can be used as a code editor for your ActionScript, ActionScript Communication, or Flash JavaScript files. This means you can take advantage of editing your code in Flash MX 2004 instead of having to round-trip edit between Flash and another program like Dreamweaver. It is a lot quicker to edit everything in one place and can be beneficial when you need to view some code in the Actions panel alongside an external script in the code editors. However, if you are using Windows, then you can also use Document Tabs to quickly switch between your code files and the FLA document you are working with.

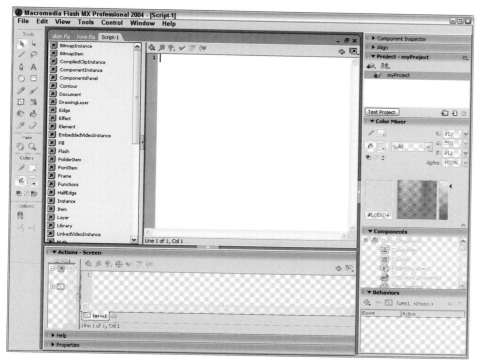

The code editor allows you to edit ActionScript and Flash JavaScript without leaving Flash MX 2004. You can use the Document tabs beneath the script pane to tab back to other files that are open.

➡ 5.7   Actions Panel

New
Ctrl N
⌘ N

Open
Ctrl O
⌘ O

Close
Ctrl W
⌘ W

Preferences
Ctrl U

———

There are some features not available in the code editors that are available when using the Actions panel. Notably, you are not able to use the Pin Script feature or Insert A Target Path. This is because the Stage is not associated with the code editor, so some of the relationship between Stage and code is not available.

———

Change the preferences for code authoring using the Preferences dialog (Edit > Preferences).

7.6   Starting Flash Projects

New
Ctrl N
⌘ N

Open
Ctrl O
⌘ O

Close
Ctrl W
⌘ W

────

This feature is only available in Flash MX Professional.

────

You still need to send all associated files along with the FLP files when transferring documents to another person working on the project. Files such as FLA and AS documents are not saved within the FLP file.

────

When you open an existing Flash project, you see it connecting to the Internet when you have designated a site for the project.

────

Check in and out using the Version Control menu.

────

You can only open one project at a time. If you open a project when another project is open, the current project is closed.

Flash is used for a lot of high-end development involving teams who sometimes work on large scale projects and applications. When projects grow, teams and the number of files used expand as well. Flash projects help organize the files, manage projects, send them around, and put the application online. You can start a new Flash project by choosing File **>** New and then selecting the Flash Project option.

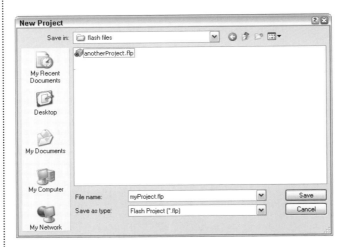

When you choose to open a new Flash project, you are asked to give that project a name. It is saved as a FLP (Flash project) file. Once you give the project a name and click Save, the Project panel opens and you can begin adding files to it.

The Project panel helps you organize the files involved with a project. When you create a new Flash project, you can add new files and folders to the project and publish and test from this panel. You need to set a default document before you can test and publish the project.

After you open a new Flash project, the Project panel opens. The name of your project is in the title bar as well as at the top of the pane. All of the files and folders involved branch out below the project's name.

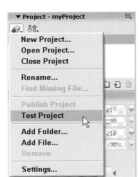

You can also open a new Flash project from the Project panel. Click on the Project menu and choose New Project.

7.7 Opening from Templates

There are several templates of varying complexity that are built into Flash. They are organized into ten categories and cover a wide range of uses. A category list groups similar templates depending on what they are used for.

1 Choose File > New from the main menu and then click the Templates tab.

2 Click the name of a category of templates that you want to open from the Category list. This opens a list of templates that fit into the chosen category; you can create and add your own templates or ones you download into these lists.

3 Click the name of a template in the center column. This opens a thumbnail and description of the template at right.

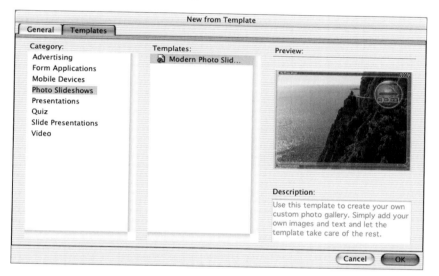

Advertising Movies templates set to standardized dimensions for some of the most common forms of online ads such as banners, skyscrapers, and pop-up ads.

Form Applications Form-based applications (Flash MX Professional only).

Mobile Devices Documents with the proper settings for some kinds of mobile devices.

PhotoSlideshows Templates that help you to easily create a photo gallery.

Presentations Templates that are very similar to common slide presentations, such as those made using PowerPoint.

Quiz Templates create quizzes that are able to send feedback and scores to a recipient.

Slide Presentations Four different styles of template upon which you can base your own slide presentations. (Flash MX Professional only).

Video A couple of templates for a video presentation and bandwidth selection.

➡ 7.12 Saving Files or Templates

New
Ctrl N
⌘ N

Open
Ctrl O
⌘ O

Close
Ctrl W
⌘ W

You can create your own templates and add them to this dialog.

Any Slide and Form templates will not open in Flash MX 2004, despite being available from the New From Template dialog. If you are using Flash MX 2004, do not try to open these templates.

7.8 Opening from Sites

➠ 7.6 Starting Flash Projects

➠ 27.9 Creating and Managing Projects

➠ 27.10 Publishing Projects

New
Ctrl N
⌘ N

Open
Ctrl O
⌘ O

Close
Ctrl W
⌘ W

Projects and version control are only available in Flash MX Professional 2004.

Supported files include FLA, SWF, AS, JSFL, and FLP.

Flash opens the proper editing environment, depending on what kind of file you select.

Flash MX Professional allows you to open files from a defined location on a server. You can open supported files in Flash directly from an FTP server (shown below), locally saved sites or through SourceSafe as long as you have a defined site in Flash. This feature is only available in Flash MX Professional.

1 Choose File > Open From Site and select a site from the drop-down menu. Flash connects to the FTP server or finds the sites on your hard drive or network and then lists available files in the pane below.

2 Select one of these files and click Open to open and edit the file in Flash. The file opens in the Flash authoring environment.

3 When you are finished making revisions, you can "check out" and upload the revisions to the server again. Choose Check Out from the Projects panel Version Control menu.

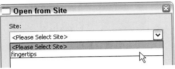

A list of sites you have defined can be opened from this menu. In order to define a site, choose File > Edit Sites and click the New button. This opens the Site Definition window where you can add a new site.

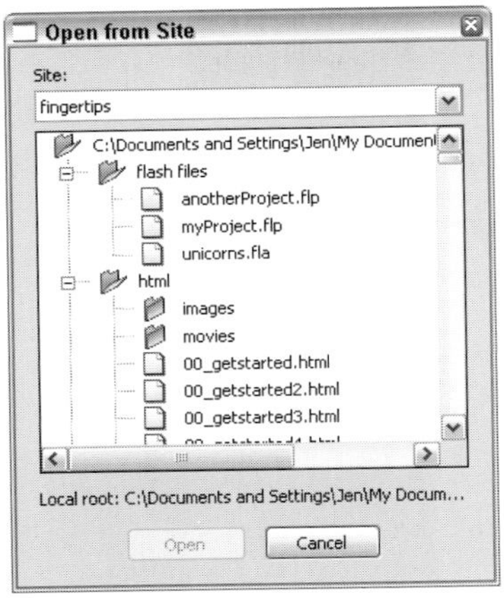

The fingertips site is defined, and its files are available to load into and edit using Flash. These files are currently on the hard drive. You can download and open them from the FTP right in Flash MX Professional 2004 if you choose to do this instead.

7.9   Printing from Movies

You can print a frame from a movie by choosing File > Print from the main menu. The Print dialog opens, and you use a drop-down to show you what printers are available on your system. The changes and settings you can make from the Print dialog depend on what printers you have installed and also what operating system you use.

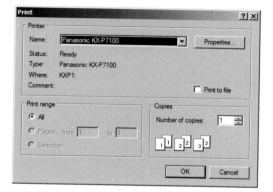

On a Windows system, you will see a Properties button on the dialog. Numerous settings and preferences are available through the Properties button located on the Print dialog. What settings are available after clicking this button differ on each computer system depending on what printer is installed.

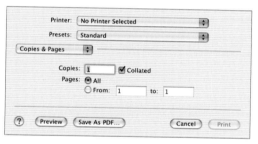

On the Mac, you will see additional drop-down menus as is standard for the operating system. One is to choose a print preset, and a second drop-down toggles between Copies And Pages, Layout, and a Summary display to make and review print settings. Toggle between these menu options to choose your print settings for the frame in Flash.

➡ 6.12   Printing and
           Sending
           Files

➡ 20.25 Using the
           PrintJob
           Class

Print
Ctrl P
⌘ P

___

On the Mac, you also have the option to save as a PDF document. If you click this button, a new dialog opens and allows you to choose a file name and location to save the file to.

FLASH WORKSPACE

AUTHORING TASKS

SCRIPTING TASKS

TESTING AND PUBLISHING TASKS

WHAT'S NEW

7.10 Using Rulers, Guides, Grids, and Snap

➡ 5.1 Align Panel

Rulers
Ctrl Alt Shift R
⌘ Option Shift R

Show grid
Ctrl '
⌘ '

Edit grid
Ctrl Alt G
⌘ Option G

Show guides
Ctrl ;
⌘ ;

Turn on rulers (View > Rulers) before trying to add guides to the authoring environment.

Choose View > Rulers to display rulers above and to the left of the Stage. Rulers are useful for precise measurement of the relationship between objects. They also allow you to use guides and help you place them on the Stage.

Guides allow you to use guide lines with your document that help you align or place objects on the Stage. You can show guides by choosing View > Guides > Show Guides. These lines are only visible in the authoring environment and are not visible when you publish the SWF file. Click within a Ruler and drag the guide over the Stage. You have four options in the View > Guides submenu:

Show Guides Makes guides visible over the Stage. Unselect this option to hide guides.

Lock Guides Locks any guides over the Stage into place, so they cannot be moved using the mouse. Uncheck this option to unlock guides.

Edit Guides Opens the Guides dialog.

Clear Guides Clears any guides that are currently open.

Ⓐ Changes the color of the guide lines.

Ⓑ Allows you to have objects snap to guides, make guides visible, or lock guides by default.

Ⓒ Allows you to select between Normal, Must Be Close, or Can Be Distant. Affects how close the object must be to the guide before it snaps to it.

Ⓓ Makes the current settings in the Guides dialog the default settings for every new document.

The grid is made visible by choosing View > Grid > Show Grid. It is used to help you align object around the Stage. The Color, Show Grid, and Snap To Grid settings are the same as for Guides.

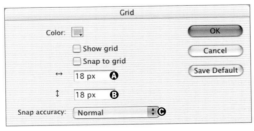

Ⓐ **Horizontal Spacing** Sets the amount of horizontal spacing between grid lines.

Ⓑ **Vertical Spacing** Sets the amount of vertical spacing between grid lines.

Ⓒ Select from Normal, Must Be Close, Can Be Distant, or Always Snap.

7.10   Using Rulers, Guides, Grids, and Snap *(continued)*

Choose View > Snapping to see a menu of several different Snapping options. It is possible to choose more than one option in this menu, depending on your preferences.

Edit Snap Align   Opens the Snap Align dialog.

Snap Align   Activates Snap Align that shows you dotted alignment guides on the Stage while moving objects. These guides help align objects to each other, or the edge of the Stage.

Snap To Grid   Snaps objects to the grid while being moved on the Stage.

Snap To Guides   Snaps objects to guidelines when they are within a certain distance.

Snap To Pixels   Displays a grid at 1 pixel increments when your magnification is set to 400% or higher.

Snap To Objects   Snaps objects to each other once they are within a certain distance of each other.

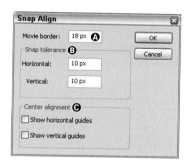

A   Sets the snap tolerance between objects and the edge of the Stage.

B   Sets the horizontal and vertical snapping tolerance between objects on the Stage.

C   Toggles whether objects will snap when their center points are aligned either horizontally or vertically.

➡ 5.4   Info Panel

Edit guides
`Ctrl` `Alt` `Shift` `G`
`⌘` `Option` `Shift` `G`

Lock guides
`Ctrl` `Shift` `;`
`Option` `Shift` `;`

Snap to guides
`Ctrl` `Shift` `;`
`⌘` `Shift` `;`

Snap to objects
`Ctrl` `Shift` `/`
`⌘` `Shift` `/`

Remember that you can snap align to the horizontal or vertical centers of objects as well as their edges. Select the Center Alignment check boxes for this functionality, which is turned off by default.

BUILDING APPLICATIONS WITH A TEAM

Macromedia Flash has developed from being largely an animation program into a full blown application development environment (and animation program). Because of this, the need for content management and version control has become more important to some of those using Flash for application development. Flash MX Professional introduces "projects," which allow you to package up an application and work with other developers in a team. Flash also supports the SourceSafe for source control.

7.11 Changing Movie Properties

Make your settings
a default if you are cre-
ating several Flash doc-
uments for a single
application with the
same original settings.

You can only set one
frame rate for the entire
Flash document.

Set a higher fps value
to make the motion
in your animations
smoother.

After you have started a new Flash movie, you might need to change the properties of the movie, such as the size of the Stage, background color, frame rate, or publish profiles. To quickly change the movie's properties, click the Stage and open the Property inspector. Clicking the Size button opens the Document Properties dialog, and the Settings button opens the Publish settings dialog.

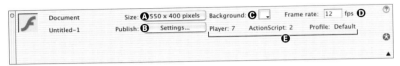

Ⓐ Displays the current dimensions of the Stage. Click the button to open the Document Properties dialog.

Ⓑ Opens the Publish Settings dialog.

Ⓒ Allows you to change the background color when you click the swatch and use the Color Picker. A hex value can also be set in the Color Picker.

Ⓓ Displays the current frame rate and allows you to change it to a new value. It is measured in fps (frames per second).

Ⓔ This area displays the target player, ActionScript version (1 or 2), and current publish profile.

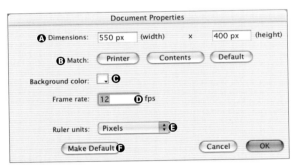

Ⓐ Sets the dimensions of the Stage in pixels. Enter values into the width and height text fields.

Ⓑ These three buttons contain default settings that are used to set Stage dimensions. Printer matches the printer page size settings, Contents matches Stage content dimensions, and Default is set to 550 px × 400 px.

Ⓒ Sets the background color for the Stage.

Ⓓ Sets movie frame rate, measured in fps (frames per second.) The default value is set to 12 fps.

Ⓔ Allows you to change the ruler units used by Flash. This can be changed to inches, inches (deci-mal), points, centimeters, millimeters, or pixels.

Ⓕ Makes current settings default. These settings are applied each time you open a new movie.

7.12 Saving Files or Templates

You can save a movie you are working on as a FLA, or you can save it as a template. A template is also saved as a FLA, but it is saved within the Flash directory.

Saving a movie is just like in many other programs: choose File > Save. This command saves the changes you've made to the Flash document, but it doesn't remove information such as a history of elements in the movie that you selected, created, or deleted. This means that the file sometimes bloats with data that you do not need in the FLA anymore.

The Save And Compact option removes unneeded data from the FLA file; this makes your FLA files smaller in size, but sometimes this command takes time to process. Choose File > Save As to save a new copy of the current document or rename it; this opens the Save As dialog, enabling you to give the file a new name and save the file as a Flash MX or Flash MX 2004 document. Do not choose File > Save after choosing Save And Compact because it will bloat the file size back to the pre-compacted size. Always choose Save And Compact again, or only run the command right before you close the file.

A Flash MX document cannot contain any elements that are specific to Flash MX 2004, such as screens and Pro Player features. If you try to save an MX document with unsupported features, you see this warning.

Saving a Template

Choose File > Save As Template to save the current document as a Flash template. You can save a FLA file as a template, allowing you to reuse the file repeatedly as a basis for other Flash work. The file is saved as a FLA, but it is placed into the Flash install directory.

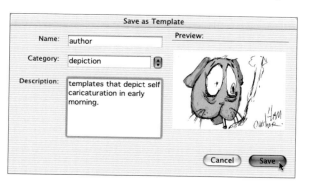

When saving a document as a template, you are asked to choose a name and category and write a description of the file. This information and a preview will be accessible in the File > New From Template dialog.

➡ 7.3 Starting Flash Documents

➡ 7.7 Opening from Templates

Save
Ctrl S
⌘ S

Save as
Ctrl Shift S
⌘ Shift S

You cannot use Save And Compact with code files.

Because Save And Compact causes you to wait for it to process, use the Save command during your authoring session, and then use Save And Compact to optimize the file when you are finished.

If you think there will be developers on your team working with an earlier version of Flash, make sure you choose File > Save As to save the movie as a Flash MX (version 6) document.

7.13 Exporting Movies

You can export many different kinds of images and image sequences from Flash. This is extremely helpful if you have to use different software to continue editing the content. Or, you can export a SWF file as well. This is a quick way of exporting a SWF file when you already have HTML files published. Choose File > Export > Export Movie to open the Export Movie dialog.

Export movie

Ctrl Alt Shift S
⌘ Option Shift S

Exporting a SWF file from the Export Movie command is done by those intending to import the files into Macromedia Director.

Export images from Flash the same way you export image sequences. The options will differ, but the process is the same. Simply choose File > Export > Export Image, and the Export Image dialog opens.

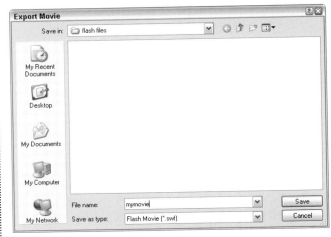

The Export Movie dialog allows you to name the file and select a file format to export to such as SWF or MOV. Click Save, and a second dialog allows you to choose various settings for the export depending on which kind of file you chose. Choose Flash Movie and click Save.

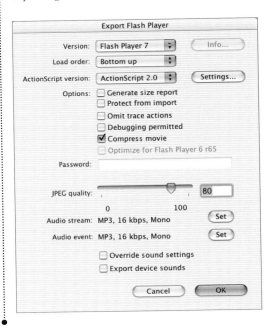

Choose export settings in the Export Flash Player dialog. Your movie is exported as a SWF file. This process is usually a lot quicker than choosing File > Publish.

CHAPTER 8

Selections and Groups

BEFORE YOU CAN USE Flash's editing features, you have to select one or more items from the Stage on which you want to apply changes. More importantly, you have to be able to define what you *don't* want to edit. This process of marking what you want to change is called *making a selection* and it is fundamental to almost all content production applications. Flash does not remember a selection. To make a selection permanent, such that you can reselect it with a single click, you should make the selection into a *group*. This allows you to treat the group as a single entity for the purposes of selection *and* animation.

8.1 Selecting with the Selection Tool

→ 8.2 Selecting with the Lasso or Free Transform Tool

Selection tool
[V]

Subselection tool
[A]

Select all
[Ctrl] [A]
[⌘] [A]

Delete selection
[Backspace]
[Delete]

Deselect all
[Ctrl] [Shift] [A]
[⌘] [Shift] [A]

———

Selecting a shape with a stroke is counted as *two* selectable elements. When click-selecting, you need to select both.

———

You can also make quick selections using the Timeline. Selecting a frame in the Timeline will also select the Stage contents of the frame.

The Selection tool is the primary means of making selections in Flash. There are two ways to make a selection with it: clicking selections and dragging marquees. Before making a selection, make sure that the content you wish to select is on a layer that allows editing (i.e., it is unlocked). With the Selection tool ▶, click the element you want to select. It will highlight with a light blue bounding box for a symbol or text or with a patterned fill for primitive graphics. You can also double-click a fill to select both the fill and its outline.

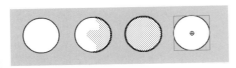

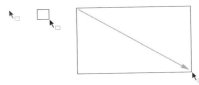

Left to right: an unselected circle, a partly selected circle primitive, a fully selected circle primitive, and a selected circle symbol. To make multiple click selections, hold down the Shift key while selecting.

To select multiple elements, use the Selection tool in marquee mode. Click-hold near one corner of the area containing the elements you want to select and drag-release the mouse to the diagonally opposite corner.

When starting a marquee, start the first corner on a blank area of the Stage (or over pixels in a locked layer); otherwise your drag will be taken to be a move. To alert you that this will be the case, the cursor will change ▶⊕; you should move the mouse slightly until it is not over selectable pixels and the cursor will become ▶. If you can't easily make the selection by clicking or dragging, you may be better off making your selection via a lasso.

All symbols that are *totally* enclosed within the marquee will be selected when you release. The first two aliens in row three are *not* selected because they are partially outside the marquee box.

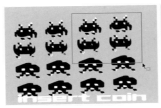

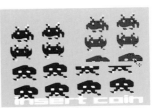

All parts of primitive graphics within the bounding box will be selected. For example, this selection selects only the top portion of the last two aliens in the third row. Using the Move tool on this selection would split them in half, with the unselected bottom halves staying put when you move.

8.2 Selecting with the Lasso or Free Transform Tool

Working with the Lasso Tool

The Lasso tool ✐ makes nonrectangular selections. It allows you to make selections by defining a freehand selection border.

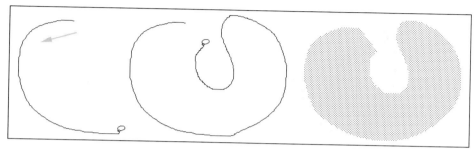

To create a lasso selection, click-drag to form a freehand shape. When you release the mouse, Flash will draw a straight line between the start and endpoint of the freehand line and will use the resulting area to define your selection. Apart from the difference in shape, a lasso selection operates exactly like a marquee selection (as described in the previous section).

The Hidden Selection Tool: Free Transform

Although the Selection and Lasso tools are fairly standard selection tools that you would expect to find in most graphic applications, Flash has a third and less obvious tool capable of making selections: the Free Transform tool ▦. The beauty of the Free Transform tool is that it makes selections the same as the Selection tool in marquee mode, except that the marquee selection box stays on stage (via the transform envelope).

 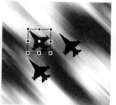 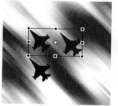 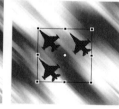

Here the user has selected the Free Transform tool and then Shift-clicked each of the jets in turn. The transform envelope in these images reflects how the selection grows as each element is selected, something that doesn't happen with the standard selection tool.

Lasso tool
[L]

Free Transform tool
[Q]

Select all
[Ctrl] [A]
[⌘] [A]

Delete selection
[Backspace]
[Delete]

Deselect all
[Ctrl] [Shift] [A]
[⌘] [Shift] [A]

The tools in this section select symbols or primitives. To select more basic elements such as points within a stroke or the fill gradient data, use the Subselection tool (to select and edit individual points within a vector curve) or the Fill Transform tool (to select and edit an individual fill area).

8.3   Editing a Stage Selection

➡ 3.6   Selection
         (Arrow) Tool

➡ 3.9   Lasso Tool

➡ 4.2   Layer Options

Delete selection
Backspace
Delete

**Duplicate selection
to the Stage**
Ctrl D
⌘ D

**Paste clipboard
in place**
Ctrl Shift V
⌘ Shift V

**Move selection
(1 pixel steps)**
↑ ↓ ← →

**Move selection (10
pixel steps)**
Shift ↑
Shift ↓
Shift ←
Shift →

Layer options play a
large part making selec-
tions. You can hide or
lock layers to prevent
them from becoming
part of a selection.

When designing a site,
arranging content into
meaningful layers helps
later when it's time to
make selections. If you
order elements that
you know you will want
to select together, you'll
only have to lock all
other layers and press
⌘/Ctrl+A to select the
contents of the current
layer only; no need for
marquees or the lasso!

Once you have formed a selection, you may want to edit parts of the selection itself before you go on to edit the elements *within* the selection.

To extend your selection by adding additional elements Hold down the Shift key and select additional elements using any of the methods described in the preceding sections.

To remove an element from the selection Hold down the Shift key and select the elements you want to remove. The Selection/Lasso tools are toggles; selecting twice will deselect your selection.

To deselect all of a selection Click an empty area of the Stage or make an empty selection.

To select the majority of the elements on the Stage Select All and then Shift-select all elements that you *don't* want to select.

The many things you can do with your selection are spread all over the interface (and not only do you have to know where they are, you have to be aware of what they are!). One of the best kept secrets is the contextual menu that appears when you right-click/⌘-click anything on the Stage (including the Stage itself). This menu always lists almost all edit options available to you and is clever enough to be context-sensitive to the contents of your selection.

8.4   Making and Editing Groups

Flash doesn't allow you to make permanent or semipermanent selections. Once you click outside a selection, it becomes deselected. The way around this is to instead form a *group* from the selection. A group is effectively Flash's way of making a selection permanent.

To create a group Make a selection and then select Modify > Group. You will see a light blue outline around your selection.

To ungroup Either select Modify > Ungroup or Modify > Break Apart.

To edit a group once you have created it Open a group by double-clicking it (this process is called Edit On Stage).

Groups vs. Symbols

It is important to understand the downside of using groups vs. symbols:

- You cannot use ActionScript to animate a group because it doesn't have the properties required to achieve this; specifically, it doesn't have an instance name.

- Groups are not bandwidth friendly if you copy them because they are not *instances*. All symbols are instances, which means they are essentially linked copies of one original (or in technical terms, they are a reference to an original rather than a true copy of it). Duplicating a 20 KB group to the Stage will result in an additional 20 KB added to your overall file size, whereas making a symbol and copying an instance of it to the Stage will result in a few additional bytes.

Group current selection
Ctrl G
⌘ G

Ungroup
Ctrl Shift G
⌘ Shift G

Break apart
Ctrl B
⌘ B

Although it is possible to create nested groups (i.e., a group that itself contains groups), this is not recommended. If you need to create nested groups to maintain depth by keeping certain symbols in front of others, you should be using a symbol instead because this process is easier to control through layers.

PLANNING TIMELINES FOR EASY SELECTION

When designing a site, arranging content into meaningful layers helps later when it's time to make selections. If you order elements that you know you will want to select together, you'll then only have to lock all other layers and press ⌘/Ctrl+A to select the contents of the current layer only; no need for marquees or the lasso!

8.5 Using Groups

→ 8.6 Breaking
      Apart Stage
      Elements

**Group current
selection**
[Ctrl] [G]
[⌘] [G]

Ungroup
[Ctrl] [Shift] [G]
[⌘] [Shift] [G]

Using groups effectively is something that even accomplished Flash designers seem to have trouble with, given that it is very difficult to see when a group has advantages over a symbol. The following example should clarify this.

Imagine that you want four jets to fly in formation from bottom-right to top-left. Halfway through the animation, you want each pair of jets to peel off to split the formation. There are three ways to do this:

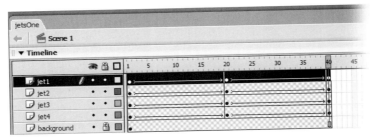

Give each jet its own tween. This will give you the most complex timeline: four separate layers, one per jet.

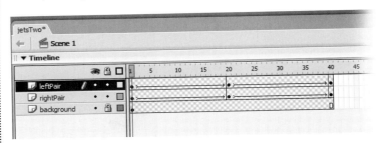

Make each pair of jets a symbol and give each pair its own tween. This is slightly better in terms of timeline complexity; you'll have two layers, one per each jet pair. However, doing this often will clutter your library with lots of symbols—not ideal!

8.5 Using Groups (continued)

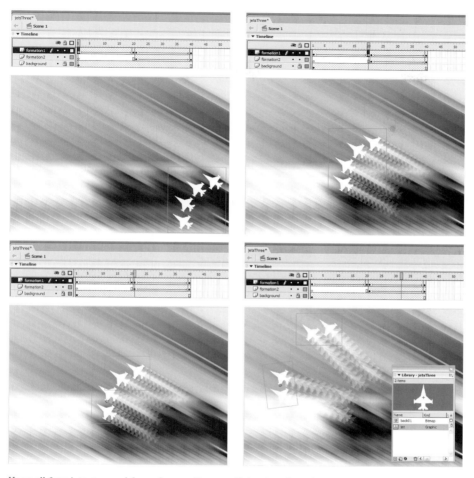

➡ 10.11 Adding
        Motion
        Tweens

➡ 12.6   Library
        Symbol
        Icons

Break apart

`Ctrl` `B`

`⌘` `G`

Although it is possible to create "nested" groups (a group that itself contains groups), this is not recommended. If you need to create nested groups to maintain depth (that is, to keep certain symbols in front of others), then you should be using symbols instead, because that makes this process easier to control through layers.

Keep all four jets grouped for as long as they are flying together. As soon as the formation splits, ungroup and regroup the jets into two pairs, as in the third step here. Between frames 1 and 20, the jets are all within one group, so the early part of the animation consists of a single tween. At frame 21, the formation group is ungrouped and regrouped into two new smaller groups. These are animated separately from frame 21 to the end.

You can see that the library is much less cluttered for the final version of the animation. The animation complexity is where it belongs—in the Timeline—without seeping into the library. This version is the easiest for another Flash animator to understand; the reasons for the changing groupings are obvious because they are done in the context of the animation and are on the Timeline. With the previous symbol-based animation, it is not immediately obvious why you have library symbols leftJets and rightJets because they have no immediate context.

8.6 Breaking Apart Stage Elements

Group current selection

⌃ Ctrl G
⌘ G

Ungroup

Ctrl Shift G
⌘ Shift G

Break apart

Ctrl B
⌘ B

When you break apart a symbol, you only affect the symbol on the Stage—you *do* not lose the version in the library.

A group that is never broken up is probably a group that needs to be a symbol. Remember that the whole point of groups is to make a selection semipermanent, and you should avoid using them as a quick alternative to a symbol.

Break Apart is useful when you want to create a number of similar graphic symbols. Create the graphics for the first one on the Stage, select them, and then select Modify > Convert To Symbol. This allows you to create a symbol from the selection. Select Break Apart to remove the symbol on the Stage and make the changes needed to create the next graphic, repeating the process.

In addition to forming groups, you will be constantly ungrouping and breaking them apart back into their separate members. To use the Break Apart option, select the items you want to break apart and then choose Modify > Break Apart. This will do the following:

- Ungroup any group(s) you have selected. You can also use the Ungroup function (Modify > Ungroup) to do this.

- Delete any symbol(s) in a selection and leave the contents of its first frame on the Stage. Using Break Apart again on the result will Break Apart any non-primitives left within the result, eventually leaving you with raw primitives.

- Separate any text field into separate letters. Breaking apart again will turn the text into primitive shapes.

- Modify a bitmap so that you can delete parts of it using the Eraser tool.

Left: The original bitmap on the Stage. Center: After Break Apart (note the stipple pattern over the image). Right: The Eraser can be used to cut the graphic out from its background, creating an effect rather like a transparent GIF, except that the edges of the cut are smooth vectors rather than pixel edges.

The original text

The text after Break Apart

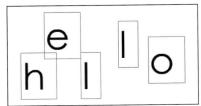

The letters have been moved to show they are now separate.

The *o* has been broken apart again, showing that it can now be edited as a primitive.

CHAPTER 9

Drawing and Shape Creation

THIS CHAPTER LOOKS AT using the Flash drawing tools to create graphics. In general, there are three issues when creating graphics; drawing, hierarchy, and optimization. Although the first is obvious, the other two are less so.

Flash is a very hierarchical system, consisting of a number of distinct types of graphic. Knowledge of this hierarchy, and where any shape you draw fits within it, is important. Flash also creates Web content, so optimizing your graphics is an integral part of the content creation process.

9.1 Basics of Primitives

➠ 3.7 Subselection Tool

➠ 9.2 Understanding Strokes and Fills

➠ 9.10 Editing Vector Points with the Subselection Tool

➠ 9.14 Optimizing Vector Shapes

Subselection tool
[A]

The big disadvantage of vector animation is that it can become slow if you use large filled areas. Filling a complex shape takes many more calculations than showing a bitmap of the same shape. The bitmap has its appearance predefined, whereas the vector shape contains the basic *definition* of the shape, and the final appearance has to be *calculated* per pixel from this.

All the content you create with the Flash drawing tools is made up of mathematically defined fill shapes and lines (called "strokes" in Flash, as in "pen stroke"). These fills and strokes are usually called either shapes, primitives, or primitive shapes. All are created using a point based geometry.

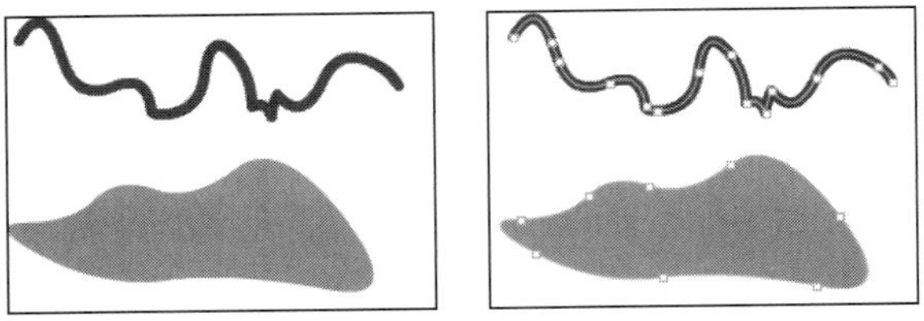

Any primitive is made up of a series of points. You can see these points by selecting any part of a stroke or the edge of a fill with the Subselection tool .

Optimization and Simplification

As with all web design, file size is important, and it is achieved with primitives by reducing the point count—unlike bitmaps, reducing the size of a primitive does *not* reduce the file size.

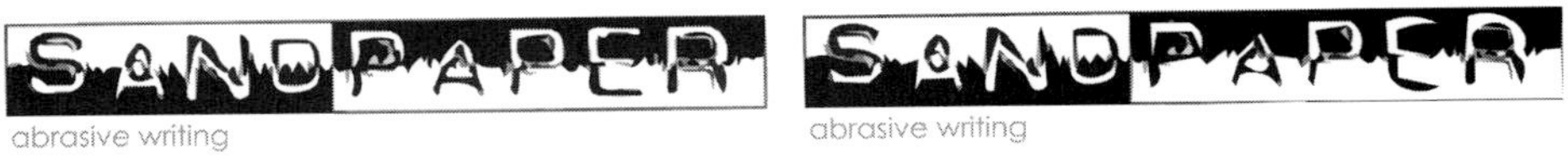
SANDPAPER
abrasive writing
SANDPAPER
abrasive writing

The logo to the right has about a third of the points of the one on the left, due to simplification and optimization. Not only does this make the graphic smaller in file size, it also makes it easier for Flash to draw it quickly. Note that in this example the change in image quality is negligible between the two examples. Unlike bitmaps, where reducing files size is strongly associated with reducing image quality, reducing the number of points in a vector image does not always reduce quality.

Primitives and Symbols

Unlike other drawing and animation tools, Flash is also a programming environment. To create animation using ActionScript, Flash needs a link between the graphical environment and the programming one, and this is the *instance name*. Only symbols (and some text fields) can have an instance name. You cannot animate a primitive shape using ActionScript unless you first make it into a symbol because a primitive doesn't have an instance name.

There are also some nonprogramming animation effects (such as motion tweens) that Flash internally changes into code or numerical descriptions, and these will not work with a primitive either (for essentially the same reason).

9.1 Basics of Primitives *(continued)*

Another major difference between primitives and symbols is that when you drag a symbol from the library to the Stage, Flash doesn't place the original symbol onto the Stage, or even a copy of it, but a *reference* to it. Flash adds information to the FLA that says "when you see this keyframe, be sure to place this symbol at this position on the Stage." This process has a number of important implications:

- If you copy the same symbol to the Stage several times and then change the primitives within the original, *all the copies of the symbol will change*. This is because an instance is simply a reference to the original (i.e., if you change the original, the instances refer to the changed original, so they change in appearance as well).

- If you copy a primitive and change the original, you end up with two different primitives (because you had two different primitives that looked the same when you copied).

WHEN YOU CANNOT OPTIMIZE A VECTOR...

For very complex vectors that don't seem to optimize well, consider importing the shape as a *bitmap*. This works well for images that have few solid color areas such as photographs or other 'real life' images.

➠ 9.20 Changing Fill Color and Gradient

➠ 9.21 Changing Stroke Color

➠ 11.1 Understanding Symbols

You don't usually have to worry about web-safe colors in Flash when creating primitives. In fact, Flash is the best way to show unlimited and precise colors to the maximum number of users on the Web at the moment!

When you drag a symbol to the Stage, you are performing the graphical equivalent of a programming process called *instantiation*. The reference is an *instance* (also called an *object*) of a template called a *class* (in this case, a movie clip, button, or graphic). Knowing where primitives sit in this hierarchy is the key to programming effects with them in ActionScript.

9.2   Understanding Strokes and Fills

Pencil tool
Y

Pen tool
P

Line tool
N

Oval tool
O

Rectangle tool
R

A stroke can only have a solid color even though the Color Mixer can sometimes imply otherwise via its color type drop-down. Gradients can be applied to fills only.

Strokes are created by the Pencil 🖉 , Pen ✒ or Line tool ╱ . They are also created as the outlines of circles and rectangles when you use the Oval ◯ or Rectangle ☐ .

A stroke has two attributes, color and thickness. A special case of the thickness attribute is a *hairline stroke*. This has zero thickness and is always drawn with a thickness of one pixel regardless of zoom level.

A fill is an area containing color. A fill can be created by the Oval ◯ , Rectangle ☐ , and Paint Bucket 🪣 tools.

A fill has one editable attribute, color, which can contain color gradients. A fill can usually be created with or without a stroke border.

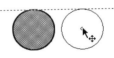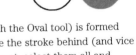

Strokes and fills remain separate. For example, this circle (created with the Oval tool) is formed from a separate fill and stoke border. If you move the fill, you will leave the stroke behind (and vice versa). To make a series of primitive strokes and fills into a single element, select them all and make the selection into a group or symbol.

USING EXTERNAL DRAWING TOOLS

Although flash has a comprehensive set of vector animation tools, there are a number of things that other applications do better. Consider drawing involved vector images in Illustrator or Freehand. Also, a bitmap editing application (such as Photoshop or Fireworks) are obligatory for Flash web design.

9.3 Understanding Color and Gradients

A shape can be filled with a solid, gradient, or pattern fill. In this section you will look at the two primitive vector-based colors, solid and gradient.

Color can be added to both fills and strokes. When using the Color Mixer, there are two color models you can use:

The **RGB (red green blue) model** creates color by simulating the way light mixes. Each of the three color components is represented by a value between 0 (no color) and 255 (maximum color). The Color Mixer panel shows this color model by default. To enter a RGB value, change the R, G, and B values to the desired component values.

The **HSB (hue saturation brilliance) model** is based around the way the human eye sees color. Hue represents the color and can be between 0 and 360 degrees on the HSB *color wheel*. The saturation specifies the intensity in percent of the hue, and is also known as *chroma*. Finally, the brilliance specifies the darkness-brightness via a 0 to 100 percent range.

Gradients

A color gradient can be applied to fills and is created by varying color in a particular direction and within a particular envelope. You can select a gradient from the color picker, or create your own via the Color Mixer. There are two types of gradient envelope, linear and radial.

  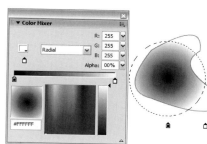

A linear gradient will vary color in a straight line from one side of a rectangular envelope to the other. You can specify up to eight colors within your gradient—here there are only two, black and white.

A radial gradient will vary color in a straight line along the radius of a circular envelope. As with linear gradients, you can specify up to eight colors within your gradient; this shows only black and white.

As well as defining colors for a gradient, you can also specify the size, position, and orientation of the gradient envelope. In general, you will want the envelope to enclose the shape, because this will show the full gradient (as per last example on the right).

Color Mixer panel
Shift F9

A shape tween allows animation of the gradient envelope, allowing your gradient to change its attributes over time. It also works with solid color.

9.4 Creating Fills and Strokes

Selection tool
[V]

Line tool
[N]

Oval tool
[O]

Rectangle tool
[R]

Pencil tool
[Y]

Brush tool
[B]

Ink Bottle tool
[S]

Paint Bucket tool
[K]

To create a regular oval or rectangle:

1 Select either the rectangle □ or oval ○ tool.

2 Select the fill and stroke color. If you do not want either a stroke or fill as part of the shape, select the No Color ☑ icon from the color picker. If you want the default colors (black stroke, white fill), select the Black and White icon ▣. To swap the stroke and fill color, select the Swap Colors icon ▤ .

3 Position the cursor on the Stage at one corner of the final shape. Drag to reveal an outline of the shape and release when the outline corresponds to the desired shape. To draw a square or circle, hold down Shift as you drag.

Creating Strokes

To create a straight line, you can use the Line Tool, and the line properties can be altered via the Property Inspector. The Options button on the Property inspector opens the Stroke Style window, which gives detailed options.

1 Select the Line tool ✏ . Select the stroke color from either the Tools panel or the Property inspector.

2 Select the stroke thickness from either the Property inspector or the Stroke Style window.

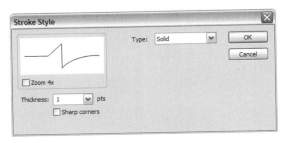

3 The Stroke Style dialog allows you to define a pattern for your stroke (options are Solid, Dashed, Dotted, Ragged, Stipple, or Hatched). Select the stroke type from either the Property inspector or the Stroke Style window. Selecting it from Stroke Style will reveal options to customize the current style.

9.4 Creating Fills and Strokes (continued)

4 Finally, click-hold at the start point of the line, and drag-release at the endpoint.

To make a line into a curve, first create a line as detailed above. Unselect the line by clicking on a blank area of the stage. Select the Selection tool ![cursor] and place the cursor over the part of the curve you want to change. The cursor will change ![cursor]. Drag and release the cursor to form a curve.

To change one of the endpoints of a stroke once it has been drawn (and then unselected as above), choose the Selection tool ![cursor] and place the cursor over an endpoint of the stroke until it becomes a ![cursor]. Click and drag the cursor to a new position and release.

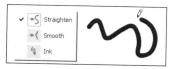

To create a freehand stroke, use the Pencil tool ![pencil]. Set the stroke options as in Step 3 above to create a straight line, then set the Pencil tool options to Straighten, Smooth, or Ink. These will straighten, smooth, or do nothing to any freehand stroke you create.

To create a nonregular shape, you can do either of the following:

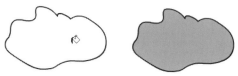

Draw a closed stroke and fill it with the Paint Bucket tool ![bucket] by clicking inside the enclosed area.

Or, paint a shape with the Brush tool ![brush]. If you want to add a stroke around the shape once you have created it, select the Ink Bottle tool ![ink] and click anywhere on the perimeter of the shape.

You can create curves using the Pen tool or edit a stroke using the Subselection tool. Both these tools create strokes by altering or creating points rather than working with strokes directly. They work at a lower level than the tools described in this section and are therefore more accurate. The downside is that it usually takes longer to draw with them.

9.5 Moving Fills and Strokes

Selection tool
V

Lasso tool
L

Oval tool
O

Rectangle tool
R

It is usually a good idea to either make primitives into symbols or groups or lock the layer they are on as soon as you have finished them. Accidentally causing overlapping primitives can quickly ruin your graphics, but the techniques listed here protect against this happening.

It is a good idea to have one finished shape per keyframe. Not only does this prevent overlapping deleting some of your shape areas, but shape tweens also rely on one shape per layer.

The way you create a shape has implications when you separate its parts as you move them.

When working with primitives on the same layer, moving a fill over any other primitive will delete hidden areas; when moving strokes, overlapped areas are preserved. When working with primitives on different layers, moving any element will not delete any areas.

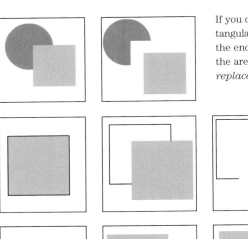

If you create these shapes (a circular fill with a rectangular fill created on top of it) on the same layer, the end result will be as shown at right. Note that the area of the circle that the rectangle overlaps is *replaced* by the rectangle.

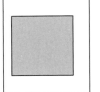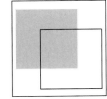

Similarly, moving the fill over the stroke for this rectangle will delete the hidden parts of the stroke.

Moving the stroke over a fill *doesn't* have the same effect.

Primitives created on different layers will *always* preserve overlapping areas. If this circle and square are on different layers, moving them apart will reveal the hidden areas.

Splitting a Primitive

Selecting only portions of a primitive or primitives will cause them to split when you move the selected area because the unselected areas will remain in place.

In this sequence, part of a circle is selected using the Lasso tool and then moved via the Selection tool. This process pulls the selection away from the rest of the circle.

9.6 Creating Faux Perspectives with the Distort Tool

The Distort tool allows you to add tapers to shapes to create quick perspective effects. The following quick example will show you how to achieve this.

1 Create some text using the Text tool. Apply Break Apart on it (Modify > Break Apart) twice to convert it to a series of primitives. When you have done this, the text will no longer be enclosed by a light blue bounding box when you select it.

2 With the text shapes selected, select the Free Transform tool ⊞ from the Tools panel. In the Options section of the Tools panel, select Distort ◰ . The text will gain a distort bounding box around it. Move the top-left corner point of the box upward as shown. This will give you the finished effect.

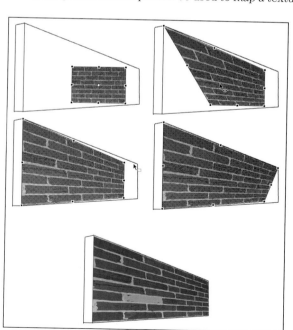

Using Distort to Map Textures

The same general technique can be used to map a texture to a 3D outline.

A brick texture is mapped to a wall outline by aligning the texture to the outline. By aligning textures to basic shapes in this way, you can quickly create realistic backgrounds for animated features.

➡ 3.17 Free Transform Tool

➡ 9.14 Optimizing Vector Shapes

➡ 9.23 Simulating Lighting with Gradients

Free Transform tool
Ⓠ

The brick texture was created by tracing a bitmap. When doing this, remember to optimize the finished shape because they can get fairly complex if you let them.

Shift-clicking a corner point of the distort bounding box will move the opposite corner point to the direction you start to drag, but in the mirror-image direction. This allows you to create symmetrical tapers.

9.7 Conforming Primitives to Curves with the Envelope Tool

➡ 3.11 Text Tool

➡ 3.17 Free Trans-
form Tool

Text tool
T

Free Transform tool
Q

The Envelope tool works best with Snap off (View > Snapping > Snap To Grid should be unchecked).

The Envelope tool is very useful for logo design. You can use it to wrap text around a logo or to change its size and orientation precisely. However, the Envelope tool in this way requires a good hand!

The Envelope tool allows you to make complex shape and size changes to primitives only via a curve-based envelope. Using this tool can be a difficult process, so it is best to use a guide layer containing the curve you want to conform to.

Here the chevron shape is made to conform to the curve in the guide layer *curve*. Before you start, lock the guide layer.

If your background is white, it is a good idea to change it to a darker color, so that you will be able to make out the different parts of the envelope. Select Modify > Document and change the background color to a mid-gray. Select the shape then select the Free Transform tool ▣. In the Options section of the Tools panel, select the Envelope icon ▣. You will see the envelope appear around the shape.

The envelope consists of control points (the squares), each with two "bowties" (the lines ending in circles). Moving them will change the shape of the envelope. This in turn forces the shape to change as it conforms to the envelope.

To make the chevron conform to the curve:

1 First, move the square points so that their *position* conforms to the curve. When you have done this for all points, you will end up with something like the image on the right.

9.7 Conforming Primitives to Curves with the Envelope Tool *(continued)*

2 Next, move the bowties so that the envelope's *curvature* conforms to the curve. When you have done this for all bowties, you will end up with something similar to the example on the left. To remove the envelope, click any blank area on the Stage. The finished shape is shown on the right.

➡ 10.23 Creating and Using Guide Layers

Modify Document
Ctrl J
⌘ J

The Envelope tool is one of the hardest tools to use. It has no Undo, and accidentally clicking on the Stage removes the envelope. Also, once you remove the envelope, you cannot get back to the last used envelope (it always starts off as a rectangle). Not a tool to use when you are working through the night to meet a client deadline!

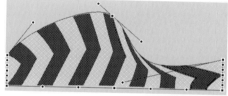

The Envelope tool can also be used to change the shape of the perimeter of a shape. This is a much easier process than the one just shown, although the principle is the same. Move the envelope's control points to change it to the desired shape.

The Envelope tool also works very well with text that has been broken apart (Modify > Break Apart) to make it into shapes, and then conformed.

9.8 Deleting Shapes, Strokes, and Areas

Selection tool
[V]

Line tool
[N]

Pencil tool
[Y]

Lasso tool
[L]

Rectangle tool
[R]

Delete selection
[Del]

Deleting parts of a primitive is mostly a case of making the right selection. On timelines with a large number of layers, be sure to lock layers that should not be part of the deleted selection or you may end up deleting more than you expect.

A primitive is easy to split once created, so deletion can occur for all or parts of a primitive. The easiest way to make a deletion is via the keyboard Delete key.

Deleting an Area

Because many shapes consist of at least two parts (a stroke and fill), the easiest way to delete them entirely is to use either the Selection tool ▶ in Marquee mode or the Lasso tool ♀ to enclose the area in which the shape is placed, then press the Delete key. You can also double-click the fill to select both the fill and its stroke before deleting them.

Deleting Part of a Primitive

To delete part of a primitive, you can do either of the following:

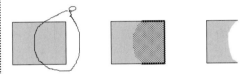

Select the part you want to delete via a marquee or lasso, then press the Delete key.

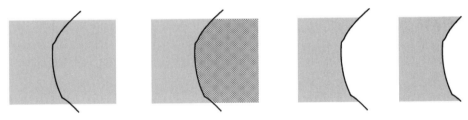

Draw a stroke via the Line ✏ or Pencil tool ✏ on the same layer as the primitives you want to delete so that it separates the part that you want to delete. Then click the part(s) you want to delete and press the Delete key. Finally, select and delete the parts of the stroke you do not want to keep. This method is useful when you want to put a stroke on the newly created edges when deleting parts of a fill.

9.9 Creating Bezier Curves

When creating a stroke, you will sometimes want more control than the Line tool allows. The Pen tool allows you to work at a greater level of accuracy by showing you the control points that are used to create the stroke.

Select the Pen tool ✒ and position it where you want to start the stroke section. A little x will appear by the side of the cursor ✒ₓ , thus signifying that a new point will be created when you click.

To draw a line section, click once to start the line, and then again to draw its endpoint. A line will be created containing two points, each of which will be displayed in the layer color.

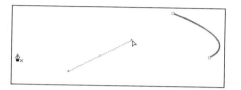

To draw a Bezier curve section, click and hold to start the curve. You will see a pair of "bowtie" handles. Dragging the mouse will edit the bowtie. The direction of these represents the direction of the curve as it goes through the point, and the length of the handles represents the "speed" or tension of the curve as it goes through the point. Once you are happy with the length and direction, release and click on the Stage once more to specify the endpoint of the curve.

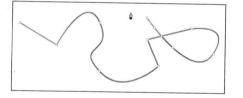

To draw a continuous stroke consisting of line and curve sections, continue to add further endpoints. Clicking will create a line or corner point, and click-holding will create a curve. Note that drawing a section that intersects another will create a control point at the intersection.

To use the Pen tool to create a fill as well as a stroke, first make sure that Snap To Objects (View > Snapping > Snap To Objects) is checked. Then, create a stroke as before. The last point should be placed in the same position as the first one. When you have placed the cursor close enough for this to happen, the cursor will appear with a little o around it to signify a closed stroke is about to be created. Click to complete the operation, and you should see the enclosed area filled.

➡ 3.7 Subselection Tool

➡ 3.10 Pen Tool

➡ 9.10 Editing Vector Points with the Subselection Tool

Pen tool
[P]

Subselection tool
[A]

Snap To Objects
[Ctrl] [Shift] [/]
[⌘] [Shift] [/]

The curves created by the Pen tool are complex and can take time to draw. For this reason, any curves created by the Pen tool are *approximated* in the final SWF. In almost all cases, you will not see the differences this creates unless you are actively looking for them.

The Pen tool does not allow you to edit points once you have created them. To do this, use the Subselection tool. The Pen and Subselection tools are closely related and are often used together for this reason.

If you see the close path *o* on the cursor but a fill is not created when you click, you probably do not have Snap To Objects enabled.

9.10   Editing Vector Points with the Subselection Tool

Pen tool
[P]

Subselection tool
[A]

———

The curves created by the Subselection tool are complex and can take time to draw. For this reason, any curves created are *approximated* in the final SWF. In almost all cases, you will not see the differences this creates unless you are actively looking for them.

———

The points are drawn in the current layer color. If you find them difficult to see, change the layer color to something more contrasting.

———

A good analogy of bowtie length on bowtie handles is the speed of a car following the stroke path—the longer the length, the faster the car. As you increase the bowtie handles, you increase the speed of the car, making the path open out to reflect the longer turning radius at higher speeds. In technical terms, the bowtie handle is actually the *velocity vector* of the car as it goes along the stroke path.

The Subselection tool allows you to edit a stroke or fill at the point level, allowing for accurate editing of primitives. It is strongly associated with the Pen tool, which allows you to create strokes and fills at the point level (although you can use the Subselection tool with primitives created with any drawing tool). You can also use the Subselection tool to see how many points are being used to make up a primitive. This is useful when optimizing.

To edit a stroke, with the Subselection tool ➤ , move the cursor over a stroke or the edge of a fill. If your primitive contains *both* a stroke and a fill, move over the stroke. You will see the cursor show a little square ➤▪ (representing a point) to the bottom right.

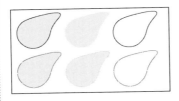

Click the shape; it will show its point data. Examples of before (top) and after (below) shapes are shown here for (left to right) a shape plus fill, fill only, and a stroke with no fill.

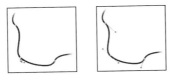

To select a point, move over it until you see a hollow square to the bottom right of the cursor ➤▫ , and then click the point. You will see the selected point and the two points either side of it change to make the point *position* and curve *direction* editable.

Changing a Curve's Direction

Use the bowtie handles to alter the direction of the curve as it goes through the three points. The handle direction represents the curve direction as it goes through the point, and the handle length represents its speed.

First: Click a handle. Second: Drag to a new position. Third: Release. Fourth: The resulting curve.

Changing a Point's Position

To change a point's position, simply click-drag it. You do not have to select a point first to do this (it becomes selected with the click).

9.11 Smoothing and Straightening Vectors

There are two ways to smooth and straighten your primitive shapes: while drawing them or after they have been placed. After creating a shape, modify your shapes as follows:

1 Select the area you want to modify. Note that you do not have to select the whole shape, and in most cases, you will not want to do this; you will usually want to apply smoothing and straightening to different areas of the same shape.

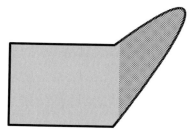

2 Select either Modify > Shape > Straighten or Modify > Shape > Smooth. You will see the selection either become smoother or straighter. In many cases, you will have to apply the change a number of times.

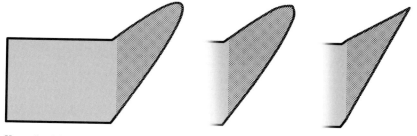

Here, Straighten has been applied twice, making the curve into a straight corner.

Note that smoothing and straightening can sometimes have no effect, particularly when the original shape has few points. If you draw a rectangle and try to smooth it, you will not end up with a circle.

INCREASING VISIBILITY OF VECTOR POINTS

When using the Pen tool, you may sometimes find that the points created are not easily visible against the current background. To fix this, consider changing the Layer color (which is used to define the point color) to something more contrasting.

➡ 3.14 Pencil Tool

➡ 9.14 Optimizing Vector Shapes

Smoothing and straightening are closely associated with optimizing, and you will find them useful to fix minor kinks and other undesirable features when importing external vector-based assets (such as clip art).

_____

After you have optimized a shape, some lines and corners may not be exact. Consider using smoothing or straightening to fix this.

9.12   Converting Lines to Fills

When converting strokes to fills, you can also select fills if it is easier (i.e., you can use a marquee to select an entire shape containing both strokes and fills). Fills are not affected by the conversion because they are already fills.

Make sure that you are happy with the curvature of a stroke before you convert it to a fill because once you convert, the resulting fill no longer has any of the editing options common to strokes.

Converting strokes to fills creates more point data, and therefore results in higher file-sizes—convert only when you absolutely have to.

It takes most beginners some time to see any reason to want to change a stroke into a fill. This is because the reasons are driven by the limitations of stroke edit options (when compared to fills), many of which are not immediately obvious:

■ You cannot vary thickness along the length of a stroke.

■ Strokes cannot be colored via gradients.

■ All strokes have rounded endpoint edges that cannot be removed.

■ Stroke edges cannot be softened.

To convert a stroke to a fill, select it and then select Modify > Shape > Convert Lines To Fills. The stroke will *not* change in appearance when you do this.

You can see the difference between a stroke and a fill by drawing a thick stroke with the Line tool ✏ , then selecting it with the Subselection tool ▶ . You will see that the line has only two points (left); one at the start and one at the end. If you select the stroke with the Selection tool ▶ and convert it to a fill (as above), before viewing it with the Subselection tool once more, you will see that the line is now defined by its *perimeter points* (right).

Squaring off a Line's Endpoints

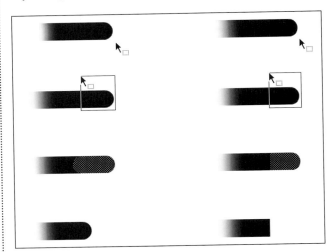

One of the most common reasons for converting a stroke to a fill is to make a line with squared-off endpoints. If you select the end of a stroke and delete it, the resulting endpoint is still rounded (left column). If you convert the stroke to a fill first, you will see a squared-off endpoint after the same operation (right column).

9.13 Expanding and Softening Fill Edges

The Expand Fill feature allows you to increase or decrease the perimeter of a shape by adding or subtracting a pixel value all around the perimeter. To expand an edge:

1 Select your fill. Choose Modify > Shape > Expand Fill.

2 Enter a distance in the Distance text entry box. This is the number of pixels the fill will change by.

3 Check either Expand (add pixels) or Inset (subtract pixels).

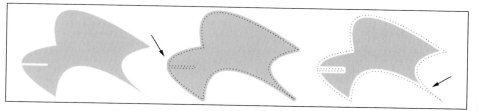

The effects of Expand Fill; dotted lines show the original shape perimeter for comparison. The original shape (left) is expanded by 6 pixels (center) and inset by 6 pixels (right). Note that the center image loses its slot shape because of the expansion, and the version on the right loses most of its tail due to the inset. Expanding and inserting a shape can lose detail if you use high values.

Softening an Edge

Softening an edge works much the same way as expanding an edge, except that the expansion or inset is made gradual by changing alpha (transparency) value over the specified pixel range. To soften an edge, select a fill as before and then select Modify > Shape > Soften Fill Edges. The Soften Fill Edges dialog is exactly the same as the Expand Fill dialog, except you will also see a Number Of Steps value. This specifies the number of "bands" around the shape. Increasing this value creates a smoother softening effect at the expense of increased file size and shape complexity.

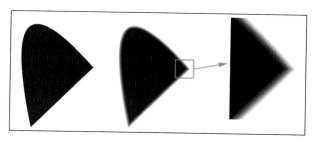

Left to right: the original unsoftened shape, the same shape with a five-step Soften Fill Edges, and a close-up showing the steps.

➧ 9.12 Converting Lines to Fills

If you want to expand the edges of a stroke, consider changing thickness instead.

If you want to soften a stroke, you have to convert it to a fill first with Modify > Shape > Convert Lines To Fills.

Softening a shape creates separate fills around it. To move a shape and its softening perimeter fills, you have to select them all. Consider making a softened shape into a group or symbol to make this easier.

Expand and Inset can be used on text that has been converted to fills via Modify > Break Apart (you will need to break apart text consisting of more than one character twice). This allows you to create extreme weight values that the font may not support directly.

Using noncontrasting colors is an efficient way of avoiding the need to soften edges.

9.14 Optimizing Vector Shapes

➡ 9.11 Smoothing
and Straight-
ening Vectors

Optimize curves

Ctrl Alt Shift C
⌘ Option Shift C

———

Always optimize any
vectors you import
from outside Flash.
External vector images,
particularly clip art, are
usually designed for
print rather than web
design, and can be sub-
stantially optimized.

———

When designing graph-
ics that will be con-
stantly moving, the eye
will not see much of
the detail, so optimiza-
tion can usually be car-
ried to much greater
extremes than with
static graphics.

———

Flash optimization does
not take into account
advanced color opti-
mizations that can
occur using gradients.
If your shapes have
subtle color gradua-
tions, consider remov-
ing all color by hand
before optimization
and hand coloring the
shapes afterward.

One of the primary aims of web design is small file size. In vector graphics, this is achieved through point and curve reduction, which reduces the amount of information needed to re-create the shape. Reduction also increases animation speed because less information needs to be processed to draw the shape.

1 Select the shape(s).

2 Select Modify > Shape > Optimize to bring up the Optimize Curves dialog.

Smoothing Defines the amount of curve smoothing. Moving this slider to the right will result in greater optimization (fewer points) at the expense of accuracy (the optimized shape may look noticeably different from the original).

Use Multiple Passes Allows you to select a slower but more accurate algorithm. For any computer less than two years old, it is recommended that you always have this checked for all but the most complex shapes, because current processors will optimize a shape in a few tenths of a second anyway.

Show Totals Message Gives an indication of the curve reduction. It is recommended that you always have this checked because it gives a good indication of the level of optimization.

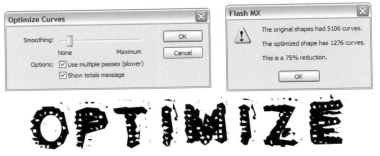

The "Optimize This" graphic was optimized by 75 percent (i.e., to 25 percent of its original size), as specified by the Show Totals window.

Although optimization creates a noticeably different set of shapes in this case, in many cases, the changes are not noticeable in the final presentation.

9.15 Working with Depth

Depth in Flash is much like depth of view in real life. An object with a greater depth than other Stage elements will appear to be behind the elements.

The trouble starts in Flash when you place two things at the *same* depth. In real life, two things the same distance away will cause no problems, but in Flash this is not allowed—the rule here is "one thing per depth."

Working at the Same Depth

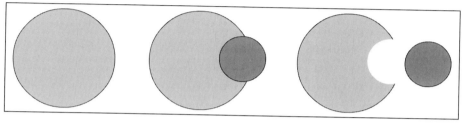

If you draw a fill and then draw something else over the top of it, the overwritten pixels are deleted. You can see this if you draw two differently colored circles, one over the top of the other, then move one of them, as in the cut-out effect shown here. This is because only one primitive can occupy any one depth, and the smaller circle is the last one drawn. It occurs even if the upper circle has an alpha value; you will *not* see the lower circle through a semi-transparent upper circle when you draw on the same layer, because the lower content will be *replaced*.

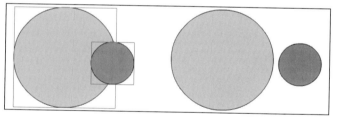

If, however, you group or make the primitives into symbols, the opposite occurs. Moving one circle will now reveal the other one behind it. This occurs because groups and symbols are nested graphics, and overlapping pixels don't interact (although they are physically in the same positions on the Stage, they are at different positions in the Flash Timeline hierarchy).

➡ 10.2 Animation Concepts in Flash

Bring To Front (move to top depth)
[Ctrl] [Shift] ↑
[Option] [Shift] ↑

Bring Forward (add 1 to depth)
[Ctrl] ↑
[⌘] ↑

Send Backward (subtract 1 from depth)
[Ctrl] ↓
[⌘] ↓ **Send To Back (move to bottom depth)**

———

To make an element appear to move from in front to behind during animation, change the layer it is in over a number of keyframes.

———

The depth value range is −16383 to 16384. Content placed on the Stage is assigned negative values from −16383 upward toward −1.

9.15   Working with Depth *(continued)*

➡ 10.21 Setting Layer
Properties
and Layer
Types

Lock

Ctrl Alt L

⌘ Option L

Unlock All

⌘ Option t Shift L

Depths from 0 to 16383
are reserved for content
that is placed onto the
Stage at runtime. You
cannot access or edit
content on these depths
without using Action-
Script.

When working with
depth, locking and hid-
ing layers is an invalu-
able way of keeping
layers separate while
you edit, and of hiding
in-front content while
you are editing behind
content.

The Lock and Unlock
options in the Arrange
submenu allow you a
finer level of control
than locking or unlock-
ing a layer; instead of
per-layer locking, you
can also selectively lock
individual primitives or
symbols *within* a layer.

Depth and Layers

The easiest way to force elements to be at different depths is to place them on different layers. Content in upper layers will always appear in front of lower ones, and primitives placed on different layers will not create gaps and holes in lower primitives.

Depth and Flash

Flash handles depth internally as a set of integer numbers. Each element placed onto the Stage is assigned a number, and the higher this number, the closer the element is to the "front" or top of the depth stack.

The final Flash SWF does not contain layers. Instead, the content on them is assigned depths at SWF compilation based on the layer ordering.

You can edit the depth of an element directly per layer with the submenu options found in Modify **>** Arrange:

COMMAND	EFFECT
Bring To Front	Move to topmost depth of current layer
Bring Forward	Add 1 to depth
Send Backward	Subtract 1 from depth
Send To Back	Move to lowest depth of current layer
Lock	Lock element
Unlock All	Unlocks all locked elements

9.16   Assigning Colors

One of the most obvious attributes of a primitive is its color. Flash allows you to edit color at any time.

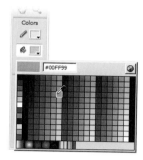

To select colors before drawing primitives, set the stroke (top) and fill (bottom) color swatches on the Tools panel.

You can select a color by doing any one of the following:

- Clicking the stroke or fill color swatches to reveal Flash's color picker. You can either select a color from the picker or select an existing color on the Stage.
- Clicking the color picker icon ⬤. This brings up the operating system color picker window.
- Using the Color Mixer panel.

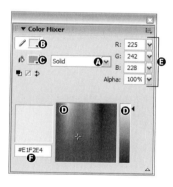

Ⓐ Choose Solid (other options are for Linear or Radial gradients).

Ⓑ Click to select the stroke color.

Ⓒ Click to select the fill color.

Ⓓ Click in the color swatch to select the color

Ⓔ Enter a color's RGB values.

Ⓕ Enter a color's hexadecimal value (in HTML format).

Editing Color

To change the color of an existing primitive:

1 Select a new stroke or fill color using any of the three methods just noted. You can also quickly select a color on the Stage by using the Eyedropper tool 🖊 to select a color from the Stage. The cursor will change to a 🖊 or 🖊 depending on whether you are about to select a stroke or fill color. Once you select either, the Ink Bottle or Paint Bucket tool will automatically become contextually selected, saving the trouble of having to select them manually in step 2.

2 For a stroke select the Ink Bottle tool 🖋 and click a stroke. All clicked strokes will change to reflect the new color. For a fill, click with the Paint Bucket tool 🖌.

Color Mixer panel
[Shift] [F9]

___

The methods for selecting and changing color apply only to primitives on the current Timeline. You cannot access nested primitives (i.e., primitives in symbols or groups) without first opening the symbol for editing. If the symbol or group is on the current Timeline, you can do this by double-clicking it.

___

The Color Swatches panel has an advantage over the color picker in that you can increase the size of the swatches by increasing the size of the panel.

9.17   Creating Linear Gradients

Color Mixer panel
(Shift) (F9)

———

Gradients contain
almost no web-safe col-
ors, although this
should not put you off
using them; if a user
cannot view much
more than the web-safe
palette, they probably
won't be able to view
Flash content either.

A linear gradient is a graduation of color along a line. A gradient can be used within a fill just like any other solid color.

These shapes all contain linear gradients.

In real life, few things have solid color, and gradients allow you to reflect this. For example, this image of a TV set consists of gradients to create the subtle shine and shadow effects that a real object would exhibit.

There are a number of default linear gradients at the bottom of the color picker, but you will usually want to create your own via the Color Mixer panel. Select Linear from the drop-down (A). The strip C is where the gradient is defined. This is done via up to eight color bricks that are placed along the strip to define the target colors. Flash will then create graduation between the target colors. A thumbnail of the gradient in progress is shown (D).

To change a target color, click it. The currently selected target color is shown with a filled triangle at the top 🔺 , and an unselected color is shown with a hollow triangle 🔺. The selected color will appear in the color brick (B). Change this by either clicking it and choosing a new color, or using the standard color variation controls on the Color Mixer.

To add a color to the gradient, click the strip (C) where you want to add (the cursor will change to 🔖). If you have already placed eight colors, the cursor will not change.

To delete a color from the gradient, click on the color brick and drag downward. Flash will not allow you to delete the last two colors because this is the minimum number needed to form a linear gradient.

To change the position of a color, drag it to the left or right.

9.18 Creating Radial Gradients

A radial gradient is a graduation of color outward from a point in all directions. This creates a circular (or radial) shaped fill pattern A gradient can be used within a fill just like any other solid color

These shapes all contain radial gradients.

In real life, many objects have rounded surfaces. These can be difficult to represent in two dimensions, but radial gradients allow you to give the impression of round surfaces via shading. The circle in the previous image (left) appears to be a sphere because of the radial gradient applied to it. The curvature of the TV screen is implied by the radial gradient applied to it.

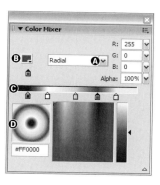

There are a number of default radial gradients at the bottom of the color picker and Color Swatches panel, but you will usually want to create your own or modify the existing ones via the Color Mixer panel. Select Radial from the drop-down (A). The strip (C) is where the gradient is defined. This is done via up to eight color bricks that are placed along the strip to define the target colors. Flash will then create graduation between the target colors. A thumbnail of the gradient in progress is shown (D).

To change a target color, select a color by clicking it. The currently selected target color is shown with a filled triangle at the top ▲ and an unselected color is shown with a hollow triangle △. The selected color will appear in the color brick (B). Change this by clicking it and choosing a new color, or using the standard color controls on the Color Mixer.

To add a color to the gradient, click the strip (C) where you want to add (the cursor will change to ⬚) and click. If you have already placed eight colors, the cursor will not change.

To delete a color from the gradient, drag it downward. Flash will not allow you to delete the last two colors because this is the minimum number needed.

To change the position of a color, drag it to the left or right.

Color Mixer panel
Shift F9

———

Gradients contain almost no web-safe colors, although this should not put you off using them; if a user cannot view much more than the web-safe palette, they probably won't be able to view Flash content either.

9.19   Adding Colors and Gradients to the Palette

Color Mixer panel
Shift F9

Color Swatches panel
⌘ F9

___

To export an ACT palette from Adobe PhotoShop for use in Flash, from Photoshop 7 select Save For Web. In the dialog that appears, click the little right-arrow to the top right of the Color table. In the drop-down menu that appears, select Save Color Table, making sure you set Save As Type to .act.

The color palette is saved as part of the FLA, so it is useful to customize it per FLA so it contains all nonstandard colors you have used. When creating separate SWFs that make up a finished site, it is also useful to save a common palette to use as the template palette for your separate FLAs.

Editing the Palette

To edit the palette, you need to use both the Color Mixer and Color Swatches panels. The general procedure is to create a new color or gradient and add it to the palette via the Color Mixer panel and to perform more complex palette edit options via the Color Swatches panel. The options to edit a palette are contained within the two panel menus.

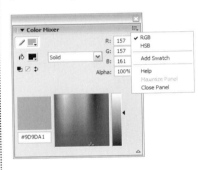
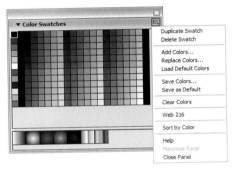

To add a color or gradient to the current palette, create your color or gradient using the Color Mixer panel, then select Add Swatch from the Color Mixer panel menu. To delete a color or gradient from the current palette, select the color's swatch on the Color Swatches panel and choose Delete Swatch from the Color Swatches panel menu.

Managing Palettes

To save a palette, use Save Colors from the Color Swatches panel menu. This will save a Flash CLR (Color Set File) 🖌.

To load a CLR file, you have two options, both from the Color Swatches panel menu. To add the colors contained in a CLR file, select Add Colors. To replace the current palette with the one in the CLR file, select Replace Colors.

To make the current palette the default (so that all new files will start with it), select Save As Default from the Color Swatches panel menu. You can still get back to the out-of-box Flash default if you do this, because the initial default is the Web 216 palette, which is also selectable from the Color Swatches panel menu.

To share palettes between other applications (such as PhotoShop and Fireworks), you should use the Adobe Color Table (ACT) format. You can select this format from the Save As Type drop-down when you save a palette, and Flash also allows you to load this format.

9.20　Changing Fill Color and Gradient

Once you have placed a fill on the Stage, you are likely to want to change the fill color or gradient. There are a number of ways to achieve this, depending where you get the replacement color or gradient from.

Changing Fills Using the Color Picker

The easiest way to change a fill color or gradient is to select a new one from the color picker:

1　Select the fill whose color or gradient you want to change.

2　Click the fill color brick from either the Tools panel or Color Mixer and select a new color or gradient from the color picker.

3　The fill will change to reflect the new color or gradient.

You can also overwrite a fill color or gradient simply by selecting the Paint Bucket tool 🪣 and refilling a fill with the currently selected color or gradient.

Editing Fills Using the Color Mixer

To edit the existing color of a fill, select the fill whose color you want to edit. In the Color Mixer, make changes to the color. All changes will be reflected in the fill as you edit.

To edit the existing gradient of a fill:

1　With the Eyedropper tool 🖊, click the fill. You will see the gradient appear in the Color Mixer.

2　Select the fill with the Selection tool ▸.

3　Make changes to the gradient in the Color Mixer. All changes will be reflected in the fill as you edit.

Copying a Fill Color Using the Eyedropper Tool

To change the color of a fill to that of something else already on the Stage:

1　Select the Eyedropper tool, and click the fill whose color you want to copy.

2　The currently selected tool will automatically change to the Paint Bucket tool 🪣. Click the fill(s) that you want to change to the color in step 1.

Note that this process does not work with gradient fills.

➡ 5.2　Color Mixer Panel

➡ 5.3　Color Swatches Panel

➡ 9.16　Assigning Colors

➡ 9.17　Creating Linear Gradients

➡ 9.18　Creating Radial Gradients

Eyedropper tool
[I]

Paint Bucket tool
[K]

Color Mixer panel
[Shift] [F9]

9.21 Changing Stroke Color and Thickness

Ink Bottle tool
⌊S⌋

Property inspector panel
⌊Ctrl⌋ ⌊F3⌋
⌊⌘⌋ ⌊F3⌋

If you only want to change stroke color, you can simply select a new stoke color from the Tools panel and then click each stroke you want to change using the Ink Bottle tool.

A stroke cannot be colored with a gradient. To do this, you first have to convert it to a fill.

A stroke's color and thickness remains editable after you have drawn it. Changes are made via the Ink Bottle tool and/or the Property inspector. To change a stroke color and thickness:

1 Select the stroke(s) you want to edit.

2 To vary color, alter the stroke color swatch in either the Tools panel or Property inspector.

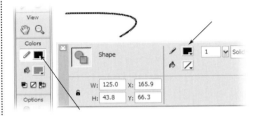

3 To vary the thickness, with the stroke still selected, alter the thickness setting in the Property inspector. You can either enter a new value in the text input area, or use the slider. The allowable thickness range is 0.1 to 10. If you want a zero (or "hairline") thickness stroke, select Hairline from the drop-down.

Note that you can also set a stroke style (such as dotted or stipple). These are not strictly an attribute of a stroke; Flash simply draws lots of single strokes to make up the pattern.

To apply the same settings to several strokes you can use the Ink Bottle tool . To use this tool, select the first stroke you want to edit, and follow steps 2 and 3 above. To apply the same changes to subsequent strokes, click them using the Ink Bottle tool.

9.22 Transforming Gradients

It is common to need to alter the orientation, size, and position of a gradient after it is applied, particularly if you are creating precise effects (such as distance fades, shadows, or highlights). This is done via the Fill Transform tool. This tool creates a bounding envelope for the gradient. Making changes to the envelope will in turn affect the gradient.

To select a gradient for editing, make sure that the fill you want to edit is currently unselected. Then select the Fill Transform tool 🎛 and click the fill. Depending on which type of gradient you have selected, you will see one of two bounding envelopes.

Linear Gradient

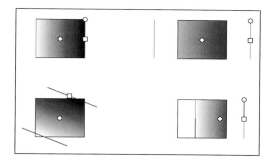

The envelope for the linear gradient looks as shown in the top-left image. There are three control handles:

The **square handle** (top right) allows you to lengthen or shorten the gradient along its line of graduation. When you are near this handle, the cursor will become ↔.

The **circular handle** (bottom left) allows you to rotate the direction (or line of graduation) of the gradient. When you are near this handle, the cursor will become ⟲.

The **center circular handle** (bottom right) allows you to change the position of the gradient center. When you are near this handle, the cursor will become ✛.

Radial Gradient

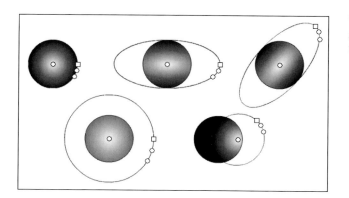

The envelope for the linear gradient looks as shown at top left.

➠ 3.17 Fill Transform Tool

➠ 3.19 Paint Bucket Tool

➠ 9.17 Creating Linear Gradients

Fill Transform tool

Although there seems to be a lot to remember about the Fill Transform tool, it is very intuitive in practice. You don't really have to remember what each handle does, because the changes in cursor appearance usually give the game away even for the most forgetful user.

Continues ●

9.22 Transforming Gradients *(continued)*

Sometimes, you may find that no envelope appears when you click a fill. There are two reasons this may happen: either the fill is already selected (unselect the fill by clicking a blank area of the Stage with the Selection tool and try again) or the envelope is too large to show up in the current view (set the Stage magnification to about 25 percent to see if this is the case). You will not see an envelope if you click a solid or pattern fill.

There are four control handles:

The **square handle** (top center) allows you to vary the eccentricity (or "ovalness") of the gradient. When you are near this handle, the cursor will become ↔.

The **lower circular handle** (top right) allows you to rotate the envelope. Because the envelope is a circle by default, this handle will have no effect unless you first add some eccentricity via the square handle. When you are near this handle, the cursor will become ↻.

The **middle circular handle** (bottom left) allows you to scale the envelope. When you are near this handle, the cursor will become ⊙.

The **center circular handle** (bottom right) allows you to change the position of the gradient center. When you are near this handle, the cursor will become ✛

9.23 Simulating Lighting with Gradients

Real life images consist of three-dimensional lighting and color graduation across surfaces caused by changes in surface angle and shade. Most of these effects can be approximated by editing gradients with the Fill Transform tool.

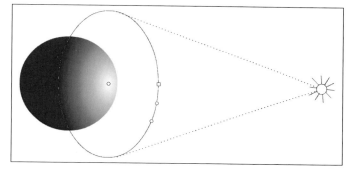

Lighting across a curved surface can be simulated by assuming the radial gradient envelope is the cross section of a cone-shaped light beam hitting the surface. To get a good 3D lighting effect, the envelope is usually an oval rather than a circle.

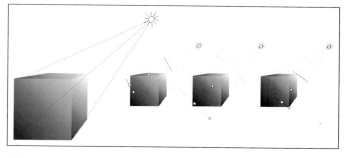

Lighting across straight edges tends to diminish the further you are from the light source. Although this diminishing is nonlinear, it is possible to get good results using linear gradients. The trick is to line each side's gradient direction so that it runs parallel with light rays coming from the light source, with the darkest side of the gradient being at the edge furthest away from the light source.

Other surfaces are simply a mixture of these two techniques. When used with other effects such as shadows and highlights, the use of gradients can create a very unvector like style, with no solid color areas whatsoever.

➡ 9.17 Creating Linear Gradients

➡ 9.18 Creating Radial Gradients

As seen by the examples, lighting effects are *much* easier to create if you use a temporary light source symbol and lines representing light rays. Consider placing such lighting construction lines on a guide layer so they are not exported in the final SWF animation

Don't forget that you can *animate* the gradients on the faux 3D shapes (using shape tweens) so that the angle made by the lighting changes over time. Atmospheric animated lighting effects, such as the effect of car headlights on a dimly lit house, or the changing direction of the setting sun, can be achieved using gradients as a base technique.

Faux 3D lighting can also be created with third-party applications such as Swift3D and then imported into Flash for simplification and optimization.

9.24 Using Pattern Fills

➡ 3.20 Eyedropper
Tool

➡ 13.2 Importing
Bitmaps

Break Apart
Ctrl B
⌘ B

Eyedropper tool
I

Import To Stage
Ctrl R
⌘ R

Many websites offer free tileable bitmaps for use as HTML backgrounds. These also make a good source of Flash pattern fill bitmaps. Better still, they tend to be already optimized for web use. Be careful not to pick some of the more obvious ones that have already passed into the realm of web design cliché, though.

As well as vector-based fills, you can also use a bitmap as your fill. Bitmap-based fills (or "pattern fills") allow you to break up or hide the clean lines of the underlying vectors with a bitmap pattern scanned in from a real life object.

The bitmap will be tiled when used as a pattern fill, so it is a good idea to choose a bitmap that allows seamless tiling. Bitmaps are also usually larger in file size than vectors, so it is recommended that you keep your bitmap small.

To make your bitmap into a pattern fill:

1 Import the bitmap onto the Stage using File > Import > Import To Stage.

2 Select the bitmap and break it apart with Modify > Break Apart.

3 Select the fill color on the Tools panel.

4 With the Eyedropper tool 🖊, click the bitmap. You will see the fill color change to the bitmap.

Now if you create any fill, the fill pattern will be formed by tiling the bitmap to the shape edges.

SOFTENING AND FILE SIZE

Softening a shape can dramatically increase the number of points, and therefore file size. This can also make animation using a softened shape *much* slower, particularly because softening also uses alpha transparency, which can take up to twice as long to redraw when compared to an opaque shape.

CHAPTER 10

Working with Timelines

AS IN MOST DIGITAL animation applications, the Timeline is fundamental to the way Flash works. A timeline is the way Flash represents the changes that are applied to the Stage over time to give *movement*.

Motion graphics is not just about animation. There are at least two other things that you can add to visual content: sound and video. This chapter will also look at embedding both these media types onto the timeline.

10.1　Understanding Animation

Many of the terms, workflows, and conventions used in Flash derive from traditional animation, which is why it is important to have at least an introduction to traditional animation before moving more deeply into Flash animation.

All film-based motion is an optical illusion, based on the fact that the eye and mind are fooled into thinking a series of consecutive still images are actually a single moving scene.

Frames, Keyframes, and Tweens in Traditional Animation

Each image is called a *frame*, named after the individual images once they are transferred to film. Two types of frame are used.

Before computers and fast video capture, onion skinning was done by flipping quickly between rough-sketched pages representing the proposed frames. The flicking between pages was rather like pulling and peeling the layers of an onion, hence the name.

A *keyframe* is used to define the major or key parts of the animation. Here, the key parts of the animation are the points where one leg is straight (because it defines how long the stride is during the walk). These are the first and last frames in the animation. To complete the animation, the frames in between (or *tweens*) are added once the keyframes are defined. These are shown grayed out in the image.

Onion Skinning and Bluing

Animators need a means to compare the individual images they are creating to make sure that they flow together with no discontinuities. This is done via *onion skinning*, where the animator flips through paper sheets showing the animation frames (rather like a flipbook animation).

10.1 Understanding Animation *(continued)*

Another way to compare frames is *bluing,* where the animation is first drawn using basic outlines on tracing paper (and usually using blue ink). Looking through the sheaf of tracing paper, you would see something like the following image.

Left: Onion skinning allows you to see errors that you would not see if you looked at each frame in isolation. Here you can see that the left foot goes slightly below ground level. Right: Although bluing creates a mess of lines to the untrained eye, to an animator it can show discontinuities in the final animation. You can see here that there is a big gap before the last frame in the animation, and it looks like an additional frame is needed to fill in the arrowed gap.

The keyframes are usually created by senior animators. The tweens are then created separately by a team of other animators. This ensures that although there are several different animators (who may even be in different countries), the animation style and pace is defined by the senior animator(s). In Flash, *you* are the senior animator defining the cool key points in the animation, and Flash automatically fills in the tweens for you.

Layering Animation

Traditional animation frames are first painted on transparent cells (from cellophane, the material used). The frame content is split into separate graphics to build up the image via layers of cells. Even a simple image such as this benefits from this process:

- If you did not use layers, you would have to completely redraw the scene for every frame. Because the only things that will actually move between frames are the man and his shadow, separating into layers means that you only need to draw the background once and can reuse the background cell in every frame. *Splitting animated content into layers allows you to separate static content from animated content.*

- The man's shadow is behind him. This is achieved by placing the shadow's cell behind the man's cell. *Splitting animated content into layers allows you to simulate depth.*

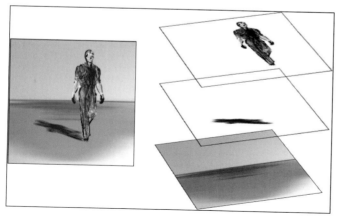

10.2 Animation Concepts in Flash

Flash allows you to add comments to a timeline, which is useful in documenting long or complex animations.

All the animation concepts noted in the preceding section are reproduced almost verbatim in the Flash Timeline.

Keep in mind the relationship between the Timeline and Stage: the Stage always shows the content displayed by the currently selected frame in the Timeline. A good analogy is to think of a film projector at a movie theater; the frames in the Timeline are the film reel in the projector room, and the Stage is what you see on the screen.

Frames, Keyframes, and Tweens in Flash

The Flash Timeline consists of frames that are very similar to animation frames:

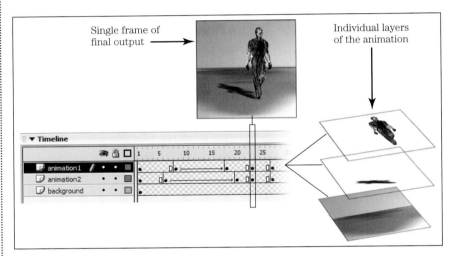

A simple timeline, like this one, is identical in concept to traditional animation frames (think of the Timeline strip as identical in function—if not in appearance—to a film strip). Unlike traditional frames, Flash frames can be stacked into layers like the breakout at the right. In this case, a Flash frame like the one at the top is more like an individual cell in a hand-drawn animation.

You can have three flavors of frame: keyframes, frames, or tweens:

A *Flash keyframe* is identical to an animator's keyframe. To edit the content of a keyframe, select it by clicking it and add content to the Stage. An empty keyframe (i.e., one that shows a blank stage) will appear with a central hollow circle (below, frame 1). A keyframe with content will appear with a filled circle (frame 5). As well as graphics, you can also attach an ActionScript script to a frame. A frame with a script attached will appear with an a (frame 10). Finally, you can add labels and comments to a keyframe. A label (frame 15) is used to name a keyframe (and is used by scripts to control the timeline). Finally, a comment (frame 25) is used to document your timeline and allows you to add information about what the timeline section or keyframe does.

10.2 Animation Concepts in Flash *(continued)*

A *frame* is a continuation of the timeline and will display the content of the last keyframe on the same layer. A frame following an empty keyframe is white to signify that the frame is blank. A frame following a filled keyframe is gray, signifying that the frame has content displayed in it.

A *tween frame* is exactly the same as a traditional animator's tween. Although tween frames are noted as a type of frame, in terms of editing (and what Flash does internally), they are really a *link* between two keyframes that defines the keyframes as the start and endpoints of a tween. Just like traditional tweens, a Flash tween requires a start keyframe and an end keyframe. Flash becomes the in-between animator, though, because it will digitally interpolate between the two endpoints to give you your tweens automatically. There are two types of tween in Flash: shape tweens (which allow you to change the shape and position of primitive lines and fills) and motion tweens (which will animate symbols, allowing you to change their size, orientation, transparency, and color over time).

Differences between Traditional Animation and Flash

Both onion skinning and bluing (described in the preceding section) are available in Flash. The only difference between traditional animation and Flash is in terminology; Flash calls bluing "onion skin outlines."

As mentioned, Flash timelines allow layers of frames, allowing you animation-cell like control of the Stage contents. Layers also come in several different flavors:

Guide layers allow you to add construction lines, comments, and other content that you do not want to appear in the final presentation. They also allow you to set up complex path-based animations by defining a line that you want a motion tween to follow.

Mask layers allow you to selectively hide other layer content.

Layer folders allow you to organize your layers much like your operating system allows you to separate content into folders or directories.

In general, layered Flash frames are more like the individual cells that make up a traditional animation frame than complete frames in their own right.

Another difference between Flash timelines and traditional animation is that Flash frames are hierarchical (i.e., you can have timelines within timelines). This has implications that will be discussed in later sections.

Finally, Flash timelines can *loop.* If you don't tell Flash to do anything when it gets to the end of a timeline, it will go back to the start and play again. The only way to prevent it from doing this is by adding a simple script or a behavior to tell it to stop.

➡ 11.10 Adding Movie Clip Control Using Behaviors

➡ 15.3 Adding a Frame Label or Comment

➡ 15.9 Controlling Timeline Flow with Scripts

Unlike traditional animation, Flash allows you to create *scripted* animation as well as Timeline-based animation. Although a totally scripted animation timeline looks different from a frame/tween animation (it typically only has one frame), the concept is still the same: it presents a series of still images quickly to give the illusion of animation. In scripted animation, however, the graphics are moved per frame via code at runtime, rather than placed manually by the designer at author time. The fundamentals of scripted animation are covered in Chapters 15-18. You can also add simple timeline controls via behaviors.

10.3   Navigating between Timelines

─────

As well as moving up
and down the timeline
hierarchy, your Time-
line itself can be split
into separate segments
called *scenes*. These are
deprecated in Flash and
are discussed briefly
in Section 10.21. Their
use is no longer recom-
mended, hence their
low prominence in
this book.

─────

You can see the entire
timeline hierarchy as
a tree diagram via the
Movie Explorer (Win-
dow > Other Panels >
Movie Explorer). A more
authoritative tree dia-
gram is shown by the
Debugger window dur-
ing test mode opera-
tions. The latter does
not display either
groups or graphic sym-
bols because neither
have a timeline.

─────

This chapter looks at a
non-code-oriented view
of Flash. Timeline hier-
archies are crucial to
the understanding of
scripted animation, and
this is discussed in Sec-
tions 16.3 and 16.4.

Timelines are hierarchical (you can have timelines within timelines) because symbols that you place on the current Timeline can also have timelines of their own. Thus, to fully edit a Flash presentation, you not only edit the current Timeline, but you also move up and down the hierarchy to edit other parts of the animation embedded in symbols.

Navigating the Hierarchy via the Stage (Edit In Place)

The Edit In Place feature allows you to edit a symbol in place, and it is also the best way to navigate forward in the Timeline hierarchy. When using it to edit timelines, bear in mind that only movie clips contain true timelines:

- Graphic symbols do not have timelines. They will only display frame 1 of their timeline, so it is pointless to edit their timelines to add more frames—although Flash will let you do this.

- A group does not have its own timeline. When you navigate inside a group, the Time-line shown is the Timeline of the previous (or "parent") Timeline.

- Navigating to a button timeline will give you a pseudo timeline that is composed not of frames but of *button states*.

To move back to the original Timeline, double-click an area of the Stage that is either grayed out or blank.

Using the Timeline Path (Path Explorer)

The Timeline path will show you where you are in the current hierarchy and is useful when you want to go backward by multiple levels. As you double-click symbols to go for-ward, the Timeline path will alter to reflect your current position. You can also use this path to navigate quickly backward.

Click the left-arrow to go back one level. All parts of the path (apart from the current Timeline) are underlined to signify a link. To go back directly to any level, click that level's name.

Note that the main timeline is always called Scene 1 by default; you can change this via the Scene panel (Window > Design Panels > Scene, then click "Scene 1" to enter a new name).

10.4 Making Frame Selections

Editing frames involves making a frame selection and then applying an edit. To select a single frame, simply click it. The frame will highlight in black. This can be used as a single frame selection (for copy or delete edit actions) or an insertion point (for frame paste or creation edit actions).

To create a multiple frame selection, click and hold the first frame in the selection and then drag toward the left or right. You can also make selections across layers by dragging up or down.

Left to right: no selection, single frame selection, multiple frame selection, multiple layer selection.

Timelines are arranged in frame sections for easy selection. To select a frame section, double-click anywhere on it. Each section starts with a keyframe and ends in a frame with a rectangle inside it. The timeline below it has three sections (the last section is only one frame long so only has enough space to show a keyframe).

When deleting, copying, and pasting sections of frames that include a tween, you should therefore make sure your frame selection includes both keyframes that make up the tween, otherwise the tween will not be correctly deleted or copied.

Here, you should select at least frames 15 to 25 if you want to edit the tween correctly. In all other respects, you can assume that tween frames will act like normal frames when editing.

➡ 10.2 Animation Concepts in Flash

➡ 10.9 Adding Shape Tweens

➡ 10.11 Adding Motion Tweens

Add frame(s)
F5

Delete selected frames
Shift F5

Be sure to include the start and end keyframe associated with a tween when copying and pasting tween sections. This is because a tween is defined by the keyframes at either end rather than the frames in between.

Copying and pasting a frame selection is done via a dedicated clipboard rather than the operating system, so you can't use the standard copy/paste shortcut keys (Control C, etc) when using frame selections.

COLOR AS A TWEENED PRIMITIVE

Shape tweens don't just change shape over time, they change *primitive attributes*. Color is also a primitive attribute, and you will find if you create a change in it between the two keyframes, this will also be reflected in the shape tween. As well as chroma, a primitive Flash color can also have alpha or be a gradient. Changes in any of these will be reflected in the final shape tween.

10.5   Adding and Deleting Frames and Keyframes

➭ 10.9 Adding
        Shape
        Tweens

➭ 10.11 Adding
        Motion
        Tweens

Add frame(s)

F5

Delete selected frames
Shift F5

Convert to keyframe
F6

Delete keyframe
Shift F6

Convert to blank keyframes
F7

There are two types of frame you need to consider when adding and deleting frames: normal frames ("frames") and keyframes. Tweens are associated with keyframes, and you do not normally need to consider them as a special case when editing.

Note that every timeline must have a keyframe at frame 1, so don't try to delete it!

Inserting a keyframe doesn't increase the length of the timeline by adding a new frame as well; rather it *converts* the current frame into a keyframe.

Deleting a keyframe is the same as deleting a frame.

Adding and Deleting Frames

To add new frames, select the place in the Timeline that you want to populate with new frames, then right-click/⌘-click the frame and choose Insert Frame, or choose Insert > Timeline > Frame.

If you select a frame or frames past the end of the current timeline, new frames will be added up to the end of your selection.

If you insert a frame or frames within the current timeline, the existing frames after your selection will be shifted forward.

To lengthen or shorten a frame section, with ⌘/Ctrl pressed, position the cursor over the rectangle ▯ at the end of the section. The cursor will become a double arrow ↔. Click and drag to the right to lengthen the section, or delete frames by dragging to the left.

To insert or delete frames from within a frame section, drag to highlight a frame section (the frames will highlight in black), then do either of the following:

■ Select Insert > Timeline > Frame or right-click/⌘-click the selection and choose Insert Frame to add the same number of frames as the selection.

■ Right-click/⌘-click the frame or frame selection and choose Remove Frames to delete the selected frames.

In both cases, the selection is preserved, so you can use it again to make further frame additions or deletions.

Adding and Deleting Keyframes

To add a keyframe, select one or more frames and choose Insert > Timeline > Keyframe or right-click/⌘-click the frame and choose Insert Keyframe. The keyframe will be added in the last frame of your selection if you select more than 1 frame.

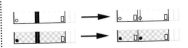

The keyframe will be filled with gray or will be plain white, depending on whether the keyframe insertion point represents a Stage with content or an empty Stage, respectively. You can see which one you will end up with by looking at the color of the frame you are adding the keyframe to.

To force insertion of a blank keyframe, choose right-click/⌘-click on the Timeline at the point you want to add the keyframe and select Insert Blank Keyframe from the context menu that appears.. To clear an existing keyframe(s), select it/them and choose Modify > Timeline > Clear Keyframe or right-click/⌘-click the frame and choose Clear Keyframe.

10.6 Moving and Copying Frames and Layers

A frame selection can be moved by drag-and-drop. The cursor will change 🔓 whenever you are over a draggable selection. If you drag a selection to a point beyond the last frame in a layer, an additional frame section will be created to fill the gap when you drop the selection. You can also drag a selection onto another layer.

Pasting Frames

Copy-paste operations are carried out via the frame contextual menu, *not* the normal operating system clipboard copy and paste options in the Edit menu. The frame copy-paste operations can be accessed by the right-clicking/⌘-clicking your frame or frame selection and selecting the appropriate option.

Apart from that, copy-paste operations work as you would expect:

- Copy a selection, select an insertion point, then paste to add a selection to a timeline.
- Copy a selection, select the same number of frames at an insertion point, then paste to overwrite frames with frames from elsewhere.

Editing Layers and Frames

To quickly select all frames in a layer, click the layer title.

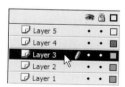 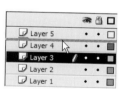 

To change the layer order, drag a layer and drop it to the new position. As you drag the timeline up or down the layer stack, a thick line will appear between layers to signify the position the layer will be inserted in if you drop it.

To add or delete a layer, use the Timeline icons at the bottom left of the Timeline panel.

To create a new layer containing a frame selection, create a new blank layer and copy-paste the required frames into it (there is no direct method for duplicating a layer in Flash).

To reverse the order of a sequence of frames, choose Modify > Timeline > Reverse Frames or right-click/⌘-click and choose Reverse Frames. Any animation associated with the frames will play backward.

To synchronize frames across timelines, choose Modify > Timeline > Synchronize Symbols. Sometimes, when you have embedded timelines where the number of frames in each does not match, you can get jerkiness in the animations due to one timeline finishing before another (particularly when one or more of the timelines loop). To fix this, select the affected frames and choose this option. This effect does not seem to occur often in later versions of Flash, and this option is hardly used.

➡ 10.20 Adding Layers

➡ 10.26 Working with Scenes

During frame-based copy-paste operations, Flash uses a different clipboard from normal operating system copy-paste, given that you usually need to copy-paste graphics to the Stage at the same time as copy-pasting frames to the timeline.

The frame clipboard is the only way to copy frames between separate timelines (i.e., between nested timelines or scenes).

If you want to repeat a selection of frames several times, you are usually better off turning the selection into a movie clip. To do this, make a selection, copy it into the Frame clipboard, then create an empty movie clip and paste the frame clipboard into it. You can then place copies of the movie clip onto a timeline. This method is much more bandwidth friendly than repeatedly pasting a frame selection.

10.7   Changing Frame View Attributes

➡ 4.4   Timeline
        Menus and
        Modes

➡ 10.8 Creating
        Frame-by-
        Frame
        Animation

Preview modes do not
show the location of
scripts or frame labels,
and you should not use
them if you are working
with scripts.

Many scripters use
compact timeline
views if they will not
need to edit tweens or
other frame-based ani-
mations.

Having a long timeline
on a single screen via a
compact view is partic-
ularly useful when you
are drag-dropping
frames. It is much eas-
ier to do this when you
can see the location
from where you want
to drag and drop to on
the same screen!

You can change the
layer height to 100 per-
cent, 200 percent, and
300 percent by chang-
ing the Layer Height
property in the Layer
Properties window
(Modify > Timeline >
Layer Properties).

Flash allows you to change the frame view to suit your current editing or authoring needs.

Animation Views

To get a better timeline view of your animations, select either Preview or Preview In Context from the Timeline panel menu (accessed by clicking the icon ⬚ at the top right). These show you the content of each keyframe in the timeline. They are particularly useful when

- You want to perform frame-by-frame animation.

- You are rearranging keyframes to change the course of your animation.

- Your animations are not working and you need to investigate the keyframe setup.

- You have not opened the FLA for a long time and quickly need reminding which keyframes contain which graphics—this is perhaps the most common reason given by honest Flash developers for using these modes!

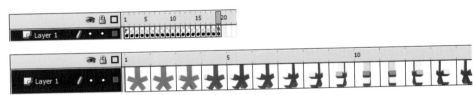

A standard timeline (top) and a timeline set to show Frame Previews (bottom), both of a frame-by-frame animation. Frame Previews gives a much better indication of what the animation actually is.

Compact Views

Where you have long timelines, it is sometimes preferable to fit as much of the Timeline as you can onto one screen without needing to scroll around the Timeline.

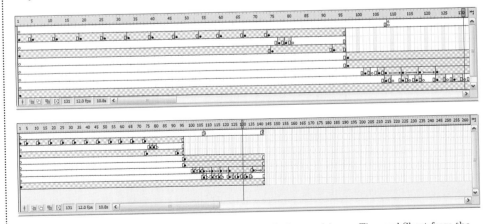

Top, the default frame size; bottom, the smallest possible frames (choose Tiny and Short from the Timeline menu). The latter allows significantly more frames and layers to be viewed without having to scroll around the timeline.

10.8   Creating Frame-by-Frame Animation

Flash uses mathematical interpolation to create tween frames automatically. In complex animations (especially organic animation involving flexing of body parts, or 3D transformations, such as a 3D logo rotation), this may not be possible using interpolation. In these cases, frame-by-frame animation is an alternative.

Importing and Simplifying Source Material

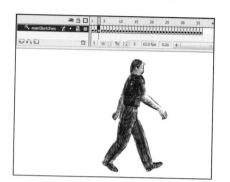

Frame-by-frame animation in Flash is very close to traditional hand-drawn animation; you have to create every frame yourself. Before you embark on this, it is recommended that you draw sketches on paper and plan your animation beforehand. Scan the images, and then import all your resulting bitmaps into Flash as a guide layer using File > Import.

You can optionally convert your bitmaps to vectors using Modify > Bitmap > Trace Bitmap and use them as the basis for your frame-by-frame animation. To do this, you should increase the contrast of your bitmaps via an application such as Photoshop (Image > Adjustments > Brightness/Contrast within Photoshop before you import them into Flash). Here, the figure on the right has been optimized for conversion to vectors (high contrast, large areas of solid color) using this technique.

Creating Vector Keys by Tracing

Frame-by-frame animation is a process of converting your source material into Flash vector graphics by using the standard Flash drawing tools to trace your source material.

Copious use of the Flash vector optimization tools (the first three commands in the Modify > Shape submenu) is recommended as you trace your graphics.

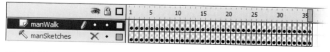

The finished timeline will appear as a sequence of keyframes.

Optimize
Ctrl Alt Shift C
⌘ Option Shift C

Insert keyframe
F6

Delete keyframe
Shift F6

Import to stage
Ctrl R
⌘ R

———

Before using frame-by-frame animation, consider simplifying so that you can use tweens. Frame-by-frame animation can be a laborious process!

———

There are third-party applications that can create frame-by-frame animation for you. For example, 3D animations can be created in Swift3D, and complex figure animation can be created in Poser 4 (Pro Edition).

———

Having a pen tablet is almost obligatory when creating Flash graphics by hand tracing.

10.9   Adding Shape Tweens

Break apart
Ctrl B
⌘ B

Insert keyframe
F6

Delete keyframe
Shift F6

———

Shape tweens are bandwidth heavy when compared to motion tweens.

———

Make the start and end shape the same, and then edit the end shape (rather than use a different shape) because it will make the primitive attributes that the tween acts on the same or similar, resulting in better animations.

———

Shape tweens work best when there is only one shape per tween. When you draw a circle or square in Flash, you actually create *two* shapes; the fill and the stroke. Consider deleting one or the other when using them with shape tweens

The shape tween allows you to create variations in a shape over time. Shape tweening is only possible with primitive shapes; you cannot shape tween using symbols.

Creating a Basic Shape Tween

1   Create a start keyframe and in it create your initial shape.

2   Create an end keyframe further along the same layer. Select this keyframe and make changes to the shape contained in it.

3   Select the start keyframe and choose Shape from the Property Inspector Tween dropdown (you can also later remove the tween using the same drop-down).

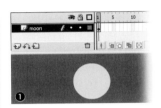  

Refining the Tween

There are a couple of options you can change to fine-tune the tween, both of which are found in the Property inspector (select the first keyframe in the tween to access them):

Ease can be set from −100 to 100. Positive values (easing out) create more frames at the end of the animation and create a transition that seems to get slower with time. Negative values (easing in) create more frames at the beginning of the animation and create a transition that appears to get quicker with time. A zero value creates a transition with equally spaced frames (no easing).

Blend can be set to either Distributive or Angular. Distributive attempts to maintain curves throughout the animation; Angular attempts to preserve straight lines (and therefore also corners).

 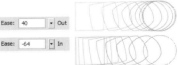

To create shape tweens using text, groups, or symbols, you have to break them apart (Modify > Break Apart) until they consist of primitive shapes only. A shape tween that is attempted with nonprimitives will not work and will appear with a dotted line through it.

10.10 Controlling Shape Tweens with Hints

Shape tweens work well when the start and end shapes have substantially the same point structure, and when there are no enclosed or separate areas in the start and end shape. When this doesn't happen, the tween consists of the start shape and end shape with a mess in the middle that seems related to neither. Shape hints are an aid in fixing this situation. View the animation with onion skin outlines set and see where Flash is going wrong.

Adding the Hints

Because the problem is where the endpoints of the rays are ending up, it is prudent to add a hint on each of them (obviously, in each situation, the problem will be different, and you will have to work out what it is). To add a hint:

1 Place the Timeline at the first keyframe and select Modify > Shape > Add Shape Hint. You will see a red circled *a* appear.

2 Mouse over the hint. When you are over it, the cursor will change to a ⬚₊. Click-drag the hint to the corner you want to add a hint to (it will try to snap to suitable positions).

3 Move to the second keyframe in the tween. You will see an identical hint. Move it to the position that you want the point to end up on the target shape. If the point is correctly associated, the hint will turn green. The hint at the first keyframe will now also turn yellow. If either are not correctly associated, then both will remain red.

4 Add further hints (they will be labeled *b, c,* and so on) in sequence around the shapes.

As you can see from the onion skin outlines of the finished tween, the transitions are now very smooth, with no confused middle section to the animation.

Once you have finished using hinting (or unchecked Show Hints from the context menu), there is no direct option to bring them back! To do this, reselect the first keyframe in the tween and add a new shape hint. This will bring all the hints back into view, and you can delete the just-added hint.

➥ 4.3 Timeline Options

➥ 10.5 Adding and Deleting Frames and Keyframes

➥ 10.9 Adding Shape Tweens

➥ 10.8 Creating Frame-by-Frame Animation

Add shape hint

Ctrl Shift H

⌘ Shift H

As a rule, hints work best when you add them in sequence around the perimeter of the shape. Starting from the top and working clockwise seems to have the best results (as in the example). Adding hints at corners or points of greatest curvature also helps.

Sometimes, adding too many hints makes Flash *more* confused. In these rare situations, you will see blank frames between the keyframes. It is best to remove all the keyframes, switch to onion skin outlines, and add the hints one by one, moving each when you add it until it give a smoother onion skin transition.

The option to add a shape hint will be grayed out if the keyframe you have selected does not have a shape in it. If this happens, check your frames!

10.11   Adding Motion Tweens

Text fields that are not set up to display embedded fonts will not animate correctly when used in motion tweening because they do not include the point information required by the process.

Unlike shape tweens, motion tweens can be implemented easily via ActionScript. For many animations, an Action-Script-based solution gives greater control than motion tweening, although it usually takes longer to set up.

A motion tween creates animation by varying a symbol's *properties*. These are most commonly the symbol's position, size, or angle. To create a motion tween:

1 Create a start keyframe, and in it place a symbol, group, or text field (which should be displaying embedded fonts).

2 Create an end keyframe further along the same layer.

3 Select either keyframe and move the symbol/group/text field by click-dragging it to a new position, and/or scale, rotate, or skew the symbol by using the Free Transform tool.

4 Select the start keyframe and make it a tween by selecting Motion from the Property Inspector Tween drop-down (you can also later remove the tween using the same drop-down).

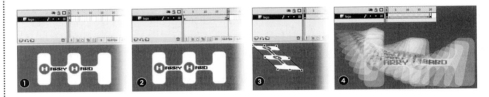

Refining the Tween

There are options you can change to fine-tune the tween, all of which are found in the Property inspector (select the first keyframe in the tween to access them).

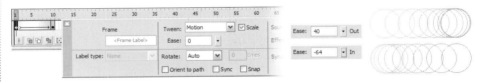

Scaling Exclude the effects of scaling in the tween by unchecking this.

Ease Can be set from –100 to 100. Positive values (easing out) create more frames at the end of the animation, causing the effect of deceleration. Negative values (easing in) create more frames at the beginning of the animation, causing acceleration. A zero value creates a transition with equally spaced frames (no easing).

Rotate You can cause rotation in the symbol through the course of the tween by selecting CW (clockwise) or CCW (counter-clockwise) in this drop-down. Auto will try to guess the rotation for you based on the shape start and end positions (it works well for rotations of less than 180 degrees or a half turn), and None ignores rotation.

A motion tween that is attempted with primitive shapes will not work and will appear with a dotted line through it.

10.12 Using Motion Tween Color and Alpha Effects

A motion tween does not simply control motion, it works by varying *properties*. A symbol has other properties that vary tint, alpha, and brightness, and they can be included within a motion tween to create color fades or even cinematic color transitions.

Create a motion tween using a symbol as described in the previous section, but don't move the symbol between the two keyframes.

Select one of the two keyframes in the tween, and then select the symbol on the Stage. In the Property inspector, a Color drop-down will appear. This is used to apply the effect. When you test the animation, you will see the symbol stay stationary, but it will change in terms of color and/or transparency.

Ⓐ None This is the default option. Select it if you want to remove a color effect.

Ⓑ Brightness A slider will appear, with –100 percent being maximum darkness (black) and 100 percent being maximum lightness (white).

Ⓒ Tint The R, G, and B values allow you to enter the Red, Green, and Blue components of the tint color, although it is usually easier to use the color brick to select a color (click it to see the available colors). The percent value goes from 0 to 100. 0 percent is no tint, and 100 percent applies a maximum tint.

Ⓓ Alpha A slider will appear, allowing you to select between maximum transparency (0 percent alpha) and maximum visibility (100 percent alpha).

Ⓔ Advanced Clicking the Settings button will bring up the Advanced Effect window. This allows you to apply all the above options at the same time. The Red, Green, and Blue values let you change the percentage value of each color component, thus applying tints. The R, G, and B values allow you to add absolute values to the three color components (i.e., color offsets). Adding the same value to each of the R, G, and B values is the same as varying brightness. The Alpha and A values allow you to change the percent value of the current alpha or add or subtract an absolute alpha offset.

Despite its name, the color drop-down allows you to apply color *and* alpha variations (given that in Flash, alpha is part of the color definition).

Color effects can be applied at the same time as motion effects. It is usually better to apply the motion effects first, then select the symbol and apply a color effect.

Brightness is useful when you want to create fade-to-white or fade-to-black effects.

Tint allows you to select a color you want to tint with and a percent value for the level of tinting.

If you don't understand a color's red, blue, and green components, you can view their effects manually via the Color Mixer panel. Play around with the sliders in this panel to get a feel for what particular values give before using color effects.

When you test in the authoring environment, the frames per second value at the bottom of the timeline will show the frame rate being *achieved* rather than the set frame rate. Although this is not indicative of the final frame rates, it does give some indication of the most processor intensive parts of your animation.

10.13   Testing Animations in the Authoring Environment

Play
Enter
Return

Rewind
Ctrl Alt R
⌘ Option R

Step forward one frame
.

Step back one frame
,

Toggle Enable Simple buttons
Ctrl Alt B
⌘ Option B

———

Scrubbing takes into account onion skinning, and the two used together are an efficient way of quick-testing your tween animations as you develop them.

———

When testing your animations, note that the playback speed is not indicative of the final speed of the animation when using the Flash Player.

———

The Enable Live Preview option allows live previewing of components - they will change to reflect their parameters as you change them in real time.

Flash allows you to test tween-based animations without having to compile and test your movie. This can be useful because it allows you to test your work without the stop-start of having to move to a different environment.

Scrubbing is the term given to moving the playhead manually through an animation. To do this, click-hold the playhead. It will turn into a black vertical line. Drag the mouse left and right along the timeline. The Stage will reflect the movements of the playhead, giving you animation at the same rate you drag the playhead and in the same direction.

The Controller toolbar (Window > Toolbars > Controller) consists of a set of video control style buttons, and you can use them to play, rewind, stop, etc, the current timeline. When a timeline is playing using the Controller, you can pause the animation by clicking and holding anywhere on the Stage. Release to resume.

Play All Scenes	
Enable Simple Frame Actions	
Enable Simple Buttons	Ctrl+Alt+B
✓ Enable Live Preview	
Mute Sounds	

Options on the Control menu allow you to control the way playback will work. Enable Simple Frame Actions makes Flash take account of simple Timeline actions such as `gotoAndPlay()`, `stop()`, and `play()`. Enable Simple Buttons does the same with button scripts, but note that it only works with Flash 5 style scripts of the form shown here:

```
on(release){
    stop();
}
```

Mute Sounds ignores sounds attached to the timeline.

10.14   Using Center Frame

When working with long timelines, it is useful to be able to be able to quickly scroll the timeline so that the selected frame(s) are seen in the center of the Timeline panel. The Center Frame icon allows you to achieve this with a single click.

1   Select one or more frames on a timeline that is longer than the current timeline view (far right, frame 100, next to the cursor in this image).

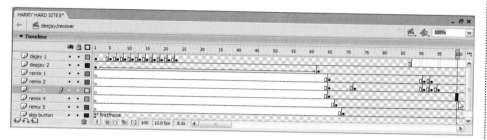

2   Click the Center Frame icon ⬍ . The timeline will scroll so that the selection will be in the center of view.

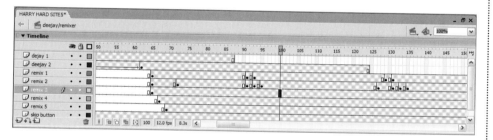

Center Frame will do nothing if the current Timeline does not extend beyond the end of the Timeline panel, which is why many Flash designers (especially coders, who generally create short timelines) don't know what this icon is supposed to do!

SCREENS VS. SCENES

In many cases, Screens are a better option to using Scenes, particularly if you are competent in ActionScript. Think of Screens as a more flexible replacement for Scenes.

10.15 Using Onion Skinning and Edit Multiple Frames

It might be useful to think of the edit multiple view as a multiframe exposure, with objects caught in the camera in several positions over time. To use this mode efficiently, you should know which parts of your multiexposure are what because it can become confusing very quickly if you have no idea which part of the Stage is the start frame and which is the end frame content!

It is a good idea to hide or lock any layers that you do not want to include in the view before entering either onion skinning or edit multiple mode.

Using onion skinning or edit multiple frames can make the Flash interface sluggish because it is being asked to redraw much more Stage content. Consider using Onion Skin Outlines or switching all layers to show outlines if this starts to affect your workflow.

Viewing an Animation in Onion Skin Mode

Onion skinning allows you to see all the graphics associated with a frame selection and gives an indication of the smoothness and direction of an animated sequence. To view an animation sequence in onion skin mode:

1 Select one of your animation frames.

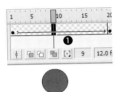 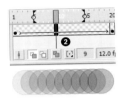

2 Click the Onion Skin icon 🔲. A pair of [ ] brackets will appear around the playhead, signifying the range of frames that are being used in the onion skinning. These can be repositioned by click-dragging to include more or less frames. The onion skinning will appear on the Stage.

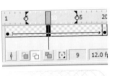

Some animations are clearer when seen in outlines. Clicking the Onion Skin Outlines icon 🔲 allows you change to such a view. The outlines will be rendered in the layer color.

Editing an Animation via Edit Multiple Frames

When developing animations, you will often want to move the contents of several frames together. Edit multiple allows you to do this. To move the contents of the start and end frame of a tween:

1 Click the Edit Multiple Frames icon 🔲. The [ ] brackets will appear.

2 Move the brackets to enclose the keyframes containing the content to be moved. You will see the content in all selected frames appear on the Stage.

3 Select the relevant Stage contents (in this case, both circles) and move, scale, or rotate them using the standard tools (Selection tool or Free Transform).

 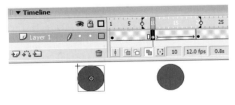

10.16   Adding Sound to a Timeline

Assuming you have already imported your sound files into Flash (using File > Import To Library), the next step is to attach the sound to a keyframe:

1   Create or select a keyframe where you want the sound to start. Select this frame and use the Properties inspector (Window > Properties) to select the sound you want to attach from the Sound drop-down menu. This menu will list all sound files you have imported.

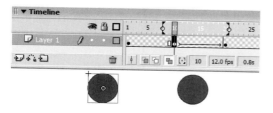

2   Once you have attached a sound, you will see a graphic of the sound waveform appear on the timeline.

Sound Options

The lower half of the Properties inspector displays available options (expand the inspector by clicking the down-arrow in the bottom right if you don't see the options).

The Effect drop-down allows you to select from sound effects to add to your sound. All the effects are based on a *volume envelope*. You can define your own sound envelope by clicking the Edit button or by choosing Custom from the Effect drop-down menu. This will open the Edit Envelope window (shown below).

The Sync drop-down allows you to select the type of sound and/or add a sound event:

Event makes the sound an "event" sound. Event sounds are stored as part of the final SWF and must be fully loaded before they can start to play. Once loaded, event sounds can be reused.

➡ 11.18 Creating Buttons with Audible Feedback

➡ 13.4   Importing Sound

A sound envelope can make a mono sound sound as if it is actually stereo. Using mono sounds and changing them to stereo at run-time can reduce your sound file sizes.

To fix some sound issues with the Flash player, it is usually a good idea to have no sound for the first 0.25 second of a FLA.

Continues ●

➡ 23.1 Understand-
ing Flash
Sound and
Video Classes

It can be difficult to
closely synchronize
event sounds to frames.
Although there are sev-
eral workarounds to
this, it is better to fix it
using ActionScript-based
sound so you can keep
close control.

ActionScript provides
better ways of loading
long sound files on
demand than the tech-
niques listed here, and
it is a better option for
creating applications
such as web-based
sound jukeboxes.

If you don't have any
sounds or need some
placeholder sounds until
the final assets are cre-
ated, some well-hidden
sound files are available
as part of Flash at Win-
dow > Other Panels >
Common Libraries >
Sounds.

Start causes the sound to restart. This is similar to Event, except that using Event again before the first sound completes creates another version of the playing sound, whereas Start *restarts* the sound. Use Start in preference to Event for longish sounds.

Stop stops all playing instances of the sound file in the Sound drop-down.

Stream makes the sound a streaming sound. A streaming sound can begin playing before it has totally loaded in, but it must be reloaded every time you want to play it. It is useful for long music files you only want to play once. Note that sometimes you have to use event sounds in preference, because event sounds provide better synchronization, and this may be needed when you are (for example) synchronizing spoken words to a speaking character animation.

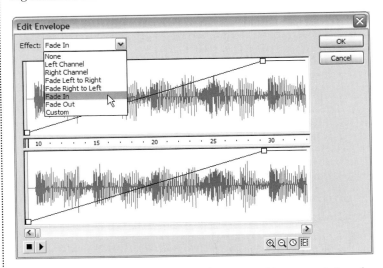

The envelope is a line graph superimposed over a graphic representation of the sound. It is edited by click-dragging the square control points to define a shape. To add a control point, click-drag anywhere on the envelope that doesn't already contain a control point, and a new one will be created, up to a maximum of 5. When editing the envelope, the icons at the bottom right of the window can be used to (from left to right) zoom in, zoom out, show time scale in seconds, and show time scale in frames.

10.17   Understanding Timeline Effects

Timeline effects allow you to quickly add preset helpers and effects. They work automatically, creating the symbols needed to create a particular effect, adding the symbols to the timeline, and renaming the timelines

Timeline effects are added by selecting an element on the Stage and then selecting an effect to apply via the Insert > Timeline Effects submenus. For all effects, a standard window will appear:

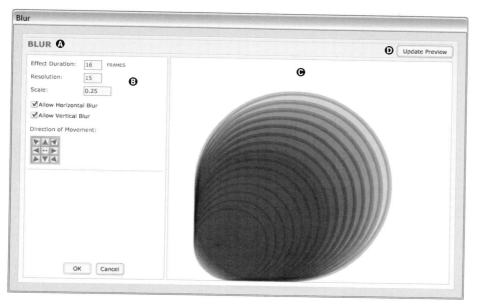

ⓐ The effect title.

ⓑ The effect parameters pane. Vary the settings here to customize the effect, and use the OK and Cancel button at the bottom to add or reject the effect.

ⓒ A live preview of the effect.

ⓓ Click to reflect any changes you have made in B to update the preview seen in C.

There are three types of effect you will see on the submenu:

Assistants Timeline assistants are helpers containing preset timeline authoring tasks.

Effects Timeline effects allow you to add animated special effects.

Transform/Transitions Allows you to add standard animated effects that would normally require tweens or masking.

⇒ 10.18 Adding and
Removing
Timeline
Effects

Timeline effects are very useful for beginners. Intermediate and advanced users may find the way the effects take control of the library and rename layers an undesirable feature.

Timeline effects can be recreated in more bandwidth-efficient form using ActionScript and/or advanced Timeline effects such as masking. The downside of this route is that the effect will take longer to create for all except the more accomplished Flash designer.

You will see the Timeline being redrawn when you exit an effect setup window. For some complex effects, this may take a few seconds.

10.18 Adding and Removing Timeline Effects

➡ 10.17 Understanding Timeline Effects

If you copy a symbol with a Timeline effect on it, and then remove the effect from the original, it will also be removed from the copy.

You can add only one effect per Stage element.

Timeline effects work by placing affected content into nested movie clips. Any scripts that are attached to (or refer to) this content may stop working because the timeline hierarchy seen by ActionScript changes. It is unwise to mix Timeline effects and your own code on the same timeline unless you understand the implications of this.

Behaviors and Timeline effects should work happily together (despite the above tip) because of the way they are written as long as you add the Timeline effect before the Behavior.

To add a Timeline effect, select the Stage element(s) that you want to apply the effect to, then select the desired feature from Insert > Timeline Effects.

You can then preview and customize the effect using the effect's window. The standard Macromedia effects have several common customization controls:

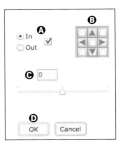

- **A** Standard checkboxes and radio buttons.
- **B** Direction boxes. Effects that are directional include a grid of arrowed buttons. Click the button corresponding to the required direction.
- **C** Text input boxes. Where the box has a slider under it, you can also vary the value by moving the slider puck.
- **D** OK and Cancel buttons at the bottom of the customization controls to accept or cancel the addition of the effect.

Once the Effect is added, note that it is added to the resulting symbol *and not the Timeline* (despite the name "Timeline Effect"). If you copy the symbol, the resulting symbol will also have the same effect.

To remove or edit a Timeline effect from a symbol, select the symbol and then select Modify > Timeline Effects > Remove Effect or Modify > Timeline Effects > Edit Effect.

10.19   Adding Video to a Timeline

Once a video clip is imported into the library, attach it to a timeline thus:

1 Select or create the keyframe you want the video to start on.

2 Select the video clip in the library as shown, then drag its image or icon onto the Stage.

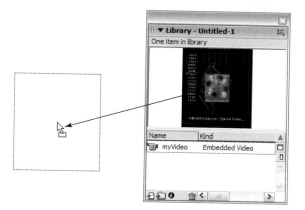

3 If the Timeline is not long enough to contain the video, you will see a dialog similar to the following. You should click Yes unless you don't mind not being able to see the entire length of the video.

4 Once attached to the Timeline, the video content can be seen just like any other animation except that you can't edit it.

5 At this point, you are strongly recommended to use the bandwidth profile to test any video content to check estimated download times (given that video assets have some of the largest file sizes).

Selecting between Preloaded and Streaming Video Content

The Timeline you attach the video clip to is important because it defines whether the clip will preload or stream in when seen on the Web:

■ If you add the video to a movie clip timeline, the video will not begin playing until all of its timeline is loaded—it will preload.

■ If you add the video to the main Timeline, the video will begin playing as soon as it starts to load into the browser—it will stream.

When streaming, try to ensure that the video starts loading some time *before* it starts playing, so that it doesn't keep pausing as it waits for the next block of video content to stream in. To do this, you need to place some bandwidth-light content on the Timeline immediately before the video (such as simple text titles).

Beware of preloading video clips; the preload pause on slow connections can be very long for even modest video clips!

If you want the imported video clip to play at the same rate as the original video clip, make sure you do *not* uncheck Synchronize To Macromedia Flash Document Frame Rate in the Video Import Wizard (if you don't see this option during the import process, don't worry, it is checked by default).

10.20   Adding Layers

Layers are needed to organize your Timeline. They are not exported to the final Flash SWF and do not add any file size to the finished presentation (so use as many as you want!). Layers make editing *much* easier. In general, you should aim to place all major parts of your Stage content on its own layer.

Layers are also useful for simulating depth; content in lower layers will appear on the Stage below higher layers. To add a layer to a timeline:

1 Select any part of the layer below the point you want the new layer to appear.

2 Either click the Insert Layer icon  or choose Insert > Timeline > Layer.

Layers are not just for graphics. You also attach ActionScript and labels to frames, and it is recommended that you place these two on their own graphics-free layer. The top layer is usually reserved as the one for ActionScript and labels.

By default, layer content is loaded "bottom-up," with the lowest layer being loaded first.

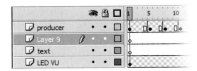

The new layer will be added with a title Layer *n*, where *n* is a number.

To Re-order Layers

You will often find that you need to re-order the new layer in the stack. To move a layer, simply drag the layer title area and drop it in the new position.

10.21   Setting Layer Properties and Layer Types

Once you have added a new layer or placed content on it, you will usually need to change its properties and type to reflect its content.

It is a good idea to rename your new layer to something consistent with its proposed use. To do this, double-click the layer title. The title will become a text entry box, allowing you to edit the default title.

To change a layer's properties, bring up the Layer Properties window. You can access this by:

- Double-clicking a layer color swatch.
- Right-clicking/⌘-clicking anywhere on a layer title bar and choosing Properties from the menu that appears.
- Choosing Modify **>** Timeline **>** Layer Properties.

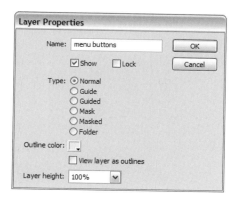

The window presents all changeable properties and attributes of a layer, most of which are self evident and selected via the radio buttons. You can also change the name by entering a new one in the Name text box or change the color by clicking the color swatch and selecting a new color from the color picker that appears. You can also change the layer height to 100% (default), 200%, or 300% via the drop-down menu, although this feature isn't used much because it doesn't change the frame heights.

The Layer Properties window options are context sensitive, and some of them will always be grayed out for certain layer types.

Sometimes a layer will be forced to become a type other than normal because of other layers around it. For example, a layer created under a Mask layer will default to masked. This can confuse and aggravate beginners who expect a Normal layer to appear. When this occurs, stay calm and remember the Layer Properties window.

10.22   Using Layer Folders

➡ 10.21 Setting Layer
     Properties
     and Layer
     Types

When changing an existing layer into a layer folder, you will lose any frames and content in the original layer. You will be given a warning dialog. It is far easier to get into the habit of always creating new layer folders.

——

Unlike file folders in an operating system, you do not have to reference the layer folder when defining a path to content inside it. In particular, when using ActionScript, dot notation does *not* refer to layer folders.

A timeline can quickly become cluttered by layers, especially if you follow the Best Practice Rule of "many layers = good." Layer folders allow you to fix this by organizing your layers into related groups; they work much like file-based folders in your operating system.

To create a new layer folder, select Insert > Timeline > Layer Folder or click the  icon. To convert an existing layer into a folder, bring up the Layer Properties window and click the Folder radio button.

A new layer folder has a folder icon to the left of its layer title and no frames of its own (you will see a gray frameless area where the frames should be). The layer title will be Layer n, where n is a number.

Moving layers into and out of a layer folder is a simple case of drag-and-drop. Click a layer and drag it within a layer folder to place it inside a layer folder (the folder icon will darken to signify the layer will end up in the folder).

To open or close a layer folder, click the little arrow to the left of the layer folder icon. Here, layer folder remix is closed, and deejay is open. As you can see, a closed layer hides its content.

All layers within a folder inherit the same Show/Hide, Lock/Unlock, and Show As Outlines settings of the folder. Hiding folder deejay automatically hides body and arms.

A timeline with folders will act exactly the same as the same timeline with no folders in the final Flash presentation. These two timelines will behave in exactly the same way.

10.23   Creating and Using Guide Layers

Guide layers are used to hold labels, construction lines, and other helper graphics that you don't want to be seen in the final Flash presentation. In most cases, content in guide layers is not exported as part of the final Flash presentation either.

To create a new guide layer, create a normal layer and then right-click/⌘-click it and choose Guide from the menu that appears.

A new guide layer has a special icon ⚒ to the left of its layer title but otherwise looks and acts like a normal layer in the authoring environment. The difference becomes apparent when you see the final compiled output: all content on the layer is ignored in the final animation.

Some assets *will* be exported in the Final Flash presentation irrespective of whether they appear in a guide layer. You should be careful when using these in conjunction with guide layers because they may increase the file size of the final Flash presentation for no benefit:

- Any code you attach to a guide layer's keyframes *will* be exported and will execute at runtime. To prevent code from running at runtime without having to delete it, consider commenting it out instead.

- Any other assets that are set to be exported for ActionScript will always be exported irrespective of guide layers. This includes components, which are set to this by default and may stop working if you attempt to change this.

→ 10.21 Setting Layer Properties and Layer Types

→ 10.24 Creating Motion Tweening with Guide Paths

———

Temporarily making a layer a guide is a good way of preventing it from being seen in the final SWF without actually deleting the layer and its contents. This is useful when updating a site; you can copy a layer, make the original a guide, and edit the copy, giving you a fall-back position if you get it wrong (or the client doesn't like the changes!).

———

If you're wondering, the guide layer symbol is a hammer (i.e., a construction tool) to represent the fact that it contains construction lines.

———

You should not confuse a guide layer with a motion guide layer; although they are similar, they are set up to do different things.

TIMELINE EFFECTS AND ACTIONSCRIPT

Timeline Effects are designed to allow you to add effects quickly and easily, but they are usually not the most efficient implementation. Designing your effects using custom ActionScript is the preferred option for the script-experienced Flash user. Not only is this more bandwidth friendly, you can make your name by creating your own effects rather than following the crowd!

10.24 Creating Motion Tweening with Motion Paths

———

Sometimes, you may want to have several layers guided by the same motion guide layer. To make other layers guided, drag them onto either the motion guide layer or a guided layer.

———

You will have to read the previous tip slowly a few times.

———

You should not confuse a guide layer with a motion guide layer—they do different things. The confusion is compounded because a motion guide layer with no guided layers associated with it automatically becomes a guide layer.

———

Onion skinning and edit multiple are very useful when using path-based animation.

Tweening works by setting up a start and end position and moving a symbol in a straight line between the two. When you want motion along any other type of path (such as a curve), you have to set up a motion path for the animation to follow. The motion path has to be inside a special type of layer called a motion guide for this to work.

Setting Up the Layers for Motion Path Animation

To create a motion guide, select the layer containing the content you want to animate, then either click the 🐾 icon or select Insert > Timeline > Motion Guide. This will insert a motion guide layer above the selected layer and make the selected layer a guided layer.

Creating a Motion Path Tween

1   Select the guide path and in it draw an unbroken line to represent the motion path. You can draw or edit it using any of the drawing tools capable of working with lines.

2   In the guided layer, place your symbol (in this case a rocket) in a keyframe so that its registration point touches the path at your start point.

3   Add additional frames to the motion guide layer so that it extends to all frames of the tween. Create a new keyframe at the end frame of the animation and in it move the rocket to the end position on the path, with the registration point touching the line.

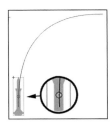 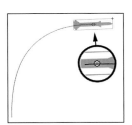 

Once completed, the timeline will look like this. When you view the resulting animation, the symbol will now follow the path rather than go in a straight line from the start to end point.

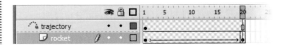

The symbol can align itself to the motion path (left) or rotate between the endpoints during the animation (right). Select the first keyframe and check or uncheck Orient To Path.

190

10.25 Creating and Using Masks and Masked Layers

A mask is any shape that defines areas that are hidden. Flash implements masks via a special type of layer called a mask layer, and these act on associated layers called masked layers. To set up a mask-masked layer pair:

1 Start with two normal layers, one directly above the other. Add the mask shape in the top one, and the content to be masked in the lower one.

2 Right-click/⌘-click the upper layer and select Mask from the menu that appears.

 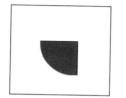

When masking in Flash, content will be revealed in the area of overlap between a mask and the masked content and hidden in areas of no overlap. The effects of masking are shown in the Authoring environment if you lock both the mask and masked layers.

Using Masks in Practice

Consider this television graphic. It consists of a television showing static. The screen is not square, but slightly rounded for an authentic TV, you need to create a nonrectangular mask.

The content in each of the three layers is shown below. The mask makes the static clip appear screen shaped by hiding all parts of it outside the mask area. When placed over the lowest layer (*filled tv*), the masked static covers the TV screen area, giving the illusion that it *is* the screen.

 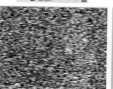  

➥ 22.8 Using Dynamic Masking

Masking is useful in creating all sorts of advanced effects once you start using complex Timeline setups—many of the more complicated Timeline effects use masking.

Masks can be any color. It is usually a good idea to make them a contrasting color from the rest of the content so they stand out.

Making the mask layer show outlines only is a good way of seeing what the nonmasked content looks like.

Masking can also be created using Action-Script, which allows for more interactive and complex effects.

More complex effects can be created. For example, if you tween animated the mask so it changes from a small dot to the full screen, you can simulate the TV being switched on.

10.26   Working with Scenes

Scenes are available
only for the main time-
line. You cannot use
them in a movie clip
timeline.

Deleting a scene
deletes all frames
within it. Do so with
caution!

Scenes allow you to split the main timeline into sections, rather like different scenes in a film. Each scene will typically be a distinct part of the overall animation. Physically, each new scene will appear as a blank timeline, much like the one you see when you open a new FLA.

You should note that Scenes are deprecated in Flash, for reasons stated below

Creating and Editing Scenes

Scenes are created and renamed via the Scene panel. Use the three icons along the bottom right of the panel to duplicate, add, or delete a scene respectively. To rename a scene, double-click a scene title and enter a new name in the text entry box that appears. When you start a new FLA, you will have one scene called Scene 1.

When the final Flash presentation is created, the scenes will be converted to one long Timeline in the order they are listed in the Scene panel. To change this order, simply click-drag the scenes until you see a horizontal line appear between the scenes you want to insert, and release.

Navigating between Scenes

Scenes are not used that often by most designers in modern Flash design. They were an early feature of Flash and are now somewhat outmoded.

To move between scenes, click the clapperboard icon (top-right of the Timeline) and select a scene from the drop-down that appears.

10.27 Setting Screen Properties and Parameters

Screens are a new way of creating Flash content where a Timeline is not necessary. They are useful for simple page-based sites, business or kiosk presentations, and forms in which you want pop-ups and menus. Screens are available in Flash MX Professional only.

There are two kinds of screens: a slide (designed for sequential content such as slide shows or business presentations) and a form (designed for nonsequential presentations that typically have greater interaction, such as web application front ends).

Starting and Configuring a Screen Presentation

To create screen-based content, select File > New and choose Flash Slide Presentation or Flash Form Presentation from the General tab, or select Flash Slide/Form Presentation from the Create New Section of the Start Page.

The screen authoring environment is different from the standard Timeline-based layout and is shown below:

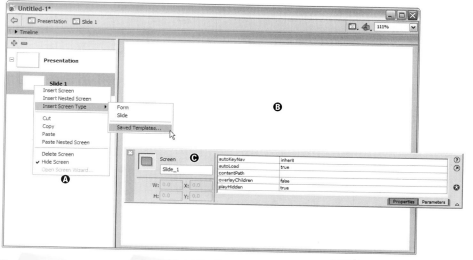

A **Screen Outline pane** Contains thumbnails of the screens in the current presentation. The hierarchy is illustrated via the tree structure. This panel has a contextual menu, accessed by right-clicking/⌘-clicking a screen thumbnail.

B **Stage** Works much like the standard Flash Stage, except that content in higher-level screens will be shown grayed out (see following discussion on screen hierarchy). You can add symbols and primitives to the Stage as per normal Flash Stages.

C **Property inspector Properties tab** Shows properties and parameters for the currently selected screen in the Screen Outline. Slides and forms have different parameters.

Note that the Timeline panel is shown but starts closed. You can open it if you need to add layers or frames, but it is possible to design screens without it.

➡ 10.29 Building Form Applications

Delete selected screen
⟦Del⟧

Selecting a slide- or form-based presentation sets the default screen type to your choice (advanced users may want to mix the two types by forcing the nondefault screen type as required).

Slides are very similar to the way other slide-based presentation applications (such as Microsoft PowerPoint) work, in that they are slide- or page-based, with simple navigation links between each slide.

When building screens, you can hide the content on screens you don't want to see while authoring by right-clicking/⌘-clicking the screens you want to hide and selecting Hide Screen from the contextual menu. The screen content will then not show through the hierarchy. You can view the content of a hidden screen by selecting it in the Screen Outline pane.

10.27 Setting Screen Properties and Parameters *(continued)*

New Document
Ctrl N

___

For users with previous experience of Flash, think of screens as a replacement for scenes. A big clue that screens are closely related to scenes is that you can't use the two together in the same presentation (the Scene panel is grayed out and inactive when you are creating screen-based content).

___

Like most page-based content (such as the book you are holding right now), it's a good idea to plan out what you want in each screen before you start. This makes the whole process much easier (as any publisher will tell you).

To set basic screen parameters (screen size, background color, and frame rate), you should use the same window as with standard Flash content, i.e., Modify > Document. The settings will be applied to *all* screens in the current presentation.

The Screen Outline Pane and Hierarchy

The Screen Outline pane shows all screens in the current hierarchy in tree form. You can change the name of a screen by clicking it within this pane. The name is reproduced with underscores instead of spaces in the Property inspector, and the Property inspector name is the string you should use when controlling screens via ActionScript or behaviors.

For a slide, all top-level (or *ancestor* screens) will show through beneath child screens. The top-level screen (called Presentation by default) is called the master screen, and all screens will show its content (making it the background for all screens).

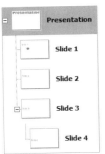

In the tree shown here, Slides 1, 2, and 3 will have the content in slide Presentation showing in them. Slide 4 will have the content in Slide 3 and Presentation showing in it. This allows you to use particular slides as backgrounds to others.

For a form application, *all* forms are visible all the time by default; you lose the ease of building applications with slides, but you can control the visibility of forms yourself (using either behaviors or your own custom ActionScript) to create a layered presentation, where content is selectively shown or hidden dynamically, rather than relying on the fixed hierarchical functionality of slides.

Editing the Screen Hierarchy

To change the position of a screen within the hierarchy, click-drag it to the new position.

To add a new or nested screen below the currently selected, select the Insert Screen or Insert Nested Screen options from the Outline Pane's context menu. You can use Insert > Screen and Insert > Nested Screen, or press the + at the top of the Screen Outline pane.

To cut, copy, and paste screens, use the Cut, Copy and Paste options in the Screen Outline pane's context menu. You can also paste a full branch of a tree by selecting Paste Nested Screen. This will copy the copied screen and all screens in the branches below it. You can also delete the currently selected screen by clicking the—at the top of the Outline pane, although you cannot delete the first (Master) screen in the hierarchy.

194

10.28 Building Slide Presentations

The content in this section is available for use in Flash Professional only.

As well as websites, the Internet is increasingly used for simple sequential (page-based) presentations, where (for example) a company may choose to use a voice conference coupled with a web-based slideshow instead of going to the expense of getting everyone in a single room and using a traditional slideshow presentation.

Slides make use of two of Flash's features: low file size (for web delivery) and behaviors (for ease of production by noncoders). Navigation can be done via the keyboard or Flash buttons.

Sequential Navigation Using the Keyboard

In simple slide presentations, all you want to do is move sequentially between slides. To do this, make sure that the autoKeyNav parameter for each screen is either set to Inherit (and no screen in the hierarchy above has it set to False) or True.

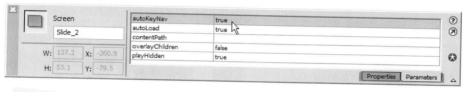

The slideshow host can then move sequentially back and forward through the screens by hitting the keyboard ← and → keys.

Navigation Using Flash Buttons

If you want to add simple navigation using traditional web conventions (i.e., rather than the keyboard, use clickable screen buttons, which is what a web-based audience would expect), you need to navigate using Flash buttons. Flash buttons also allow you to navigate to slides out of sequence.

To add a button that takes the user to a screen, add a button in your chosen screen. Select it and, in the Behaviors panel, click the + icon and select a behavior from the Screen submenu. This will typically be Go To Slide if you want to go to a slide out of order, or Go To Next/Previous Slide if you want to do it following the hierarchy.

➡ 5.8   Behaviors Panel

➡ 10.27 Setting Screen Properties and Parameters

➡ 10.29 Building Form Applications

➡ 10.30 Controlling Screens and Adding Transitions

➡ 11.2   Understanding Behaviors

➡ 11.15 Creating Buttons

➡ 11.16 Adding Basic Button Navigation Using Behaviors

Behaviors panel
Shift F3

If you don't alter the autoKeyNav property of any slide in your presentation, they will all respond to the keyboard ← and → keys, given that it is the default functionality. You typically change this property only if you wanted to add Flash buttons instead.

10.29 Building Form Applications

➡ 5.8 Behaviors Panel

➡ 10.27 Setting Screen Properties and Parameters

➡ 10.28 Building Slide Presentations

As seen by this example, not only is it a good idea to plan your form content before starting (as with slides), it is also important to get your form *rules* (i.e., on what conditions particular forms become visible or invisible) defined before implementation.

Forms are used where you don't want a sequential presentation. Forms are not in any real sequence as slides are, and all forms are visible by default. The downside of this is that you have to create more control yourself (via Behaviors or, more often, ActionScript), but the upside is that you are not constrained by hierarchy in what can or cannot be shown; it's totally up to you.

Forms are best illustrated via a simple example. Suppose you want a simple menu front end as shown here. When you click each of the two buttons, an associated set of content will be overlaid in the main screen area:

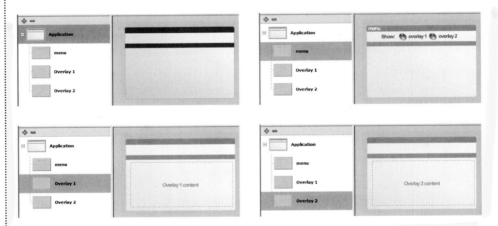

Four forms make up this application: the background form Application, the menu form Menu containing your buttons, and the two content forms Overlay 1 and Overlay 2.

The following rules will drive this application:

A When the application first loads, hide both Overlay 1 and Overlay 2.

B When the Show Overlay 1 button is clicked, show Overlay 1 and hide Overlay 2.

C When the Show Overlay 2 button is clicked, show Overlay 2 and hide Overlay 1.

10.29　Building Form Applications *(continued)*

To add a behavior to a form (i.e., to implement rule A):

1 Select the menu form by selecting it in the Screen Outline pane (making sure nothing on the Stage is also selected). Using the Behaviors panel, click the + and select Screen > Hide Screen.

2 The Select Screen dialog will appear. Either by directly typing into this window's text entry box (recommended), or by selecting from the tree diagram in this dialog's bottom pane, select `this._parent.Overlay_1` as the target screen.

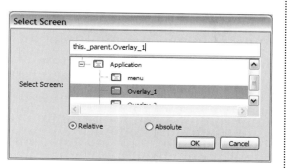

3 You will now see a behavior appear in the Behaviors panel. Click in the Event column for this behavior and select Load. This ensures Overlay 1 is hidden when the application starts via a behavior attached to the form menu.

4 With the form menu still selected, repeat steps 1–3 for Overlay 2, targeting `this._parent.Overlay_2`. When you are done, you should see two behaviors attached to form menu.

➡ 10.30 Controlling Screens and Adding Transitions

➡ 11.2 Understanding Behaviors

➡ 11.10 Adding Movie Clip Control Using Behaviors

Forms are most useful when you use Action-Script rather than behaviors because of the added flexibility of ActionScript in defining custom code. Usually, you won't want to show or hide forms on simple interactions such as button clicks, but you will want to show or hide them on more complex logic states, such as "the text just entered is incorrect, reveal the form displaying the error pop-up window until the user clicks the OK button on the error window."

Continues ●

Behaviors panel
Shift F3

___

When building forms,
you can hide the con-
tent on forms you don't
want to see while
authoring by right-click-
ing/⌘-clicking any you
want to hide and select-
ing Hide Screen from
the context menu that
appears. A hidden form
will only show up when
it is selected in the Outline pane.

To add a behavior to a symbol on a form (i.e., to implement rules B and C):

1 Select the first (left) button and add a Screen **>** Show Screen Behavior, targeting
   `this._parent.Overlay_1`.

2 With the first button still selected, add a Screen **>** Hide Screen Behavior to it, targeting
   `this._parent.Overlay_1`. You have now added behaviors to the first button to show
   Overlay 1 and hide Overlay 2 when it is click-released.

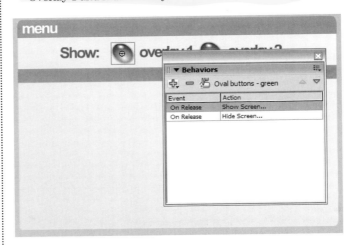

3 Do the same for the right button, this time showing Overlay 2 and hiding Overlay 1.

10.30 Controlling Screens and Adding Transitions

The control of screens is different for slides and forms. Forms are typically controlled by ActionScript only, although you can get some basic control using behaviors. Slides are controlled in a much simpler way; you simply move up or down the hierarchy, usually in sequence, with the occasional nonsequential button jump.

➡ 5.8 Behaviors Panel

➡ 10.27 Setting Screen Properties and Parameters

➡ 10.28 Building Slide Presentations

➡ 10.29 Building Form Applications

➡ 11.2 Understanding Behaviors

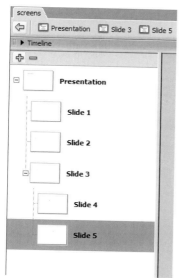
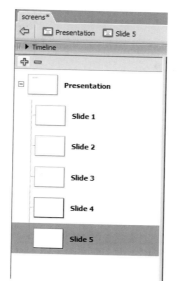

One thing to bear in mind when creating sequential slides is the way Flash will walk through the hierarchy. In the tree at the left, you will see the following if you press the → keyboard key to move forward through the hierarchy:

1 Slide 1 with Presentation as a background

2 Slide 2 with Presentation as a background

3 Slide 4 with Presentation and Slide 3 as a background

4 Slide 5 with Presentation and Slide 3 as a background

You can see how the slide order will work by looking at the path at the top of the Screen Outline pane. For Slide 5 it is 📄 Presentation 📄 Slide 3 📄 Slide 5, signifying that Slide 5 will appear in front, followed by Slide 3 and Presentation in the background.

If you want to see Slides 1 to 5 in sequence, you need a flat hierarchy, as shown at the right.

Continues ●

10.30 Controlling Screens and Adding Transitions *(continued)*

Behaviors panel
⟨Shift⟩ ⟨F3⟩

———

When you add transitions, you may want other behaviors not to work until the transition has completed. The OnTransitions events allow you to do this.

Adding Transitions

You can select from some predefined transitions for your screens (both slides and forms). The most obvious event to attach a transition to is when a new screen appears; the reveal event. To add a transition on a new screen appearing:

1 Select the screen that will appear, making sure nothing is selected on the Stage.

2 From the Behaviors panel, click the + and select Screen > Transition. This will bring up the Transitions window.

3 The Transitions window has a list of available effects at the top-left corner, a thumbnail of the effect at the bottom-left corner (the bold *A*), and controls to customize the transition effect to the right. Once you have selected your effect and customized it, click OK.

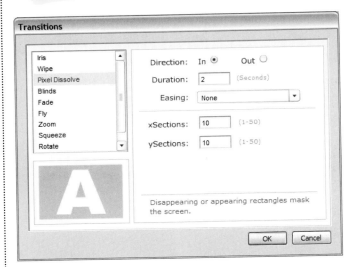

4 In the Behaviors panel, select the event you want the transition to trigger on by clicking in the Event column and selecting an event from the drop-down. The default event is usually reveal, so you won't normally have to change anything.

Other common events to trigger transitions on are when you hide or reveal a form (hide and reveal in the drop-down).

CHAPTER **11**

FLASH WORKSPACE

AUTHORING TASKS

SCRIPTING TASKS

TESTING AND PUBLISHING TASKS

WHAT'S NEW

Symbols and Behaviors

SYMBOLS ARE THE MAIN assets you will use in Flash. They include graphics (a static graphic), buttons (a clickable graphic that provides the easiest way to add interactivity and navigation to a Flash presentation), and movie clips (an animated sequence).

The big secret of Flash symbols is that they can be *nested*—you can have a symbol that itself contains other symbols. Nesting gives you a much richer palette of options it might seem on the surface.

ActionScript must be added to symbols to create interactivity, but this is made easier by the availability of drag-and-drop behaviors.

- 11.1 **Understanding symbols**
- 11.2 **Understanding behaviors**
- 11.3 **Creating graphics**
- 11.4 **Using the Color Instance effects**
- 11.5 **Using graphics in tween animations**
- 11.6 **Creating movie clip animations**
- 11.7 **Using movie clips in tween animations**
- 11.8 **Creating nested movie clips**
- 11.9 **Navigating between nested movie clips**
- 11.10 **Adding movie clip control using behaviors**

- 11.11 **Testing movie clips**
- 11.12 **Creating movie clips from bitmaps**
- 11.13 **Creating movie clips from videos**
- 11.14 **Adding video control using behaviors**
- 11.15 **Creating buttons**
- 11.16 **Adding basic button navigation using behaviors**
- 11.17 **Creating text buttons**
- 11.18 **Creating buttons with audible feedback**
- 11.19 **Creating invisible buttons**
- 11.20 **Creating animated buttons**

11.1 Understanding Symbols

When you edit a symbol on the Stage by double-clicking it, you are not editing the instance; you are following the reference back to the Library symbol and editing that. This means that all instances of the current symbol will change, even though it may appear that you are not editing the Library symbol.

Even if you don't know about properties, you have probably already used them. Whenever you move a symbol on Stage, you are really only changing the properties that define position. Physically, a property is simply a number (such as 56.7) or a text string (such as "ben"), and Flash is really changing these (and not the symbol itself) when you move or scale a symbol.

Primitive strokes and fills are the basic elements that can be created in Flash, but to make them useful, you usually need to combine primitives to form *symbols*. Symbols are the next step up from primitive fills and strokes:

- Primitives have features that change or set appearance.

- Symbols have added features that allow them to *do* things as well.

For example, a button is a particular symbol that allows you to combine a set of primitive shapes so that when you click it, it can change appearance to signify button up and down states. A primitive that is not part of a button can be made to *look* like a button, but you can click it all day and nothing much will happen!

Flash is an object-oriented programming (OOP) system, and even if you don't intend to go anywhere near ActionScript, it is wise to use the correct OOP-based terminology when discussing symbols.

Classes, Instances, and Properties

All three types of symbol are *classes*: `Graphic` class, `Button` class, and `Movie Clip` class. The class defines the blueprint that each of the three symbols conform to and is the thing that makes buttons different from movie clips and both of them different from graphics.

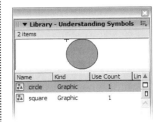 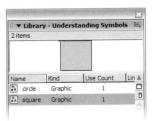

When you create symbols in the Library, you take the basic graphic, button, or movie clip and fill it with a timeline and/or graphics. The graphic symbols *square* and *circle* are both still graphics, but they look different from each other. The graphical appearance of the symbols in the Library has been defined, but they still cannot do anything because many of the underlying class structures (especially properties) are not yet defined.

Symbols in the Library have no real status until you place them on the Stage, when they become *instances* (also referred to as *objects,* which means the same thing). An instance has all the features of the Library version, plus a set of unique data associated with it called *properties*. Properties include things such as position, size, transparency, and orientation.

11.1 Understanding Symbols (continued)

Using properties, two instances of the same symbol can be made to look (and act) differently. These two *circle* instances are created via the same symbol but look different because they have been given different property values. The circle on the right was originally the same as the one of the left, but has been turned into an oval by increasing the property associated with height, and rotated clockwise slightly by increasing the property related to angle. It has also undergone a color change, again via properties.

The relationship between classes, Library symbols, and instances can seem a little tenuous, and an analogy may help make the distinctions easier.

If you assume there's a class called `Human`, then you could create two Library graphic symbols, `male` and `female`. Both are symbols of the class `Human`, but they look different. `male` and `female` may be different from each other, but are still not individuals and are not *real* in the sense that you cannot interact with a real-life version of either; they are really just templates for the two types of `Human` you will meet. To create unique instances (or to follow the analogy, *individual people* who actually exist), you would drag `male` and `female` to the Stage and give them properties.

For example, you could have an instance (or individual person) of `female` called `Jende-Haan`, which would have a hairLength property set to `long` and a position property of `Canada`. An instance of `male` called `ShamBhangal` would (at the moment) have the hair property set to a much shorter value, and a position of `England`. These two instances are true individuals and are *real* in that they are physical entities you can interact with; you can point to one at a Flash convention and say "Ooo quick, look, there's Jen deHaan, the author...."

References and Copies

When you drag a Library symbol to the Stage, you create an instance. An instance is not a copy of the original Library symbol, but a *reference* to it, in the same way that `shamBhangal` is not `male` but *a* `male`.

 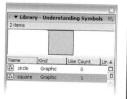 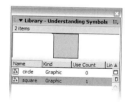

Although it may look as if you are dragging a copy of the symbol square onto the Stage, Flash does not see the process this way; rather, Flash sees you adding a "marker" on the Stage that says "put one of those symbols at this position on the Stage, and give it a unique set of properties."

➡ 11.15 Creating Buttons

The only way to break the reference between an instance and its Library symbol is to convert the instance back to a set of primitives via Modify > Break Apart. You may have to do this several times if your symbol has embedded symbols inside it.

One of the most important properties of an instance is its instance name. This property is used to differentiate between particular instances (rather like an individual person's name). Once an instance has an instance name, it can be controlled via ActionScript.

FLASH WORKSPACE

AUTHORING TASKS

SCRIPTING TASKS

TESTING AND PUBLISHING TASKS

WHAT'S NEW

Continues ●

11.1   Understanding Symbols *(continued)*

Something not mentioned in this section is that a class has methods. These are a part of ActionScript that lets you control symbols via ActionScript, and they are a major feature for the Flash programmer.

The process of creating references to the original Library symbol when you drag an instance onto the Stage has a number of implications:

- All you actually add to the SWF file size is the reference, not a full copy of the symbol. This makes adding instances much more efficient in terms of file size than copying elements that are not symbols (i.e., groups or primitives). When copying groups or primitives, you create a true copy, which is usually a much bigger addition to the SWF file size than a simple reference.

- If you change the Library symbol, all references to the symbol will point to the changed symbol, causing all instances of the symbol on the stage to also change as well. Although all instances of the same Library symbol are the same, you can alter individual instances via properties to create versions that look different. This is much more efficient than creating totally separate versions.

Here, the man and boy are references to the same symbol, but they are scaled differently via the size-related properties. In terms of the `Human` analogy, if you changed the `male` template (version of `male` in the Library) to include long hair instead of short hair, all male individuals (or male *instances)* would have long hair.

- A symbol can itself contain embedded symbols. This leads to further file size efficiency through reuse.

 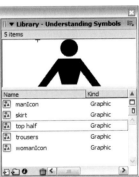

The man and woman symbols are made of three different embedded symbols; both share the same "top half" symbol.

11.2   Understanding Behaviors

Tween-based animation is linear and unchanging. To make anything in Flash interactive or nonlinear, you have to add ActionScript. For the designer who doesn't want to use coding, an alternative is behaviors. These are drag-and-drop elements that attach the relevant code without you having to touch a line of the stuff. Behaviors are aimed at beginners and noncoders.

Behaviors can be attached to either symbols (movie clips or buttons) or keyframes. Behaviors are attached or deleted via the Behaviors panel.

Behavior Workflow

The general workflow of using behaviors is shown here.

1   *Select* the item you want to attach a behavior to.

2   Select the behavior you want to *attach* to the item via the + icon at the top of the Behaviors panel. This brings up a contextual menu of available behaviors for your selection.

3   *Customize* your behavior via a dialog that appears as soon as you attach the behavior.

4   *Manage* your behaviors after attaching them by reselecting the item and adding, deleting, or modifying the behavior by selecting it from the list of attached behaviors in the Behaviors panel. If you double-click it, you can get back to step 3 and edit the customizations. If you click the – icon, you can delete the behavior.

When to (and When Not to) Use Behaviors

Behaviors are useful when you cannot or do not want to write raw ActionScript yourself. They allow you to add ActionScript to your Flash content via easy to manage and encapsulated packages using a nonprogramming, dialog-based system.

The default behaviors are generally less useful for the advanced programmer, who would rather either write their own custom ActionScript, or prefer third-party functionality to be added via more advanced and flexible structures (i.e., component-based methods, linked ActionScript AS files containing class-based definitions, or general function libraries).

➡ 5.8   Behaviors Panel

➡ 11.10 Adding Movie Clip Control Using Behaviors

Behaviors panel

———

Behaviors use Flash 5 style attached on(event) structures that are no longer in common use for hand-coded ActionScript. They are difficult to interface to using a more modern Action-Script coding style and are therefore more suited to noncoders and beginners (who would not look at the code in any case) rather than experienced scripters.

———

Behaviors are only useful for adding standard or general features (e.g., when building a standard button-based site interface). For most nonstandard or non-general applications (such as advanced custom interfaces or Flash games), you have no other option than to write your own Action-Script.

11.3   Creating Graphics

Convert To Symbol
F8

New Symbol
Ctrl F8
⌘ F8

Note that a graphic has a one-frame timeline. Although you can add additional frames, a graphic will only show its first frame. When creating graphic symbols, use as many layers as you need, but don't add additional frames to the Timeline because they will not be seen.

You cannot control a graphic symbol via ActionScript, and any ActionScript you add to its Timeline will not run. If you need to do either, use a movie clip instead.

Although it is possible to create an animated graphic symbol by embedding a movie clip inside it, there is usually no real reason to do this; using a movie clip embedded inside another movie clip is usually the way to go.

The graphic symbol is used for static and noninteractive content, or as a building block for more advanced symbols.

When to Create Graphic Symbols

The following examples show typical uses of graphic symbols.

A static logo. Because such a logo will be used in several places within a site, it is a good idea to make it into a graphic symbol.

A static background may be fairly complex, and creating it as a separate graphic symbol helps keep its parts separate from the main animation.

A static graphic that will be used to form a button should be made into a graphic, because you will typically re-use the same graphic in more than one button state.

Shown here is a series of static graphic symbols that will form the frames of a movie clip animation. Because they are fairly complex, creating them as separate graphics helps break the overall effect into separate 'building blocks'. Notice that one of these graphics is also used in the logo design above. This re-use would lead to efficiencies in the final site design.

Creating a Graphic Symbol

To create a graphic symbol you can do either of the following:

- Make a selection on the Stage (which will typically consist of primitive shapes) and select Modify > Convert To Symbol. In the dialog that will appear, make sure the Graphic radio button is selected and enter a name for your new graphic.

- Choose Insert > New Symbol to create a new graphic from scratch. A window identical to the Convert To Symbol dialog will appear, except it will be called Create New Symbol. Configure it as in the last bullet point and, in the Timeline that appears, add your symbols graphics.

11.4   Using the Color Instance Effects

Symbols are more versatile than raw primitives because symbol instances can be modified to change their appearance without needing a separate symbol for each change. One of the most common changes is to vary color.

To add a color instance effect:

1   Select a symbol instance (graphic, movie clip, or button) on the Stage.

2   In the Property inspector, select an effect from the Color drop-down.

Brightness and Alpha effects vary the brightness and transparency of the instance. When selecting either of these effects, you will see a % value slider appear. For brightness, the range is –100% (black) through 0% (no effect) to 100% (white). For Alpha, the range is 0% (transparent) to 100% (opaque).

You can set the Tint effect anywhere from 0% (no effect) to 100% (full effect); use the RGB sliders to specify the color you want to tint with. You can also select the tint color by clicking the color brick to open the color picker.

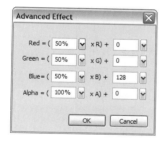

Advanced Effect allows you to add all the other effects simultaneously. When you select this option and click the Settings button that appears on the Property inspector, you will see the Advanced Effect window. The sliders on the left allow you to make relative percentage changes to the Red, Green, Blue, and Alpha color channels; the sliders on the right allow you to make absolute changes.

➡ 11.5   Using Graphics in Tween Animations

➡ 22.10 Changing Color via Scripts

To remove a color instance effect, select None in the Color drop-down.

———

Color effects can be applied to tweens. If for example, you set a blue tint in the start tween keyframe and a red one in the end keyframe, you would see a color transition from a blue tint to a red tint. This can be useful for animated color fades for video effects and lighting effects in Flash cartoons.

———

Color effects can be applied to video clips. Embed the video into a movie clip and apply the effect to the movie clip. This allows you to create film like video transitions (fade to black, fade to white, filter effects, etc).

———

Color instance effects can be controlled via ActionScript to create interactive transitions.

———

Flash includes the alpha channel as part of a color; instead of RGB (red-green-blue), you really have RGBA (red-green-blue-alpha). This is reflected in all color-based panels, such as the Color Mixer panel.

11.5   Using Graphics in Tween Animations

**Convert selected
frame to keyframe**
F6

———

Although you can ani-
mate a graphic symbol
using tweens, you can-
not animate it using
ActionScript. To do this,
you must use movie
clips. This is because the
graphic symbol is not
accessible by Action-
Script (it has no associ-
ated ActionScript Class).

Although graphic symbols are themselves static, you can use them as a building block in tweens to create animation.

A static graphic can be used as part of a tween to add incidental or background graphics. In this animation of a skier,
only the skier is animated, but the animation looks much
better because of the static foreground and background
scenery. Note that the trees are actually the same instance
repeated, scaled, and placed on "foreground" and "background" layers to give a sense of depth.

A graphic is the simplest thing you can animate in a tween animation:

1 Add an instance at the start keyframe (below left).

2 Create a second keyframe further along the Timeline (below center).

3 Make the first keyframe a motion tween by selecting it and doing one of the following:

  ■ Selecting Insert > Timeline > Motion Tween.

  ■ Right-clicking/⌘-clicking it and choosing Create Motion Tween from the context
menu that appears.

  ■ Choosing Motion from the Tween drop-down on the Property inspector (below right).

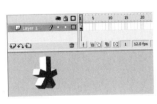 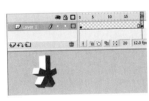 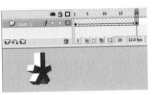

4 Finally change one or both of the graphic instances (as illustrated below):

From left to right: Moving an instance (using the Selection tool) to create movement, scaling an
instance (using the Free Transform tool) to create change in size, and rotating an instance (also
using Free Transform) to create change in orientation.

11.6   Creating Movie Clip Animations

One of the major features of Flash animation is the movie clip. A movie clip has its own timeline, something that may seem like a rather superficial point, but it is actually one of the most powerful features in Flash! Movie clips are useful when you:

- Want to create a repeating animation (also called a *walk cycle* or *animation cycle* in traditional animation). If your animation included a figure walking, you would create a movie clip of the figure walking one complete walk cycle (walking on one foot, then the other), and then move this movie clip to give the impression of a continuous walk.

- Want several versions of the same animation to occur.

For example, if you were creating this wintery scene, you could create the falling snow by creating lots of separate motion tweens, but you may be still putting it together next winter. A better way would be to create an animation of a single snowflake falling, and then add many instances to the Stage to create many falling snowflakes.

- Have a complex animation and want to structure it. Rather than create a complex animation on a single timeline, it is usually better to create separate movie clips, each containing a part of the full animation. This also allows you to add several effects that would not be possible if you placed all your tween animations on the main Timeline.

A movie clip is very similar to the main Timeline, so creating an animation inside a movie clip is much the same as creating the same thing on the main Timeline. To create a movie clip, do one of the following:

- Choose Insert > New Symbol, or choose New Symbol from the Library panel menu. In the Create New Symbol dialog, check Movie Clip and add a name. The movie clip will appear in the Library and you will be in edit mode within the movie clip's Timeline on the Stage/Timeline panel. Then add content and tweens as you would for the main Timeline.

- Select any content on the Stage and choose Modify > Convert To Symbol. You will see almost exactly the same dialog as the Create New Symbol, except that it is now called Convert To Symbol. A new movie clip is created as before, but you are not currently editing it. To do this, double-click the movie clip on the Stage. You will find that the content you selected is now on frame 1 of the movie clip's Timeline. Edit as you would the main Timeline.

For both methods, the quickest way you can return to editing the main Timeline is by using the Path Explorer (above the Timeline).

A movie clip animation will behave differently from the same animation placed on the main Timeline when seen over the Internet. The main Timeline will start almost immediately (called "streaming"), whereas the movie clip will not start until all frames are loaded in.

The main Timeline is really just another movie clip. This is something that becomes much more apparent when you start using ActionScript; the main Timeline and movie clips are part of the same class, and can be controlled in much the same way.

Movie clips are often referred to as simply "clips."

11.7   Using Movie Clips in Tween Animations

Note that an animation cycle has to be seamless; the start and finish point of the movie clip animation can't have any glitches. This makes the repeating animation cycle look like one long continuous animation. The best way to create a seamless animation is to have the first keyframe in the animation identical (or nearly identical) to the first one.

The most common animation cycle is the walk cycle: the animation of a character walking two paces.

Implementing the main (movement) animation via ActionScript allows you to make the birds move in an interactive way; although the bird flapping animation is a fixed tween, its flight path is now interactive.

When you use movie clips in a tween animation, you effectively have two timelines to work with: the main Timeline and the Timeline inside the movie clip. Using movie clips in this way allows you to create *animation cycles*.

Suppose you wanted to create an animation where a bird flies across the screen. The bird will do two things: it will flap its wings, and it will fly forward. This is actually two *subanimations*. You could do both animations on the main Timeline, but if you want to make the bird flap its wings 50 times as it traverses the screen, you would have to tween 50 wing flaps.

A better method is to use the fact that a movie clip contains its own Timeline and create a smaller, repeating animation (the wing flap); then use the main Timeline to create the bigger, nonrepeating animation (the traverse).

To create the wing flap, create a movie clip and inside it create a tween of a stationary bird that moves its wing in one complete flap (e.g., down-up and back to down). This is the animation cycle.

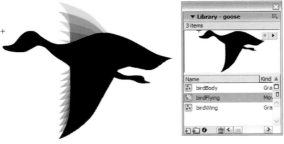

Going back to the main Timeline, create a tween using the newly created "bird flying but not moving forward" movie clip. This tween creates the "moving forward" part of the animation

You will not see both animations working together in the authoring environment, because it only shows animation on the current Timeline you are editing. If you test the main Timeline in the test environment, you will see the bird flapping its wings and moving forward at the same time.

11.8   Creating Nested Movie Clips

Most real-life motion consists of many moving parts within a system. A car moves forward, but its wheels also rotate relative to the car. As a man walks forward, his arms swing, his upper body moves up and down slightly, and his legs move to and fro. Rather than a single animation, there's a hierarchy of movement; the body parts move relative to the man's center point, but all of them also move together as a whole. To implement this type of hierarchical animation, you use nested movie clips.

Suppose you wanted to create the ubiquitous cartoon car animation. As the car moves forward, the car body rocks slightly and the wheels rotate.

The first thing to do is create separate building blocks. First, create the car body and wheel graphic symbol. Then, create the two subanimations:

First, the rotating wheel movie clip. Note that the wheel animation starts and ends with the wheel in the same position. This ensures that the animation can be repeated seamlessly.

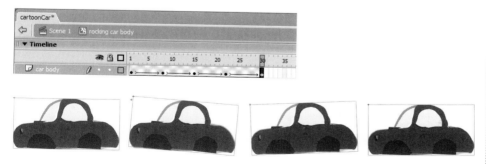

Second, the seamless rocking car body movie clip.

Continues

11.8   Creating Nested Movie Clips *(continued)*

Most real life animations have lots of obvious subanimations, but a realistic animation includes the more subtle subanimations as well, such as the rocking body subanimation in the car example. In a walk cycle, a realistic animation would include a slight body bob as well as the more obvious arm and leg movements.

In complex animations, you should have no part of the tween animations on the main Timeline; everything should be encapsulated within movie clips. The main Timeline is used simply to introduce and remove movie clips that contain the separate animations that make up the overall production. Think of the main Timeline as the story script and the movie clips and nested movie clips as the actors.

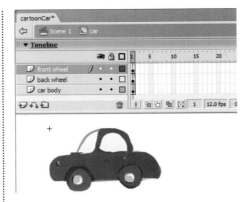

To create the fully animated car, take the two subanimations and place them in a third movie clip.

To recap, the following symbols were used:

■ The basic graphics are static graphic symbols (`car body` and `wheel`).

■ The subanimation movie clips `rocking car body` and `rotating wheel` use these graphic symbols to create the moving parts.

■ The two subanimations are finally nested in the complete animated movie clip `car`.

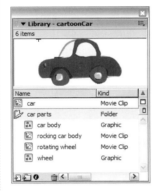

11.9 Navigating Between Nested Movie Clips

As you create your nested animation, you may need to tweak the embedded animations and graphics. You move around the nested movie clips via the Path Explorer. To edit a cartoon car animation, you can do either of the following:

■ Double-click an instance of the car on the Stage. This will put you in Edit In Place mode.

■ Double-click the car symbol in the bottom pane of the Library panel, or click the car symbol in the Library and then double-click its thumbnail in the top pane of the same panel. Either of these will put you in Edit Symbol mode.

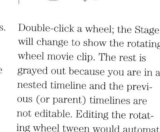

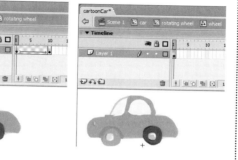

You will see something like this. The Timeline of **car** becomes visible. Notice that the Path Explorer shows the path Scene 1 > car.

Double-click a wheel; the Stage will change to show the rotating wheel movie clip. The rest is grayed out because you are in a nested timeline and the previous (or parent) timelines are not editable. Editing the rotating wheel tween would automatically alter the animation of the other wheel because they are instances of the same symbol.

Finally, double-click the wheel again to get to the lowest nest; the **wheel** graphic symbol.

Although the graphic on the Stage has not changed, both the Path Explorer and Timeline have changed to show the wheel graphic. It is important to realize that you are now editing a graphic and not a movie clip. Although you can add more frames to the Timeline, they would not show up because a graphic is static; it only shows its first frame. The clue to this is the Path Explorer shows the Graphic icon in front of the wheel part of the path.

To go back through the animation's nesting, you can either:

■ Click the back arrow ⇦ to go back one level.

■ Click any part of the path to go directly back to that level. Each part of the path is a link, as signified by their <u>underlining</u> every time you mouse over them.

In Edit In Place mode, the contents of the Timeline(s) the symbol is on stay visible. They are shown grayed out because they are not part of the symbol you are editing.

In Edit Symbol mode, you only see the contents of the symbol as you edit.

It is important to keep in mind what type of Timeline you are currently editing as well as where it is in the nested animation hierarchy. You should be constantly checking both of these factors via the Path Explorer.

11.10 Adding Movie Clip Control Using Behaviors

Behaviors panel
Shift F3

Although you don't have to add the actions layer (you can simply attach the behaviors to the animation keyframes), it is good practice to keep code in a separate layer from your graphics. Note that adding layers does not increase file size of the final SWF, so this is a win-win technique!

Although you must know about instances and frame labels to use behaviors (two core features of ActionScript), you don't have to write any ActionScript.

This section assumes you have read Sections 11.7 to 11.9, and uses terms and examples developed in those sections. Behaviors are a form of ActionScript, and to use them you need to know the basics of frame labels and instances; this section therefore also assumes you have read Sections 15.3 and 15.4.

Tween animations work in a linear frame-by-frame fashion, and they continue to cycle around forever. In many animations, you may not want this to happen. The easiest way to prevent this is via behaviors. There are two ways you can use behaviors; to stop the current Timeline or to stop other timelines.

Using Behaviors to Stop the Current Timeline

A timeline will usually go back to frame 1 when it reaches its last frame—that is, it will continue to loop. To prevent this, you need to attach a *stop* behavior at the last frame.

Suppose you wanted your car movie clip to go across the screen and stop. Begin by creating a tween that moves the car across the screen.

To stop the tween Timeline from looping:

1 Add a new layer above the current one and call it `actions`. Add a keyframe on the last frame in the tween and label it **end**.

2 Select the keyframe you just added. In the Behaviors panel, click the ⊞ icon. In the menu that appears, select Movieclip > Goto And Stop At Frame Or Label. In the window that appears, enter **end** in the text entry box at the bottom left, then click OK.

3 The Behaviors panel should now include a behavior, whenever you select the keyframe. The keyframe itself should now also have a little a in it, signifying it has attached ActionScript. Test the movie; the car stops when it reaches the far right.

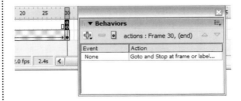

11.10 Adding Movie Clip Control Using Behaviors (continued)

Using Behaviors to Stop Other Timelines

Although the car has stopped, the nested animations continue; the wheels keep turning and the body keeps swaying as if it was still moving. This is because the stop behavior only stops the Timeline it was asked to stop. You must also stop the *nested* timelines.

To stop a movie clip other than the current one, you must give Flash some way of knowing which movie clip(s) you want to stop; to do this, you *name* each one with an instance name.

To name each nested movie clip: Double-click the `car` instance on the Stage and then click the car body and each wheel in turn. Using the Property inspector, give the body, front wheel, and back wheel instance names of `body`, `frontWheel`, and `backWheel`.

 +

You also need to give an instance name to the `car` symbol. Go back to the initial Timeline using the Path Explorer, select the full car symbol on the Stage, and call it `mainCar` on both the first and last keyframe in the tween.

To stop the nested movie clips: Go back to the frame to which you added your first behavior and select it. Perform the same procedure as before to add three more Stop At Frame Or Label behaviors, but open the tree diagram in the top pane, and for each one, select one of the nested movie clips within `mainCar`.

 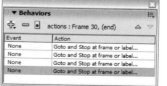

You should end with four behaviors in all, one for each Timeline involved in the car animation. When you test the movie now, all parts of the animation should stop when the car stops.

Using behaviors in the way shown is a very powerful feature and allows you to create complex animations. For example, instead of stopping movie clips, you could create another movie clip, `driver`, to start when the car stops. This would show the driver getting out of the car. This triggered animation would be difficult to achieve without ActionScript or behaviors.

The behaviors here are still not interactive. The process of making them so is discussed in Sections 11.13 to 11.16.

FLASH WORKSPACE

AUTHORING TASKS

SCRIPTING TASKS

TESTING AND PUBLISHING TASKS

WHAT'S NEW

11.11   Testing Movie Clips

Test Movie
Ctrl Enter
⌘ Enter

Test Scene
Ctrl Alt Enter
⌘ Option Enter

_____

When developing your animation, it is a good idea to test it online every so often using at least the top two browsers (Microsoft Internet Explorer and Netscape Navigator). This will show up any nonanimation issues that may be hidden when testing using other methods, such as download or browser compatibility issues. Better to discover such issues earlier rather than later!

When testing animations involving movie clips (and especially nested movie clips) it is important to know which parts of your animations will be executed and which parts won't.

The Authoring Environment

When in the authoring environment, anything on any other timeline except the current one will *not* execute. The following *will* be executed when you play the current Timeline via the Controller Toolbar (Window > Toobars > Controller)

- Animations on the current Timeline

- Simple (Flash 5 style) ActionScript and most movie clip control behaviors attached to frames in the main Timeline, or attached to buttons and movie clips on the current Timeline

- Sound attached to the current Timeline

The second and third bullet points depend on the settings you specify on the bottom segment of the Control menu. Some are disabled by default, so you may have to enable them by checking them.

The Test Environment

To test any complex Flash content (i.e., anything that includes nested movie clips or Flash 2004 style ActionScript) you should test your content using the test environment. Control > Test Movie will run the current animation, including all nested movie clips and *all* ActionScript and behaviors.

Sometimes (especially when debugging an animation) you may want to test the current Timeline upward. To do this, choose Control > Test Scene.

Testing in the Browser

The best way to test your animation is via your default browser because this will show you the content as the end user will see it: in a browser. To do this, choose File > Publish Preview > HTML.

11.12 Creating Movie Clips from Bitmaps

Using bitmaps in Flash is a common way to break up the "cleanness" of vector graphics; bitmaps are obligatory in certain web design styles. Bitmaps can also form a major part of your site's content. It is therefore important to be able to animate them using as many of Flash's features as possible.

Unfortunately, Flash cannot animate bitmaps well directly. Although a raw bitmap can be used directly in tween-based animations, there are several things you can't apply to it, including Color Instance effects, ActionScript, and ActionScript control. To get around this, place your bitmap inside a movie clip. This gives the bitmap all the features of the movie clip it is in. To create a movie clip "wrapper" for a bitmap:

1 Import your bitmap with File > Import > Import To Library.

2 On the Stage, create an empty movie clip with Insert > New Symbol. In the Create New Symbol dialog that appears, select the Movie Clip radio button and give the movie clip a name.

3 The Stage will change to show the Timeline of the movie clip you just created. Drag the bitmap from the Library to the Stage of this movie clip, being careful to place it near the registration point of the clip (the little + in the center of the Stage).

You will now have the bitmap and a movie clip in the Library, both of which will look exactly the same, except that the movie clip version can use all the Flash animation techniques available to movie clips.

➡ 11.7 Using Movie Clips in Tween Animation

➡ 13.2 Importing Bitmaps

_____

Because bitmaps have a much larger number of colors in them than a typical vector-based graphic, they work particularly well with Color Instance effects.

_____

Flash is predominantly a vector-based system, so it can handle small bitmaps or bitmaps that do not move much, but it will become very sluggish if you use large ones.

_____

Flash will really slow down if you combine the two things it finds hardest to work with: alpha effects applied to bitmaps. Avoid this if you want fast and responsive graphics!

11.13   Creating Movie Clips from Videos

Behaviors panel
Shift F3

———

Flash can import the QuickTime (MOV), Windows video (AVI), MPEG Movies (MPG/MPEG) and digital video (DVI) formats, as well as being able to import its own embedded video (Flash Video or FLV) format.

———

A movie clip does not start playing until all of its contents are loaded (i.e., it must be pre-loaded). When using video clips, be aware of this issue; a video clip can take a long time to load even on a broad-band connection.

———

If you place video on the main Timeline rather than into a movie clip, it will start playing before all of its content is loaded (i.e., it will stream). You should use this for larger video clips, even though you will lose the animation abilities that placing it in a movie clip would allow.

A video clip must be placed on a timeline. Placing it inside a movie clip rather than on the main Timeline gives you the ability to animate the video while it is playing.

1   Create a new movie clip with Insert > New Symbol, and in the Create New Symbol dialog select the Movie Clip radio button and give your movie clip a name.

2   The Stage and Timeline will change to show the (currently empty) movie clip you just created. To embed a video into it, choose File > Import > Import To Stage and select a video clip from the Import file browser window that appears. This will set the Video Import Wizard running. On the first page, select the Embed Video In Macromedia document. For the remaining pages in the wizard, select values that match your video.

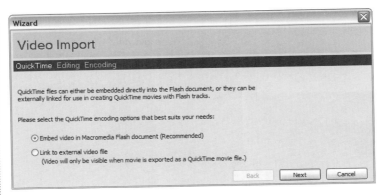

3   A dialog asks you whether it is okay to extend the movie clip Timeline to match the video length. Click Yes.

The video is now embedded into the movie clip. You can animate the movie clip using any of the methods you would use with a normal movie clip. Particularly useful are Instance Color effects, which allow you to add fades and color tints to give you many standard video effects. You can also move through the video frames by moving around the Timeline it is embedded in. Finally, you can add several instances of the movie clip onto the Stage to create a "video wall" effect.

11.14   Adding Video Control Using Behaviors

Although there is no built-in video player user interface in the Flash Player, a subset of the default behaviors allow you to quickly build your own.

Adding the Video to a Timeline

Assuming you have imported your video, either embed it inside a movie clip or drag it from the Library and onto the Stage to embed it onto the main Timeline. You will most likely see a pop-up with a text message that starts, "This video requires *XX* frames to display its entire length." This message occurs if the timeline is not long enough to display the entire video file. You will most usually want to click 'Yes' to this dialog (which will allow Flash to lengthen the timeline to fit the video).

Behaviors require that all movie clips and video clips have instance names. If you attached the video to the main Timeline, select the video on the Stage and give it an instance name. If you embedded it into a movie clip, select that also and give it an instance name.

Adding the Video Controls

To create a video interface, you will need button symbols for each of the standard video controller buttons (play, stop, rewind, etc). Luckily, you use some of the default buttons that ship with Flash. Choose Window **>** Other Panels **>** Common Libraries **>** Buttons and take your pick from the Library that appears. Add a menu of buttons below your video (the gel buttons are shown here 🔘 🔘 🔘).

USING GRAPHIC SYMBOLS VS. MOVIE CLIPS

Many designers never use graphic symbols, and instead only use buttons and movie clips. This practice is normal for designers with a strong ActionScript background, and they do it so that they retain the ability to control all their symbols via ActionScript (a graphic symbol cannot be directly controlled via ActionScript, whereas a movie clip can). For everyone else, 'always using movie clips' is probably a bad habit, and to be avoided! The advantage to a non-ActionScripter in using graphic symbols is that Flash uses slightly less memory when displaying graphics than when displaying movie clips.

➡ 5.8   Behaviors
         Panel

➡ 11.2 Understand-
         ing Behaviors

It's recommended you keep the video (or the movie clip containing the video) on a separate layer from the buttons. Make the two layers the same length (one frame long if you have embedded into a movie clip, or a number of frames equal to the video length if you have embedded directly onto the main Timeline.)

Continues ●

11.14   Adding Video Control Using Behaviors

(continued)

Behaviors panel
Shift F3

___

The images here show
the sample AVI file that
ships with the latest
version of QuickTime. If
you have installed
QuickTime, you should
have this video file on
your hard drive as
`sample.avi`.

Adding the Video Control Behaviors

Finally, you need to attach the video control behaviors to the appropriate buttons. For the
play button, do the following:

1 Select the button. In the Behaviors panel, click the ✚ icon at the top left and select
Embedded Video **>** Play.

2 In the Play Video dialog that appears, find and select the video clip you want to control
from the tree diagram. Click OK.

3 Repeat for any other video control buttons you have added, attaching the appropriate
behavior under the Embedded Video submenu for each.

11.15 Creating Buttons

Buttons are used in Flash to create basic interactivity; click a button and something happens.

A button timeline looks like this. It is different from a movie clip timeline in the following way.

A movie clip plays rather like a film reel and is time based; one frame is seen after the next in a time-sequential manner. A button changes frames due to interaction rather than time. When you are not over the button, the Up frame is shown; when you are over the button, the Over frame is shown; and when you click the button, the Down frame is shown. In this way, the button Timeline changes frames based on what the user does, and this creates button animation between the Up, Over, and Down interactive events.

The final frame, Hit, defines the active button area (also called the *hit area*). The graphic defined in this frame defines the pixels that will be detected to be part of the button by the mouse when you roll over it. Normally, the hit area is defined so that it totally encloses the Up graphic.

Creating the Button's Graphic States

To make use of the button Timeline moving between frames, you must add a keyframe in each frame that represents that state:

- Add a button up graphic in the Up keyframe.
- Add a button over graphic in the Over keyframe.
- Add a button down graphic in the Down keyframe.
- Add a graphic or shape in the Hit keyframe to define the hit area pixels. The hit area is sometimes known as the button "hotspot" in other web design fields.

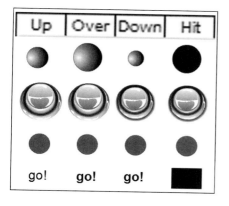

The image here shows several different buttons and the associated graphic for each state.

→ 11.16 Adding Basic Button Navigation Using Behaviors

→ 11.17 Creating Text Buttons

→ 11.18 Creating Buttons with Audible Feedback

New Symbol

Ctrl F8

⌘ F8

The final frame, Hit, is not part of the graphic appearance but defines the pixels that will be detected as part of the button. If this frame contains no content (i.e., it is an empty keyframe), the button will not work, because it has no hit area.

The hit area is defined by "nonzero" pixels. Even if the hit area has zero alpha, the transparent pixels are counted; you might not be able to see them, but Flash can.

Continues

11.15   Creating Buttons *(continued)*

———

In this section you have only defined the button's graphical transitions when the user interacts with it. You have not yet told Flash what to do when the user clicks it. Like an unconnected light switch, the buttons will flick up or down when you use them, but they won't cause anything to happen. To do that, you need to add Action-Script or a behavior.

———

One of the best ways to learn how Flash button timelines are set up is to look at the default buttons in Windows > Other Panels > Common Libraries > Buttons.

The first button changes its shape for each state. Note that the hit state is defined as the same size as the biggest graphic state. When doing this, make sure that none of the states is that much bigger than the up state; otherwise, your hit area will become noticeably bigger than the up state, and the button will go to the down state before the user is over the up graphic.

The second button uses buttons of the same shape and size for all states, and each button is a solid area of pixels with no gaps. In this case, you can use the last graphic state (down) as the hit area. The Timeline would look like this one.

The third button is just a filled circle. Because of this, the button will not show animation between states; all the graphic states show the same circle. In cases like this, you can use the same button state (up) as all of your states. Use this type of button when the button is small (i.e., it would be difficult to see the button animations) or when you are using sound to signify the different button states rather than changes in appearance.

The final button uses text as a button. The area of the visible states has gaps, so you should *not* use any of them as the hit state graphic. Instead, use a solid rectangle that totally covers the text.

11.16   Adding Basic Button Navigation Using Behaviors

A button symbol will do nothing interactive (apart from change button appearance when rolled over or clicked). To make the button actually do something, you need to add an *event handler* to the button. The easiest way to do this (without learning ActionScript) is to use a behavior.

To attach a behavior to create Timeline navigation, do the following:

1 Create a button (or use one from Window > Other Panels > Common Libraries > Buttons).

2 Place it on the Stage and select it.

3 In the Behaviors panel, click the ⇦ icon and select Movieclip > Goto And Play At Frame Or Label, or Movieclip > Goto And Stop At Frame Or Label, depending on which one you require.

4 In the window that appears, select the target movie clip you want to control from the top pane (it must have an instance name, as must all movie clips it is embedded in). In the lower left text entry box, enter a frame number (not recommended) or a frame label (recommended) for the frame you want to go to in the target.

When you click the button in the SWF, the target Timeline will go to the specified frame.

To attach a behavior to create web navigation, repeat steps 1 and 2 above, then proceed here:

3 In the Behaviors panel, click the ⇦ icon and select Web > Goto Web Page. In the dialog that appears, enter the full URL (i.e. including the http//: part) of the web page you want to load (below left).

4 In the Open In drop-down menu, select where you want to new page to appear. For traditional (nonframed) web pages, the most usual choices are _self (replace the current flash content with the new page) or _blank (open a new browser window to display the new page in) (below right).

5 Click OK.

When you click the button in the SWF, the page specified will open as requested.

➡ 11.2   Understand-
          ing Symbols

➡ 11.14 Adding
          Video Con-
          trol Using
          Behaviors

➡ 11.15 Creating
          Buttons

➡ 18.1   Understand-
          ing Event-
          Driven Code

➡ 18.5   Writing But-
          ton Scripts
          for Flash
          Movie Navi-
          gation

➡ 18.6   Writing But-
          ton Scripts
          for Web
          Navigation

When controlling a timeline with buttons, you usually want to stop it first. Consider adding a Goto And Stop At Frame Or Label behavior at frame 1 of the Timeline you want to control, and specify it to stop at frame 1.

Goto and Play at frame or label

Choose the movie clip that you want to begin playing:

`this`

🖼 _root

○ Relative   ○ Absolute

Enter the frame number or frame label at which the movie clip should start playing. To start from the beginning, type '1':

`page01`

OK   Cancel

Go to URL

URL: `http://www.macromedia.com`

Open in: `"_self"` ▾

OK   Cancel

FLASH WORKSPACE

AUTHORING TASKS

SCRIPTING TASKS

TESTING AND PUBLISHING TASKS

WHAT'S NEW

11.17 Creating Text Buttons

New Symbol

Ctrl F8

⌘ F8

___

To make the button actually do something, you need to either attach a behavior to it or define your own event handler for it using ActionScript.

One of the easiest types of buttons to create is text buttons. Not only are they easy to create, but they are also easy to use for the end user because the text tells them what the button will do.

To create the Button up, over, and down states;

1 Create a new button symbol with Insert > New Symbol. In the dialog that will appear, make sure you select the Button radio button. Give your button a name.

2 The Timeline of the button you have just created will appear, and you can start creating it. Select the Up keyframe.

3 Enter some static text near the + on the Stage (this is the center or *registration point* of the symbol) with the Text tool **A** .

4 Add a keyframe for the over state. With it still selected, make a change to the text. The most popular change is to use the Property inspector to make the text either bold or italic. When you do this, the text may get longer, so you may have to move it to the left a little to keep it in the same general position.

11.17   Creating Text Buttons (continued)

5 You may also add a down state, but this is not always needed. If you want one, add a new keyframe on the down state and with this keyframe still selected, make a change to the text. A popular change to make is to change the text color to something lighter or darker.

6 Finally, add a keyframe in the Hit frame, and with it selected, use the Rectangle tool ☐ to add a contrasting rectangle that completely covers the text. This defines the hit area of the button; the mouse pointer will change to the hand cursor when it goes over this shape.

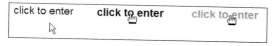

Finally, go back to the main Stage (click scene 1 from the Path Explorer, top left of the Timeline) and place an instance of your button on the Stage. When you test this button using Control > Test Movie, you should see the button text change as shown when you are (left to right) not near it, roll over it, or click it.

click to enter   **click to enter**   click to enter

➡ 18.5 Writing But-
        ton Scripts for
        Flash Movie
        Navigation

➡ 18.6 Writing But-
        ton Scripts
        for Web
        Navigation

Text tool
Ⓣ

If you want to create HTML type text links within plain text, you can do so by adding HTML formatting to a text field.

USING BEHAVIORS VS. HAND-WRITTEN ACTIONSCRIPT

Given that writing simple button scripts is an easy task, many users will move away from using behaviors quickly. This is to be recommended; writing your own scripts can lead to optimization in code and bandwidth, as well as allowing you to create more complex interfaces.

11.18 Creating Buttons with Audible Feedback

New Symbol
Ctrl F8
⌘ F8

Keep sounds designed for buttons short; anything longer than a half a second will carry on playing after the user has moved on from clicking the button.

Only add sounds to a button's visual states. You should never add a sound to the hit state, because the sound will never be heard.

As part of good net-etiquette, it is recommended that you don't use loud full volume sounds for your buttons; a visitor to your site may be in a busy office or worse, working late at home!

Users expect buttons to click when they are pressed. The most usual place to add a click sound on a button is when it is pressed or in the down state. You can also add a sound to the over state. Adding sound to any other state is not recommended, although Flash will let you do it.

Assuming you have already set up a button with the visual states set up, the process of adding sound is as follows:

1 Import your button sound(s) into the Library using File > Import > Import To Library. You can hear each sound by selecting the sound file in the Library lower pane and clicking the ▶ icon to the top right of the sound thumbnail (top pane).

2 Add a new layer and call it **sound**. Lock all other layers. Add keyframes in this layer for all button states to which you want to add a sound.

3 Select each keyframe that you want to add sound to. In the Property inspector, select the sound you want to add via the Sound drop-down. This will list all sound files in your Library. Ensure that the Sync drop-down is set to Event (A Stream sound would load from the Internet every time the button was pressed and would therefore play with a delay, whereas an Event sound is loaded as part of the SWF and is immediately available).

You will see the sound attached to the keyframe as a little soundwave thumbnail. Every time the button moves to this state, in addition to showing a new button state, the sound will also be played.

11.19   Creating Invisible Buttons

Some designers use only one button: an *invisible one*. An invisible button is simply a transparent hotspot; any area of static graphics you place it over becomes a button.

An invisible button can be placed over anything else to make that thing appear as if it is a button. Although the "anything else" will not give any visual feedback when you place the mouse over it in the final Flash movie, the cursor will change to the hand icon, signifying to the user that they are over a button hotspot area.

To create an invisible button:

1   Create a new button symbol with Insert > New Symbol. In the dialog that will appear, make sure you select the Button radio button. Give your button a name.

2   Select the hit state and add a keyframe. Create a hit area by adding either a round or rectangular shape (color is not important). Do *not* add anything in the other states.

3   Go back to the Stage by clicking scene 1 on the Path Explorer (top left of the Timeline). Drag an instance of the invisible button onto the Stage from the Library. No matter what color you used to create the hit area, you will see a light blue translucent shape. This signifies an invisible button.

Using an Invisible Button

home | **about** | **products** | **links**

In this example, invisible buttons are placed over the static text "home | about | products | links". This creates hotspots over each item of text.

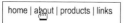

When the movie is run, you will see the mouse reacting to the hotspots as if the text itself were button areas, but the whole menu is being driven by instances of a *single* button.

➡ 3.12   Oval Tool

➡ 3.13   Rectangle Tool

➡ 11.15 Creating Buttons

➡ 11.16 Adding Basic Button Navigation Using Behaviors

New Symbol
Ctrl F8
⌘ F8

————

Although the invisible button provides no visual feedback, you can provide audible feedback by adding a click sound to its down state. This is a common technique in Flash web design when using invisible buttons.

————

One of the great things about invisible buttons is that you don't have to create lots of separate buttons; every symbol or raw graphic can become a button just by slipping an invisible button over it. This can really cut down on file size because you have only one simple "true button" in your Library.

11.20   Creating Animated Buttons

➡ 11.15 Creating
        Buttons

The three visual states of a button can each be represented by an animation rather than a static image. This is done by using movie clips for each animated button state.

Create a movie clip for each state that you want to animate. The button state you are most likely to want to animate is the over state.

Animating the up state is only recommended if you stop the animation after one loop (for example, by adding a behavior at the last frame of the animation to stop it); a button that is always constantly animating even when the user is not interacting with it can become annoying very quickly! The down state is very short lived (it usually lasts a few tenths of a second; the time it takes a user to click then release the button), not long enough to consider adding animations. It goes without saying that the hit state should not usually be animated; because the hit area is not shown, if it changes it will only confuse the user.

Adding animation is very easy: simply place the movie clip you want to use for the animation on the required button Timeline's event frame. In this case you would add the `animatedOver` movie clip to the button over keyframe.

CHAPTER 12

Managing Symbols

ALMOST ALL OF THE viewable content in a Flash site will consist of symbols. You will usually find yourself faced with having to manage a large number of them—experience shows that you can end up with a couple hundred in even modest sites. The way you create and manage symbols efficiently is important to the overall workflow, and this chapter looks at how to do this.

- 12.1 **Basics of symbol use**
- 12.2 **Creating and editing symbols**
- 12.3 **Setting the symbol registration point**
- 12.4 **Changing Stage symbol behaviors**
- 12.5 **Swapping symbols**
- 12.6 **Library symbol icons**
- 12.7 **Organizing the Library**
- 12.8 **Working with multiple libraries**
- 12.9 **Making your site accessible**

12.1   Basics of Symbol Use

The Stage and Library

The Library is the store where all your symbols (graphics, buttons, and movie clips) are kept. All symbols you create will automatically appear in this panel. You can share libraries between FLAs (author time sharing) or SWFs (runtime sharing). Symbols are listed within the Library in alphabetical order by default. You can add Library folders to structure the symbols in a more meaningful way.

Symbols are created in two ways:

■ By selecting content on the Stage and then making it into a symbol with Modify **>** Convert To Symbol.

■ By creating a new symbol from scratch with Insert **>** New Symbol.

The Stage is where symbols are used as *instances*. To create an instance, click-drag a symbol from the Library and release it onto the Stage.

Symbols and Instances

An instance is a reference to (*not* a copy of) the symbol. The difference between a reference and a copy is that if you change the original in the Library, the instances also change; the instances are *linked* to the symbol so that they will reflect changes made to it. An instance is created by dragging a symbol from the Library to the Stage.

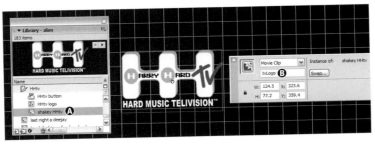

Ⓐ The symbol name is a label for your benefit. Use it to differentiate your symbols, giving each a descriptive title. To edit it, double-click the name in the Library. The name field will change to a text entry box.

Ⓑ The instance name is used by ActionScript and behaviors to control the instance. In this text entry box, give each instance a unique name containing no spaces. An instance without an instance name will appear as <instance name>.

12.1 Basics of Symbol Use *(continued)*

Editing Symbols

Editing can be done in two display modes, Edit Symbol and Edit In Place.

When you edit a symbol, you see only the contents of the symbol Timeline in isolation.

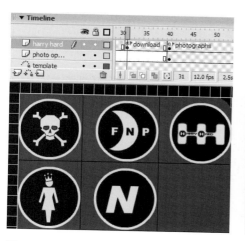
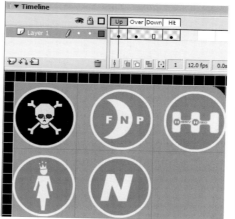

When you Edit In Place, the symbol maintains its position on the Stage and you see all other content on the Stage grayed out. Left: Normal Stage view; right: Edit In Place view, after clicking the skull & crossbones button.

Create New Symbol
Ctrl F8
⌘ F8

Instance names can have no spaces in them. To get over this, use "camel case." This uses a capital letter at the start of each word except the first, so "my movie clip" becomes *myMovieClip*. Camel case is commonly used for all instance and variable names in Flash and is so called because of the "humps" the capitalization creates.

Graphic symbols do not have an instance name because they cannot be controlled by ActionScript (there is no Graphic class to allow ActionScript to access them).

12.2 Creating and Editing Symbols

Create New Symbol
Ctrl F8
⌘ F8

There are a number of ways to create and edit symbols in Flash, and that's great, but the large number of options can also be confusing. This section lists each option and why you would use each.

There are three ways to create a new symbol:

- Select some content on the Stage and then choose Modify > Convert To Symbol. Use this method when

  You have just started a new FLA and have an empty Stage on which to experiment creating new symbols; as soon as you see something that you will be able to use, make it a symbol.

  You have placed a number of symbols on the Stage that you want to copy several times. Making them a symbol rather than a group is more bandwidth efficient.

  You have just imported some content onto the Stage (via File > Import > Import To Stage) and want to convert it to a symbol.

- Select an instance on the Stage and choose Modify > Symbol > Duplicate Symbol, or right-click/⌘-click a symbol in the Library and select Duplicate from the context menu that appears. Use this option when you want to base a new symbol on an existing one.

- Choose Insert > New Symbol or click the New Symbol icon ⊞ at the bottom left corner of the Library. Use this method when

  You want to create a new symbol from scratch, starting with an empty timeline.

  You have just imported some content into the Library (via File > Import > Import To Library) and want to drag it into a new empty symbol.

  You want to create an empty movie clip to attach ActionScript to.

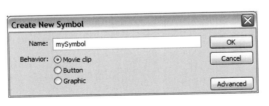

When you create a new symbol or duplicate from the Library, you will see the Create New Symbol dialog. Enter a name in the text entry box. This will show up in the library as a label for the symbol. Select the symbol type (movie clip, button, graphic) via the radio buttons.

When you create a new symbol via duplication from the Stage, you will see the Duplicate Symbol dialog. Enter a new name for the duplicate in the text entry box.

12.2 Creating and Editing Symbols (continued)

Editing Symbols

There are two ways to edit an existing symbol.

Edit

In Edit, you see the content on the symbol's Timeline only. Use this mode to edit a symbol in isolation. To get into this mode, either:

- Double-click a symbol in the bottom Library pane or double-click the thumbnail in the top pane.
- Right-click/⌘-click an instance on the Stage and select Edit from the context menu that appears.

Edit In Place

In Edit In Place, you see the symbol on the Stage with all content around it in place but grayed out. Use this mode to edit the symbol in context so that you can (for example) alter it to fit into a space or position in the final site design. To get into this mode, either:

- Double-click an instance on the Stage.
- Right-click/⌘-click an instance on the Stage and select Edit In Place from the context menu that appears.

Edit Symbol
Ctrl E
⌘ E

Convert To Symbol
F8

___

When you use shared libraries, make sure that you edit symbols in the FLA that has the Library containing them. If you do not do this, the symbol stops being shared and becomes part of the current Library, something that may increase download times. Flash will warn you if this is about to happen.

DELETING SYMBOLS FROM THE LIBRARY

Rather than delete unused/unneeded symbols in your library, it may be wise to create a library folder called 'deleted' or 'bin' into which you place them. The advantage of this is that you are covered if you ever change your mind (or most likely, the client changes their mind!). Note that leaving unused symbols in the library does not affect the size of the final SWF file.

12.3   Setting the Symbol Registration Point

➡ 11.3 Creating
        Graphics

Unwanted movement
occurs when you offset
the registration point
because scaling works
around the registration
point.

When you edit or create a symbol, you will see the registration point as a little + icon. Unless you have a good reason not to, keep this somewhere near the middle of your content so it will scale correctly.

The reason is shown here: the dark rectangle will scale correctly because its registration point is near its center. The light one has an offset registration point. If you scale now, you get unintended *movement*—the rectangle moves towards its registration.

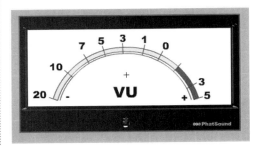

Here, the registration point of the VU meter symbol is just above the "VU" text, which will ensure correct scaling.

There are two situations when you would intentionally not place the symbol registration at the center:

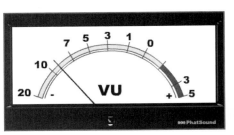 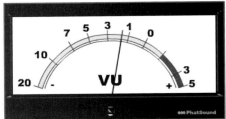

Rotation around a pivot   To create a needle for the VU meter, it has to rotate, as shown here.

12.3   Setting the Symbol Registration Point *(continued)*

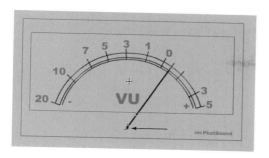

The needle needs to rotate from its bottom edge where the arrow points (the rest of the meter is shown in outline mode so you can see this pivot point).

New Symbol
Ctrl F8
⌘ F8

Convert To Symbol
F8

You can achieve complex motion using offset registrations and nested movie clips. For example, if you have a ball moving toward its registration in one movie clip and place this movie clip in another that rotates the former clip around its registration, the ball will move in a *spiral* toward its registration.

To achieve this, create the needle symbol, making sure that the registration point is at the end you want to use as your rotation pivot point—in this case to the far left (left) of the VU needle. *The registration point is the pivot point used in rotation, and you sometimes need to make this noncentral.*

Scaling in a direction Suppose you want to create an animation of a digital meter that uses a bar graph. If you scale the bar graph to increase or reduce its length, it will change length from *both ends* if the registration is at its center.

To make it scale directly (from one end only), you place the registration point so that it touches the edge you don't want to move when the scale occurs. *The registration point defines the center of scaling, so if you want a particular point on a graphic to remain stationary during scaling, put the registration at that point.*

Defining the Registration Point with Convert To Symbol

When you convert a selection to a symbol, you can define the position of the registration point as part of symbol definition via the Convert To Symbol dialog. The 3×3 matrix allows you to define the position of the registration. Simply click the dot best representing the position relative to the content that you want the registration to be.

12.4 Changing Stage Symbol Behaviors

———

Don't confuse symbol behaviors with behaviors...something that is easy to do given that behaviors are attached to symbols!

The symbol behavior defines whether the symbol will act as a movie clip, button, or graphic. You can change this so that the behavior of a symbol on the Stage is different from that implied by the symbol in the Library.

To change the behavior of a symbol on the Stage, select it and in the Properties inspector, use the drop-down shown to select a new symbol behavior.

Why would you want to change a symbol behavior? There are several reasons:

- You want to control a graphic symbol via ActionScript or behaviors. You cannot control a graphic in this way, but changing its symbol behavior to a movie clip will allow it.

- You want a button to stop at one of its states (usually the button down state). If you change a button's symbol behavior to a movie clip, it becomes a 4-frame movie clip, allowing you to make it go to and stop at the down state (frame 3) using either Action-Script or behaviors.

- You have swapped a symbol for another using the Property inspector's swap button. When you do this, the behavior does not change if you (for example) swapped a movie clip for a button. When swapping a symbol for another type, you should usually also change the symbol behavior.

- You want to add accessibility text to a graphic. Accessibility text can be added to movie clips and buttons, so you would typically have to change the symbol behavior to a movie clip.

12.5 Swapping Symbols

After placing a symbol on the Stage, you may decide you would rather use another symbol from the Library. Instead of deleting the original and carefully placing the new one in the same place, you can use the Swap Symbol command and let it do it all for you.

To swap a Stage symbol, select it and either choose Modify > Symbol > Swap Symbol or click the Swap button on the Properties inspector.

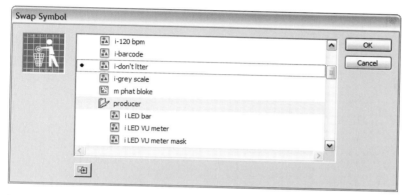

Using either method, you will see the Swap Symbol window appear. The current symbol used is shown with a bullet point to the left of it, and the other symbols are listed in the same order they appear in the Library. To swap, select any other symbol by double-clicking it or by single-clicking and clicking OK.

There are reasons you would want to swap symbols in normal workflows. The most obvious (at least for commercial web design) is that you are using *placeholders* for the early stages of the design. When you start a new site, you may not have the final assets from the client, or you may not want to build them until you do something else (usually write the ActionScript to drive the site). In this case, you will start with simple placeholders; that is, symbols that are roughs of the final assets. When you have the final assets, you use Swap Symbol to switch to the final assets.

Another reason to swap symbols is to simply try different ideas or redesign parts of a site. Deleting a symbol and replacing it with a new one is far more destructive than swapping, because you lose any behaviors that are attached to a symbol as soon as you delete it. If you swap, you can *swap back* to get to the original starting position if you decide you don't like your changes.

Finally, it is normal to start a FLA with all content in the current Library, and later convert to using shared libraries. Swapping between content in the shared and nonshared assets is the way to go because exact positions and scripting are preserved.

➡ 12.4 Changing
Stage Symbol
Behaviors

If you swap a symbol for another type (for example, swapping a button for a movie clip), you will also have to change the symbol behavior.

If you try to swap a symbol with scripts attached to it for one that does not allow this (e.g., swapping a movie clip for a graphic), Flash will warn you via the Symbol Conversion Loses Script Warning window.

If the symbol you want to swap is part of a multikeyframe animation, remember to swap it on all keyframes it appears on.

12.6   Library Symbol Icons

The icon shown for components is the general one. The default components that ship with Flash each have a separate icon.

The Library panel displays all symbols using a number of different icons. This section lists them all with cross references to the section that best describes the symbol or asset. More general references are included in the sidebar.

Icons for Library Symbol Types

ICON	SYMBOL TYPE	SEE ALSO
	Movie clip symbol	11.6 Creating Movie Clip Animations 22.3 Animating via Scripted Property Changes
	Button symbol	11.15 Creating Buttons 18.5 Writing button Scripts for Flash Movie Navigation
	Graphic symbol	11.3 Creating Graphics 11.5 Using graphics in Tween Animations
	Component	19.1 Introducing V2 Components 19.2 Using components
	Bitmap	11.12 Creating Movie Clips from Bitmaps 13.2 Importing Bitmaps
	Sound	10.16 Adding Sound to a Timeline 13.4 Importing Sound 23.2 Defining a Sound Object
	Video	11.13 Creating Movie Clips from Videos 13.5 Importing Video
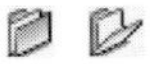	Closed and open layer folder	12.7 Organizing the Library
A	Font symbol	24.4 Creating Font Symbols

SYMBOL NAMES AND INSTANCE NAMES

Because a symbol name (i.e., the title that appears next to each symbol in the library) is for your benefit only, feel free to add spaces, punctuation, and make them as long as you need. An instance name, on the other hand, is used by ActionScript, and should follow the same rules as variable names. This means no spaces and no punctuation. Don't confuse the two sets of rules when creating these two names!

12.7 Organizing the Library

The Library panel is the repository for all assets included in the final SWF. Even a small Flash site can have a couple hundred separate items in the Library, so, as with a real Library, it is important that your Library panel is well organized.

Managing Symbols

If you widen the Library panel, you will see that it has a number of columns that are normally not visible, all of which are useful in managing your symbols.

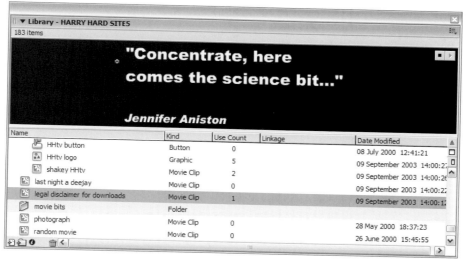

The Use Count column will tell you how many times each symbol appears on the Timeline. A use count of zero may mean that you have symbols in the Library that you can safely delete. You can also keep track of when symbols were last edited by looking at the Date Modified column.

Arranging, Deleting, and Renaming Symbols

All Library content is arranged alphabetically by default. You may sometimes want Flash to order by Kind, Use Count, or Date Modified. To order by any of these columns, simply click the column title.

It is a good idea to always use layer folders to keep your Library tidy. Layer folders work in exactly the same way as folders in your operating system. To create a layer folder, click the icon at the bottom of the Library.

To move symbols in and out of your folders, simply click-drag the icons.

Deleting symbols is performed with the icon.

To rename a symbol name, double-click it. The name will change to a text entry box, allowing you to enter a new name.

➡ 12.8 Working with Multiple Libraries

➡ 22.3 Attaching and Duplicating Movie Clips to the Stage

Library Panel
Ctrl L or F11
⌘ L or F11

——

You can use ActionScript to *attach* symbols to the Stage dynamically at runtime, which cannot be included in the use count. The clue as to whether this occurs is to look at the Linkage column; if there is something entered in it for a symbol with a zero use count, *don't delete the symbol* without checking whether your Action-Script requires it.

——

If the Use Count column contains only '-'s, you need to update it; in the Library panel menu (click the icon in the top right of the panel) select Update Use Counts now, or better still, check Keep Use Counts Updated).

——

After deleting a number of symbols from the Library, be sure to save the File with File > Save And Compact. Deleted content is not removed from the FLA until you do this.

——

Note that an unused symbol is not exported to the final SWF file unless you override Flash to make it do so.

12.8   Working with Multiple Libraries

Open External Library

Ctrl Shift O

⌘ O

Because there is no immediate way of telling whether a symbol is shared or not, consider using a naming strategy that makes it obvious; adding "_shared" to the end of all content in the shared Library is one way of doing it.

If you want to share many assets, consider putting them all into a folder called shared. Dragging this across from the shared folder will copy all assets at once. Any subdirectory structure you place in the folder will also be preserved.

Flash allows you to share between libraries during author time. This allows a number of designers working on the files that make up a site to access the same Library, while at the same time allowing control of this Library so that a change to a symbol within it will be reflected across the site files. You can also copy assets between libraries using simply drag and drop between libraries.

Setting Up a Shared Library and Copying Assets

1   Create a FLA whose Library contains all the assets you want to share. This is your Shared Library (for the purposes of this example, called shared.fla).

2   Create one or more FLAs that you want to have use the Shared Library (for example, sharedUser.fla).

3   With sharedUser.fla open, select File > Import > Open External Library. This will open the normal file browser, except it will be called Open Library. Find and select shared.fla. The Library for shared.fla will open (but not its Stage).

4   Drag all content you want to share from this new Library into sharedUser.fla's Library. These are your shared symbols. You can rename the versions in sharedUser.fla if you wish (but it is not recommended).

If you simply want to copy assets from one Library to another without sharing, you can treat the copied items as you would any other Library symbol, and you can ignore the next section.

Using a Shared Library

To manually update one or more shared symbols in the Library of sharedUser.fla (so that they change to the latest version in shared.fla):

1   In the Library of sharedUser.fla, select all symbols you want to update.

2   Right-click/⌘-click anywhere on the selection and select Update from the context menu that appears.

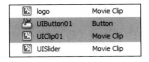

12.8 Working with Multiple Libraries *(continued)*

3 In the Update Library Items window that appears, check all entries that you want to update, then click Update. Note that any symbols you selected in step 2 that are not shared will not appear in the list.

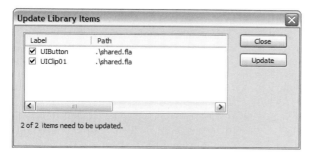

To automatically update shared symbols in the Library of `sharedUser.fla` (so that the versions found in `shared.fla` are used every time a SWF is published):

1 Right-click/⌘-click each symbol in turn and, in the context menu that appears, select Properties. This will bring up the Symbol Properties window.

2 At the bottom of this window, you will see the Source Section (if you don't, click the Advanced button). Check the Always Update Before Publishing box.

When you have a Library with shared items set to automatically update in it, you should edit the version in `shared.fla`, *not* the one in `sharedUser.fla`. Flash will warn you if this is about to happen. Editing a shared item in this way will make the item nonshared.

Note that you do not have to share all assets in the shared Library; you should only drag across the items that you actually want to use.

The final SWF created using runtime shared libraries will be exactly the same as a SWF that contains the same content but that was built without using shared libraries.

Note that the shared Library structure *does not* by itself contain any version control. This may be problematic on large projects.

12.9   Making Your Site Accessible

Accessibility panel
Alt F2
Option F2

———

You may have to enable accessibility features to add accessibility to components. The method to do this is enable-Accessibility().

———

When adding tab indexes, go up in steps of 5 rather than the more obvious 1. That way, you won't have to renumber everything every time you add a new button or movie clip.

———

You can use ActionScript to detect whether the current user has a screen reader. Accessibility.isActive() will be true if the user has a screen reader.

An accessible site is usable for the sight impaired using a screen reader. A screen reader converts a website into synthesized spoken text. For a screen reader to create intelligible output, you have to correctly format your site by adding meaningful text strings to each button and movie clip on the Stage. For a Flash site, this is done via the Accessibility panel.

The ⊕ icon will appear on the Properties inspector every time you select something that is compatible with accessibility options.

Defining Accessibility Options for the Whole SWF

You can define accessibility for the whole SWF by either clicking

■   the Stage and then clicking the accessibility icon

■   the Stage and then selecting Window > Other Panels > Accessibility.

In either case, the Accessibility Panel will appear:

Make Movie Accessible sets accessibility options.

Make Child Objects Accessible sets whether the screen reader looks at nested symbols or not.

Auto Label sets whether the screen reader reads text close to symbols as part of their description.

Defining Accessibility Per Item

Selecting a button or movie clip brings up slightly different Accessibility panels: they're identical, except that the Make Child Objects Accessible option isn't available for buttons.

You can choose to make buttons accessible or not. You can also specify a name, description, and keyboard shortcut that can be read by most screen readers. Finally, you can specify a numerical tab index number that specifies the order in which buttons are selected when the user presses the Tab key. Lower tab index numbers occur earlier in the tab ordering. The first three will be read by most screen readers. The user can use the last one to move between buttons and movie clips by pressing the Tab key; its value should be an integer number (lowest numbers come earlier in the tab ordering). The same options are available for a movie clip, except that you can also make nested movie clips and buttons ("child objects") be read or ignored by the reader.

In general, to design a site for accessibility:

■   Do not make accessible any movie clips that contain animation only.

■   Make all UI buttons accessible.

CHAPTER 13

Importing and Optimizing Media Assets

FLASH MX 2004 ENABLES you to import and optimize media assets such as images, sound, and video. Flash also allows you to import certain file formats directly into the authoring environment. This means you can create a file in Toon Boom Studio or Swift 3D, save it as a native format, and then import that native format right into Flash. You can maximize the quality of your work while speeding up the workflow.

FLASH WORKSPACE

AUTHORING TASKS

SCRIPTING TASKS

TESTING AND PUBLISHING TASKS

WHAT'S NEW

13.1 Media Overview

Often when building complete applications using Flash, you will want to import graphics from another program rather than creating all images and assets from within Flash. Having a thorough knowledge of image types and the differences between each type is very important if you want to keep file sizes as small as possible while maximizing image quality. GIF files are often a good choice if you require the use of transparency or have few colors within an image. JPEG images are better if you have lots of colors, such as a photograph, and JPEGs generally have good compression. A drawback to using JPEG images is that they are *lossy*, meaning that data is discarded to keep file sizes low. This can lead to images that look very poor if they are constantly saved and recompressed as JPEGs. You also cannot save transparency in JPEG files.

A good file format to use for importing images into Flash is PNG. PNG images are *lossless*, meaning they don't lose quality when being compressed and uncompressed, unlike JPEG images. PNGs also allow for transparency like GIF images, but they let you set the level of transparency (or opacity) in the file. This allows you to create PNG images with complex gradient transparencies that can easily be imported into Flash. As you will learn in this chapter, there are a few file formats that can only be imported into Flash if you have QuickTime Player 4 or greater installed.

Many other kinds of media can be imported into a Flash document. Video and sound files can be imported into a FLA file that can help you create multimedia presentations. Many kinds of video files, such as MOV and AVI, can be imported into Flash, as can audio files such as AIF, WAV, and MP3. Not only can the files be directly imported into and manipulated in Flash, but you can dynamically import selected media formats into a SWF file at runtime. These videos and sounds can be placed within movie clip or graphic symbols in Flash so you can manipulate them in many of the ways that a movie clip can be manipulated.

Native files from other programs can be imported into a FLA file. Adobe Illustrator, Photoshop, and Acrobat (PDF) files can be directly imported into Flash. With the aid of third-party importers, native Swift 3D, Plasma, and Toon Boom Studio files can also be imported into the Flash environment. All of these options help you build almost any kind of presentation you want without the quality loss you might experience when exporting it to a different file format. Importing native files also helps you retain some of the editability you might otherwise lose as well. Whether it's for a corporate slide show, web presentation, or instructional CD-ROM, Flash is truly a dynamic multimedia authoring tool.

13.2 Importing Bitmaps

Like most other formats, bitmap images can be imported into a FLA file. To import an image directly to the Stage, choose File > Import > Import To Stage. The image appears on the Stage after it imports, and a reference to the image is placed into the Library.

To import a bitmap image directly into the Library, choose File > Import > Import To Library. The bitmap appears in the Library with the same name as that of the file you imported. You can import JPEG, GIF, PNG, and BMP bitmap images into a FLA file. You will need Quick-Time 4 or greater to import the following image files: PTNG, PICT, QTIF, TGA, and TIF.

Remember that Fireworks PNG files can be imported as bitmap (rasterized) files or as vector files. To import a Fireworks PNG file, follow these steps:

1 Choose File > Import > Import To Stage or Import To Library. The Import dialog appears.

2 Choose a PNG file to import and click the Open button (or Import on the Mac). The Fireworks PNG Import Settings dialog appears.

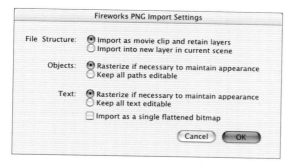

3 You can choose between several paired options in the Fireworks PNG Import Settings dialog. Here's what the options mean:

Import As Movie Clip And Retain Layers imports a PNG file within a movie clip symbol. Frames and layers are retained within the symbol.

Import Into New Layer In Current Scene imports a PNG file into the FLA on a new layer at the top of the layer stack on the Timeline. Fireworks layers are flattened, but Fireworks frames are retained.

Rasterize If Necessary To Maintain Appearance preserves PNG strokes, fills, and effects. This option can be enabled for both objects and text individually in order to maintain the look of your PNG.

Keep All Paths Editable ensures that Fireworks objects are still editable vectors after being imported. Some strokes, fills, and effects might be lost in the process. This option can be selected for both objects and text individually.

Import As A Single Flattened Bitmap will gray out the rest of the options in the Import dialog and flatten the PNG image into a single layer bitmap image.

➠ 13.3 Compressing Bitmaps

You can import JPEG images into a SWF file at runtime. However, you must make sure that the JPEG images are not saved as a progressive file. When you save the JPEG image, make sure this option is not selected.

You can import Fireworks PNG graphics, which retain editability if you import them as vectors. Alternatively, you can flatten the images and import them as a bitmap.

Bitmap images are treated like symbols in a FLA file. You can reuse the bitmaps, and they are similar to adding instances of a movie clip or button symbol.

13.3   Compressing Bitmaps

➡ 13.2 Importing
Bitmaps

_____

If you don't modify an image's properties, it will use the default JPEG quality defined in the Publish Settings or Export Flash Player dialogs. Both of these have a slider for JPEG quality that lets you specify a default bitmap quality between 1 and 100. The higher the value you set, the better the quality—but it also means a higher file size.

After an image is imported into Flash, you can modify its compression settings by using one of the three following methods:

- Highlight the symbol in the Library and click the Properties button near the lower-left corner of the Library.

- Right-click the symbol in the Library and select Properties from the contextual menu.

- Highlight the symbol in the Library and select Properties from the Options menu.

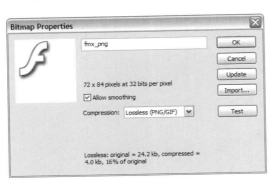

Each of these methods will display the Bitmap Properties dialog, where you can modify which compression method you wish to use; either Photo (JPEG) or Lossless (PNG/GIF). Selecting the Photo (JPEG) option allows you to specify whether to use the document's default quality or override the value and specify a new quality setting for the symbol.

Clicking the Test button in the bottom of the Bitmap Properties dialog will display the original file size of the image, the compressed size of the image, and the level of compression gained by compression.

In the Bitmap Properties dialog, you can change an individual image's compression settings by selecting Photo (JPEG) from the Compression drop-down menu, deselecting the Use Document Default Quality check box, and entering a new value in the Quality text field.

The upper-left corner of the Bitmap Properties dialog displays a preview of the image you are modifying. If the image is larger than the preview pane, you can move your mouse over the preview pane and move the image by using the hand cursor. If you modified the compression or quality, you can view your changes by clicking the Test button. You can zoom into the preview by right-clicking in the preview pane and selecting either Zoom In, Zoom Out, 100%, or Show All.

13.4   Importing Sound

Sound is imported into a Flash document in the same way as bitmap images. A single audio clip can be selected, or you can select multiple sound clips by holding down the Ctrl/Command or Shift keys while clicking filenames. Sound properties can be changed much the same way as changing the properties of the bitmap image. Selecting a sound in the Library and choosing Properties from the contextual menu, or clicking the Properties button in the Library, opens the Sound Properties dialog.

When defining a sound's properties in the Sound Properties dialog, there are five options for compression: default, ADPCM, MP3, Raw, and Speech.

➧ 6.11 Publish
       Settings

➧ 23.3 Starting and
        Stopping a
        Sound

You can preview the compressed audio in the Sound Properties dialog by clicking the Test button on the right-hand side of the dialog. If you want to stop the audio clip before it is finished playing, click the Stop button.

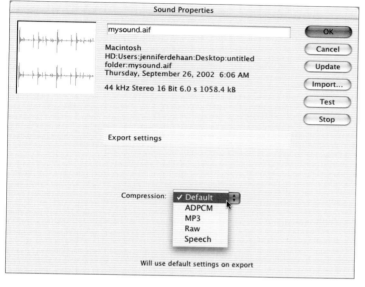

Default   Uses the sound settings defined in the Flash tab of the Publish Settings dialog.

ADPCM   Short for *adaptive digital pulse code modulation*, ADPCM tends to introduce noise and is a good choice for short event sounds such as button clicks. You can convert the audio clip to mono by enabling the Convert Stereo To Mono check box beside the Preprocessing label. There are four available sample rates to choose from: 5 kHz, 11 kHz, 22 kHz, and 44 kHz. 44 kHz offers CD-quality sound, but it also provides the least amount of compression, meaning your file sizes will be larger. 22 kHz is half the standard CD audio rate and a good choice for web audio. 11 kHz is one quarter the standard rate and typically the lowest quality you'd want. 5 kHz is barely acceptable for compressing a speech track.

Continues ●

The top of the dialog displays the original, uncompressed settings of the audio clip as well as its duration (in seconds). The bottom of the dialog displays the compressed settings, the new file size of the audio clip, and how much the audio was compressed. The rate of compression is displayed as a percentage of the original file size.

MP3 Selecting MP3 allows you to set a bit rate and quality level for the imported sound. The Bit Rate drop-down menu allows you to set a bit rate from 8 Kbps up to 160 Kbps. The default is 16 Kbps; using a higher rate results in larger file sizes. Flash recommends using 16 Kbps as a minimum value to ensure good results. The Quality drop-down menu provides three options:

Fast is the lowest quality but fastest compression.

Medium offers a higher sound quality than Fast but it's slightly slower to compress.

Best offers the best sound quality, although it takes the longest to compress.

Similar to ADPCM, you can set the sound to mono instead of stereo by checking the Preprocessing check box, although the check box is only enabled if the bit rate is set to 20 Kbps or higher.

Raw Sounds are exported without any sound compression. Similar to MP3 and ADPCM, you can convert the audio from stereo to mono by checking the Preprocessing check box. There are four options available for the sample rate: 5 kHz, 11 kHz, 22 kHz, and 44 kHz. The higher the sample rate, the higher the sound quality, but this results in a larger file size. You cannot set the sample rate to a value higher than the audio was imported at; meaning if an audio track is imported at 22 kHz, you cannot set the sample rate to 44 kHz within Flash.

Speech This option works best when exporting sounds containing speech. The sound will automatically be converted to mono, and you can select the same four values for Sample Rate as seen in previous options: 5 kHz, 11 kHz, 22 kHz, and 44 kHz. Using a higher sample rate results in larger file sizes but also yields the best quality.

13.5   Importing Video

Importing video into Flash MX 2004 is different from importing sounds or images. When you select a video file to import, Flash opens the Video Import wizard, which walks you through the steps of editing and optimizing the video before bringing it into Flash.

When importing the file, Flash provides the option of embedding the file within a Flash document or linking to an external QuickTime movie. Selecting the Embed Video In Macromedia Flash Document option leads to a wizard screen that asks whether you want to import the entire video or trim the video, create several small clips, and join them together.

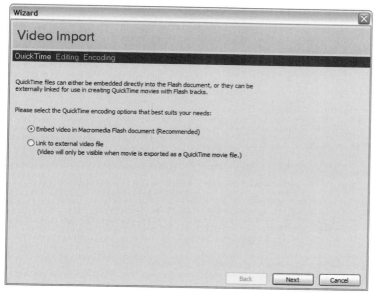

Selecting Edit The Video First takes you to the Editing (Customize) screen of the Video Import wizard, which allows you to create several smaller video clips from the clip being imported and optionally join the list of clips into a single clip after importing. (See the following section for details about this wizard screen.) By setting markers you can create new clips and add them to the list on the left-hand pane in the dialog.

The next wizard screen is the Encoding step, which allows you to use a predefined compression profile based on standard settings. You can edit an existing profile or create a new one by selecting Create New Profile from the drop-down menu. Clicking the Edit button beside a compression profile takes you to the Encoding (Compression Settings) screen of the wizard.

Video keyframes are different from Flash keyframes. When a video is compressed, the keyframe interval determines where the compressor will completely redraw the video frame. Between each video keyframe, pixel changes are approximated.

Continues ●

A video keyframe interval of 12 means that a new video frame is drawn every 12 frames. If your video is rendered at 30 frames per second, more than one keyframe per second is drawn.

Always try to import the best quality video possible. If you can import uncompressed video, you will get the best results. If you are importing video that someone else compressed, make sure you have the proper codec installed.

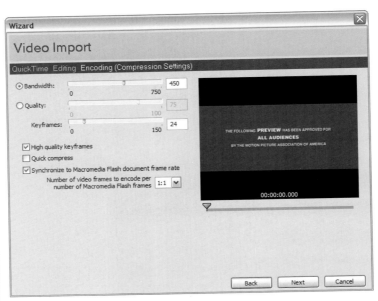

Here you can use sliders to define the bandwidth or quality of the video being compressed. You can also set the keyframe interval for the current video. The keyframe interval in video refers to the number of frames between each video keyframe. Typically, the lower the number, the higher the video playback quality. Setting the keyframe interval to 0 means that no keyframes will be created. This dialog also has three check boxes that determine overall video quality:

High Quality Keyframes Ensures that image quality is consistent in video keyframes.

Quick Compress Increases the speed in which the video is compressed, although it sacrifices video quality.

Synchronize To Macromedia Flash Document Frame Rate Synchronizes the frame rate of the embedded video to the frame rate of the Flash document.

13.6 Editing Video into Clips

If you want to edit a video clip before importing it into your Flash Library, choose either File > Import > Import To Stage or File > Import > Import To Library from the main menu to begin the Video Import wizard. Flash will open the Import or Import To Library window depending on whether you're importing the video to the Stage or Library. From this window, select the appropriate video file you want to import and click the Open button to continue the import process.

The next steps might vary depending on the type of video file you are importing. If you are importing a QuickTime movie, you will have the option to embed the video in Macromedia Flash document or to link to an external video file. Select the Embed option and click Next; the next step of the wizard allows you to choose whether you want to import the entire video or edit before importing. If you aren't importing a QuickTime movie, you are instead immediately taken to the option to import the entire video or edit the video first and are not given the option to link to an external file.

If you chose the Edit The Video First option while importing your video into Flash, you will be taken to the Editing (Customize) step of the Video Import wizard, where you can specify which video clip or clips get imported into Flash. Click the Next button, and you are taken to the Editing part of the Video Import wizard process.

➡ 13.5 Importing Video

➡ 13.7 Understanding Video Encoding Settings

➡ 13.8 Understanding Advanced Encoding Settings

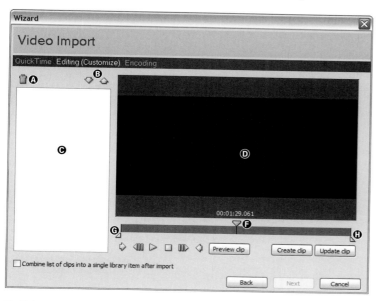

Ⓐ Delete currently selected clip

Ⓒ Scroll pane

Ⓔ Playhead time

Ⓖ In point

Ⓑ Move clip down, move clip up

Ⓓ Editing pane

Ⓕ Scrubber

Ⓗ Out point

Continues ●

13.6   Editing Video into Clips *(continued)*

Editing your video into
clips allows you to trim
out parts of the video
you don't need in your
FLA file. It also lets you
take parts of a longer
piece of footage into
Flash and manipulate
each part separately.

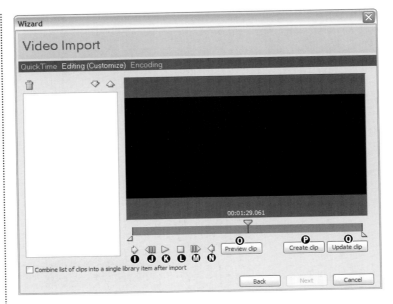

ⓘ Set in point to current scrubber position

Ⓙ Step back one frame

Ⓚ Play video from current playhead position

Ⓛ Stop playing

Ⓜ Advance by one frame

Ⓝ Set out point to current playhead position

Ⓞ Preview clip between current in point and out point

Ⓟ Create a new clip in the list

Ⓠ Update a selected clip in the list

To create a new clip, drag the in point and out point along the scrubber bar. To preview
the current clip, click the Preview Clip button. If you need to modify the clip, move the in
and out points until you are satisfied or move the playhead frame by frame using the step
back one frame and advance by one frame buttons in the controller. After you are happy
with the clip, you can click the Create Clip button to add the clip to the list in the list box
to the left of the Editing pane. If you want to create multiple clips, reposition the in and
out points and click Create Clip again to add another clip to the list. If you want to combine each of the clips in the list into a single video, click the check box in the lower left-
hand corner of the dialog. To reorder the clips within the list, select a clip in the list of
clips and click the move clip down or move clip up buttons.

When you have at least one clip in the list, you can click the Next button to proceed to the
Encoding step of the Video Import wizard.

13.7   Understanding Video Encoding Settings

During the encoding process of importing a video, Flash prompts you for the compression profile you want to use. Either clicking the Edit button beside an existing compression profile or selecting the Create New Profile option in the Compression profile drop-down menu takes you to the Encoding (Compression Settings) section of the wizard.

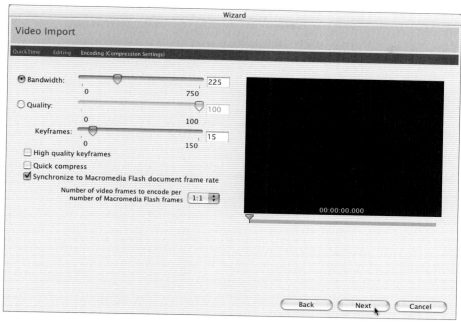

Flash uses the Spark codec to compress video footage. Sorenson Squeeze includes the Spark Pro codec that offers you several different options for encoding your videos.

Always try to encode the best quality video footage you can. Recompressing already compressed video can lead to unexpected results.

There are two main ways to control the quality of the imported video: setting the approximate bandwidth (in kilobits) using the Bandwidth slider, or setting the value using the Quality slider. The Quality slider sets a consistent quality for each frame while ignoring the available bandwidth. By moving the playhead along the scrubber bar, you can see a preview of the quality at different locations of the video. This lets you see if the quality is too low and needs to be adjusted without having to import the entire video and rerun the Video Import wizard. The third slider, Keyframes, sets the keyframe interval for the video clip. Video keyframes are different from keyframes in Flash. A video keyframe is where the importer draws an entire frame of video. Between each video keyframe, pixel placement is approximated depending on the two surrounding keyframes.

If you check the radio button beside Bandwidth, you are able to select the High Quality Keyframes check box, which ensures that image quality is consistent in the video keyframes. The second check box, Quick Compress, will increase the encoding speed but will cause the video to lose quality if there is a lot of motion in the clip. The final check box, Synchronize To Macromedia Flash Document Frame Rate, determines if the frame rate of the video clip will match the frames per second in the Flash document. Finally, there is a drop-down menu that allows you to set the number of video frames that are encoded for each Flash frame. If you want one imported frame in the video footage to play for every frame on the Flash Timeline, then leave it at the default ratio of 1:1.

13.8 Understanding Advanced Encoding Settings

When importing videos into Flash using the Video Import wizard, you can not only modify and create your own custom compression profiles, you can also define advanced settings such as color correction, resizing the video, and cropping options for your imported videos. After choosing the video file to import and optionally editing the video, you are taken to the Encoding step of the wizard.

In the Encoding step, click the Edit button beside the Advanced Settings drop-down menu to display the Encoding (Advanced Settings) screen. You can also create your own custom advanced settings profile by selecting the Create New Profile option from the Advanced Settings drop-down menu.

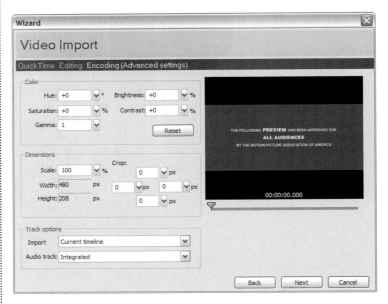

This step allows you to customize the color settings for the video clip as well as scale the imported video or crop the edges of the video clip. You can also remove the audio track from the video clip. The color in the movie can be modified by changing the following options:

Hue Sets the color value and is measured by a degree amount between $-180°$ and $180°$.

Saturation Measures the strength of the color by measuring the amount of gray in contrast to the color hue. You can set the saturation between -100% and $+100\%$. Higher values indicate more color, lower values indicate more gray.

Gamma Measures the lightness of the footage; a value can be between 0.1 and 1.8. Smaller values mean you will output a darker image.

13.8 Understanding Advanced Encoding Settings *(continued)*

Brightness Sets the lightness or darkness of the color using a value between –100% and +100%. More black is represented by small values and more white by higher values.

Contrast Measures the contrast between dark and light on a scale of –100% to +100%. Higher values mean more contrast.

In the Dimensions section of the dialog, you can set the scale of the imported video clip by moving the slider in the drop-down menu or by typing in a new percentage value in the input text field. Changing the scale updates the Width and Height values in the text fields below it.

You can also crop parts of the video by setting values in the four text fields under the Crop heading. Each of these fields crops the corresponding number of pixels off a different side of the video frames. For example, by setting the top text field's value to 100, you will crop 100 pixels from the top of the video. Flash makes it easy to see how the imported video will look by drawing a rectangle around the final video's dimensions. If you crop 100 pixels from the top of the video, a rectangle appears in the Preview area and shows you how much video will be removed when the video imports into Flash. You can also use the other three text fields to control how much video is cropped off the left, right, and bottom of the video.

The Track Options section has two drop-down menus: Import and Audio Track. The Import menu has the following choices:

Current Timeline Imports the clip(s) as a video object in the FLA's Timeline.

Movie Clip Imports the video as a movie clip. The movie clip is placed in frame 1 of the FLA.

Graphic Symbol Imports the video as a graphic symbol in the FLA's Timeline.

The final drop-down menu in the Track Options, Audio Track, has the following three choices:

Separate Imports the audio track as a separate symbol in the Library and removes it from the imported video.

Integrated Imports the audio as part of the video file.

None Discards the audio information in the imported video.

➥ 13.9 Optimizing Video

➥ 13.10 Creating Effects with Video

You cannot apply effects to a video object. However, effects can be applied to movie clips that contain video footage. Some effects can also be applied to graphic symbols.

13.9   Optimizing Video

It's always a good idea to keep a frame rate at a ratio of its original rate. Therefore, if you have a video that's created at 30 frames per second, you should always compress it at 15 fps or 7.5 fps. This typically affords better results.

It's always a good rule of thumb to keep videos as small and short as possible and to trim off as much footage as possible. This is easy to do when you have the video editing capabilities built right into Flash MX 2004.

When you use video in a SWF file, you have to be careful to take into account the people that will be viewing your presentation. If you make the video too large in frame or file size, some viewers might decide not to download your video. You can limit the size of a video by trimming its length as much as possible and making the frame size as small as you can. The frame size is the pixel height and width of the video itself. This size should typically be limited to 320 (width) by 240 (height) for a standard 4:3 aspect ratio video file. For less bandwidth, you could change the height and width to 160 (width) by 120 (height). Naturally, how you encode the video in the Video Import wizard also dictates how large or small your video is. This is largely controlled by your quality and keyframe settings.

Additionally, if you load too much video into the SWF player, playback might slow down or you could max out the RAM on someone's computer. It's always a good idea to test your SWF files on a variety of computers and also to place preloaders (progress bars) on SWF files containing video files. Older computers will really struggle to keep up with any SWF file at a high frame rate, particularly if it's playing a lot of video.

When you choose Synchronize To Macromedia Flash Document Frame Rate in the Video wizard, the Flash Timeline might drop frames to keep up with the video footage that you import. Dropping frames might speed up playback, but it also might make a video appear quite choppy. You should also be aware that if you choose to drop frames any Action-Script that's on a dropped frame will be lost.

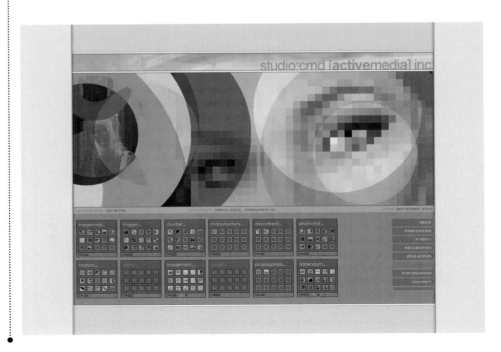

13.10   Creating Effects with Video

You cannot affect the properties of a video symbol in a SWF. However, you can control the properties of a movie clip in a SWF file. When you import video into a movie clip, you can control the movie clip as you would any movie clip and, by doing so, control the video. You can change the alpha, rotation, size, and other properties of the movie clip to make interesting effects on the video footage.

A video's Timeline is not the same as that of a movie clip. However, if a video is running along a movie clip Timeline you can control the video by controlling the Timeline within the movie clip. Therefore, you can stop and start the movie clip Timeline (or create Action-Script cues and the like) and affect the video as well.

Interesting effects can be created by layering video underneath other elements on the Stage. You might have vector illustrations, photos, or navigation that layers over the video. Creative presentations have been made by adding footage that appears to have a black or white background and then changing the FLA file to have the same color background. This creates the illusion of a transparent alpha layer in the video and can make for some very professional looking results. However, you will have to shoot your footage in a very specific way to achieve this effect.

You cannot retain a video's alpha layers when you import that footage into Flash MX 2004. You will have to mimic the transparency by editing the video or shooting it with a particular background color that you match with the SWF background color.

IMPORTING PLASMA

Discreet's Plasma software is a top-notch 3D animation software that's specifically targeted at the Web, including Flash and Director integration. Save a Plasma file into an SWFV file format and this file can be directly imported into Flash MX 2004. You can install the importer that's offered at www.discreet.com/support/plasma/download/download.php3 into the Importers folder, a process that's described in Sections 13.15 (for Swift 3D files) and 13.16 (for Toon Boom Studio).

13.11   Importing FreeHand Files

A new folder is created in the Library for the FreeHand elements that you import into the document. Inside this folder are the symbols from your Free-Hand file.

Macromedia FreeHand files are imported into Flash by choosing File **>** Import from the main menu. Importing a FreeHand file opens the FreeHand Import dialog. If you only want to display FreeHand files in the Import dialog, you can select the FreeHand (*.fh*; *.ft*) option from the Files Of Type drop-down menu. FreeHand files have extensions named after the version of FreeHand that they were created in. For example, if a file was created in FreeHand 9, it would have the extension `.fh9`; the extension for a file created in FreeHand MX would be `.fh11`.

This dialog allows you to control how the FreeHand document is imported and what pages you choose to import from the file. FreeHand MX integrates wonderfully with Flash MX 2004 because it allows you to preserve layers, text blocks, Library symbols, and pages when importing into Flash. FreeHand MX is also a vector graphics program; therefore, any vector images imported into Flash look crisp and do not appear blocky when you zoom in on the images.

When importing FreeHand files, the Mapping settings can cause a dramatic difference in how the file is imported:

Scenes Converts each page in FreeHand into a Flash scene.

Keyframes Converts each page in FreeHand into a keyframe in Flash.

The Layers section has three settings:

Layers Each layer in the FreeHand document is preserved and created as a new layer in the Flash document.

Keyframes Each layer in the FreeHand document is converted into a new keyframe within Flash.

Flatten All of the layers in the FreeHand document are flattened into a single layer within the Flash document.

In the Pages section you have two options, importing all pages from the FreeHand document or importing a range of pages from the FreeHand document. The final section of the FreeHand Import dialog is the Options section:

Include Invisible Layers Imports both visible and invisible layers into the Flash document.

Include Background Layer Imports the FreeHand document's background layer.

Maintain Text Blocks Imports the FreeHand text blocks so that they are still editable within Flash.

13.12   Importing Illustrator Files

Adobe Illustrator is a very common vector illustration program that saves in the AI file format. Importing Adobe Illustrator files is very similar to importing a FreeHand file. Adobe Illustrator files typically either have an .eps or .ai file extension and can be filtered by selecting the Adobe Illustrator (*.eps, *.ai) option from the Files Of Type drop-down menu. Importing an Illustrator document brings up the Import Options dialog.

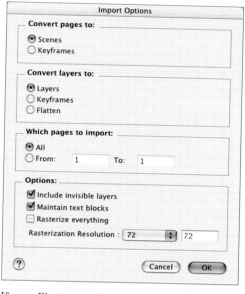

When importing a multipage Illustrator document, you can either convert each page within the Illustrator document into a new scene (or screen if you are working in a screens-based document) or a new keyframe.

➡ 13.11 Importing FreeHand Files

➡ 13.13 Importing PDF Files

➡ 13.14 Importing Photoshop Files

Illustrator is perhaps the most common program for creating drawings and technical illustrations. You will probably receive AI files from clients or friends for using with Flash.

If your Illustrator document has multiple layers, you can choose from the following options in the Convert Layers To section:

Layers Maintains existing layers from the Illustrator file.

Keyframes Converts existing layers in the Illustrator file into new keyframes in the Flash document.

Flatten Flattens layers in the imported file into a single layer in the Flash document.

If your Illustrator file has multiple pages, you can choose to import all layers or you can select a range of pages to import by specifying a value in the From and To text input text fields.

The Options section controls whether invisible layers are imported into the Flash document, or if only visible layers are included. You can also choose whether text blocks should be editable once they are imported into Flash by checking the Maintain Text Blocks check box.

Check the final check box if you want to rasterize everything. Enabling this option rasterizes the document, which means it converts the Illustrator file from vector into a bitmap image. When you select Rasterize Everything, Flash automatically deselects and disables the Maintain Text Blocks check box and forces you to set the Convert Layers To option to Flatten.

13.13   Importing PDF Files

PDF files are a very common format for saving text-based documents or documents with text and images. They are also a common way of saving image files on a Mac. Therefore, being able to import a PDF directly into Flash is very useful if you receive a lot of files from clients for importing into a FLA.

Adobe PDF files can be exported by many different programs, particularly Adobe Acrobat and Adobe InDesign. Many people use PDFs to export their page layouts, advertisements, and e-books. PDF is a more commonly used format for saving image files on the Macintosh as well. Flash MX 2004 introduced the ability to import PDF files. The import process for a PDF document is the same as when importing an Adobe Illustrator document. Although there is no option in the Files Of Type drop-down to filter only PDF files, you can select the All Post Script option, which displays files with the extensions `.ai`, `.pdf`, and `.eps`.

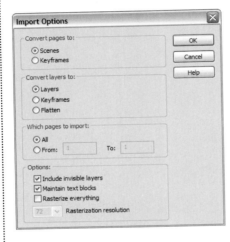

Scenes Converts each page in PDF into a Flash scene.

Keyframes Converts each page in PDF into a keyframe in Flash.

The Layers section has three settings:

Layers Preserves and creates each layer in the PDF document as a new layer in the Flash document.

Keyframes Converts each layer in the PDF document into a new keyframe within Flash.

Flatten Flattens all of the layers in the PDF document into a single layer within the Flash document.

In the Pages section you have two options: importing all pages from the PDF document, or importing a range of pages to be included from the PDF document. The final section of the PDF Import dialog is the Options section:

Include Invisible Layers Imports both visible and invisible layers into the Flash document.

Maintain Text Blocks Imports the PDF text blocks so that they are still editable within Flash.

Rasterize Everything Rasterizes the PDF pages.

If you are importing a PDF file with a lot of text, setting Maintain Text Blocks might not work like you expect it to. When Flash imports the file, each line is turned into its own separate text block, meaning if you had 30 lines of text on a page you would have 30 individual static text fields within your document. This can make editing text within Flash a very time consuming task.

13.14   Importing Photoshop Files

In order to import Photoshop files into Flash MX, you must have QuickTime 4 or later installed on your computer. Photoshop files have the extension .psd and can be filtered in the import dialog by selecting the (poorly named) PhotoShop 2.5, 3 Image option from the Files Of Type drop-down.

Choose File > Import and choose a Photoshop file to reach this dialog. Clicking Yes imports the Photoshop PSD image and places it in the Library or Stage, depending on what import method you selected. You can edit the file in Photoshop directly by right-clicking the symbol in the Library panel and selecting Edit With Photoshop from the contextual menu. You can also select the instance on the Stage with the Selection tool and click the Edit button within the Property inspector. If you want to edit the image in a different program, you can select Edit With from the Options menu, or right-click (or Control-click) the symbol and choose Edit With from the contextual menu.

If the PSD file changes outside of Flash (by editing the Photoshop file, for example), the image should automatically update within the FLA. However, you can easily update the image within Flash as well by choosing Update from the Options menu or by right-clicking (or control-clicking) the symbol in the Library and choosing Update from the contextual menu.

It is important to note that after a Photoshop file is imported into the Flash authoring environment, the graphic is rasterized (converted into a flattened bitmap) within Flash's Library and is no longer editable within Flash. That means the layers within the PSD are not transferred into Flash, and the text is no longer editable, although the Photoshop PSD file is not affected in any way.

➡ 13.11 Importing FreeHand Files

➡ 13.12 Importing Illustrator Files

➡ 13.13 Importing PDF Files

————

You can update the PSD in Flash by opening the Bitmap Properties dialog and clicking the Update button. This will update both the preview and the instance on the Stage.

————

You may notice a few slight problems if you try importing a PSD file with a complex gradient on a transparent background. In some circumstances, it might be a better idea to try using a transparent 24-bit PNG instead of a PSD because the PSD image sometimes appears to have a white glow around the edges of the gradient.

13.15 Importing Swift 3D Files

➡ 13.16 Importing
     Toon Boom
     Studio Files

Go to www.erain.com
for more information on
3D software that inte-
grates with Flash MX.

Swift 3D and the
importer are available
both for Mac and Win-
dows platforms.

Even though the erain
website says that the
importer is for Flash
MX, it also works with
Flash MX 2004—how-
ever, the directories
are slightly different
between versions.

Swift 3D is a third-party program that allows you to create 3D presentations and content and export them as SWFT files that can be used in your FLAs. It is quite easy to get started using Swift 3D.

There is a Swift 3D importer that enables you to directly import native Swift 3D SWFT files into a FLA file. This helps you in the following ways:

- Improves workflow by avoiding exporting, saving you time
- Allows you to take advantage of SmartLayers right in Flash
- Provides more flexibility over your 3D content
- Lets you make smaller, more resourceful SWF files

You will need to install the SWFT importer by copying a DLL file that is included with Swift 3D into the Importers folder within the Flash MX 2004 install directory. This directory is most likely:

```
Windows: C:\Program Files\Macromedia\Flash MX 2004\en\First Run\Importers
Mac: Applications\Macromedia Flash MX 2004\First Run\Importers
```

When you restart Flash and then import a file by choosing File > Import, an additional file type is added to the File of Type drop-down. This enables you to import the SWFT files into Flash. SWFT files are created by outputting the 3D file as this kind of file using Swift 3D's Preview and Export Editor. When you import the file into Flash, a new movie clip with the Swift 3D layers is created for you.

13.16 Importing Toon Boom Studio Files

Toon Boom Studio is a comprehensive two-dimensional animation program perfect for animation professionals and easy to use for those who are new to animation. Featuring support for all major sound and image formats, Toon Boom Studio features a powerful array of drawing tools as well as tools to simplify lip-synching and amazing three-dimensional camera and scene planning. You can download a trial copy of the latest version of Toon Boom Studio from the manufacturer's website at www.toonboomstudio.com. This site also features downloadable clip art, various tutorials, and the Toon Boom Studio importer for Flash MX (for both Windows and Mac OSX).

The Toon Boom Studio importer allows you to import .tbp projects directly in Flash MX 2004. You can control which scenes, layers, and frames are imported into your Flash document and whether sound files and any sound edits applied in Toon Boom Studio are imported into the FLA. The importer tool can preserve the order of the layers within your animations or compress the animations onto a single layer. To install and use the importer, follow these steps:

1 Download the importer for Flash MX from Toon Boom Studio's website.

2 Move the contents of the ZIP file into the Importers directory, which is probably at:

Windows: C:\Program Files\Macromedia\Flash MX 2004\en\First Run\Importers
Mac: Applications\Macromedia Flash MX 2004\First Run\Importers

3 Restart Flash to copy the files into your profile folder within Documents and Settings.

4 When you restart Flash, you will be able to import Toon Boom Studio project files by selecting File > Import > Import To Stage or Import To Library, and choosing Toon Boom Studio (*.tbp) from the Files Of Type drop-down menu.

If you are importing more than one scene, the Toon Boom Studio importer requires that you import all elements and frames as well.

Even though the Toon Boom Studio website says that the importer is for Flash MX, it works perfectly with Flash MX 2004. The only difference is that the directories are slightly different between the two versions.

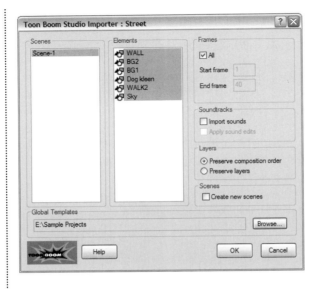

After you find a Toon Boom Studio project file to open, the Toon Boom Studio Importer dialog appears. This dialog allows you to select which scenes and elements will be imported into your Flash document. By default, each element in every scene of the Toon Boom document is imported into Flash; however, you can choose to import only the elements you want by selecting them. Different scenes and elements can be selected by clicking items in the list box with your mouse. If you want to select several consecutive elements or scenes, click one item and drag your mouse over the other items in the list. You can also use the Shift and Ctrl keys to select multiple items.

Within the Frames section, you can choose to either import all frames within the scene or a range of frames. If you are only importing a couple of elements from the Toon Boom Studio file, the importer will tell you how many frames the elements are on.

The Soundtracks section allows you to import the sound into the Flash document or discard the sound when the file is imported. The second check box, Apply Sound Edits, defines whether the audio fade-ins and fade-outs are preserved. If this check box is deselected, all edits and fades will be lost and entire sounds will be imported into the Library. Deselect the Import Sounds check box to disable the Apply Sound Edits check box as well.

The Layers section of the importer determines how layers are handled in Flash MX 2004. Choosing Preserve Composition Order imports all selected elements into a single layer, whereas selecting the Preserve Layers option imports the elements into their own layers.

The final check box, Create New Scenes, creates additional scenes as needed during the import process. If you uncheck this option, Flash imports all elements into the current scene.

CHAPTER 14

Working with Extensions and Commands

ONE OF THE MOST powerful features of Flash MX 2004 is how it allows developers and designers to add new extensions, also known as modules or plug-ins, into the Flash application. Some excellent free third-party extensions built for Flash MX are almost mini-applications in themselves: a free version of Macromedia's DataGrid component built for Flash MX, a rich text editor, photo gallery components, and a text effects extension, to name a few. Standalone third-party applications, including Swift 3D, allow you to convert two-dimensional artwork into three-dimensional objects, which can be rotated and animated and imported back into Flash.

- 14.1 **Installing and using the Extension Manager**
- 14.2 **Finding extensions on the Web**
- 14.3 **Installing and uninstalling extensions**
- 14.4 **Installing and uninstalling components**
- 14.5 **Installing and uninstalling commands and behaviors**
- 14.6 **Installing the FLV Exporter and understanding codecs**
- 14.7 **Exporting FLV files**

14.1   Installing and Using the Extension Manager

———

Macromedia Extension Manager 1.6 (or greater) is required to install extensions for Flash MX 2004.

———

The Extension Manager allows you to install extensions for Flash MX 2004, Dreamweaver MX 2004, and Fireworks MX 2004 as well as Flash MX, Dreamweaver MX, and Fireworks MX.

———

You can launch the Extension Manager directly from Flash by selecting Help > Manage Extensions.

Macromedia's Extension Manager allows you to install new extensions like components, effects, tools, screen types, behaviors, and commands and manage existing ones from a single interface. The Extension Manager can be downloaded from:

`http://www.macromedia.com/exchange/em_download/`

After downloading the Extension Manager, close all open Macromedia products and run the installer. When you have installed the Extension Manager, it can be accessed via Windows' Start menu or from within Flash by selecting Help > Manage Extensions. Components are distributed using MXP files, which can be installed into Flash using the Extension Manager 1.6 (or above).

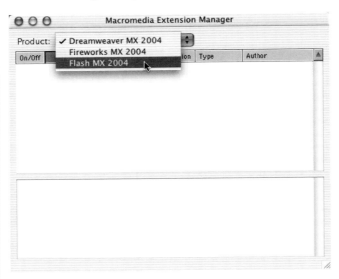

Use the Extension Manager to organize the extensions on your system for your installed Studio MX 2004 (or earlier) software.

Find out more information about the Extension Manager in the following PDF:

`http://download.macromedia.com/pub/exchange/mxi_file_format.pdf`

After you install the Extension Manager, a `ReadMe.htm` document opens. Make sure that you check out the release notes for the software listed on that page, which are also found at

`http://www.macromedia.com/support/extension_manager/releasenotes/1/`
`releasenotes_1_6.html`

14.2　Finding Extensions on the Web

The most common place to find extensions and components for Flash is at the Macromedia Exchange at www.macromedia.com/go/flash_exchange. You can access the Exchange site directly from Flash by selecting Help > Flash Exchange, or by selecting Macromedia Flash Exchange from Flash's Start page. These components and extensions are created by Macromedia as well as the Flash community and for the most part are free of charge, although some third-party extensions (plug-ins) are sold commercially. Sometimes you will be required to pay for extensions or components before you are allowed to download them, although this typically means you will receive a higher quality component or extension that includes some level of support.

➡ 14.1　Installing and Using the Extension Manager

➡ 14.3　Installing and Uninstalling Extensions

➡ 14.4　Installing and Uninstalling Components

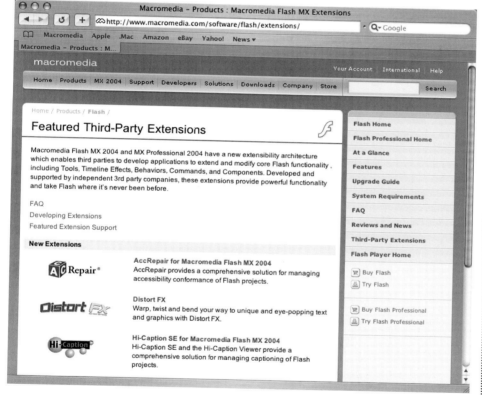

You can access the Macromedia Flash Exchange from Flash MX 2004 by selecting Macromedia Flash Exchange from the Start page or by selecting Help > Flash Exchange from the main menu.

———

At the time of writing, third-party extensions are largely for sale, mostly because documentation is not publicly available. If you do purchase these extensions, you will receive a professionally developed extension. It's likely over time that, when documentation and help is available to the community at large, more inexpensive or free extensions will become available.

———

You can access Macromedia Exchange directly from the Extension Manager by clicking the Macromedia logo to the right of the drop-down menu. You can also access the Exchange by selecting File > Go To Macromedia Exchange.

Macromedia has published a list of companies that have created third-party extensions for Flash MX 2004. The list, located at www.macromedia.com/software/flash/extensions/, includes extensions that perform text effects, image effects, and Flash charts as well as tools to help convert your two-dimensional text and artwork into three-dimensional animations.

Numerous sites are also dedicated to providing components for Flash MX and Flash MX 2004. Some sites that exclusively feature components are www.flashcomponents.net, ghostwire.com, and www.flashcomponent.com.

14.3   Installing and Uninstalling Extensions

_____

You can also import publish profiles into Flash using the Publish Settings dialog.

Extensions are separate files that you can install on your computer that are equivalent to the plug-ins that you find in other programs such as Photoshop. When Flash MX 2004 was released, many companies began offering third-party extensions. Macromedia even published a list of extensions on their website at www.macromedia.com/software/flash/extensions/. This list includes charts, text effects, and image effects as well as tools to help you convert your 2D artwork into 3D animations.

Installing extensions often requires that you download an EXE file, and each of these works in its own way. They typically involve some sort of licensing system with serial numbers or activation when you install. Where you access the new functionality depends on the extension you install. For example, if you install one with effects, then you will find the new functionality under the Insert > Timeline Effects submenu.

Some extensions appear within the common libraries, the Components panel, or the Behaviors panel and might be installed using the Extension Manager instead of an EXE file. If you install an extension using an EXE, you might have an uninstall option offered in a new directory the installer created. Consult the support documents supplied by the third-party extension creator for more information. If you installed the extension using an MXP and wish to disable the extension, you can use the On/Off check box or select the File > Remove Extension option, or you can select the extension and click the garbage can icon.

FINDING HELP FOR DEVELOPING EXTENSIONS

Creating extensions, components, and behaviors can quickly become complicated. However, there is a lot of online information and help on how to build components. At the time of writing, information about building components and extensions for Flash MX 2004 is not yet released. However, forums like www.flashmx2004.com are a good place to start for additional help and information from members of the community. You can also find information on the latest available resources on extensions and components at www.flash2004.com/resources.

14.4 Installing and Uninstalling Components

To install components using Macromedia Extension Manager, launch Extension Manager, then choose File > Install Extension or press Ctrl+I to open the Select Extension To Install dialog. (These commands are phrased this way because components are one type of extension.) From this dialog, you can select any MXP file you wish to install.

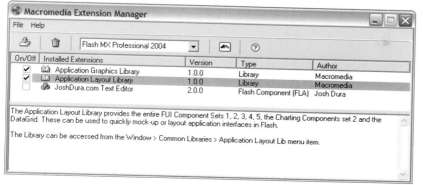

After components have been installed, they can be toggled, sorted, or removed using the Extension Manager. Click a component to see a brief description of it as well as additional information by the author of the component, such as how to access it in Flash.

Components can be installed using the Extension Manager or by manually moving the component files into the proper directories. If you are working in a multiuser environment (Windows NT, 2000, XP, or Mac OS X), the Extension Manager installs components and extensions for the currently logged in user only. This allows each user to have their own set of extensions and components installed that is not available to all users on the machine. If you are using a Windows operating system, you can find the user configuration folder in the following folder:

`C:\Documents and Settings\<USERNAME>\Local Settings\Application Data\ Macromedia\Flash MX 2004\en\Configuration`

Of course, this path differs slightly if you've changed the location of the `Documents and Settings` folder or changed your default settings in any way. The `Configuration` folder contains dozens of directories, including `Behaviors`, `Components`, `Effects`, `Libraries`, `Panel Sets`, and `Templates`.

In order to see all of these folders, it might be necessary to modify your folder options so your Windows Explorer displays hidden files. This is accomplished by selecting Tools > Folder Options from Windows Explorer's main menu. In the Folder Options dialog, click the View tab and, in the Advanced Settings pane, make sure that Show Hidden Files And Folders is selected under the Hidden Files And Folders folder.

➡ 14.1 Installing and Using the Extension Manager

➡ 14.2 Finding Extensions on the Web

➡ 14.3 Installing and Uninstalling Extensions

➡ 14.5 Installing and Uninstalling Commands and Behaviors

Components panel
Ctrl F7
⌘ F7

Component Inspector panel
Alt F7
Option F7

———

If you are installing a Flash MX (version 6) component, the help documentation that installs into the Reference panel in Flash MX is not compatible with the Help panel in Flash MX 2004 unless it is rewritten by the component's creator to be so.

———

If you install components by directly placing them in the user's folder, you will be unable to manage them via the Extension Manager.

14.5 Installing and Uninstalling Commands and Behaviors

Behaviors panel
Shift F3

————

Commands are saved as Flash JavaScript files and have a JSFL extension. If you create your own custom commands using the History panel, then the JSFL file will most likely be saved to the Commands directory.

When it comes to software, "command" is often used as an ordinary, generic word. But a *command* is something specific in Flash: it's a tool for saving or remembering an action and repeating tasks numerous times. In some ways, Flash commands are similar to "macros" or "actions" in other applications. You can download commands from the Flash Exchange, or create them yourself by saving steps from the History panel. To create your own custom commands, follow these steps:

1 Perform a common task in Flash.

2 Open the History panel.

3 Select the step or steps in the History panel that you want to save as a command.

4 Right-click (or Control-click) the History panel and choose Save As Command from the contextual menu.

A dialog appears and prompts you for a name for this command. After you have assigned a name for your command, you can replay it by choosing the command name from the Commands menu. You can also choose Commands > Run Command, in which case an Open dialog appears and you can locate a specific command on your hard drive to execute.

You can easily rename commands and download them by using the Manage Saved Commands dialog, accessed by selecting Commands > Manage Saved Commands. Downloading new commands from the Internet is as simple as going to the Flash Exchange, which you can do by selecting Commands > Get More Commands. Commands for the current users are then stored in the following folder:

```
C:\Documents and Settings\<USERNAME>\Local Settings\Application Data\
Macromedia\Flash MX 2004\en\Configuration\Commands
```

Commands placed in this folder are visible in the Commands menu in Flash.

Behaviors make your SWF files more interactive without your having to write Action-Script code in the Flash authoring environment. Behaviors are added to symbol instances, components, screens, or frames and can be triggered on a handful of different *events*. To manually install a behavior, you can move it to the user's folder. This can be found at

```
C:\Documents and Settings\<USERNAME>\Local Settings\Application Data\
Macromedia\Flash MX 2004\en\Configuration\Behaviors
```

After placing a behavior in the Behaviors folder, you must restart Flash or select Reload from the Options menu in the Behaviors panel. To delete a behavior, simply delete the behavior's XML file from the user's folder listed above.

14.6 Installing the FLV Exporter and Understanding Codecs

The Flash Video (FLV) Exporter comes with Flash MX Professional 2004 but must be installed separately. The FLV Exporter allows you to export video from professional video editing and encoding applications such as Apple Final Cut Pro, Adobe After Effects, QuickTime Pro 6.3, Discreet Cleaner 6 or XL, Avid Express, or Avid Media Composer directly into Flash. Video support and playback in Flash Player 7 has been radically improved and even allows for dynamic loading of FLV files at runtime, a task that was previously possible only if you were using Flash Communication Server. External FLV files with dynamic playback are a huge boost for the Flash video movement because they eliminate many of the limitations that previously existed when working with Flash and video.

Progressive download allows you to download the file from a web server and have the video begin playing before the entire video has been downloaded, although it does not "stream" the video in the true sense of the term. Although video capabilities in Flash MX 2004 are not nearly as great as those found in Flash Communication Server, they have greatly increased from previous versions of Flash.

To install the Flash Video Exporter, double-click the Flash Video Exporter installer file. You will be prompted to accept a license agreement before you can proceed. After you've accepted the license agreement, the installer can begin copying the necessary files to your hard drive. Click Next to continue and begin the installation. Click Close to quit the installer after the installation is complete.

Some files are very large, so they need to be compressed with the help of special software, including the FLV exporter. When working with video files, a term you will often hear referred to is Codec which is the kind of software that is used within a program that compresses files. Codec is an acronym for compression/decompression and is software that reduces the amount of disk space required by large files. For example, if you had a video that you shot with a DV camera, the raw, uncompressed footage would be much too large to stream over the Internet, perhaps measuring a few gigabytes. However, if the video was compressed it would be a significantly smaller file size that could be downloaded by visitors on many different Internet connections. To reduce the size of the video, the footage is compressed, and when the user plays back the footage it is decompressed and displayed on their screen. This would allow you to convert a 10-second, 20 MB raw video file to a 1 MB clip suitable for downloading online. Common video codecs include Sorenson Spark, Sorenson Video 3, RealVideo, H263, Cinepak, and MPEG.

The Spark codec is based on the H263 codec, which is a common codec used for video conferencing. The codec is impressive because it is not intensive on the CPU.

The codecs being used for FLV playback are the same as in earlier versions of the Flash Player, thus making the files compatible between the two versions.

If you are using Cleaner XL to create FLV files, you need to download the latest (free) service pack from www.discreet.com/support/cleanerxl/.

14.7 Exporting FLV Files

The FLV Exporter is only available if you have installed Flash MX Professional 2004.

After you install the FLV Exporter (for Flash MX Professional), you can export FLV video from many different video editing programs. If you have QuickTime Pro installed, you can easily convert a movie from a MOV to an FLV by selecting File > Export. In the Save Exported File As dialog, make sure that the value in the Export drop-down menu is Movie To Macromedia Flash Video (FLV) in order to save it as an FLV. To customize the export settings, click the Options button beside the Export drop-down menu to open the Flash Video (FLV) Exporter dialog.

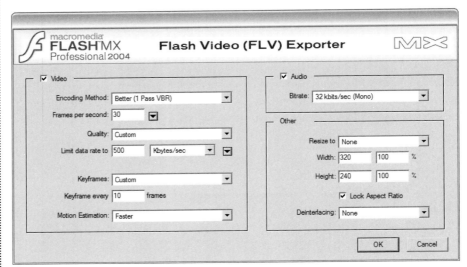

This dialog allows you to set the encoding method, quality, and various video and audio settings that will be used when exporting your movie. There is even an option to resize the movie from its original dimensions. Once you're satisfied with the settings, click OK to close the FLV Exporter options and return to the Save Exported File As dialog, then click OK to encode the movie.

When the SWF file has been exported into an FLV, you will be able to load the video file dynamically using Flash MX Professional's Media Components or by using ActionScript to load the file at runtime using `NetStream` and `NetConnection`.

THE LANGUAGE OF FLASH EXTENSIONS AND COMPONENTS

JSFL is "Flash JavaScript," the language used to create extensions (plug-ins) for Flash. This language will be recognizable to you if you are an experienced ActionScript user. ActionScript 2 is used to build components, which are wrapped up into SWC files, which are "compiled clips." This helps stop people from finding the code inside your components. However, keep in mind that there are tools that can be used to look inside (decompile) your SWF and SWC components.

Color Section

Color Panels

In Flash MX 2004, there are several ways you can select colors using color controls, swatches, and palettes. You can also choose colors using the System color pickers, Color Swatches panel, Color Mixer panel, and color controls in the Tools panel. How you arrange and choose colors differs depending on how you arrange your palettes, as well as the operating system you are using.

The Color Swatches Panel

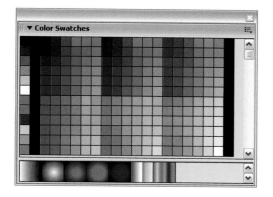

The Color Swatches panel allows you to add, remove, and save swatches and palettes in Flash. Gradients can be chosen from the bottom row.

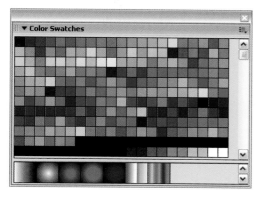

You can reorder the arrangement of the Color Swatches panel. Choose Sort By Color from the Color Swatches panel Options menu to reorder the swatches to the arrangement seen here. The best palette arrangement depends on which one you find the easiest to select colors from.

Continues

Color Panels *(Continued)*

The Color Mixer Panel

The Color Mixer panel is where you can choose colors from a palette or by mixing colors. You can use a hexadecimal value or use RGB or HSB modes and enter values and percentages into the text fields on the right. The current color selection is the large green box in the bottom left of the panel.

Gradients can be created in the Color Mixer panel as well. The current gradient is the large box that changes from red to white in the lower left corner. Choose a radial or linear gradient from the drop-down menu, and then click the color pointers (here one is red and another white) to change the colors in the gradient. You can also create bitmap fills in this panel by choosing Bitmap from the drop-down menu. A dialog box opens where you can browse to a bitmap on your hard drive, which is then loaded into your document to use as a fill.

Color Pickers

On the Mac, you can Option+double-click the Fill or Stroke color control to open the System color picker, or you can click the Color Wheel button at the top right of the Color pop-up window. On the Mac there are several different ways to access the system colors in the System color picker. Click one of the buttons at the top of the dialog (here "Color Wheel" is selected) to select a mode for choosing a color.

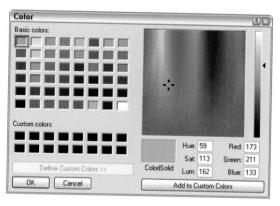

The system color picker differs on the Windows and Mac operating systems. You can access these windows by clicking the Color Wheel button in the upper right of the Color pop-up window (the windows that pop up when you click a color control button). Alternatively, in Windows, you can Alt+double-click the Fill or Stroke color control to open this system color picker.

Color Spaces

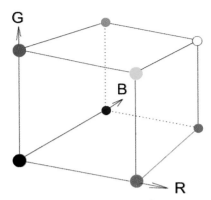

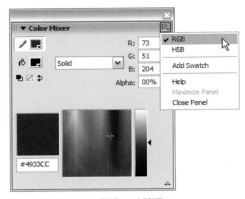

The RGB model uses three color components: Red, Green, and Blue. The RGB model is best visualized as a cube, with the three components representing the x, y, and z axes. The corner points of the resulting cube are black, white, and the primary and secondary colors, and the diagonal line between the black and white corners contains neutral grays. When changing the R, G, and B sliders in the Color Mixer, you are effectively selecting the color of the point (R,G,B) in the (x,y,z) space of the cube.

To switch between RGB and HSB sliders, select the Color Mixer panel's menu (via the icon at the top-right corner) and select either RGB or HSB.

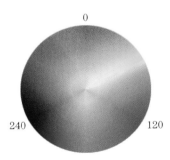

In the HSB color wheel, colors on the perimeter are fully saturated (S = 100%) and the center of the wheel is 0% saturation (no color), or white. Reds are at around 0 degrees, with pure red at the top edge of the wheel. Similarly, green and blue are at 120 and 240 degrees, respectively. When changing the HSB sliders in the Color Mixer, the angle is the H value, the S value is the distance from the center of the circle, and the B value is the depth downward in the HSB cone (see the following section for more information on the HSB cone).

Relationship between HSB, RGB, and the Color Mixer

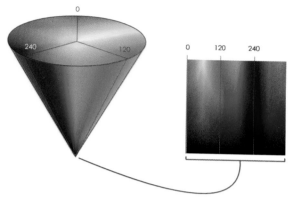

The full HSB color model is best represented as a cone, with the color black being the lower tip of the cone. The Color Mixer's rectangular area is the unwrapped side edge of the cone, with the lower edge of the rectangle being the tip stretched out, and the top edge being the perimeter of the cone. The vertical bar in the Color Mixer that varies brightness is analogous to moving up and down the cone.

In the RGB model, the rectangle is an approximation of the three cube faces that do not include the white corner.

Video Color

You can change many color values and attributes when you import videos into Flash using the Video Import Wizard. For example, the hue, gamma, and brightness of the video footage can be changed when you import the footage. Here are several different ways that you can control the color and quality of the video in the Video Import Wizard. These color settings are found under Advanced Settings in the Encoding section of the wizard. Click the Edit button to change the settings seen here.

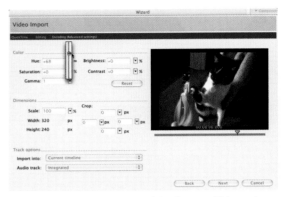

Original This is the original appearance of the video that is being imported into Flash. Notice the color values of the video are somewhat dark; you can change this with the controls in the Video Import Wizard.

Hue Changes the color value of the footage. This setting helps you correct the color if there are problems with your footage. The range here is between –180 degrees and 180 degrees (*degrees* refer to the position on a color wheel).

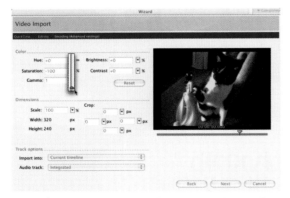

Saturation Changes the level of gray in your footage, in proportion to the amount of color. You can take away color from the footage or add to it. You can desaturate the video by dragging the slider to the bottom (as shown at left) or saturate it by dragging the slider upward (as shown at right).

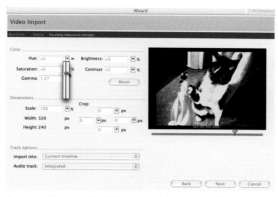

Gamma Controls the lightness of the video, which is particularly useful if you want to control the gamma for computers that do not have correction (like many Windows machines). The values here range between –0.1 and 1.8.

Brightness Changes the footage by adding more black or white. This can help if you have a video that is leaning toward one end of the scale in brightness, which might make the action hard to make out.

Contrast Changes the amount of contrast between the light and dark areas of your footage. Make the lights and darks more similar to each other by dragging the slider downward (less contrast). Make the changes between light and dark more apparent by dragging the slider upward (more contrast).

Compression Greatly affects the quality of the video as well. When you highly compress a video (perhaps by decreasing quality), you will notice blockiness in the imported video. You can see a great difference between these two files. The video on the left uses a high-quality compression (100), while in the video on the right the quality has been reduced to 50.

Gallery

`www.chewman.net`

Though he formerly created digital imagery solely for the Web, James Chew has expanded his focus to design for other mediums as well, including print and CD-ROM. Chew endeavors to push personal boundaries, and his work has evolved and taken form over the years. Working first with Macromedia Flash, Adobe Photoshop, Discreet 3ds max, and more recently an integration of Internet programming technologies, Chew's intention is to cultivate a firm foundation in a gamut of design applications and programming languages

© Adam Phillips
www.biteycastle.com

These are screenshots from a couple of the animated shorts on Adam Phillips' website, www.biteycastle.com. For any illustration or animation work, Phillips uses Flash and sometimes tweaks images for blur and other effects using Fireworks.

All Phillips' work is drawn directly into Flash using a Wacom Intuos 9″×12″ graphics tablet. Occasionally for movies he uses swift3D v3 for 3D elements or guides for animating backgrounds.

One of the core Flash skills is "basic" tweening, but when used by a real animation master, the effects can be anything but basic. Phillips is a trained Disney animator, and it shows! Look for future collaborations between Phillips and one of the authors of this book, Sham Bhangal.

Continues

Gallery *(Continued)*

© Adi Sideman at Oddcast, Inc
`vhost.oddcast.com`

Flash is a very versatile web tool, so it comes as no surprise that it is used for novel and nonstandard applications. Oddcast's Site Pal (`vhost.oddcast.com`) allows you to create a customized virtual host (the "[V]host"), a Flash-powered talking avatar.

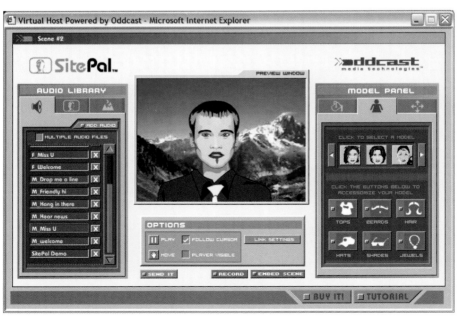

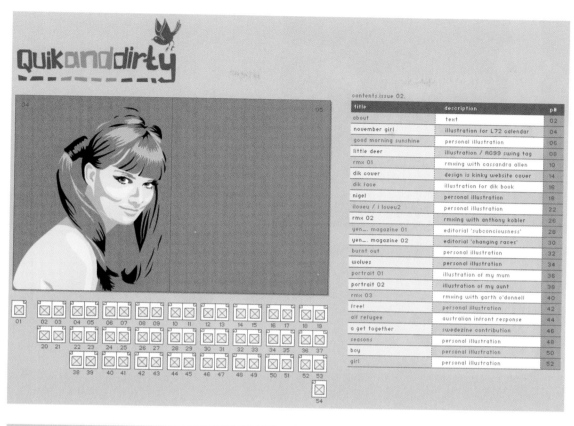

contents.issue 02.

title	description	p#
about	text	02
november girl	illustration for L72 calendar	04
good morning sunshine	personal illustration	06
little deer	illustration / AG99 swing tag	08
rmx 01	rmxing with cassandra allen	10
dik cover	design is kinky website cover	14
dik face	illustration for dik book	16
nigel	personal illustration	18
iloveu / i loveu2	personal illustration	22
rmx 02	rmxing with anthony kobler	26
yen_. magazine 01	editorial 'subconciousness'	28
yen_. magazine 02	editorial 'changing races'	30
burnt out	personal illustration	32
wolves	personal illustration	34
portrait 01	illustration of my mum	36
portrait 02	illustration of my aunt	38
rmx 03	rmxing with garth o'donnell	40
free!	personal illustration	42
oil refugee	australian infront response	44
a get together	swedezine contribution	46
seasons	personal illustration	48
boy	personal illustration	50
girl	personal illustration	52

© Anna Augul

anna@quikanddirty.com, www.quikanddirty.com

One of the emerging uses of the Internet is web art. Anna Augul's site Quikanddirty shows Flash used in Web art and illustration. The clean lines and vibrant colors created by vector art are used by Augul to good effect, creating a distinct and retro style.

Continues

© Magnetic Studio—Digital Artist: Peter Lacalamita
www.magneticstudio.com

Magnetic Studio is a Toronto-based company led by Peter Lacalamita that specializes in digital art and animated content. Clients include Pepsi, Yoplait, Hypnotic, MTR Entertainment, Atom Films, Microsoft, Pearson Education, and Macmillan Publishing. Magnetic's animated shorts have appeared in festivals around the globe, including Seoul Net and Cinema Paradise. Preview this work online at **www.magneticstudio.com**.

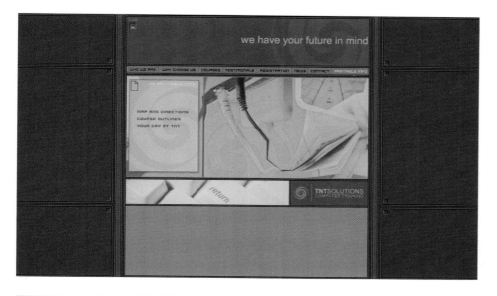

www.studiocmd.com, www.nemesisgroup.ca

Jason Chesebrough is a digital artist at studio:cmd [activemedia] incorporated. (www.studiocmd.com) and creative director at Nemesis Group, Inc. (www.nemesisgroup.ca).

Continues

Gallery *(Continued)*

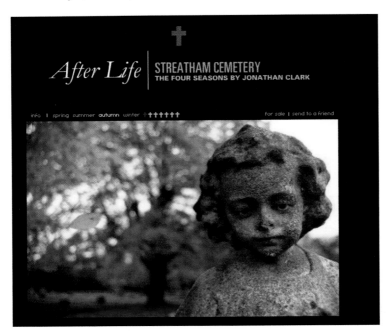

© Jonathan Clark
www.jonathan-clark.com/
afterlife

Ever had that feeling that the paintings and pictures in the room were looking at you or, even worse, moving? That's exactly what they do in Jonathan Clark's After Life—still photography that is anything but "still."

What lifts this site from the ordinary is the way the core idea is so well implemented, with excellent typography and layout and a subtle but atmospheric soundtrack.

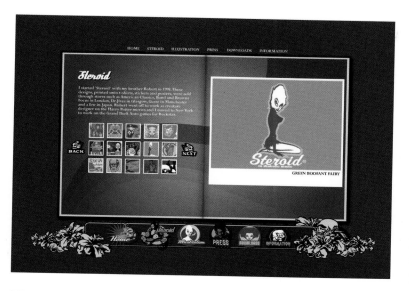

© Stephen Bliss
www.stephenbliss.com

Stephen Bliss has been working for several years at Rockstar Games (on, for example, covers for the Grand Theft Auto game series), but he needed a personal website because people were showing increasing interest in his designs. He wanted to show such work as his designs for Burton snowboards, a CD cover for trip-hop group Massive Attack, and T-shirts he had produced for his company, Steroid.

Bliss worked with Futaba Hayashi, who did the site design and production, discussing her art direction and animation ideas to make the site (www.stephenbliss.com) both informative and entertaining.

COLOR PANELS

COLOR PICKERS

COLOR SPACES

VIDEO COLOR

GALLERY

Continues

Gallery *(Continued)*

© Peter O'Dwyer SIXSIDIA
www.sixsidia.com, www.zachgold.com

From the quirky to the corporate, all from one designer…

Flash is a really cool medium for getting your more way out ideas out of your head and into the public domain. For Peter, this is *sixsidia* (www.sixsidia.com), a world inhabited by "Ponkas" and their adventures, as told via Flash animation features.

Of course, you have to be able to do traditional sites as well, and Peter shows the other side of Flash design at the Zach Gold site (www.zachgold.com), a perfect example of a site that complements its subject matter with a cool-looking and fast-loading user interface.

SCRIPTING TASKS

CHAPTER **15**

FLASH WORKSPACE

AUTHORING TASKS

SCRIPTING TASKS

TESTING AND PUBLISHING TASKS

WHAT'S NEW

Working with Basic Scripts

TWEEN-BASED ANIMATION IS GREAT for noninteractive animation, and behaviors are useful for helping out with adding basic or common scripted features. There comes a time in every Flash designer's career when neither will do, though; you have to write some Action-Script for yourself. This chapter is for those times.

- 15.1 **Script overview**
- 15.2 **Understanding scripted animation vs. Timeline animation**
- 15.3 **Adding a frame label or comment**
- 15.4 **Adding an instance name**
- 15.5 **Entering code in the Actions panel**
- 15.6 **Basic syntax**
- 15.7 **Dot notation**
- 15.8 **Attaching a script**
- 15.9 **Controlling Timeline flow with scripts**
- 15.10 **Error checking and formatting scripts**
- 15.11 **Working with properties**
- 15.12 **Using external scripts with #include**
- 15.13 **Managing scripts with the Movie Explorer**
- 15.14 **Best practices in Flash coding**

15.1   Script Overview

ActionScript is Flash's *scripting language.* It allows you to build truly interactive and intelligent Flash content such as advanced user interfaces and application front ends, desktop applications, and games. Along with the simple animation system and small file sizes, ActionScript is one of the three core features that makes Flash so versatile in web design.

Programming vs. Scripting

Perhaps the first point of confusion for people new to ActionScript (and web-based code in general) is the word *script.* Unlike a true programming language, a scripting language is not designed to create large, standalone applications. Instead, it is a feature of an existing application that tells that application what to do. For Flash, the application is the Flash Player, which must be installed before you can view Flash content. The upside of this is that a scripting language is easier to learn. It doesn't contain the low-level and complex features needed to interface directly to an operating system, and it runs in a much friendlier environment than a true programming language such as C++ or ADA. Action-Script also gives the scripter total control of the graphical environment, which makes it a lot more immediate and cool than other, more intense languages; ActionScript is just more fun to work with!

Tweens vs. Scripts

A tween-based animation is fixed; it will do the same thing every time you run it. With a scripted solution, the animation not only can become totally interactive so that it responds to mouse clicks and other user inputs, but it can also be made to act intelligently, something tweens have a hard time doing.

Scripting languages such as ActionScript and the closely related JavaScript are designed to be easy to learn, making them suitable for designers whose first discipline may not be programming...so if you have not had any real experience in programming, don't panic.

Flash sites are famous for their clever and novel user interfaces. It is difficult to create such interfaces without using ActionScript.

Scripted animation is usually more band-width friendly than tweens because the former uses the same small code section every frame to create motion, whereas a tween is converted to a unique set of static positional data per frame.

One of the big advantages of knowing ActionScript is that you can then use components, which are general movie clips that allow you to quickly build user interfaces with common building blocks.

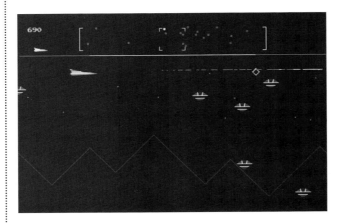

The remake of the video game Defender (shown here) was written entirely in ActionScript. Flash is not just for websites once you learn scripting!

15.2 Understanding Scripted Animation vs. Timeline Animation

As soon as you start using scripted animation as opposed to Timeline animation (motion and shape tweens), or using scripts to control tweens, you open up a world of interactive animation and navigation.

Tweens and ActionScript

Tween animations work via a system of *interpolation*. Flash looks at the beginning and ending keyframes of each tween section and mathematically calculates what needs to go into every frame between the two to create a smooth animation. In the published SWF, the calculations for each tween frame are fixed when you create the SWF and cannot be changed at runtime.

With ActionScript, you can create the opposite; animation that doesn't repeat itself every time it runs, and animation that can react to events.

The easiest way to start controlling animation is to make the playhead move around the Timeline through user interaction, in much the same way that you can fast forward, rewind, and jump through sections on a DVD or video player. Although the DVD/video you are watching is a linear story, the video controls add some level of interactivity, allowing you to fast forward, rewind, pause, and (on a DVD) skip to named sections of the film. In the same way, you can add navigation controls that make the Flash playhead move to particular frames in your Flash site when the user clicks a button or uses other interface controls.

For example, you can attach a script that causes the playhead to move to the part of the Flash Timeline that deals with the Home section of the site so when the user clicks a button labeled Home, they are returned there.

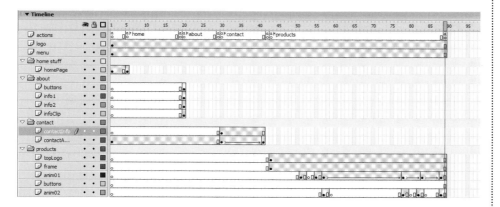

Note the Actions layer at the top of the Timeline with a number of labeled frames: Home, About, Products, and Contact. These are specially labeled frames that the Timeline can be made to go to when the appropriate button is pressed by the user.

Continues ●

The secret to effective use of Flash is making your graphics appear interactive and intelligent without forcing Flash to run performance-intensive or long code. The skill is not in being able to code well (although you should also do that), but in being able to strip a motion problem down to simple and basic goals so that you don't have to do much coding.

15.2 Understanding Scripted Animation vs. Timeline Animation *(continued)*

In addition to the creative process of designing a Flash site's visuals, scripted animation requires novel coding techniques for emulating motion. Many of the pioneers of Flash design (Yugo Nakamura, Joshua Davis, Manny Tan, et al) looked to nature and physics to work out how to simulate realistic motion, collisions, and other effects, then incorporated the ideas into user interfaces.

When programming Flash-based motion graphics, it is always a good idea to review how video games solve motion problems; the video games industry has solved a lot of the advanced animation coding principles that web motion graphics scripters face. Often the solution to Flash animation problems can be solved by looking in a games programming book.

home | about | products | contact

A simple button menu might look like this. When the user clicks the Products button, the playhead will jump to the frame labeled Products and start playing from there. In this way, the Timeline can be split into page sections, emulating the standard HTML page-based navigation—but of course, the pages are animated Flash content.

The harder way to control animations is to control them directly. This is how graphics in a Flash game work. Each game "character" will do the following every frame:

- Look at where it is
- Calculate where it wants to be ("the goal"), based on one or more conditions
- Move a small increment towards this goal

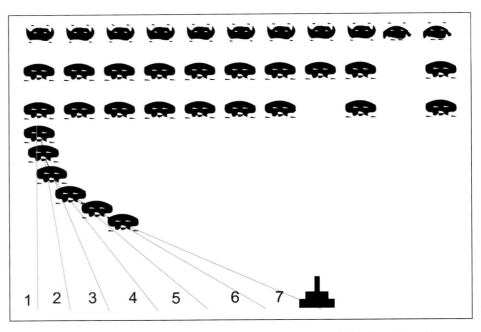

In this simple example, an alien breaks formation and attacks the player's ship. Its only goal is to go to the same position as the player's ship. If the player moves left to right to avoid the alien during frames 1 to 7, the alien's goal constantly changes through the same frames, and, although its simple goal-based path is always a straight line, the resulting path is a complex curve. Further, the alien's movement suggests it is aware of the player, given that it changes its direction as it swoops, when all it is really doing is following a very basic and brain-free path. This is the secret of scripted animation with the appearance of advanced interactivity; let the user do all the thinking, and make your content respond to the user's actions in a way that suggests the animation is responding intelligently.

15.3 Adding a Frame Label or Comment

Before you can start controlling your timelines via scripts, you are strongly advised to add labels (and comments) to keyframes in your movie's Timeline. These name your keyframes in a meaningful way, making the interface between the code and Timeline more obvious than if you just refer to keyframes by raw frame numbers. A label can be used by ActionScript (or certain other applications that can embed Flash content, such as Macromedia Director) to control the Timeline. A comment is for your benefit only as an aid to documenting your timelines and is not exported as part of the final SWF.

A label appears as a little red flag on the Timeline in the keyframe. A comment appears with a pair of green slashes.

To add a label or comment to a frame:

1 If the frame is not already a keyframe, make it one by selecting it and right-clicking/⌘-clicking the frame and selecting Convert To Keyframes from the context menu that appears.

2 With the keyframe selected, add your text in the text input requester to the top left of the Properties inspector. To signify a comment, start the text with two slashes (//); text without the leading slashes will be a label.

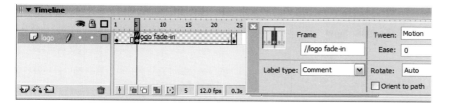

If the number of frames in the Timeline before the next keyframe is large enough, you will see the entire comment on the Timeline. If there aren't enough frames, you can see the entire comment by hovering over the keyframe with the mouse; the comment will appear in a tooltip.

➡ 15.9 Controlling Timeline Flow with Scripts

Properties inspector
Ctrl F3
Cmd F3

It is a good idea to keep labels fairly short because you have to type them exactly when referring to them in ActionScript.

Comments are not exported to the published SWF, so feel free to use as many as you need and make them as long as you want. The more you add, the less you have to struggle to recall when you look at the FLA six months later.

Adding a comment that contains the name and date of the originator, plus any specific instructions, in the first frame of a new FLA is common practice and a good idea. For example: "// (c) 2003 Sham Bhangal. Can be freely distributed as long as this FLA is made available with the associated readme file."

15.4   Adding an Instance Name

➡ 15.6 Basic Syntax

➡ 15.7 Dot Notation

➡ 16.3 Understanding Scope and Dot Notation

Properties inspector

Ctrl F3
Cmd F3

Because Flash requires that instance names are replicated exactly when you refer to them in ActionScript, don't use names that are so long that the chances of typos occurring is high.

Although you cannot have two identical instance names on the same frame, you can use the same instance name in different timelines. This is because Flash takes into account an instance's location when identifying it. The beauty of this is that, given the same instance names, you can use the same code.

You should *always* give every button an instance name if you are using ActionScript (and you are using the Flash MX 2004 coding styles), because every button needs to be referenced by code (to add the event handler) before it will work.

The interface between the environment of the symbol on the Stage and the code environment of ActionScript is the *instance name.* This is what Flash uses to reference individuals on the Stage. Without it, Flash has no way of controlling a specific instance. If you want to control a movie clip via ActionScript, you must give the clip an instance name.

To add an instance name to a movie clip or button on a timeline:

1   Select the symbol on the Stage.

2   In the Property inspector (Window > Properties) add an instance name in the text input box to the left of the Swap button.

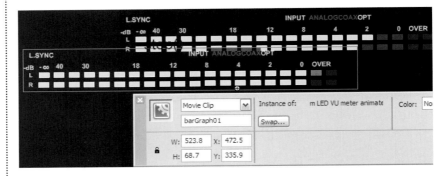

Naming Conventions

An instance name is a part of ActionScript and must comply with the same naming conventions as variable and object names:

- An instance name cannot begin with a space or a number.

- An instance name cannot contain characters that could confuse Flash into thinking the name is an expression, such as -, +, / (so start-page-button is not an acceptable name).

- Don't use a reserved word as an instance name. Reserved words appear in blue in ActionScript listings, and include names such as MovieClip, Button, and add.

- Instance names are case sensitive; *myClip* and *myclip* are different instance names in ActionScript 2. (Previous versions of ActionScript were not case sensitive.)

The standard naming convention used by the Flash community is *camel case:* in this format, all words that make up the instance name are run together with no spaces or punctuation between words. The first word is lowercase and all additional words have initial caps: *thisIsAnExampleOfCamelCase.*

Acceptable instance names include *camelCase, alien2343,* and *homeMenuButton.* Unacceptable names include *camel case, 2343alien,* and *home-menu-button.*

15.5 Entering Code in the Actions Panel

There are two ways to enter code in the Actions panel: typing all the code yourself, or letting Flash enter common keywords and paths for you via the user interfaces. In the latter method, you usually only have to add arguments and other parts of code that Flash cannot second guess for you.

The Actions panel also includes options to help you format and check your code. The panel consists of three panes:

➤ 5.7 Actions Panel

➤ 15.6 Basic Syntax

➤ 15.7 Dot Notation

Actions panel
F9

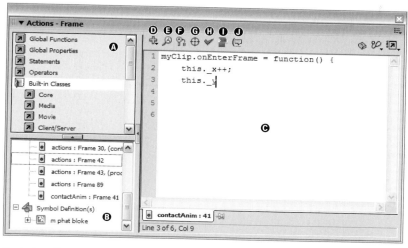

- **Ⓐ** Actions Toolbox pane: Allows you to select common ActionScript elements without having to type them yourself.

- **Ⓑ** Script Navigator pane: Contains a tree diagram of all scripts in the current FLA, allowing you to quickly find one.

- **Ⓒ** Script pane Where you enter ActionScript.

- **Ⓓ** Drop-down menu containing the same options as the Actions Toolbox.

- **Ⓔ** Finds text within the script in the Script pane.

- **Ⓕ** Finds and replaces text within the script.

- **Ⓖ** Opens the Insert Target Path window, which automatically adds dot notation paths for you.

- **Ⓗ** Checks the syntax of the current script.

- **Ⓘ** Autoformats the current script. You have to have a syntax error free script before you can auto format, so you must typically check syntax before clicking this.

- **Ⓙ** Toggles the appearance of code hints. These typically appear every time Flash detects that you are about to enter an argument, and they list the arguments you need to add.

Continues

15.5 Entering Code in the Actions Panel *(continued)*

Before you can write anything other than basic ActionScript, you will need to familiarize yourself with basic syntax, dot notation, variables, and scope.

The Script pane is used like a normal text editor; it normally shows the script on the currently selected frame or symbol. Scripts appear color-coded with the colors defined in the ActionScript tab of the Preferences window (Edit > Preferences).

At the bottom of the Script pane are the Script pane tabs. If you click the pin icon next to the tab so that it changes to a pushpin, the current script will be retained ('pinned') and a tab for it will appear to the right of the pin icon. You can thus quickly tab between a number of pinned scripts.

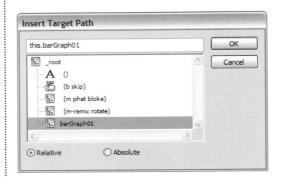

To insert a dot-notation path in your script, move the text cursor to the place in the script you want to add the path. (If you have used the Actions Toolbox, you should instead highlight the `instanceName` part of the text the toolbox added.) Click the Insert Target Path icon and, in the dialog, find and double-click the instance you want to control. The path created will always include the reserved word `this`; the word `this` is only required in certain situations (dictated by scope, but it is generally only needed within an event handler or function that is being used as an event handler), so you can (and sometimes must) remove it.

The Actions Toolbox pane can be used to add the actions and methods that make up most ActionScript. The Actions panel consists of a series of book icons 📘 that can be opened 📖 by clicking them to reveal either subbooks or actions/method icons ➘. Double-clicking one of these adds the associated ActionScript. For example, if you add the `gotoAndPlay()` method (Built-in Classes > Core > MovieClip > Methods > gotoAndPlay), the following will appear in the Script pane:

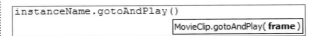

The hint will appear to remind you that you need to enter a frame number or name as an argument. You will also have to change the `instanceName` part to the appropriate instance name or dot notation path. The main statements in the code will have already been written for you.

15.6 Basic Syntax

Syntax refers to the structure of a language rather than its meaning. As with most computer languages, ActionScript structure has far fewer rules than a human language such as English, but it is not as tolerant to variation; you have to follow the syntax *exactly* or Flash will raise an error.

ActionScript is arranged as a series of lines of code. Each "line" must end with a semicolon:

```
line;
line;
line;
```

You do not have to physically place each line of ActionScript on a new line because the semicolon is all Flash needs, so you can write `line; line; line;`

Rather as human languages use paragraphs, ActionScript uses *blocks.* A block starts with an opening brace ({) and ends with a closing brace (}).

```
{
  line;
  line;
  line;
}
```

Unlike human languages, where paragraphs are used to logically separate text into related sections, thus making them easier to read and write, Flash uses blocks to define what each line section *does.* For example, if the block is an event handler, the block definition has the following functional appearance;

```
event handler for myButton{
  line;
  line;
  line;
}
```

The block definition tells Flash when to run each section of code. The preceding code block will run (for example) whenever the instance `myButton` is pressed.

➡ 15.7 Dot Notation

➡ 17.1 Overview of Code Structures

By convention, lines within a block are indented. This makes it easier to see the blocks in a listing.

15.7   Dot Notation

➡ 11.1 Understand-
      ing Symbols

➡ 16.3 Understand-
      ing Scope and
      Dot Notation

➡ 16.7 Understand-
      ing Classes,
      Objects,
      Methods, and
      Properties

Dot notation is fundamental to ActionScript.; every line of code you write will use it, although it may not appear so. For example, if you create a variable called myVariable on the Timeline myClip, Flash handles it internally as _root.myClip.myVariable. Learning dot notation is therefore one of the big steps to learning ActionScript.

ActionScript consists largely of instances, methods, and properties. To access them, you use dot notation. When used in this way, there are two forms of dot notation:

```
instance.property
instance.method(arguments)
```

Accessing Properties

To change a property , use the instance.property form of dot notation. The following line will move a movie clip with instance name myClip 200 pixels to the right by changing its horizontal position property, _x;

```
myClip._x = myClip._x + 200;
```

When using variables, you do not have to include the property, because a variable has only one property—its value. The following line will change the variable myNumber to 10.

```
myNumber = 10;
```

Accessing Methods

To access a method, use the instance.method(arguments) form of dot notation. The following line will make a movie clip called myClip go to a frame labeled "start" on its timeline and continue playing from there:

```
myClip.gotoAndPlay("start");
```

Most basic methods also have a nonmethod-based version of the same ActionScript called an *action*. This is a feature passed up from previous revisions of Flash when ActionScript did not use methods, but they are useful for raw beginners. They assume an instance of "the current Timeline this script is attached to."

If your code is attached to the Timeline of the movie clip myClip, this code will do the same as the previous line:

```
gotoAndPlay("start");
```

You can see all available properties of each Flash class by looking in the Actions panel's Toolbox pane. For example, look in Built-in Classes > Core > Movie > MovieClip > Properties to see all the basic properties of the movie clip. The methods of all classes can be found in the same way by looking in the corresponding methods book.

———

Although you can sometimes get away with not using dot notation, it is always a good idea to know why this is the case; in all such situations you are actually still using it, it's just that it is implied. As with real life, not knowing what you are implying can (and usually does) lead you into trouble!

———

Understanding dot notation will move you from being a beginner to intermediate user of ActionScript. Once a beginner learns it, they will have moved up a level in their use of Flash.

15.8 Attaching a Script

Flash is a visual environment that includes timelines and symbols. Rather than having a single script, Flash requires you to attach each script you write to one of the visual, graphical elements in the environment.

To attach a script to a keyframe, button, or movie clip, click in the keyframe on the Timeline, or click the button or movie clip on the Stage, as appropriate. As long as the Script pane in the Actions panel does not read "Current selection cannot have actions applied to it," you're good to go. If the Script pane does carry this message, check that you have not inadvertently clicked a graphic symbol, primitive, or locked layer.

You can attach a script to the following:

- Any keyframe
- A symbol after it has been placed on a time
- A frame in the Timeline of a symbol that's in the library

There are some places you *can* attach a script (i.e., Flash will let you) but you should avoid doing so:

On any keyframe in a button Use button event handlers instead. Scripts should not be placed on keyframes within a button. They should be placed on the *instance* of the button that's on the Stage.

On any keyframe in a group If you attempt to attach to a group, you will actually attach to the Timeline the group is on.

On any keyframe in a graphic symbol The script won't run because a graphic symbol has a static timeline and doesn't run itself, so any scripts you attach to it will not run either.

On a button or movie clip if you want to write code in the ActionScript 2 style Use callbacks instead.

A LITTLE ACTIONSCRIPT GOES A LONG WAY

Although learning ActionScript is a daunting prospect to most beginners, you don't actually need to know much of it to start creating compelling interactive content. A good understanding of event handlers, dot notation, and a smattering of movie clip methods will usually suffice as a good starting point.

➡ 15.5 Entering Code in the Actions Panel

➡ 18.1 Understanding Event Driven Code

➡ 18.2 Attaching Scripts to Buttons or Movie Clips

➡ 18.4 Attaching Scripts to Events Using Callbacks

Rather than attaching scripts directly to buttons and movie clips by selecting the symbol and attaching a script to it, callbacks, available in ActionScript 2/ Flash MX 2004, attach scripts to only keyframes and events, and refer to buttons and movie clips by their instance name. Thus, the code references the instance by name rather than being attached directly to it.

Behaviors use a Flash 5 style of attaching scripts that is not compatible with ActionScript 2. If you do not read or modify the behavior code, this won't matter to you, but intermediate or advanced level scripters should avoid behaviors if they want to interface their code with ActionScript 2 or Flash MX (Flash 6) scripts.

15.9   Controlling Timeline Flow with Scripts

The method-based versions of the goto-AndPlay(), gotoAnd-Stop(), and stop() actions are much more flexible because they allow you to control timelines other than the current one. This allows you to control nested timelines.

It is usual to add all ActionScript to the top layer on a timeline and call that layer Actions.

One of the easiest ways to start using scripting in Flash (and the way most beginners start introducing ActionScript into their FLAs) is Timeline control. By creating standard tween animations and keyframes on a timeline and then jumping around that timeline using ActionScript, you can control the Timeline almost as if you were using super-fast video recorder controls; by jumping forward, stopping, jumping back, or going to a particular frame, you can create fairly complex navigation.

The basic Timeline controls are very like video recorder controls. To add them to a timeline, follow these steps:

1 Add a keyframe where you want to change the way the Timeline is playing (i.e., you want the playhead to stop or jump to another frame). It is standard practice to add all scripts and labels in a layer called Actions, which is the topmost layer, so you may also have to add this layer.

2 Select this keyframe and open the Actions panel.

3 Select an action from the Global Functions > Timeline Control book in the Actions panel's Actions Toolbox pane.

The following actions are suitable for attaching in this way: gotoAndPlay(), gotoAndStop(), stop(). The easiest action to use is stop();, which simply stops the Timeline. You can use this action to stop the Timeline on a keyframe that contains buttons that allow the user to restart the Timeline (usually by jumping to other frames to form interactive navigation).

Both gotoAndStop() and gotoAndPlay() require a frame number or name to jump to. It is best to add a frame label at the frame you want your movie to jump to and use that as an argument. For example, the following line will cause Flash to go to frame label stopHere and stop:

```
gotoAndStop("stopHere");
```

All Timeline control actions can be used as event handlers. The following code will stop the Timeline and make it go to and play from frame label "homePage" when button instance myButton is click-released:

```
myButton.onRelease = function() {
  gotoAndPlay("homePage");
};
stop();
```

15.10 Error Checking and Formatting Scripts

Flash can find syntax errors in your scripts and format scripts so that all lines contain the correct number of indents and a semicolon at the end of every line that needs them.

Checking for Syntax Errors

To check for syntax errors in the Script pane of the Actions panel, click the Check Syntax icon ✔. If syntax errors are found, a listing of all errors will appear. Typical errors include:

- Not including a closing brace (}) for every opening brace ({)
- Incorrect number of arguments
- Incorrectly formed expressions
- Adding spaces where they are not allowed
- Incorrectly formed dot notation, i.e., where there are two dots instead of one:

```
1  myButton..onRelease = function () {
2      gotoAndPlay("homePage");
3  };
4  stop();
5
```

```
▼ Output
**Error** Scene=Scene 1, layer=Layer 1, frame=1:Line 1: Expected
a field name after '.' operator.
        myButton..onRelease = function () {

Total ActionScript Errors: 1      Reported Errors: 1
```

Auto Formatting

To add proper formatting, click the Auto Format ≣ icon.

```
198  placeContent = function () {
199
200  if (page[currentPage].pID != "non") {
201
202      _root.attachMovie(page[currentPage].pID, "content_mc", 10000)
203  } else {
204
205          _root.createEmptyMovieClip("content_mc", 10000)
206          loadMovie(page[currentPage].pURL, content_mc)
207      }
208  _root.content_mc._x=middleX
209      _root.content_mc._y=middleY
210  };
```

```
198  placeContent = function () {
199      if (page[currentPage].pID != "non") {
200          _root.attachMovie(page[currentPage].pID, "content_mc", 10000);
201      } else {
202          _root.createEmptyMovieClip("content_mc", 10000);
203          loadMovie(page[currentPage].pURL, content_mc);
204      }
205      _root.content_mc._x = middleX;
206      _root.content_mc._y = middleY;
207  };
```

The first script is the result of a typical late night scripting session. Click the Auto Format button and you get the much tidier second script.

➡ 15.6 Basic Syntax

Check Syntax
Ctrl T
⌘ T

Checking for syntax errors is not the same as checking for bugs. A bug is something that your code does that is syntactically correct but is wrong for another reason. For example, attaching the wrong instance name to an event would pass the syntax check, but your script would not work as you intend.

The Auto Format feature will work only for a script that is free of syntax errors. It is always a good idea to check the syntax of your script before auto formatting.

There are several errors that will cause Flash to fail silently. For example, if you specify an instance name that does not exist (usually because of a typo), Flash will not tell you; it just won't work when you test the movie.

15.11   Working with Properties

➡ 22.3 Animating via
        Scripted Prop-
        erty Changes

The instance name is
also a property, and it's
one of the most impor-
tant ones. Without it,
Flash cannot access any
of the other properties
of an instance.

———

Methods also work by
varying instance prop-
erties. They are usually
the preferred way of
accessing properties
because they contain
dedicated routines to
make the process more
transparent; you don't
have to worry about
the properties and can
use methods that do it
all for you. This process
is called abstraction.

———

Many properties can be
accessed manually via
the Properties inspector
and the Transform
panel.

All Flash instances have properties. Properties are values that can change the way an instance works or appears. In the case of movie clips, properties can change both. Properties are the link between the graphic environment and ActionScript because they define the way the Stage and everything on it appears, and because they can be read and updated by ActionScript, thus allowing ActionScript to change the Stage appearance and cause motion.

An instance's properties are accessed by creating a dot path to the instance, and then adding the property you want to access at the end. The following line will change the rotation property of a movie clip myClip to 45 degrees:

```
myClip._rotation = 45;
```

If you want to read the same property into a variable, use something of the form:

```
clipRotation = myClip._rotation;
```

When you want to create animation via properties, you have to run a script every frame. The onEnterFrame event of a movie clip allows you to do this. The following code will create animation by increasing the rotation property by 1 degree every frame:

```
myClip.onEnterFrame = function() {
    this._rotation = this._rotation+1;
};
```

The result of changing the
rotation property once

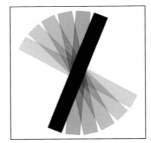

The result of changing the rotation property on each frame

15.12   Using External Clips with #include

Most Flash content consists of short scripts that you write each time you come across the same problem (e.g., button scripts and standard movie clip animation scripts). As you get more advanced in ActionScript, you may decide to write general functions and other code to address problems that you see time and again. This code has to be reusable so it can be quickly referenced in multiple FLAs. The way to do this is via a standalone script file—the AS file. There are two ways to write an AS file, depending on which version of Flash you are using.

The #include does not have a semicolon at the end of its line. This is because it is a compiler directive and not really part of ActionScript.

Creating an AS file

In Flash MX 2004, the way to create an AS file is as follows:

1   Create your script as you would normally, typically by attaching it to a keyframe.

2   To save the AS file, open the Actions panel menu (via the icon at the top right ☰▾) and select Export Script.

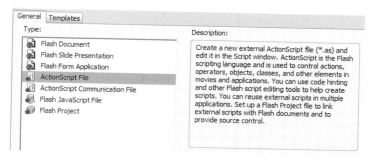

In Flash MX Professional 2004, the interface provides a dedicated full screen editor specifically to create AS files. To access this editor, select File > New and choose ActionScript File from the New Document window's General tab.

Using an AS File

To use the AS file in a FLA, add a line containing the code `#include "myfile.as"`, where `myfile.as` is the document name of your AS file. If the AS file is not in the same directory as the FLA you are adding it to, you will have to add the full file path; thus for a Windows XP system, you might use something like

```
#include "C:\Documents and Settings\ShamB\My Documents\ASFiles\myfile.as"
```

Continues

Flash will insert the script in the AS file at the point where the include directive is seen during compilation to create a single SWF file; the fact that you use an AS file will not add any new output files.

The #include doesn't check to see whether the imported file is an AS file. You can import any file, however inappropriate (such as an executable), but Flash can get confused! Because of this, it is a good idea to only import files with the .as extension.

The contents of the AS file is added to the SWF at compilation, so you will never need to upload the AS file to the server when you deploy your site onto the Web. You wouldn't want to do this anyway, because it would allow anyone who came across your AS file to read your code.

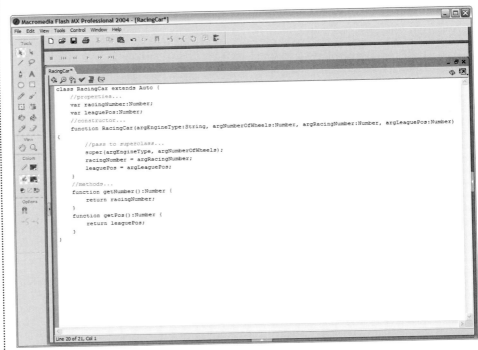

Once in the ActionScript editing environment, you will find a full-screen Script pane within which to write your script (close all panel docking areas to achieve this view).

15.13   Managing Scripts with the Movie Explorer

The Movie Explorer is a larger version of the Script Navigator pane in the Actions panel. It allows you to view the whole FLA as a tree diagram and is useful because it you can search the whole FLA for scripts containing your search text or for any symbol or instance that has your search text associated with it.

The Movie Explorer output can be filtered to add/remove text, symbols, scripts, video/sound/bitmaps, or frames/layers by clicking the first five icons in the Show bar at the top of the panel. The sixth icon, Customize Which Items To Show, provides a pop-up that allows you detailed customization of which content to show.

Movie Explorer panel
[Alt] [F3]
[Option] [F3]

For large timelines, or timelines that use several scenes, the Movie Explorer is useful for finding that script you wrote a week ago but can't find anymore.

If you follow Action-Script 2 best practices, you probably won't need to use the Movie Explorer much, given that you will have a number of large scripts on only a few keyframes (as opposed to the Flash 5 coding style, which puts scripts all over the place).

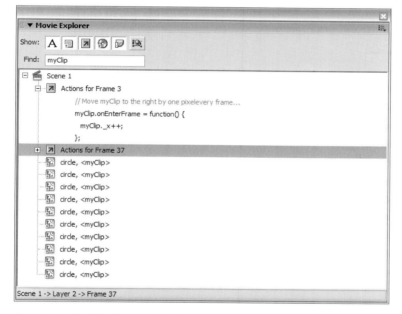

Type text in the Find box, and the lower pane will display all scripts and instances containing that text. Clicking any found item will give you a short message at the bottom left telling you where to find the item. If you enter nothing in the Find box, the lower pane will show you all content of the types specified by the Show icons.

Finally, you can print any listing created in the lower pane by selecting Print from the panel's menu.

15.14 Best Practices in Flash Coding

Flash is very forgiving when you are creating content and allows you a great deal of flexibility in developing movies and sites. As your sites get bigger or more intricate, though, following some basic guidelines helps to manage the increasing complexity.

Keep code together It is standard practice to attach all code to keyframes in the top layer and to name that layer Actions. Attaching code to symbols tends to fragment your code and spread it across the FLA and makes it difficult to manage.

Intermediate and advanced users should consider placing the majority of code in a single frame, using either functions or object-oriented definitions, and then calling this code from the rest of the FLA using single-line function calls. When created with this structure, the single long script can easily be separated out from the FLA and added as a series of AS `include` files and libraries. This is desirable because you'll be able to reuse your code elsewhere.

Add lots of comments Thoroughly comment code and label timelines. Use meaningful names: `menuButton` instead of `button6`.

Use a naming strategy This allows you to know what each item in your FLA is just by looking at the name. For general variables, run all words together and capitalize each new word: camelCase. For values that will stay constant, use all caps with words separated by underscores: CONSTANT_VALUE. Macromedia also recommends using suffixes for instance names so the Actions panel will know what type each instance is and be able to use the auto-complete facility. The suffixes for the most common instances are `_mc` (movie clip), `_btn` (button), and `_txt` (textfield).

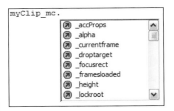

If you use the instance name `myClip_mc`, Flash would know it represents a movie clip and will display a drop-down menu showing all available methods and properties for a movie clip as soon as you write this instance name in the Script pane.

Use a standard code structure It is a good idea to adopt a standard order for various elements in your code: place functions and events first, then initialization (setting all variables and instances to their initial value), then the main code.

Keep code as general as possible Avoid using absolute references such as `_root` and instead use relative references such as `this` or `_parent`. This makes your code less position-dependent and more reusable.

Know what you want to do and debug often Understand the problem before you start the solution. As soon as you start writing your code, test it often by running it, both locally and on the Web. Whatever you do, don't put off testing your content on the Web until last because it never works out the way you expect it to.

CHAPTER 16

Working with Variables and Objects

BEFORE FLASH CONTENT CAN behave in an intelligent way, it has to be able to *remember* things such as user inputs. It also has to internally remember pieces of information to keep track of what it is doing. Both these issues are addressed by using variables, which are general containers that can hold single items of information. More specialized information structures are needed to manage multivalue or specialized data, and this is done via objects.

16.1   Understanding Variables

Anything that acts in a manner that suggests intelligence has to have *memory*. Without it, getting anything done (other than unthinking reflex actions) it doesn't just become impossible to keep track of any goal, it becomes difficult to even remember what the goal is!

In Flash, the "unthinking reflex action" is Timeline animation and simple scripts. To get Flash to remember any user inputs and to internally keep track of what it is doing, you use *variables*.

Raw and Variable Information

It is sometimes useful to think of variables as boxes inside the computer holding information. The variable name is the label on the outside of the box that allows you to differentiate between the boxes, and the value is what is inside the box.

Suppose you had some money in your pocket, including a dollar bill. A dollar bill is always worth 100 cents; its value is *fixed* and unchanging. Such a value is called a *literal* (short for *literal value*). Typical literals include raw number values (e.g., 10, 20023, 3.1415) and words or phrases (e.g., "ten", "Monday", "Pete").

Expressions in computing are very much like formulas in math and use essentially the same symbols (+, -, parentheses, and so forth).

The total amount of money in your pocket will change from day to day, as will the name of the day itself. For example, on the day with the literal name "Wednesday", you might have $7.95, but by the day called "Friday", you might have $56.00. Both the day of the week and the amount of money in your pocket are *changing,* or *variable*, values. Using variables, you can describe what happens on Wednesday as:

```
day = "Wednesday";
moneyInPocket = 7.95;
```

The variables are *day* and *moneyInPocket,* and the way they are used to store simple pieces of information is how Flash remembers things.

A line of code that includes a variable on the left side of the equal sign and an expression to work it out on the right side is called an *algorithm*. Although it looks like a math *formula*, it isn't the same. Computers allow you to have things like x = x + 1, whereas math does not. A math formula should always allow you to find the value of *x* without knowing anything about its past, whereas an algorithm assumes the last value of *x* for the right side of the equal sign.

Processing Information

Variables enable Flash to act intelligently via *expressions*. Rather than define literal values to Flash, you give it instructions on how to work out its *own* values.

Suppose that two people went out for a beer. If the money each of the two had was *person1Money* and *person2Money*, then you could work out if they could make it a big night out:

```
money = person1Money + person2Money;
```

The value of money is worked out by equating it to the expression (*person1Money+person2Money*). The beauty of this is that using the *same* expression will give you the correct value on different days; the value of *money* is no longer defined literally but via other variables that may themselves be calculated by other expressions. This interrelationship of variables allows Flash to create its *own* information internally in a way that appears intelligent; this is how computers in general appear to "know" and remember things.

16.2 Understanding Variable Types

As well as knowing different bits of information about something, there are a number of different *kinds* of information you might want to know. In computing, this feature of variables is called *type*.

You can, for example, describe your book collection in several ways:

- You can describe it in terms of numbers. If you had 5 Flash books and 3 Photoshop books, you could take the two numbers and add them to work out how many books you had altogether; 8.

- You can describe them non-numerically: "one of them is called *Flash at Your Fingertips*". If you also described one of your Photoshop books with "one of them is called *Photoshop at Your Fingertips*", you could *concatenate* the two descriptions along with "and" to give you "one of them is called *Flash at Your Fingertips* and one of them is called *Photoshop at Your Fingertips*".

- You can make comparisons using the numerical and non-numerical information about your books to form true and false statements. For example, you might want to see if your collection can be moved to a shelf with space for 10 books. If you found that you had less than or equal to 10 Flash and Photoshop books in total (i.e., a comparison between 10 and the number of books in your collection revealed that you have 10 or less), then "I can move all my books to that shelf" would be a *true* statement. If you had 12 books, it would be *false*.

Most problems contain elements of all three types (numerical, non-numerical, and true/false) of information, and there are three types of variable to handle them.

→ 15.1 Script Overview

→ 15.6 Basic Syntax

→ 15.11 Working with Properties

ACTIONSCRIPT2.0 AND STRONG TYPING

Flash MX 2004's dialect of ActionScript (ActionScript2.0) uses strong typing. This means that Flash will raise an error if you (for example) create a string variable but then try to equate it to a number value. The following code will create a string variable called myString, and then attempt to set it to the number literal '10';

```
var myString:String = "I am a String";
myString = 10;
```

The code will raise a *type mismatch error*. By using strong typing, you will generally create more robust code, because your variables and objects are more tightly defined.

Continues

———

Numbers, strings, and Booleans are the three simplest *objects* available in Flash. They are called variables only because of historic reasons; variables existed before modern object-oriented languages (such as ActionScript). Variables are actually objects with one real property: value.

Defining Different Types

You need numerical values to allow Flash to know math. A *number* is a variable that holds a numerical value.

Although computers work best with numbers and math, at some point they have to communicate with *people,* and people like to talk—that is, use a nonmathematical system involving words and strings of text. A *string* is a variable that holds non-numerical text. The problem with text is that you can't easily differentiate it from other types of code because *all code consists of text anyway.* To make defining a text string unambiguous, you should always enclose string literals in quotes:

- `pets = cats+dogs` asks for the variable `pets` to be set equal to the total of two other variables. If you have 3 cats and 2 dogs, *pets* would be given the value 5.

- `pets = "cats+dogs"` asks for the variable `pets` to be equal to the text *cats+dogs*. No matter how many animals are involved, the variable is storing the phrase, not a count.

A computer needs to make *comparisons* and save the results of them so that it can make decisions based on what is remembered to be true and false. A variable holding a true or false value is called a *Boolean*. Flash will deem an expression to be true if it is correct and false if it isn't. For example, if you wanted to decide whether you need more dogs, three being the maximum you want to have, you could do this:

`getMoreDogs = dogs < 2;`

The expression is `dogs < 2`. If `dogs` is 2 or less, then `getMoreDogs` is true, telling you that you can get another dog.

ACTIONSCRIPT2.0 AND COMPILED CODE

Although ActionScript2.0 is advertised as allowing strong typing and a new class-based structure, these features are generally compiled to internal structures that are very similar to the old ActionScript 1.0 compiled code. In particular:

Strong typing errors will only occur at compile time—the compiled SWF will have no runtime typing features

ActionScript2.0 Classes are there for ease of authoring, and create no new compiled structures over those that would be created using ActionScript1.0.

Despite this, ActionScript2.0 is a much more robust programming environment, and much more suited to creating large applications than previous versions of ActionScript.

16.3 Understanding Scope and Dot Notation

Dot Notation

Dot notation is the way ActionScript allows you to describe the Flash hierarchy.

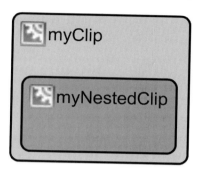

When you want to access an instance that is on another Timeline, you form the path to it using a series of dots; *myClip.myNestedClip* accesses a movie clip that is in *myNestedClip*.

You usually access an instance because you want to change one of its properties. You do this either by changing them directly (as in the first line below), or through the methods available to the instance's class (as in the second line):

```
myClip.myNestedClip._currentframe = 10;
myClip.myNestedClip.gotoAndPlay(10);
```

Scope

Sham and Jen wrote this book. They split the writing equally between them. He wrote this chapter, and she wrote Chapter 17.

You know who "he" and "she" are in the preceding paragraph because "Sham" and "Jen" were defined as the *subject* at the start of the paragraph. Assuming that you already know that Sham is a man and Jen is a woman, you know which is which in the third sentence.

Code blocks are equivalent to paragraphs, and scope is exactly the same thing as using "he" and "she"; it allows you to name the subject of a block using a general term because it is defined as the subject of the code block (or, in computing terms, *scoped by the code*). Instead of "he", "she", "it" or "they", you use only one general substitution in Flash; this. The following rules apply:

1   If you use this inside a code block, it refers to the currently scoped thing.

2   If you use this outside a code block, it refers to the Timeline the code is on.

3   If you omit this, the code will assume the Timeline the code is on. For example, the scope of this block is given at its start (myClip). Thus, the x_property is taken to mean myClip._x.

```
myClip.onEnterFrame = function(){
   this._x = this._x + 1;
};
this._y = this._y + 1;
```

➡ 16.5 Creating Timeline Variables

➡ 16.6 Creating Global Variables

Actions panel
`F9`

The code blocks where scope is most important are event handlers written using callbacks or class-based and prototype definitions. In both cases, you should use this within their code blocks

---

Using this or omitting it doesn't matter in Flash 5–style scripts (as described in 18.2).

Programmers use the word 'scope' to identify 'visibility'. In Flash this translates to the timeline or code block within which a variable 'can be seen', or the timeline which a code block is 'looking at'.

As well as this, you can also use the general path this._parent, which refers to the parent Timeline (i.e., the Timeline the scoped Timeline is on).

From rules 2 and 3, you can see that scope is only really important in code blocks when using post Flash 5-style coding. Outside them, it doesn't matter whether you add the this or not; Flash assumes the same thing.

16.4   Creating Local Variables

Test Movie

[Ctrl] [Enter]

———

The trace() action allows you to debug code within the test environment by sending the value of the action's argument to the Output panel.

———

If you wanted to use the nonlocal version of myVariable within the block, you would typically have to use the full dot notation path to it, in this case _root.myVariable.

———

Local variables exist only within a code block for the duration the code block is running. If you set a local variable to a value and then exit and later re-run the block, the local variable will be reset on the re-run. If you want *persistent* variables, you have to use Timeline or global variables.

A local variable is one that exists within a code block and ceases to exist once the block has ended. It is useful for creating modular code.

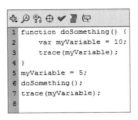

```
1  function doSomething() {
2      var myVariable = 10;
3      trace(myVariable);
4  }
5  myVariable = 5;
6  doSomething();
7  trace(myVariable);
8
```

To create a local variable within a code block, use the var action at the top of the code block. Any variable created this way will exist only within the code block.

If the doSomething() code shown is attached to the first keyframe in a new FLA, you will see this result when you test it (Control > Test Movie).

The myVariable within the code block within the function block is given a value of 10, and the one on the main Timeline is given a value of 5. When you trace myVariable within the block (line 2), you see 10, and when you return to the main code, myVariable is traced as 5 (line 7). This occurs because the two versions of myVariable are different:

- The one within the function block exists only within the block (it is *local to the block*). If there is a variable of the same name outside the block, the local variable is the one to be used by code within the block. The local version ceases to exist as soon as the block ends.

- The one outside the block is a *different* variable. It is unaffected by the local version.

The implications of local variables are that you can create separate sections of code. Local variables *localize* data to the function block that handles it, which helps ensure that bugs and other effects caused by the code block do not affect the main code.

This is particularly useful when creating function libraries and adding them to a FLA via #include. If the function code uses only local variables, then its operation is transparent to the main code. This is an important feature of modular code; one code module should not be able to affect the operation of another except by well-defined interfaces (in this case, the arguments of the function call).

16.5 Creating Timeline Variables

A Timeline variable is one that exists on a particular Timeline only. This is the default variable created by ActionScript. The trick to Timeline variables is not creating them (that's the easy part!); the challenge is always knowing the correct path to them once they have been created so that you can refer to them. This can be confusing because code within blocks has scope, and you must take this scope into account when you refer to Timeline variables.

To create a Timeline variable on the same Timeline as your script, simply define a new variable as follows:

```
myVariable = 0;
```

The following special cases apply to make this easy situation slightly more complicated:

- If you define a Timeline variable within a code block, adding the path `this` in front of the variable name will create a variable at the scope of the code block, which is usually not the same as the current Timeline. You should make sure you know whether or not you need the `this` (you usually do).

- If you want to create a Timeline variable on a timeline other than the current one, you should define this other timeline via a dot path.

Both of these are shown at work in the following code, which is attached to the main Timeline:

```
1  myClip.onEnterFrame = function() {
2      this._x = this._x+this.xSpeed;
3      this._y = this._y+this.ySpeed;
4  };
5  myClip.xSpeed = 5;
6  myClip.ySpeed = 5;
7
```

Here, you are creating animation by increasing the values of the movie clip myClip's _x and _y properties. You increase them every frame by adding the Timeline variables xSpeed and ySpeed. Note that outside the event handler block, you use a dot path to create them (which creates them in the Timeline myClip rather than the main Timeline). When you refer to xSpeed and ySpeed in the event handler block, you refer to them with this.xSpeed and this.ySpeed. This is because the event handler scopes myClip, so this is taken to be myClip within the code block.

Actions panel
F9

———

The Timeline that a Timeline variable exists on is referred to as its *scope*.

———

A Timeline variable will only exist as long as its Timeline exists. If you remove a movie clip, its Timeline, and thereßfore everything on it (including scripts and Timeline variables), will also be removed.

———

A common error (and closely related issue to the preceding tip) is what happens if you try to define a Timeline variable on a timeline that doesn't currently exist. Flash will not be able to find the specified Timeline but won't raise an error. Instead, the Timeline variable just won't be created.

16.6   Creating Global Variables

Actions panel
F9

To change the value of a global, you *must* use the _global path; otherwise Flash will assume you are referring to a Timeline variable. The rule is that when a global variable appears on the left side of an equal sign, you *must* add the _global in front of it. When it is on the right side, don't.

Global is a good place to put constants that you will be accessing from several places in your SWF.

Components and other generic code or ActionScript add-ons or third-party #include libraries may make extensive use of the global space. They will stop working if you clutter it up and overwrite some of their definitions with the same-named globals. Use global only when you must, and not because it is easier!

A global variable has a scope of "global"—that is, it exists throughout the Flash hierarchy. Among other things, a global variable (or object) is available from any timeline without the need for a dot path.

It is important to realize that the global scope is *not* a timeline; it is a *scope* (or rather, it is the absence of scope, so a global variable is available everywhere without restriction).

To make a variable global or change its value, use the _global path when defining it:

```
_global.myGlobalVariable = 20;
```

To read this global variable from any timeline, you simply refer to the variable without a path:

```
myClip.myTimelineVariable = 10 + myGlobalVariable;
```

ActionScript also exists in the global scope: ActionScript actions and methods are available from any timeline. This is why you don't need a path to access many actions, such as gotoAndPlay() or the + operator. You can actually create your own "actions" by defining them as function objects in the global scope:

```
1  _global.myAction = function() {
2      trace("you can access me directly from anywhere");
3  };
4
```

You can run this function from any timeline simply by using myAction(); without needing to use dot notation.

Avoiding Scope Collisions with Global Naming

If you have a global variable and local or Timeline variable of the same name in the current scope, you will have two different variables that can be referenced by the same name. For example, you may have a situation like the following:

```
_global.myVariable = 20;
myVariable = 30;
```

Here, you have a global variable and a Timeline variable both with the same name and both available from the current Timeline. If you try to read the value of myVariable from the Timeline this code is attached to, you will see a value of 30 because the Timeline variable masks the global. This is scope collision; two same-named variables created in two scopes are both accessible from the current scope, because one of them is global (and is by definition available everywhere).

If you refer to myVariable from any other timeline (and without a path), you will see the global version that is equal to 20, because no scope collision exists on other timelines.

To avoid collisions, it is common practice to prefix the names of all global variables with a lowercase g; "myVariable in global" would be named gMyVariable.

16.7 Understanding Classes, Objects, Methods, and Properties

Flash is an object-oriented (OO) environment. Even if you do not wish to write code using the associated style (object-oriented programming or OOP), an understanding of the OO hierarchy is useful as an overview of how Flash itself works.

Classes

A class is a blueprint of how its members are constructed. Think of a car blueprint. This defines the position of the engine, how many doors the car should have, and so on. The blueprint is *not a car itself*, it's a *definition* of what a car is.

In Flash, the class defines methods and properties. Class *defines* what each class member is and is the reason a button behaves differently from a sound object.

Methods and Properties

A class definition contains only two things: methods (which in Flash also includes a subset called "events") and properties (Flash also calls properties that cannot be changed "constants"). Properties are bits of data that can be different for each object. For a car, a property might be its color; each individual car has a color that is different. Another might be the car's mileage or its current position (note that even two *identical looking* cars will never have the same set of properties because not all properties describe appearance). Properties thus *describe* each *individual* car.

Although you can control an object through its properties, often-used operations are prewritten via methods. A method is a command to do something to the object. For a car, starting involves moving a number of electronic switches to fire the starter motor at the same time as firing the sparkplugs in such a way to set the engine working. You *could* set this configuration up manually, but it would most likely take you an hour every time you wanted to go anywhere! Far easier to just turn the car key and let the starter electronics (which have been set up to follow a *method* of starting the car automatically) do it for you. Methods allow objects to *do things* by acting on the properties and are usually easier than working with properties directly for many complex or specialized tasks.

Object

An object is simply an individual member of a class (or in the example, it is the car itself or "a car"). It has its own personal set of properties so that it can look different from other objects in the same class, but it complies with (or acts fundamentally the same as) other objects in the same class because it has the *same methods*. For example, a car you buy will be fitted out in the way you specify (color, engine size, external and internal trim, optional extras) so that it looks different from other cars from the same series, but it is still recognizable as a particular car model; the similarities between cars of the same model are greater than the differences, and (for example) the starter key will always work the same across the model series.

➡ 11.1 Understanding Symbols

➡ 16.8 Using Flash Classes

➡ 16.9 Using Flash Instances

Flash terminology commonly uses "instance" instead of "object." This is because "instance" is the term implied by the Flash interface ("instance name" rather than "object name", etc.) and because there is a class called Object, so using "instance" to denote class members is less confusing.

The graphic symbol does not have an associated class because a graphic symbol doesn't actually do anything but sit on the Stage and look pretty so methods and ActionScript–accessible properties are not required.

The process of avoiding writing your own code that works by changing properties, and instead using methods is part of the general OO concept of *abstraction*.

16.8   Using Flash Classes

———

Flash classes were
called "objects" in pre-
vious versions of Flash.
This terminology should
now be avoided as it is
outdated.

———

Although you can use
the Actions Toolbox to
add properties and
methods to your script,
most people can hand-
code faster and more
efficiently after just a little experience. When
you hand-code, you
tend to understand your
scripts faster because
you are forced to read
the ActionScript Refer-
ence more often (and
you'll probably discover
better ways of writing
code during some visits).

A nonprogrammer can use the Timeline, tweens, drawing tools, plus the *two* visual classes (movie clips and buttons). You can definitely do a lot with these tools, but once you learn ActionScript, there are around 40 other classes you can access. Learning ActionScript and its class-based structure is the only way to access this other side of Flash.

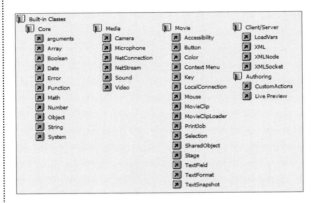

Using Flash classes is simply a matter of picking the one you want your instance to be a member of. You can see the full list of available classes by looking in the Built-in classes book in the Actions Toolbox (top-left pane of the Actions panel). For each class, you can view the methods, properties, and constants (i.e., read-only properties) via subbooks within each class book.

To define a new member (or *instance*) of a class, you can do either of the following:

■ Drag a symbol from the Library panel to the Stage and give it an instance name via the Properties inspector. This applies to classes that have a graphical representation (Movie Clip and Button).

■ Create a new instance in ActionScript with the **new** constructor (for "data only" Flash classes that have no visual representation—this includes all Classes *except* Movie Clip, Button and Video);

```
carData = new Object();
carColor = new Color();
```

In both these cases, the process of using the class blueprint to create a new instance is called *instantiation*; a new instance is created and given an instance name.

Sometimes a class is *static,* in that you do not have to define any instance to use it, because there is only one instance that is already defined within ActionScript. You can tell if this is the case because the class will not include a **new** constructor. Static classes include Math and Key, and you can use them without instantiating.

16.9 Using Flash Instances

Unless you are in the business of creating custom classes or extending the existing ones, the concept of classes is simply some interesting background reading. What you are *really* concerned with is using the instances they define. Once an instance is created, you can control it directly via its properties or indirectly via its methods.

Once you have defined a new instance, you can use dot notation to access the properties and methods of the class. You can see all the methods and properties of a particular class by looking at the contents of the Class book in the Actions Toolbox, and you can add these methods and properties to a script by double-clicking the arrow icons ⌐ .

The first example below sets the alpha property of a movie clip `myClip` embedded in another movie clip `myOtherClip` to 50 (50 percent transparent).

```
myOtherClip.myClip._alpha = 50;
```

```
1  printButton.onRelease = function() {
2      var myPrint = new PrintJob();
3      var printerOk = myPrint.start();
4      if (printerOk) {
5          myPrint.addPage(myPrintableClip);
6          myPrint.send();
7      }else{
8          trace("error in printing")
9          // add your print error code here...
10     }
11  };
12
```

This script shows how methods can be used to control a nonvisual instance (i.e., all instances except movie clips, buttons, and video). When the `printButton` is press-released, a local `PrintJob` instance is created for the duration of the event handler block (line 2). This also creates a local variable `printerOk`, which will be returned as true (via the `PrintJob` start() method) if the print has succeeded—i.e., if nothing is wrong with the printer and the user did not cancel the print—or false otherwise. If it is true, you can send something for the printer to print, in this case the content in movie clip `myPrintableClip` (lines 5 and 6). If `printOk` is false, the code in the `else` part of the `if` will be executed (lines 8, 9).

Note that the `PrintJob` instance is controlled *totally via ActionScript*. To be able to move on from movie clips, buttons and video, and use the 40 or so nonvisual Flash classes, you *must* learn ActionScript. If you don't, you will not be able to use the full features Flash has to offer.

A variable is the simplest form of instance (of class, number, string, or Boolean). You don't need to think about properties with a variable because it has only two—*value* and *name*—and you use them both implicitly when you refer to it. You also don't have to instantiate it (although you can, but this gives no real benefit).

FLASH WORKSPACE

AUTHORING TASKS

SCRIPTING TASKS

TESTING AND PUBLISHING TASKS

WHAT'S NEW

16.10   Creating and Using Arrays

One of the biggest points of confusion about arrays is that they start at item 0. Expressed another way, if you use the length property of an array, the last item is at position *length* but has an index of *length-1*.

Arrays are strongly associated with loops. A loop can move through an array and apply the same code to each item, as shown in the example.

Variables are *unstructured* data; every variable has a single value. An array is the simplest structured form of data, and consists of a numbered list of values. Arrays are most useful when you want to:

- Order a list or sort through it

- Apply the same code to many values

- Work with sequential systems that are not numeric (such as the month expressed as the month name; January, February, etc.

- Relate one set of non-numeric values to another (such as English-to-Russian language translation).

Creating and Populating an Array

To create an array, use the new constructor:

```
myArray = new Array();
myArray2 = new Array(4);
myArray3 = new Array("January", 6, true);
```

myArray1 is an empty array. myArray2 is an array with 4 array items, numbered 0 to 3, each of which has an undefined value. myArray3 is an array of 3 elements, with values "January", 6, and true.

Using an Array

To add items to the list, you use an array just like you would a variable, except that you use a numeric value called the *index* in square brackets after the array instance name. This number reflects the *position* in the list of the item you are accessing.

```
calendar[2] = "March",
```

```
1 myNumbers = new Array(1, 2, 39, 42, 15, 9006, 7.1, 8, 0.9);
2 for (i=0; i<myNumbers.length; i++) {
3     myNumbers[i] = myNumbers[i]*2;
4 }
5 trace(myNumbers);
6
```

```
▼ Output
2,4,78,84,30,18012,14.2,
16,1.8
```

One of the easiest ways to use an array is via a *loop*. This code will double all values in an array, as shown in the Output panel (which shows the items in the array after the loop has run).

Line 1 creates and populates an array myNumbers with some numeric values. Line 2 creates a loop that steps from 0 to myNumbers.length. length is the only property of the Array class and defines the number of entries. Line 3 looks at each item in the array list by using the loop variable i. Finally, you trace the array to see the final values.

16.11   Creating and Using Custom Classes

Although Flash has a rich set of variables and classes, you will sometimes need to create a custom or modified class. There are three ways to do this: using a *constructor*, a *prototype*, or the new Flash 2004 class-based structures. This section looks at when and how to set up the first type.

The following code is the skeleton code to create custom instances via a custom constructor function, each of which has two properties and one method (line numbers are not part of the code):

```
01. function myCustomized(prop1, prop2) {
02.   function methodDefinition(arg) {
03.     trace("you have just called my custom method with argument: ");
04.     trace(arg);
05.   }
06.   this.property1 = prop1;
07.   this.property2 = prop2;
08.   this.method1 = methodDefinition;
09. }
10. myCustom1 = new myCustomized(10, 5);
11. myCustom2 = new myCustomized("yes", "no");
12. myCustom1.method1(10000);
13. trace(myCustom1.property2);
```

The first line is the constructor. The first thing this function does is define another function, which is later used to define method1 (line 8). The two arguments prop1 and prop2 define the initial values of the two properties, property1 and property2 (lines 6 and 7). The last 4 lines of the listing put the constructor through its paces by making it define two custom instances (myCustom1 and myCustom2) of the custom class myCustomized.

➡ 16.12 Understanding Flash MX 2004 Class-Based File Structures

➡ 16.13 Creating Flash MX 2004 Classes

A custom instance created via a constructor creates a separate set of method functions per instance, whereas a prototype acts as a common template for all its instances. A prototype-based solution therefore creates only *one* function and is much more memory efficient.

Custom class names start with a capital letter. This is a standard convention to differentiate classes from instance and variable names. Built-in classes do the same…now you know why!

A prototype was the main way of creating classlike structures in ActionScript revisions before ActionScript 2. It is still a quick way to create custom classes based on the built-in classes, but you are better off using Flash MX 2004 classes for ease of use and ease of understanding.

16.12 Understanding Flash MX 2004 Class-Based File Structures

---

The structure described here is only applicable to Flash MX 2004 and ActionScript 2 and does not appear in Flash MX or previous versions.

The advantage of the Flash MX 2004 structure is its extensibility and reusability caused by generating underlying classes in a structured and modular way.

Flash MX uses the *prototype* in place of class. After using the new Flash MX 2004 system for a while, it becomes apparent that the new system is more flexible, especially for large projects.

Class-based programming is a useful skill set to learn if you will be writing FLAs with lots of ActionScript in them, or if you want to structure your code production in a modular way. Class-based programming in Flash uses AS (ActionScript) files that are linked to the main FLA, and these are used to *define* and *extend* your classes.

Object-oriented programming revolves around forming a basic (or low-level) classes to create the most common solution, and then refining it with further classes that create more specific ones. The specific classes are further refined if necessary before being used to finally create instances you can use. Sounds a bit high-brow and otherworldly huh? Time for the trusty auto analogy...

Suppose you want to define a number of autos. You start with the basic auto framework; engine, and a number of wheels. That is your basic blueprint or "superclass"; Auto. There are lots of different variations on this basic blueprint:

RacingCar In addition to the basic properties of Auto, this will have a racing number and league position.

FamilyCar As well as the basic properties, this will also have some type of audio entertainment system.

These two autos *extend* the basic Auto class to more well-defined types of auto, but they are both still based around the Auto superclass.

Finally, you need to create instances of the RacingCar and FamilyCar classes.

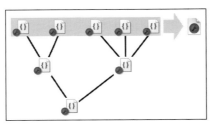

In Flash, the instances are created in your FLA and the definitions for them refer to AS files that define the class structure. The class definitions may themselves refer back through one or more levels of class definitions (toward the root superclass) as part of their definition. The basic structure is thus treelike as per the diagram, which (it is shows the flow of class *inheritance*).

The linkage between the AS files depends on the names you give the files *and this must be the class name defined, and it is case sensitive*:

- The file containing the Auto definition must be called Auto.as.
- The file containing the RacingCar definition must be called RacingCar.as.
- The file containing the FamilyCar definition must be called FamilyCar.as.

From this, it becomes obvious that you should only define *one* class per AS file.

The compilation process produces *one* file from the various FLA and AS files used: the SWF. You *do not* need to upload any of the AS files when deploying your content to the Web.

16.13 Creating Flash MX 2004 Classes

Flash MX 2004 class-based structures provide features not included in previous (proto-type-based) object-oriented code implementations, including automatic type checks, and force you to use a well-defined file structure. If you make errors in these areas, the compiler will tell you.

The best way to show the Flash MX 2004 structure is via an example, assuming a continuation of the last section, this section creates the car example using ActionScript 2 classes.

Starting a Standalone AS (ActionScript) File

Although Flash MX 2004 Professional has special features that make working with Action-Script 2 classes easier, it is still possible (and no more difficult) to create class-based content in Flash MX 2004:

- If you are using Flash MX 2004, open a new FLA (File > New), select frame 1 of the Timeline and then open the Actions panel (Window > Development Panels > Actions) to start entering your script. Make your script pane as big as possible (you do not need to use either the Stage or Timeline). When you have finished the AS file, select Export Script from the Actions panel's panel menu.

- If you are using Flash MX 2004 Professional, open a new ActionScript file. This will open a full-screen text editing environment dedicated to creating standalone scripts. You can save the file using the standard File > Save or Save As menu options.

Creating the Classes

You need to create two AS files to define the `Auto` superclass and the `RacingCar` classes, both of which should be in the same folder. The following two screen shots show you the two files you need to create:

```
Auto  RacingCar  FamilyCar
 1  class Auto {
 2      //properties...
 3      var engineType:String;
 4      var numberOfWheels:Number;
 5      //constructor...
 6      function Auto(argEngineType:String, argNumberOfWheels:Number) {
 7          engineType = argEngineType;
 8          numberOfWheels = argNumberOfWheels;
 9      }
10      //methods...
11      function getEngine():String {
12          return engineType;
13      }
14      function getWheels():Number {
15          return numberOfWheels;
16      }
17  }
```

➡ 5.19 Project Panel

➡ 16.7 Understanding Classes, Objects, Methods, and Properties

Most of the Flash MX 2004 class-based syntax checks are *compile time only*. The class-based structures are compiled down to standard ActionScript structures, and because the Flash player is inherently untyped, it will not catch *runtime* type violations.

Continues

The class definitions created here use methods
to access the instance
properties, which is rec-
ommended practice for
well-defined classes.

If you are using Flash
MX 2004 Professional,
it is strongly recom-
mended you manage
your FLA and AS files
using the Project panel.

```
class RacingCar extends Auto {
    //properties...
    var racingNumber:Number;
    var leaguePos:Number;
    //constructor...
    function RacingCar(argEngineType:String, argNumberOfWheels:Number, argRacingNumber:Number, argLeaguePos:Number) {
        //pass to superclass...
        super(argEngineType, argNumberOfWheels);
        racingNumber = argRacingNumber;
        leaguePos = argLeaguePos;
    }
    //methods...
    function getNumber():Number {
        return racingNumber;
    }
    function getPos():Number {
        return leaguePos;
    }
}
```

Note that:

- Each property defined under **properties…** has a type associated with it. Any definition
  deeper within the class structure that breaks these types will raise a syntax error. This
  helps to force you to create robust code.

- The constructor function has the same name as the class. This is the only way Flash
  recognizes the constructor, so you must name it correctly (including case).

- The **RacingCar** class use the keyword **extends** to refer back to the superclass (line 1)
  and **super()** (in the constructor) to inherit from it.

```
// define an instance of Racing Car
var myRacer:RacingCar = new RacingCar("Flat V12, 6 Liter Big Dude", 4, 45, 3);
// use this instance to prove it works...
trace("looking at myRacer:");
trace("Engine type: "+myRacer.getEngine());
trace("Position in league: "+myRacer.getPos());
```

To use the custom class definitions to create custom instances based on them,
start a new FLA called **testAuto.fla**, save it in the same folder as the AS files, and
on frame 1, attach this script. This creates two instances. *myRacer* is an instance
of the class *RacingCar,* and *myBoringCar* is an instance of *FamilyCar.*

If you test this FLA, you will see that
MyRacer has a property *myPos* that is part of
the *RacingCar* class definition, but it also
has properties such as *engineType* that it
inherited from its superclass, *Auto.*

CHAPTER 17

Code Structures

LEARNING HOW TO USE different kinds of code structures in a Flash document adds a level of complexity into your applications. You can build error checking and handling, write custom functions that debug or display values describing a certain kind of element in a SWF file, or figure out how various parts of your application are functioning after the application is published. Learning these code structures helps you understand many of the scripts you encounter when working with Flash. The statements you find on the following pages are probably the kind you find yourself working with daily when writing ActionScript, because they cover a wide array of the functionality of the scripting language.

- 17.1 **Overview of code structures**
- 17.2 **The** if, else..if, **and** else **statements**
- 17.3 **The** switch **and** case **statements**
- 17.4 **The** for **statement**
- 17.5 **The** for..in **statement**
- 17.6 **The** while **statement**
- 17.7 **The** do..while **statement**
- 17.8 **Using functions**
- 17.9 **The** try, catch, **and** finally **keywords**

17.1 Overview of Code Structures

Code structures are the backbone of the ActionScript language. A code structure is one or more keywords that controls the choice and sequence of statements that are executed—everything from looping over objects to looping over numbers or through arrays to making decisions based on user input or variables within the current SWF file. Using these code structures allows you to build applications that validate user input, such as checking that the appropriate fields have values, or looping through each of the properties within an object and displaying the values to the Output panel.

Flash MX 2004 introduces significant new code structures and keywords such as `try`, `catch`, and `finally`, which can be used to write code to perform more robust error handling. If problems occur during runtime, your SWF file can throw an appropriate error and handle that error accordingly.

If there are functions you think you need but they aren't in ActionScript, you can write your own custom functions to use within Flash documents. For example, if you need a more advanced way of generating random numbers, you can write your own function that takes two numbers as parameters and returns a random integer between the two specified values. You can also write a function that connects to a web service allowing you to send e-mails when an error occurs in your SWF file. This helps you build an extra level of error reporting to your Flash application.

Using ActionScript, you are able to "loop over" statements, which are lines of code. While you are looping over code, Flash continually executes that block of code a given number of times. You can execute the same block of code for that given number of times or while a condition is `true`.

A *condition* is a statement that evaluates to either `true` or `false`. When you write Action-Script, at times you will have a particular situation in which you need to execute a block of code based on the value of a variable. A conditional statement allows you to do this. You set a condition and when that condition is `true` (for example, when `cat == hungry`), then the conditional statement executes a block of code (such as, `feed the cat`).

17.2 The *if*, *else..if*, and *else* Statements

The if, else..if, and else statements are used to test a condition or series of conditions that you set in the script and then execute a statement based on the condition(s). If the condition is true, the statement executes. You can even write a script using else that executes some code if no conditions in the statement are met. That is, if no conditions evaluate to true, then the else statement executes. Examine the following statements to understand how each of these statements are slightly different in their functionality.

Examining the *if* Statement

The if statement is extremely useful in ActionScript for testing if a particular variable is defined, if an instance on the Stage is colliding with another instance, or if two values match. The basic format of the if statement is as follows:

```
if (condition){
  statements;
}
```

This means that if a particular condition is met, such as the length of text equaling 0, then a particular statement is then executed. This is shown in the following code snippet. To check whether a specific variable is defined, write code similar to the following:

```
if (message_txt.text.length == 0) {
  error.text = "Please enter a value for message";
}
```

Examining the *else* Statement

The else statement performs a task that is opposite to the if statement. While the if statement executes a block of code only if the condition evaluates to true, the else statement executes a block of code only if the if statement evaluates to false. This is shown in the following code, which checks whether a string of text in a text field matches a specified value. If the condition evaluates to false, then a trace action outputs you aren't Skip.

```
if (name_txt.text == "skip") {
  trace("your name is Skip");
} else {
  trace("you aren't Skip");
}
```

➡ 17.3 The switch and case Statements

The conditional operator is a great way to shorten your source code, but it often makes it much more difficult to read and modify unless you include a lot of comments in your code. Code is much more readable and easier to understand when you use traditional if, else..if, and else statements.

Continues •

Examining the *else..if* Statement

To test for several different possible values, you can use the `else..if` statement. While you can only have a single `if` or `else` statement in the `if` block, you can use as many `else..if` statements as you need. In the following code, you can see that there is exactly one `if` statement, which is followed by two `else..if` statements and finally an `else` statement at the bottom:

```
if (score_txt.text >= 90) {
  trace("very good");
} else if (score_txt.text >= 80) {
  trace("good");
} else if (score_txt.text >= 70) {
  trace("ok");
} else {
  trace("needs practice");
}
```

In this ActionScript, the following situation occurs. If the value of the `score_txt` text field is 90 or above, the `if` statement evaluates to `true` and the `else..if` and `else` statements are skipped. The text "very good" displays in the Output panel. If the score result is between 80 and 89, then the first `else..if` statement is executed and the word "good" displays in the Output panel. The `else` statement only executes when the `if` statement and two `else..if` statements do not evaluate to `true`. This happens when the value of `score_txt` is 69 or below, and the text "needs practice" is then displayed in the Output panel.

Using the Conditional Operator for Simple *if..else* Statements

Another way of representing simple `if..else` statements is by using the conditional operator, `?:`. Although the code is a bit trickier to read, the conditional operator can simplify setting a variable based on a condition. For example, to set a variable based on an `if` statement, you could use ActionScript similar to the following:

```
var thisWidth:Number = (myMovieClip._width > 100) ? 100 : myMovieClip._width;
```

The above code is shorthand for:

```
if (myMovieClip._width > 100) {
  var thisWidth:Number = 100;
} else {
  var thisWidth:Number = myMovieClip._width;
}
```

If you are working with Boolean values, Flash allows you to use the variable directly in your `if` statements instead of having to compare the Boolean value to `true` or `false`. This allows you to write code that simply says `if (userLoggedIn) {…}` instead of having to write `if (userLoggedIn == true) {…}`.

When checking Boolean values, you can also use the logical NOT operator (`!`) in your code. The not operator tests for the opposite value of the Boolean, so if you are testing a Boolean value that is set to true and you use the `!` operator, Flash inverts the true and says if NOT true (which equals false). For example, `if (!userLoggedIn) {…}` would only evaluate to true if the value of userLoggedIn was initially false.

17.3 The *switch* and *case* Statements

A switch statement tests a condition and executes a block of code if the condition returns a value of true. In a nutshell, a switch statement is like a very fancy series of if..else statements.

The case statement defines a condition for the switch statement, just like the condition found in an if or else..if statement. The case statement is only used in conjunction with the switch statement to provide functionality similar to the if, else..if, and else statements. The following code snippet checks the value in the state_txt text field and then determines what condition to execute.

```
switch (state_txt.text) {
case "CA" :
  trace("California");
  break;
case "FL" :
  trace("Florida");
  break;
default :
  trace("unknown state: "+state_txt.text);
}
```

If the value of state_txt.text is CA, then Flash traces "California" to the Output panel. If the value of state_txt.text is not CA or FL, then the default case is executed, if it exists. If break is encountered, then the SWF stops processing and exits the switch statement. In the above code, the default condition is to trace "unknown state" and the characters that were entered into the text field.

The switch and case statements are also case sensitive, so if the user enters ca into the state_txt text field, Flash will display "unknown state: ca" in the Output panel. You can get around this by converting the value of state_txt.text to uppercase or lowercase before evaluating it, as shown below:

```
switch (state_txt.text.toUpperCase()) {
case "CA" :
  trace("California");
  break;
...
}
```

→ 17.2 The if, else..if, and else Statements

The switch statement is often more efficient and readable than using a significant number of if..else blocks.

Switch statements and if..else blocks are not always interchangeable. If you need to test different values in each else..if block, then it is likely that you're unable to convert the statement into a switch statement. Switch statements evaluate the condition once and try to find an appropriate case to pass control to. Each condition is evaluated separately if you write a series of else..if blocks. This allows you to use multiple conditions.

Continues

When working with case statements, don't forget to add the break statement. If you do not add the break statement, the code keeps processing any future case statements it encounters

When working with the switch and case statements, don't forget that the values are case sensitive. For example, CA and ca require two separate case statements. Consider converting the condition to all uppercase or all lowercase when working with switch statements.

Now if a user enters CA, ca, Ca, or cA into the text field, Flash will convert the string to CA before evaluating the switch statement. The case statement is very useful if you have many case statements where you want to execute the same block of code. For example, the following code assigns a region based on which U.S. state a person is from:

```
switch (state_txt.text.toUpperCase()) {
case "CA" :
case "OR" :
case "WA" :
  var region:String = "West Coast";
  break;
case "AZ" :
case "NM" :
case "NV" :
case "OK" :
case "TX" :
  var region:String = "Southwest";
  break;
//…
}
```

If the value of state_txt.text is CA, OR, or WA, then Flash sets the user's region to West Coast. Remember, when the break statement is found, Flash stops processing and exits the switch statement. If the visitor enters their state as AZ, NM, NV, OK, or TX, then a region of Southwest is set.

COMPLEX DATA STRUCTURES

There are simple and complex data structures as well as code structures. When it comes to data structures, you can have something as simple as a name/value pair, or you can have something more complex, such as those that might be returned from a server. Using these complex data structures in Flash varies in difficulty and must be supported by whatever you are using. For example, if you are using the LoadVars class to load data, it can only handle the simple name/value pair. However, Flash Remoting handles complex structures such as the RecordSet. This means that not only is code structured in a particular way, but so is data.

17.4 The *for* Statement

The for statement executes a block of code a specific number of times. This is useful if you want to create ten objects on the Stage or loop through every item in an array and perform a particular action (such as setting the visibility, or performing a calculation) on each element in that array.

```
var myArray:Array = new Array("one", "two", "three", "four");
for (var i:Number = 0; i<myArray.length; i++) {
  trace(i+": "+myArray[i]); // will trace "0: one", "1: two", etc.
}
```

The preceding code loops through each of the items in the array and then displays the current loop index (i) and the current value of the array at that index. It is very important when looping through arrays to take into account that arrays in ActionScript are zero-based (that is, the first element is numbered 0, the second is numbered 1, etc.) and not one-based. If the for loop loops from 1 to the length of the array, it will disregard the first element within the array.

A for loop can loop through each character in a string to test if the string is a valid e-mail address by using the following code:

```
var myEmail = "test@email.com"; // sample e-mail address
var hasAtSymbol = false;  // does the e-mail address have a "@" symbol
var hasTLD = false;       // does the e-mail have a "." after the "@"
for (var i = 0; i < myEmail.length; i++) {
  if (hasAtSymbol == false && myEmail.charAt(i) == "@") {
    hasAtSymbol = true;
  } else if (hasAtSymbol == true && myEmail.charAt(i) == ".") {
    hasTLD = true;
    break; // if both a "@" and "." found, consider it valid email.
  }
}
if (hasAtSymbol && hasTLD) {
  trace("valid email");
} else {
  trace("invalid email");
}
```

This code is a fairly crude test of an e-mail address because it only checks for the existence of an ampersand (&) and a period. If you were testing e-mail addresses in a production environment, you'd want to test that the address has at least one character before the @ symbol, as well as at least one character for a domain name and a valid third-level domain (.com, or .org, and so on).

➡ 17.2 The if, else..if, and else Statements

➡ 17.5 The for..in Statement

➡ 17.6 The while Statement

➡ 17.7 The do..while Statement

The for statement is an excellent way to loop through each item within an array and display the array's values or perform calculations. Simply loop from 0 to the length of the array.

In the for loop, the counter should usually be incremented by one each time using the increment operator (++). To loop through only even or odd numbers, set the starting number accordingly and increment the counter by two values each time using i+=2 instead of i++. The i+=2 is the same as using the longer version i=i+2.

17.5   The *for..in* Statement

The for..in statement loops through an object. It loops over all of the properties of the object and can then be used to display those properties in the Output panel.

```
var myObject:Object = new Object();
myObject.username = "NateW";
myObject.password = "mightymouse";
for (var i in myObject) {
  trace(i+": "+myObject[i]);
}
/* the above will display the following in the Output panel:
    password: mightymouse
    username: NateW
*/
```

This code first creates a new object using the Object constructor, and then sets two variables within the myObject object. Next, the for..in loop loops through each item within the object and displays the name/value pair in the Output panel. You can see that the order in which the values are returned from the Object is not necessarily the same as the order in which they are defined.

The for..in statement can be invaluable while debugging your SWF file. If you use the LoadVars class, integrate with external web services, or use Flash Remoting and don't necessarily know the structure or contents of the data being passed back, you can use the for..in syntax to loop through the Object. This displays the Object's structure in the Output panel.

The for..in loop allows you to quickly debug your applications by iterating (looping over, one at a time) through each of the properties of an object and displaying the values in the Output panel. This allows you to easily see which methods and properties exist within a movie clip or component instance. Also, it allows you to loop through the results of a web service call or LoadVars object.

17.6   The *while* Statement

The `while` statement loops over a block of code as long as the condition evaluates to `true`. The `while` loop can be used much like the `for` loop in many cases, but it can also be useful when you don't know exactly how many times you need to loop and therefore cannot use a `for` loop.

The syntax for the `while` loop is shown below:

```
var images:Array = new Array("img1.jpg", "img2.jpg", "img3.jpg");
var i:Number = 0;
while (i<images.length) {
  trace(images[i]);
  i++;
}
```

The first thing this script does is create an array of items to loop over. Next, it initializes a counter variable, which keeps track of where you are within the array. The `while` loop repeats as long as the value of the counter variable, i, is less than the number of items in the array. Within the `while` loop, the script traces the value at the current index of the array and finally increments the counter variable. The preceding code could have been rewritten as a `for` loop, as follows:

```
var images:Array = new Array("img1.jpg", "img2.jpg", "img3.jpg");
for (var i:Number = 0; i < images.length; i++) {
  trace(images[i]);
}
```

Both code snippets have about the same amount of code. Each example initializes a counter variable, has the same loop condition (the value of the counter is less than the number if items in the array), and increments the counter.

Avoid Infinite Loops

When using a `while` loop you have to be very careful to not write what is called an *infinite loop*. Infinite loops are loops that go on forever because the ending loop condition can never be met. You know you have an infinite loop if your SWF begins to run really slowly, and eventually you'll see an alert notifying you that a script in your SWF is causing the Flash Player to run slowly, similar to the following:

➡ 17.4 The for
       Statement

Use extreme caution so you do not accidentally create infinite loops when using `while` and `do..while` loops. Although you can exit an infinite loop using the break statement when a certain condition is met, you should only do this when absolutely necessary to avoid possible looping problems. This also makes writing clear, concise documentation (such as comments in your ActionScript) very important so you and fellow developers can understand the code at a later date if you need to edit the FLA file.

Continues

FLASH WORKSPACE

AUTHORING TASKS

SCRIPTING TASKS

TESTING AND PUBLISHING TASKS

WHAT'S NEW

17.6   The *while* Statement *(continued)*

———

Often while loops can be rewritten as simple for loops, although not always. You should use for loops when you can, so your code is more readable at a future date.

The following code is the same as the previous while loop example, except the variable i is no longer being incremented within the loop:

```
var images:Array = new Array("img1.jpg", "img2.jpg", "img3.jpg");
var i = 0;
while (i < images.length) {
  trace(images[i]);
}
```

The value of the counter variable, i, is always less than the length of the array (which is 3), and therefore the loop can never terminate. Thankfully, Flash gives the option to stop running the ActionScript code if it runs for too long, enabling you to terminate the endless loop and fix your code.

17.7 The *do..while* Statement

The `do..while` statement is very similar to the `while` loop. The main difference between the `while` loop and the `do..while` loop is that the `while` loop evaluates the end loop condition before any code in the loop is evaluated, and the `do..while` loop evaluates the end condition at the end of the loop. The difference seems very small, but there is one important thing to note: because the `do..while` loop evaluates the end loop condition at the end of the loop, the loop is always executed at least once. The `do` loop can be changed into a `do..while` as seen in the following code snippet:

```
var images:Array = new Array("img1.jpg", "img2.jpg", "img3.jpg");
var i = 0;
do {
  trace(images[i]);
  i++;
} while (i < images.length);
```

Breaking Out of Loops

To break out of a loop before the end condition is met, you use the `break` statement. If you have an array with dozens of records and are only interested in the first record matching your criteria, you can use the `break` statement to end the loop early instead of having to check several more items in the loop that you aren't interested in. Here's an example:

```
var users:Array = new Array();
users.push({name:"Abe", manager:false});
users.push({name:"George", manager:false});
users.push({name:"Lenny", manager:true});
users.push({name:"Walter", manager:true});
var i:Number = 0;
do {
  if (users[i].manager) {
    trace(users[i].name);
    break;
  }
  i++;
} while (i<users.length);
```

➡ 17.2 The `if`, `else..if`, and `else` Statements

➡ 17.4 The `for` Statement

Whenever possible, use a `for` loop rather than a `do..while` loop; `for` loops are typically more readable and easier to maintain.

Always make sure your `do..while` statements have a definite and achievable end condition; otherwise, you'll encounter infinite loops that cause problems in your Flash movie.

Continues

17.7 The *do..while* Statement *(continued)*

➡ 17.5 The for..in
Statement

➡ 17.6 The while
Statement

When using the con-
tinue statements,
make sure you properly
increment or decre-
ment the counter vari-
able. Otherwise, you
might find that your
counter no longer
works properly and
you are stuck in an
infinite loop.

The preceding code loops through an array of users; when it encounters a user who is also a manager, the user's name is traced to the Output panel and the code breaks out of the loop. Note that even though there are two users who are managers, only the first manager found is returned.

The break statement isn't limited to do..while loops, it can also be used with for, for..in, and while loops.

Skipping Items While Looping

ActionScript has a continue statement that is very similar to the break statement. The continue statement skips a single iteration of the loop instead of exiting the loop altogether. For example, the following code loops over a range of numbers using a for loop and disregards any number divisible by 4:

```
for (var i = 0; i < 100; i++) {
  if (i%4 == 0) {
    continue;
  }
  trace(i);
}
// this code will trace "1,2,3,5,6,7,9,…"
```

This code loops from 0 to 99 if the current loop index is divisible by 4 with a remainder of 0. Then the code skips the rest of the loop body and goes to the next iteration.

17.8   Using Functions

Functions are used throughout Flash, from loading in data with `LoadVars` to sending and receiving XML packets to creating objects on the Stage or loading style sheets into Flash. The ability to create your own functions in ActionScript is one of the most powerful features of Flash. If there is a function that you need to create and Flash doesn't provide it, you can write your own custom functions. Writing functions is very important when building applications in Flash because it allows you to wrap your own business logic into a function. This logic can be reused repeatedly without having to duplicate code throughout your application. This way, if your business logic ever changes, you only have to update the code in one central place instead of searching throughout your FLA files looking for places where the code requires repair.

Creating your own custom function is simple. For example, if you have a Button component instance on the Stage with an instance name of `submit_btn`, you can execute a function when the button is pressed by using the following code:

```
function buttonClicked() {
  trace("the submit button was pressed");
}
submit_btn.addEventListener("click", buttonClicked);
```

The first step to creating custom functions is to define the function and name it using the function keyword. This tells Flash that you're creating a custom function (sometimes called a *named* function). In the functions body, you then define the ActionScript to execute when the function is called. The function seen previously is a very simple function that simply outputs a message to the Output panel stating the button instance has been clicked. This script also uses one of Flash's own functions, in this case the `addEventListener` function belonging to the button instance.

You can also write your own functions that take arguments, as shown next:

```
function traceObject(objInstance:Object) {
  trace("Tracing object");
  for (var i in objInstance) {
    trace("   " + i + ": " + objInstance[i]);
  }
  trace("-------------");
}
var myObj = {name:"Brad", phone:"555-1234", city:"St. Louis"};
traceObject(myObj);
```

This code is a simple function that takes a single argument, called `objInstance`. It displays each of the values within the object using a `for..in` loop. To display the contents of an object within the SWF file, you can write a custom function, instead of always having to write `for..in` loops.

Style sheets refer to cascading style sheets (CSS), which format and change the appearance of text, such as change the color, size, font face, or text alignment. CSS are frequently used to format HTML pages in order to separate the stylistic appearance from the document's overall structure, allowing greater flexibility and reuse.

17.9   The *try*, *catch*, and *finally* Keywords

➡ 17.2 The if,
          else..if,
          and else
          Statements

➡ 17.5 The for..in
          Statement

Try and catch blocks
allow you to build
applications with more
robust error handling.

Using a combination of
try and catch blocks
and web services, Flash
Remoting, or LoadVars,
it is possible to build
applications that fully
integrate with the client
and server. The applica-
tion can notify you by
e-mail whenever an
error in the Flash appli-
cation is thrown or
caught, thus enabling
you to track how many
errors occur in your
application.

Flash MX 2004 introduced the try, catch, and finally keywords into ActionScript. These allow developers to build much more robust applications with greater control in catching errors. The try keyword tells Flash to attempt executing a block of code, and if an invalid result is caught then you can throw your own custom error. A custom error might skip the rest of the code within a try block and go to a corresponding catch block if one exists.

```
try {
  var res:Number = 1/0;
  if (res == Infinity) {
    throw new Error("divide by zero error.");  // throw new error.
  }
  trace(res);  // if an error was thrown, this would not be traced.
} catch (error) {
  trace(error.message);  // displays "divide by zero error."
}
```

This block of code begins with a try statement. Next, a simple division is performed, and the result is stored in a variable named res. If the value of res is Infinity, a number has been divided by zero and therefore an error can safely be thrown. Processing within the try block is stopped when the error is thrown, and control passes to the catch block, where you can display the error message. Therefore, in the preceding example, the value of res is not displayed in the Output panel because an error is thrown. When the error is caught within the catch block, the value of the error attribute is an object holding the name of the error, along with the message and a function named toString. To display the contents of the error object, use a for..in loop as shown next:

```
//...
} catch (error) {
  for (i in error) {
  trace(i+":"+error[i]);
  }
}
```

The finally keyword cleans up any variables or errors that might have occurred in the try block. Unlike the catch block, which is only executed if an error was thrown, the finally block executes every time, whether there is an error or not.

CHAPTER 18

Working with Events

EVENTS ARE AN EXTREMELY important part of working with Flash. You probably use them daily if you like to write code, because they create most of the interaction in a SWF file. Events occur when your visitors click buttons or press keys to trigger the actions you've built into your FLA file or to activate built-in functionality. Events are the listeners that wait for something to happen and act upon those events. In this chapter, you find out how to add all sorts of events to a FLA document to help create interactivity in your SWFs.

18.1   Understanding Event-Driven Code

An event in Flash is an action that occurs during the playback of a SWF file. Events can be generated when a user clicks a button, presses a key on the keyboard, changes text in a text field, or scrolls a scrollbar (these are referred to as *user events*). Events can also be generated by Flash when an XML file has received data, a certain frame is reached in the Timeline, a file finishes loading in a Loader component, or even if a sound object has received ID3 data. Each of these events needs to be handled in slightly different ways.

One of the most difficult concepts for beginner and intermediate users alike is the fact that Flash operates *asynchronously,* which means that Flash continues playing the SWF file instead of pausing and waiting for a reply from the server before proceeding. This means that you have to be much more careful when loading external data because you cannot make sure that the data is available immediately after you call the `load` method.

```
var exampleLoadVars:LoadVars = new LoadVars();
exampleLoadVars.load("samplefile.txt");
exampleLoadVars.onLoad = function(success:Boolean) {
  trace(exampleLoadVars.age);
};
```

This ActionScript creates a `LoadVars` object called `exampleLoadVars` and loads a text file in the current directory named `samplefile.txt`. If you were to immediately trace the value of `exampleLoadVars.age` after performing the load, you would most likely see **undefined** in the Output panel. You must use the `onLoad` event to listen for a response because Flash continues processing the SWF instead of waiting for a response from the server. When Flash receives a result from the server, the function defined in the `onLoad` event is triggered and Flash traces the contents of the `age` variable to the Output panel.

USING KEYPRESSES WITH THE *ON()* EVENT HANDLER

You can listen for special keys such as Left, Right, Home, End, Insert, Delete, Backspace, Enter, Up, Down, PageUp, PageDown, Tab, Escape, and Space. To use these special constant values, surround them in angle brackets (<>), like so: on (keyPress "<Space>") { trace("You pressed the space bar."); }.

18.2   Attaching Scripts to Buttons or Movie Clips

You can write event-based code by putting event handlers directly on movie clip or button instances instead of on a frame. There are a couple of different methods you can use for placing code on an instance on the Stage: you can use the **on()** event handler or use the **onClipEvent()** event handler. The **on()** event handler listens for keypresses and mouse interactions, whereas the **onClipEvent()** listens for movie events.

Using the *on()* Event Handler

The on() event handler is able to listen for eight different mouse or keyboard events to trigger and execute a block of code accordingly. It listens to the following events:

dragOut Triggers if the mouse button is pressed while the cursor is over the selected symbol and the mouse is still pressed as the visitor drags the cursor outside of the symbol.

dragOver Triggers if the mouse button is pressed while the cursor is over the selected symbol, the cursor is dragged out of the symbol, and then dragged back over it.

press Triggers when the mouse button is pressed while over the selected instance.

release Triggers when the mouse button is clicked and released while over the selected instance.

releaseOutside Triggers when the mouse button is pressed while over the selected instance but released outside of the instance.

rollOut Triggers when the cursor rolls out of the selected instance.

rollOver Triggers when the cursor rolls over the selected instance.

keyPress Triggers when the user presses a certain key.

The following ActionScript code, when placed directly on a movie clip instance, allows you to click the instance and drag it around the Stage. When you release the mouse button, the instance stops moving along with the cursor:

```
on (press) {
  startDrag(this);
}
on (release) {
  stopDrag();
}
```

➠ 11   Symbols and
         Behaviors

➠ 15.8 Attaching a
         Script

Macromedia used to discourage the practice of placing ActionScript throughout your FLA file, but with the introduction of behaviors, object-based code seems to be acceptable again. However, it is still a good practice to centralize as much code as you can to make it easier for you to update, debug, and maintain your FLA files at a later date. Another practice is to use external code (.as) files as much as possible.

Be very cautious when using onClipEvent-(enterFrame) because it executes code many times every second and therefore can degrade performance. By default, Flash movies run at 12 fps, so the code in an enter-Frame block runs 12 times each second; this can cause the user's CPU to max out and play back your movie very slowly.

Continues ●

18.2   Attaching Scripts to Buttons or Movie Clips

➡ 22.2 Attaching
Events
Dynamically

———

Button scope and movie clip scope are different from each other. When you place code on a button, any methods are called for the Timeline that the button is placed on—in other words, not the Timeline inside the button instance. However, if you put code on a movie clip instance, the method calls the Timeline inside the movie clip.

———

When using on (key-Press), remember that the keys are case sensitive. It may be necessary to check for both the R and r keyPress events, depending on what you've set out to do.

(continued)

If you test this code sample, move your mouse very fast, and let go of the mouse button, the movie clip could still follow your cursor. This could happen because the mouse might not be directly over the instance temporarily. If this happens, the `release` event might not register. You can work around this by listening for the `releaseOutside` event as well as the `release` event. The easiest way to do this is to add the `releaseOutside` event to the same code block as the `on (release)` event handler, instead of duplicating code:

```
on (release, releaseOutside) { ...
```

If you want to listen for a specific key to be pressed, you need to use the following code:

```
on (keyPress "A") {
  trace("you pressed the 'A' button.");
}
```

Keys are case sensitive, so if you enter lowercase *a*, you will not see the `trace` statement. To listen for multiple keys, you must use separate `on (keyPress)` event handlers—for instance, one for uppercase *A* and a separate one for lowercase *a*.

Using the *onClipEvent()* Event Handler

The other method of handling events, `onClipEvent()`, is only permitted on movie clip instances and handles generally different events than the `on()` event handler:

load Triggers when the selected instance first appears on the Timeline.

unload Triggers when the selected instance is first removed from the Timeline.

enterFrame Triggers several times a second based on the current frame rate of the Flash document. If the document is set to12 frames per second (fps), then the `enterFrame` event handler triggers 12 times per second.

mouseMove Triggers when the X and Y coordinates of the mouse change (these values can be found by tracing `_xmouse` and `_ymouse`).

mouseDown Triggers when the user clicks the primary mouse button.

mouseUp Triggers when the user releases the primary mouse button.

keyDown Triggers when the user presses a key.

keyUp Triggers when the user releases a key.

data Triggers when data is received from the `LoadVariables` action or `LoadMovie` action.

18.3 Attaching Scripts to Events Using Functions

Scripts can be attached to events using named or inline functions instead of placing code directly on the instance. This allows you to centralize much of your code in a single frame within a specific layer, which makes it easier to maintain than having to hunt throughout your FLA file for a symbol you placed some code on. There are a couple different methods of attaching code to an event: using an *inline* (or *anonymous*) function or using a *named function*.

Here's an example of a named function that handles an event:

```
sayHello_btn.onPress = sayHello;
function sayHello() {
  trace("you clicked the shiny red button.");
}
```

The first line of code defines the name of the function that handles the `onPress` event. Every time a user clicks the button with an instance name of `sayHello_btn`, the `sayHello` function executes. When working with named functions and handling events, be careful not to add parentheses to the function name in the top line of code. (If you accidentally add parentheses before the semicolon, Flash will execute the `sayHello` method in your ActionScript and then no longer listen for the `onPress` event to be called.) Then the function is actually defined in the code snippet and traces a string to the Output panel.

Another benefit of using named functions is that if you want to reuse a function on multiple instances, you don't have to rewrite as much code.

```
square_mc.onPress = doPress;
square_mc.onRelease = doRelease;
circle_mc.onPress = doPress;
circle_mc.onRelease = doRelease;
function doPress() {
  this.startDrag();
}
function doRelease() {
  this.stopDrag();
}
```

This code relies on two movie clip instances on the Stage: `square_mc` and `circle_mc`. The purpose of the code is to allow users to drag the circle and square instances around the Stage and stop dragging the symbol once the mouse button has been released. You can see that the `doPress` and `doRelease` functions have been recycled and then used as a handler for both the `square_mc` and `circle_mc` instances.

Using named functions to handle events makes it much simpler to recycle code; however, sometimes these functions are a bit longer to write than anonymous functions.

18.4 Attaching Scripts to Events Using Callback Functions

Info panel
Ctrl I
⌘ I

———

Some callbacks pass a Boolean value stating whether or not the action successfully completes. You should always check the status of the action to see if it is successful or not before you attempt to use variables or style sheet objects.

———

When you provide the name of a function within the event handler, do not use parentheses after the function name.

Certain events can also be handled using a callback function. For example, when loading a style sheet into Flash, the style sheet triggers an event named onLoad after a file has been loaded and the results have been parsed. In order to handle this event you need to create a callback function that executes when the onLoad event occurs:

```
var css_styles = new TextField.StyleSheet();
css_styles.load("styles.css");
css_styles.onLoad = function(success:Boolean) {
  if (success) {
    myText_txt.styleSheet = css_styles;
    } else {
    trace("Error loading CSS file.");
  }
};
```

This code creates a new style sheet object and loads the contents of the styles.css file into the css_styles variable. Next, you assign a callback function for the style sheet's onLoad event. When Flash loads in the external file, the onLoad event triggers and the function then executes. When Flash triggers the onLoad event, it passes a single variable to the function. The variable is a flag stating whether or not the file can be successfully loaded and parsed. If there is an error loading the file then the value of success is false and a message traces to the Output panel. Otherwise, the style sheet object is assigned to a text instance on the Stage.

You can also create a named function instead of using the anonymous/inline function:

```
var css_styles = new TextField.StyleSheet();
css_styles.load("styles.css");
css_styles.onLoad = someStyleSheetFunction;
function someStyleSheetFunction(success:Boolean) {
  if (success) {
  myText_txt.styleSheet = css_styles;
  } else {
  trace("Error loading CSS file.");
  }
}
```

The only difference between this code and the earlier is that instead of adding the function directly to the onLoad event, you provide the name of the function in the onLoad event and define the function separately.

18.5 Writing Button Scripts for Flash Movie Navigation

Perhaps the most useful part of listening for events is when you want to build some sort of navigation in Flash. By adding a few menu buttons in your site, it is extremely easy to add navigation so you can jump between different sections of the site from any timeline.

For example, if the following code were placed directly on a movie clip instance on the Stage, the movie clip would go to a frame with the label `aboutus` when the mouse button is released over the symbol:

```
on (release) {
   this._parent.gotoAndStop("aboutus");
}
```

Note the use of scope within the code. When placing code within a movie clip instance, `this` refers to the movie clip itself. Then, `_parent` refers to the Timeline the movie clip resides on, and therefore the `gotoAndStop()` action moves the playhead to a frame with the label `aboutus` and stops. If you simply used the code `gotoAndStop("aboutus")` without using `this.parent`, Flash would try and move the playhead in the movie clip's Timeline to a frame named `aboutus`. This probably isn't what you want to see happen.

You need to modify the source code slightly if you are using a button instance instead of a movie clip. When working with buttons, the `this` identifier refers to the Timeline that the button is on. This is unlike movie clips, where `this` refers to the Timeline of the movie clip itself. If you were using buttons the code would need to change to the following:

```
on (release) {
   this.gotoAndStop("aboutus");
}
```

If you wanted to place the code on the Timeline instead of directly on the button or movie clip instance, you could add the following code to a frame:

```
buttonInstanceName.onRelease = function() {
   this._parent.gotoAndStop("contactus");
};
```

Be careful when placing code directly on instances: using `this` on a button refers to the Timeline the button instance is on, but using `this` on a movie clip refers to the movie clip's Timeline.

18.6 Writing Button Scripts for Web Navigation

➠ 11.15 Creating Buttons

➠ 11.16 Adding Basic Button Navigation Using Behaviors

➠ 15.4 Adding an Instance Name

➠ 18.2 Attaching Scripts to Buttons or Movie Clips

Remove Transform
Ctrl Shift Z
⌘ Shift Z

Using getURL can be very useful if you want to integrate a Flash site with an HTML site. You can easily pass variables to an HTML form and send users directly to a search results page or a login results page after entering their user-name and password in a secured Flash area.

If you want more control and functionality when creating hybrid Flash and HTML sites, look into the `LocalConnection` object.

If you want to launch a window with a specific size and attributes, it may be necessary to use JavaScript to launch a new window and then use the window's target name from ActionScript.

One of the great things about Flash is that it can interact with a web browser. Flash makes it simple to open a new or existing browser window using ActionScript's `getURL` function. This can be useful if you want to integrate a Flash application with a server-side script. Perhaps you want the user to be able to enter a keyword in a Flash text field and show search results in a regular HTML page. To launch a new browser window, you can use the following code:

```
mm_btn.onRelease = function() {
  getURL("http://www.macromedia.com/", "_blank");
}
```

When a user clicks the `mm_btn` instance on the Stage, Flash triggers the `onRelease` event and executes the function. The function calls the `getURL` function, which opens a new browser window at the specified URL. Much like an HTML link, the `getURL` function accepts different values for the target window. You can use one of four reserved target names (`_self`, `_blank`, `_parent`, or `_top`) or the name of an existing window or frame.

The `getURL` function can also be used to send variables to the remote page as well by adding an extra parameter. The easiest way of sending variables is to create an empty movie clip using ActionScript and call the `getURL` function for that particular object, as shown here:

```
createEmptyMovieClip("getURLparams", 1);
getURLparams.q = "flash2004";
getURLparams.getURL("http://www.google.com/search", "_blank", "GET");
```

This code creates a new empty movie clip that you use to hold the variables which are sent to the remote site. Next you assign a single variable, which in this example is a keyword to be searched on the Google site. Finally, you call the `getURL` function for the movie clip. This call sends the variables contained in the `getURLparams` movie clip to the target URL (Google) in a new browser window (denoted by the `_blank` parameter) and sends the variables in the address bar (denoted by the GET parameter). If you want to send the variables in the HTML header instead of the address bar (query string), you can change the GET to POST, the same as if you were building an HTML form. When passing variables along the address bar, you're usually limited by the browser as to how much data can be transmitted (usually between 128 and 1024 characters), plus the values can be seen and changed by the end user more easily than if the values were passed using the POST method.

18.7 Writing Button Scripts for Interactive Control and Animation

Using listeners and buttons is an excellent way to write ActionScript to control playback of the main Timeline, MP3s, or movie clips. You can add several button instances on your Stage that will each wait to be clicked by a visitor. The buttons then pause, stop, play, or control the interactive element depending on the button that's selected. Here is an example:

```
var myMP3:Sound = new Sound();
myMP3.loadSound("sounds of the ocean.mp3", true);
myMP3.onID3 = function() {
  trace("ID3 loaded");
};
play_btn.onRelease = function() {
  myMP3.start();
};
stop_btn.onRelease = function() {
  myMP3.stop();
};
```

The above code creates a new sound object and then loads in a streaming MP3 file. Next, an event handler is set up for the sound object. You could use this technique to display the song title, album, length, size, or any other available information in the Sound.id3 property. Depending on whether ID3 v1 or ID3 v2 tags are present, only certain attributes might be available in the id3 property. Then event handlers are added to two button instances on the Stage: play_btn and stop_btn. The two buttons allow visitors to control playback of the SWF file by starting or stopping the stream whenever the buttons are pressed.

➡ 10.19 Adding Video to a Timeline

➡ 13.5 Importing Video

➡ 15.4 Adding an Instance Name

➡ 15.7 Dot Notation

➡ 18.2 Attaching Scripts to Buttons or Movie Clips

Although Flash MX Professional 2004 provides media components that play back audio and video, sometimes you will want to use your own custom interface to play back audio and video files that is possible to build using ActionScript.

UNDERSTANDING DEPTH

Remember that you can only have one instance at each depth in a single SWF file. If you load a second instance at the same depth, the new instance will overwrite the old one. This is great if you intend to delete instances and replace them with new ones; however, this isn't good if you don't want to delete anything. You can avoid deleting instances by incrementing your depth numbers using ActionScript or using getNextHighestDepth().

Continues ●

_____

Calling the stop()
method on a streaming
MP3 causes the sound
file to stop and return to
its starting position. Calling the stop() method
on an embedded video
stops the playhead
within the movie clip,
which causes the video
to pause rather than
return to the first frame.
If you want to move the
playhead back to the
beginning of the
embedded video, you
need to use gotoAnd-
Stop(1) in the embed-
ded video clip.

_____

If you are loading an
MP3 containing both
ID3v1 and ID3v2 tags,
the onID3 event han-
dler is called twice,
once for each version
of ID3 tags.

18.7 Writing Button Scripts for Interactive Control and Animation *(continued)*

To control an embedded video that's placed within a movie clip, the code would be similar to the MP3 example above with a few small differences. Because the MP3 file is being streamed, calling the stop() method causes the sound to stop playing and sets the play-head back to the beginning of the sound file. When working with movie clips, calling the stop() method essentially stops the playhead at the current frame being played back. This pauses the clip. The following code adds a stop button that calls the gotoAndStop() method that moves the playhead to the first frame of the clip:

```
pause_btn.onRelease = function() {
  movie_mc.stop();
};
play_btn.onRelease = function() {
  movie_mc.play();
};
stop_btn.onRelease = function() {
  movie_mc.gotoAndStop(1);
};
```

The embedded video is placed within a movie clip symbol, which automatically begins playback. Therefore, there is no code needed to create the movie clip or initialize the playhead. The only code needed is that for the three button instances on the Stage: the pause button, the play button, and the stop button. These buttons have the instance names pause_btn, play_btn, and stop_btn, respectively. You can also add buttons and sliders on the Stage that affect the volume of the movie clip's audio, or even fast forward or rewind the video by incrementing or decrementing the playhead by a certain number of frames each time the button is pressed. Remember that this code will work for other content that's placed within a movie clip.

18.8 Creating Scripts for Runtime Symbol Creation

One of the most powerful features of Flash is the ability to create symbols at runtime. This means if a user clicks a button in the Flash SWF file, ActionScript can create a new symbol at runtimethat can be manipulated on the Stage. This allows you to easily create image galleries and other dynamic content. A SWF file should dynamically load content if you don't know when you create the SWF how many images might exist, particularly if the data is being retrieved from a remote web service or is based on user input.

Loading JPEGs and SWFs on the fly is accomplished using the `MovieClipLoader` class. This class is new to Flash MX 2004; it allows you to easily load remote SWF movies or JPEG images and to monitor the progress of the loading using callbacks. The following code takes a list of images from an array and uses the `MovieClipLoader`'s `loadClip` method to load each JPEG file and position it on the Stage:

```
var xPos:Number = 10;
var yPos:Number = 10;
var imgArray:Array = ["thumbs/DCP_2663.jpg", "thumbs/DCP_2681.jpg"];
var gallery_mcl:MovieClipLoader = new MovieClipLoader();
var listenerObject = new Object();
listenerObject.onLoadInit = function(target_mc) {
  target_mc._x = xPos;
  target_mc._y = yPos;
  xPos += target_mc._width+10;
};
gallery_mcl.addListener(listenerObject);
for (var i = 0; i<imgArray.length; i++) {
  this.createEmptyMovieClip("img"+i, this.getNextHighestDepth());
  gallery_mcl.loadClip(imgArray[i], "img"+i);
}
```

The first five lines initialize variables that are used throughout the SWF file. The `imgArray` variable holds all of the variables that load into the Flash document. This example uses a static array, although you could just as easily receive the data from a web service, by parsing an XML document, or via Flash Remoting. Then you call the `MovieClipLoader` constructor method and create an object serving as the listener for the `MovieClipLoader`. The listener object waits for a single event, `onLoadInit`, which sets the X and Y coordinates of the images as they load. The next line of code binds the listener object to the `MovieClipLoader` instance, `gallery_mcl`. The final block of code loops through the array of images and creates an empty movie clip on the Stage at a new depth. If you didn't assign a unique depth for each image, only one image loads into your document because there can only be one instance at each depth. Finally, the `MovieClipLoader`'s `loadClip` method is called and loads the current image in the array into the newly created empty movie clip instance on the Stage.

Behaviors panel
Shift F3

Apart from the MovieClipLoader class, you can also create symbols on-the-fly using create-MovieClip and duplicateMovie-Clip and by loading external movies using loadMovie().

18.9   Understanding Listeners

Components panel
Ctrl F7
⌘ F7

Flash has *listeners*, which are similar to event handlers, and they sit in the background waiting for events in a document to be triggered by Flash. For example, these events can be anything from a click on a Button component to a user changing the value of a List component or scrolling a TextArea component. For example, you would use a listener when you want to listen for the Button component being clicked at runtime. The click tells the SWF file to display the next image, submit a form filled out by a visitor, or any other number of possibilities. The ActionScript code for listening for a button click is this:

```
function wasButtonClicked(evt:Object) {
  trace("the button was clicked.");
}
myBtn_btn.addEventListener("click", wasButtonClicked);
```

In this example, `myBtn_btn` is the instance name of the button object and `click` is the event that is broadcast by Flash when the user has clicked the button on the Stage. You assign the name of the function within the `addEventListener` function that handles the event. The code above simply traces a message to the Output panel, but you could easily change the code to trigger a web service or change the contents of the SWF file at runtime.

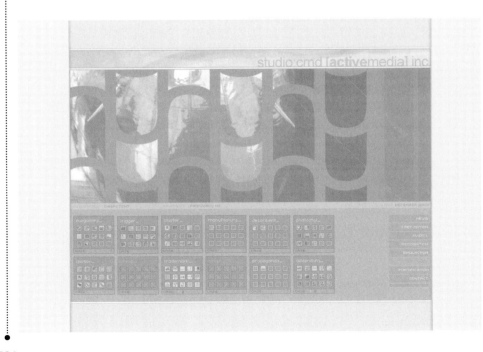

18.10　Creating Listeners

There is an alternative method for creating listeners to the one in the preceding section. Instead of passing a function name as the event handler, you pass an object that contains a function:

```
var listenerObject:Object = new Object();
listenerObject.click = function(evt:Object) {
  trace("the button was clicked.");
};
myBtn_btn.addEventListener("click", listenerObject);
```

The differences between this code and the code from the preceding section are fairly minor. The only real difference is that the function defines within an object now. You'll also notice the function is bound to the `click` parameter within the object, just as the event listed in the `addEventListener` method is.

You might have noticed that the inline function in this code takes a single parameter, `evt`, which is an object. The object contains two parameters, `target` and `type`. The `target` parameter holds the path to the instance the listener is bound to, which in this case is the `myBtn_btn` Button component instance. This can be extremely useful if you have an event listener waiting for a List component to change on the Stage. When the user changes the currently selected row in the List, the change event is triggered and you can use the `evt.target` property to get the currently selected list item by checking the values in the object `evt.target.selectedItem`. The `selectedItem` property contains an object that holds the data and label for the currently selected item in the List component.

If you are a fan of object actions, you could also rewrite the above code and place it directly on the button instance, like so:

```
on (click) {
  trace("the button was clicked.");
}
```

CHAPTER 19

Setting Up and Using Components

IF YOU'VE USED FLASH MX, you probably already know the power of Flash components. Components allow you to quickly make sites by adding premade user interface elements. In Flash MX 2004 the number of components has been increased, and Flash MX Professional 2004 includes entirely new kinds of components: Data components (focused mainly on server-side integration) and Media components (support for "streaming" MP3 audio and FLV video playback).

Components in Flash MX 2004 have been rewritten from the ground up with support for ActionScript 2. Also there is support for setting a global theme style, which applies to all components on the Stage, giving them a consistent look and feel.

19.1   Introducing v2 Components

———

Components in Flash
MX 2004 are called
"v2 components"
because they're built
on version 2 of the
Macromedia Compo-
nent Architecture.

The components in Flash MX 2004 have been completely rewritten from the ground up in ActionScript 2.0. Sporting a more consistent and modern look and new event model, these components allow you to quickly build robust applications without having to write lots of complex ActionScript. The v2 components in Flash MX 2004 are designed to reuse as much code as possible to keep file sizes down. For example, adding a TextArea component to the Stage adds approximately 40 KB to your SWF file; adding a TextInput component adds about 25 KB. However, if you use both a TextArea and a TextInput in a movie, the SWF only increases by 42 KB. Flash is able to reuse classes to reduce by more than a third what would otherwise have been a 65 KB increase.

Components in Flash MX Professional are divided into several sub-folders, including Data components, Streaming Media components, and the UI components. Flash MX 2004 includes one folder when you install it: UI components and it does not quite include all of the UI components found in Flash MX Professional.

Because v2 components behave differently and have a different architecture from the v1 components (components built for Flash MX), you may see some conflicts and inconsistencies when using v1 and v2 components together in a single Flash document. If you can, avoid mixing v1 and v2 components in the same FLA file, or (if you must use both) test your application thoroughly.

19.2   Using Components

Components in Flash allow developers and designers to build feature-rich applications without having to write large amounts of ActionScript. In fact, it is possible to build minia-ture applications in Flash MX Professional without writing a single line of code if you are using bindings (typically used to bind dynamic data to a visual UI component) and Data components.

Adding a component to your Flash document is as simple as dragging a copy of the com-ponent from the Components panel on to the Stage. The component instance can be cus-tomized by setting its parameters in either the Property inspector or the Component Inspector panel. Typically, the Property inspector allows you to modify the most common parameters for a component and the Component Inspector panel allows you to modify a wider range of parameters, but in some special cases (most notably the Media compo-nents in Flash MX Professional), you are limited to customizing the component in the Component Inspector panel.

Deleting components from a FLA is only a little bit more complicated than adding them. Much like working with any symbol in Flash, deleting an instance from the Stage will still leave a copy of the symbol in the Library. To completely remove a component from a Flash document, select the symbol in the Library panel and delete the component using the con-textual menu, the trashcan icon, or the Delete command from the Library Options menu.

If you're only using one or two components in a Flash document, you may notice an increase of 25-50 KB in file size. However, adding more components to your Flash document will often only increase the file size of the SWF movie a few KB for each additional component.

CUSTOM COMPONENTS

A component is a movie clip with predefined parameters. This means that you can easily make your own simple component using a movie clip and ActionScript in Flash. However, full-fledged components that do complicated or diverse things are not that easy to make because you have to accommodate for all the different ways a person might use that component (if it is for distribution, that is). This book doesn't cover building components, but as time progresses more resources on the subject will emerge in the bookstores or online. There is limited documentation on creating components available within the Help panel as well.

19.3   Changing a Component's Appearance

➡ 5.9   Components
        Panel

➡ 19.2 Using
        Components

___

It bears mentioning that the default Halo themes have one very important difference from simply defining a custom color. Halo theme colors have slight variations in transparency in some components such as the List or ComboBox. However, setting the themeColor to a specific color shows the color as a flat color without the same alpha effect.

___

You can also set your own custom theme-Color by using a hexadecimal value prefixed with 0x, such as 0x336699.

By default, the components that install with Flash have a slight greenish tint to them when you roll over the Button, List, ComboBox or most of the rest of the components when running a SWF file. This greenish tint is what is called a *Halo* theme. Themes in Flash MX 2004 are a collection of styles and "skins," and the default skin and color is Halo green. If you wanted to change the color you can select one of the three special Halo themes: haloGreen, haloBlue, or haloOrange. In order to change the default theme—for the entire document or for a single component—you can use code similar to the following:

```
_global.style.setStyle("themeColor", "haloOrange");
```

This gives all of the components on the Stage an orange glow instead of the default green. It is important to note that you aren't limited to the three predefined Halo theme colors either because you can use any hexadecimal color in place of the halo theme. For example, you can use the following code to bless each of the components with a rather unattractive purple color:

```
_global.style.setStyle("themeColor", "0xFF00FF");
```

Also, if you only wanted to assign a color to a single instance on the Stage instead of every component on the Stage, you could use the following code (where **send_btn** is the instance name of a Button component instance on the Stage);

```
send_btn.setStyle("themeColor", "0xFF00FF");
```

The **setStyle()** method can also change other properties and styles for components; for example, you can use the following code to remove the outline on a TextArea component:

```
myTextArea_txt.setStyle("borderStyle", "none");
```

You can even change the font globally for components by using the following (these changes are demonstrated in the following illustrations):

```
_global.style.setStyle("fontFamily", "Comic Sans MS");
```

There are many other customizations you can make to components, either by using styles or adding icons (small images) onto Button or List components. You will see several examples of customizing components throughout the rest of this chapter.

19.4   Adding Data to the List and ComboBox

You can add values to List and ComboBox components in several different ways. Values can be added manually by using the Property inspector or Component Inspector panel, using either the component's `addItem()` or `addItemAt()` methods, or setting the component's `dataProvider` property. If you're using Flash MX Professional, you can even bind an array returned from a web service or XML document directly to a List or ComboBox instance's `dataProvider` property.

You can access the Values dialog by clicking the magnifying glass icon in the Property inspector or Component Inspector panel, which allows you to set values directly into the dialog. Setting values directly using the Values dialog might reduce the amount of Action-Script you have to write, but it is also likelier to introduce errors. Be especially careful that the values in the data column match up exactly with the values in the labels column in each of the Value dialogs.

ActionScript allows you to easily add items to the List or ComboBox component, via the `addItem()` or `addItemAt()` methods. The difference between these two methods is that `addItem()` appends the item to the end of the List or ComboBox, whereas `addItemAt()` allows you to add the item to the component at a specific index.

```
myList.addItem("label1", "data1");
myList.addItem({label:'label2', data:'data2'});
myList.addItemAt(0, "label0", "data0");
myList.addItemAt(3, {label:'label3', data:'data3'});
```

As this shows, to add an item to the top-most entry in a List or ComboBox, use the `addItemAt()` method and specify an index of 0.

| label0 |
| label1 |
| label2 |
| label3 |

The item `label0` is added to the first entry in the List component and the other values are shifted accordingly. You can also see that there are two ways to specify objects when adding them to the List, either by specifying the label and data values within the function directly, or by creating an object and specifying `label` and `data` properties.

The final way of assigning values to a List or ComboBox component is by setting the `dataProvider` property. You can assign an array directly to this property:

```
myList.dataProvider = [{label:'label0', data:'data0'}, {label:'label1',
data:'data1'}];
```

➡ 5.9   Components Panel

➡ 16.10 Creating and Using Arrays

If you add an item to a component using the `addItemAt` method, you may encounter errors if you try to use nonconsecutive indexes.

Continues ●

19.4 Adding Data to the List and ComboBox

When adding items to a List or Component instance using a data-Provider array, you can easily sort the items in the components by using the array's sort method.

(continued)

This code creates an array of two objects, where each object has a `label` and `data` property. The List and ComboBox components also support a property called `labelFunction` that tells Flash to determine the label for an item for you based on a function you specify:

```
var customer_array:Array = new Array();
customer_array.push({name:'customer 1',
    company:'Sprockets', data:1});
customer_array.push({name:'customer 2', company:'Cogs',  data:2});
myList.dataProvider = customer_array;
myList.labelFunction = function(item) {
    return item.name + ' (' + item.company + ')';
};
```

The code begins with creating an array, which is used as the `dataProvider` for the List component on the Stage. The `labelFunction` property creates the label for each array item by concatenating (joining together) the name and company values for each record in the array.

The value of the labels for this array would be `customer 1 (Sprockets)` and `customer 2 (Cogs)`, respectively.

If an array, such as the one above, is being returned from a web service or external source, using a `labelFunction` makes it much simpler to populate a ComboBox or List component because you don't have to manually add each item using the `addItem()` method or create a temporary array with a manually concatenated label.

19.5   Adding Basic Event Handling

Events are generated by Flash when certain criteria are met, such as when a Loader component has finished loading content, a Button component is clicked, or a web service receives a result. You can add basic event handling to your FLA file by adding an event handler directly to the object that you want to wait for the events. If you are using a Button instance, you can add the following ActionScript directly onto the Button by selecting the instance and then entering this code into the Script pane of the Actions panel:

```
on (click) {
  trace("the button was clicked, do something profound.");
}
```

This is similar to the ActionScript that may be generated by adding a behavior to a Button instance on the Stage. Behaviors add code directly to instances on the Stage or to frames or screens and allow you to modify which event triggers the behavior. For example you could add a Trigger Data Source behavior to a Button component using the Behaviors panel, which would call a web service when the button is clicked which you can find out how to do in section 25.4. Using the Behaviors panel, you can use the drop-down menu in the Event column to modify which event will trigger the block of code.

If you're using Flash MX Professional and have a WebServiceConnector component on the Stage, you can add the following code which would be executed when the component receives a result from a web service:

```
on (result) {
  trace(this.results);
}
```

This code displays the value returned by the web service to the Output panel (assuming it is a simple value such as a string or number and not a complex value such as an object).

Each component has its own set of events that can be handled, and they execute blocks of code accordingly. These different kinds of events allow you to build complex applications. An example of this could be adding an event handler to a component and having the event call a remote web service when the value in the List component changes. When the web service returns a result, another event handler can modify the values in a Data-Grid component.

➡ 18.2 Attaching Scripts to Buttons or Movie Clips

➡ 19.6 Adding Listener-Based Event Handling

➡ 19.8 Using the Button Component

It is possible to add event handlers directly to instances on the Stage, although it is often better to put the code on the Timeline instead whenever possible. Leaving code on the Timeline in an "actions" layer makes it easier to find code when you edit the FLA file in the future.

19.6   Adding Listener-Based Event Handling

Using event listeners allows you to handle events generated by Flash, except the code can be placed on the Timeline rather than having to be placed directly on instances on the Stage. Typically, this makes your FLA files much easier to maintain because the code doesn't have to be spread all over, and it makes code more reusable because you can have one event listener handling events for many instances. Although writing event listeners takes a bit more ActionScript than coding the basic event handling explained in the preceding section, listeners are more portable so they're usually worth the extra effort.

Using basic event handling, you can catch a Button instance being clicked by adding the following code to the component directly. Select the Button instance, and then add the following code into the Actions panel:

```
on (click) {
    trace(this.label + " was clicked.");
}
```

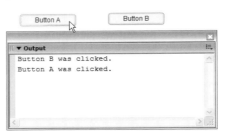

When the Button instance is clicked, the code executes and displays the button's label and a short message in the Output panel.

Whenever possible, use listener objects instead of adding code directly to instances. Macromedia's ActionScript best practices document states that it is easier to maintain Timeline-based code than object-based code.

Here is the equivalent code written using an event listener:

```
var btnListener:Object = new Object();
btnListener.click = function(evt) {
    trace(evt.target.label + " was clicked.");
};
buttonB_btn.addEventListener("click", btnListener);
```

This code creates a new object that holds the handlers for any events you want to listen for. In this case, you're only waiting for the **click** event ("listening" for it to be "thrown," in programming parlance). When the event is generated, the listener object executes the defined inline function. You add an event listener to a component instance by using the **addEventListener** method and passing two parameters: the event you wish to listen for and the listener object. Notice how the parameter in the listener object, **click**, matches the event being added in the **addEventListener** method.

The inline function for the **btnListener** listener object takes a single parameter named **evt**, which is an object. This value contains a parameter called **target** that refers to the component instance the listener object was bound to. In this case, the value of **evt.listener** is the Button instance, **buttonB_btn**.

19.7 Setting Up Symbols as Component Icons

Certain components allow you to define icons that can be used to customize the component's look beyond the default appearance. Defining an icon will add a small graphic to the face of a Button instance or to the left of a List item. Perhaps the easiest components to add an icon to are Button component instances because you can assign an icon to a Button without having to write a single line of code. All you need to do is specify a *linkage identifier* within the Library. The linkage identifier links the symbol in the Library by giving it a name so it can be used in other parts of the FLA.

Creating a Symbol and a Linkage

Before you can create a linkage, you must add a symbol to the Library that will be used as an icon. The symbol can be either a graphic symbol or a movie clip. After you create a symbol, right-click/Control-click the symbol in the Library and select Linkage from the contextual menu. A Linkage Properties dialog appears where you check the Export For ActionScript check box and provide a value for Identifier. This Identifier value is used within the FLA as the name of the icon. With the Button instance selected on the Stage, add the Identifier value from the dialog into the `icon` parameter in either the Property inspector or Component Inspector panel. You can then see on the Stage that the Button instance has a gray square where the icon will be placed. If you publish the document, you'll see the icon that you linked to the instance placed within the Button.

The process for using buttons with the List component is similar, except it requires a bit of ActionScript to link the icons to the list items. When adding items to the List component, you can specify an icon to be used by adding another column that will hold the value of the linkage identifier containing an icon. Next, you need to tell Flash which column holds the icon, and this is where the `iconField` property comes in. When you worked with the Button component, you were able to define the icon directly via the Property inspector or Component Inspector panel so this step wasn't necessary. An example of this is the following:

```
var dp:Array = [];
dp.push({label:'item1', data:1, theicon:'check'});
dp.push({label:'item2', data:2});
myList.dataProvider = dp;
myList.iconField = "theicon";
```

This code creates an array of items that are used as the DataProvider for the List component instance, named `myList`, on the Stage (and appears just like the following figure). You can see that the first item has an additional property named `theicon` that holds the linkage identifier for the icon symbol. It is important to note that the property name, `theicon`, isn't special in any way; you can use any other name just as easily. The important part is that the value in the `iconField` property matches the property name in the `item1` record.

➡ 16.10 Creating and Using Arrays

The gray square of a linked icon that's within the Button component before it's published is 12 pixels by 12 pixels. The Button component itself is, by default, 22 pixels high, which means that there is a 5 pixel margin above and below the icon within the Button. If you want to use icons larger than 16X16, it might be necessary to resize the button instance.

Continues ●

19.7   Setting Up Symbols as Component Icons

(continued)

➡ 19.4 Adding Data
        to the List and
        ComboBox

➡ 19.5 Adding
        Basic Event
        Handling

Whenever possible, use listener objects instead of adding code directly to instances. Macromedia's ActionScript best practices document states that it is easier to maintain Timeline-based code rather than object-based code.

You can also see that the second item in the array doesn't have an icon defined and therefore no icon shows up beside its label in the List component. If you want to add a default icon to be displayed if an icon hasn't been specified, use the `defaultIcon` property, which can be seen in the following ActionScript:

```
/* defIcon is a linkage identifier of a symbol in the Library */
myList.defaultIcon = "defIcon";
```

When you add this line of code to the previous example, after you publish the Flash movie you will see that even though the second item doesn't have an icon explicitly defined, the default item will be used.

Automatically Choosing a Symbol

Similar to the `labelFunction` discussed earlier, there is a comparable `iconFunction` method, which executes a function for each item in a List or ComboBox component and allows you to assign an icon based on certain criteria:

```
myList.iconFunction = function(item) {
    if (item.data == 1) {
      return "check";
    } else {
      return "defIcon";
    }
};
```

When using icons with the ComboBox component, there is one very important gotcha that you should be aware of. You would expect, and rightfully so, that you would be able to assign an `iconField` property using the following code:

```
myComboBox.iconField = "theicon";
```

Unfortunately this code does *not* work as you probably would expect. When using the ComboBox component you must use the `dropdown` property in order for the icons to work properly. The `dropdown` property is a reference List component contained within the ComboBox component. This is another example of components reusing classes and assets in order to reduce the file size. So the complete code to set an `iconField` within a Combo-Box component is as follows:

```
myComboBox.dropdown.iconField = "theicon";
```

Left: The icon assigned based on criteria in an `iconFunction`.
Right: The icon assigned as a property of the `dropdown` property.

19.8   Using the Button Component

The Button component can be very useful for submitting forms or executing a block of code—you can even use the Button component to act as a toggle. If you are using Flash MX Professional, you can use the Button instance to trigger a WebServiceConnector or XMLConnector component easily by selecting the instance on the Stage and choosing Data > Trigger Data Source from the Add Behavior menu in the Behaviors panel. This displays a dialog where you select the Data component you want to trigger. The following code is added to the Button instance:

```
on (click) {
    // Trigger Data Source Behavior
    // Macromedia 2003
    this._parent.thatWebServiceConnectorInstance.trigger();
}
```

In order to use the Button component as a toggle, you need to first set the Button's `toggle` property to true. Then whenever the user clicks the Button instance, the Button is toggled between a selected and unselected state. To test whether the Button instance is currently pressed or not, you need to check the instance's selected property, as shown here:

```
trace(myButton_btn.selected);
```

In order to use the selected property, you need to make sure the Button instance's `toggle` property has been set to true, otherwise the selected property will always return false. You can set the property by using the Property inspector or Component Inspector panel, or by setting the selected property for the instance using ActionScript.

➡ 19.6 Adding Listener-Based Event Handling

The Button component can be set to toggle between a selected and deselected state by setting the Button instance's toggle property.

The Button component is one of the more useful components and can trigger WebServiceConnector components and XMLConnector components to load or send data.

HOW MANY INSTANCES IS TOO MANY?

Macromedia does not recommend using more than 125 component instances within a single SWF file. This is just a suggestion, though; there is no technical limit to the number of components you can use in a file. However, performance will begin to suffer as the number increases because the time that components take to initialize will cause the startup time of the SWF file to seriously lag.

19.9   Using the CheckBox Component

Similar to the check box input type in HTML, the Flash CheckBox can be used within Flash forms to allow users to provide answers to simple yes or no questions. A CheckBox consists of two items, a check box and a label. You can customize the CheckBox by changing the placement of the label in relation to the CheckBox.

If you set the `label-Placement` property to top or bottom, it may be necessary to resize the component instance in order to accommodate a check box and label.

———

Unlike HTML, Check-Box instances must be given separate instance names.

The label can be moved by setting the `labelPlacement` property to one of four values: left, right, top, or bottom. Setting this property to bottom places the CheckBox above the label. Each CheckBox instance on the Stage must have a unique instance name which allows you to track which check boxes are currently selected.

The CheckBox component has only a single event, `click`, which is triggered when the user clicks either the check box or the label. Using ActionScript, you can modify a Check-Box's label by setting the `label` property for the instance. By placing the following Action-Script code directly on a CheckBox instance, you can display the CheckBox's `label` property when the user selects or deselects the check box:

```
on (click) {
   trace(this.label);
}
```

To test if a CheckBox instance on the Stage is currently selected, you must make sure that the component has an instance name and then add the following code to your Flash movie:

```
trace(checkbox1_ch.selected);
```

19.10 Using the ComboBox Component

A great feature of the ComboBox component is the ability to make *editable* ComboBoxes. This allows users to enter their own values if they cannot find a suitable one. You can set a ComboBox as editable from the Property inspector or Component Inspector panel by setting the editable parameter, or by using ActionScript and setting the `editable` property to true, as seen here:

```
myComboBox.editable = true;
```

When `editable` is set to true, the topmost item in the ComboBox is a TextInput field that allows users to specify their own value or use a value from the drop-down menu. You can access the text entered by the user by using the text parameter, as seen in the following code:

```
trace(myComboBox.text);
```

You can use the `enter` event when you are working with editable ComboBoxes. The `enter` event triggers when the user types a value into the ComboBox and presses the Enter key. You can use this event and the `addItem` or `addItemAt()` method to add new items to the ComboBox list depending on user input. By adding the following code directly on the ComboBox instance on the Stage, you can insert new items into the ComboBox each time the user presses the Enter key. The ComboBox instance must be set to editable for this to work:

```
on (enter) {
  this.addItem({label:this.text});
}
```

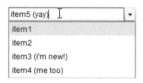

Whenever a user types in a new value and presses the Enter key, a new item is added to the end of the ComboBox. It is important to note that you're only specifying a label property for the item, and because the user can only enter one string into the editable text field in the ComboBox, the value is used for the label and the data property will be undefined.

Much like the Button component, the Combo-Box also supports the use of icons; however, they are not as easy to set up as the Button component.

When entering text into an editable ComboBox, the change event is thrown each time the user presses a key. Be aware that if you are calling a web service, each time the value of a ComboBox is changed, you may call the web service numerous times. You probably don't want to do this.

19.11　Using the List Component

When specifying colors, make sure that you prefix hexadecimal color values with 0x, such as 0xFF0000 for a red.

Whenever possible, use listener objects instead of adding code directly to instances. Macromedia's ActionScript best practices document states that it is easier to maintain Timeline based code rather than object based code.

The List component is very similar to the ComboBox component except it allows you to select multiple entries and displays many options at the same time. In fact, the ComboBox implements the List component to display its values. It is possible to customize the List component to alternate row colors by specifying the `alternatingRowColors` property. This property takes an array of colors, as shown here:

`myList.alternatingRowColors = ["0xFFFFFF", "0xE7E7E7"];`

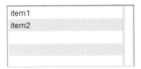

The preceding line of code alternates colors between white (#FFFFFF) and a light gray (#E7E7E7). The array of colors can be any length (but the List component behaves quite unexpectedly if you specify an empty array). Defining a single color in the array means that each item will have the same background color and therefore the List background will appear as a solid color.

You can allow for multiple selections within a List component by setting the `multiple-Selection` property to true in the Property inspector or Component Inspector panel or by using ActionScript. Then when you test the SWF file, you can select multiple items in the List by holding down either the Shift key or the Ctrl key. If you have multiple items selected, you can access the items by using the `selectedItems` parameter, which is an array of the currently selected items.

19.12   Using the Loader Component

The Loader component allows you to load JPEG or SWF files into Flash at runtime. This is very useful when you want to create photo galleries or bring in different parts of a site when the user visits a particular section, for example, if you have a website that's broken up into many smaller, separate SWF files. When the user visits the different sections of the site, those SWF files can be loaded in on-the-fly instead of having to be embedded into your Flash document. This allows you to build sites that load very quickly as you don't have to wait for one large SWF file and can instead load them on demand.

Using the Loader component is fairly straightforward, but there are a few tricks. To use this component, drag an instance on to the Stage and define a value for `contentPath` either using the Property inspector, Component Inspector panel, or ActionScript. The value of `contentPath` can be either a local file, such as `contactform.swf`, or a remote file, such as `http://www.amazon.com/images/bookcover.jpg`. If you wanted to use Action-Script then you would use the following code, where `loaderInstance` is the instance name of the Loader component, and `myFile.swf` the name of the file you want to load:

```
loaderInstance.contentPath = "myFile.swf";
```

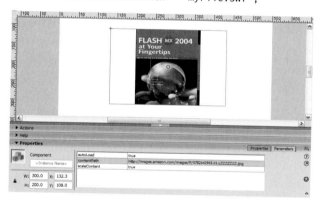

There are three parameters for the Loader component that you can modify using the Property inspector: `autoLoad`, `contentPath`, and `scaleContent`. The `autoLoad` parameter determines whether the content will load automatically or whether you must explicitly use the Loader component's `load()` method to trigger the data to load. You should set `autoLoad` to false if you are loading in files dynamically via ActionScript. The `contentPath` parameter is the URL or linkage identifier of the content you want to load.

The final parameter, `scaleContent`, is the one that has the most impact on your SWF files. It is a Boolean value that determines whether the content or the component will be resized. If `scaleContent` is false, the Loader component will resize itself to match the dimensions of the content being loaded in. If `scaleContent` is true, the content being loaded will scale itself to match the dimensions of the Loader component. It is important to note that the content being loaded will maintain its aspect ratio so it doesn't look distorted or stretched.

➡ 19.14 Using the ProgressBar Component

➡ 19.16 Using the ScrollPane Component

You can even load symbols from your Library into the Loader component by assigning a symbol a linkage identifier and entering that as the `contentPath`.

The Loader component is very similar to the ScrollPane component. The main difference between the components is that ScrollPane will add scrollbars if the content is too large for the component instead of resizing the content or component instance.

When using the Loader component, setting the `scaleContent` property to false will cause the component to resize itself to match the dimensions of the JPEG or SWF being loaded in. Setting `scaleContent` to true will cause the content being loaded in at runtime to scale itself to match the dimensions of the Loader component on the Stage.

19.13 Using the NumericStepper Component

By default, the step-Size property is set to 1, which increments and decrements the currently value by 1 digit. Setting this value to 2 will allow only even or odd digits to be entered.

The NumericStepper component allows you to select a number from a specified range of values. The NumericStepper has a TextInput field that enables you to type in a number directly, or you can use two arrow controls to increment or decrement the current number.

The Property inspector and Component Inspector panel allow you to modify the four main properties of the NumericStepper: minimum, maximum, stepSize, and value. Not surprisingly, the minimum and maximum properties control the lower and upper limit of allowable numbers that can be entered into the NumericStepper. The stepSize parameter defines how much the number increments or decrements with the up or down arrows. By default, the value of stepSize is 1, which means that if the current value in the Numeric-Stepper is 7, the value increases to 8 if the user clicks the up button or decreases to 6 if they click the down button. If the stepSize is set to 2 and the initial value of the Numeric-Stepper is 7, the value increases to 9 when the up button is clicked or decreases to 5 if the down button is pressed.

The final important parameter that can be set is the value property, which controls what the starting value of the NumericStepper component will be. If you are using Action-Script, the value property reports the current value of the NumericStepper, and there are two additional properties you can use: previousValue and nextValue. These properties tell you the previous and next values for the NumericStepper, which are simply the current value plus or minus the stepSize. So if your current value is 3 and you have a step-Size of 1, the value of previousValue is 2 and nextValue is 4. The one situation where this isn't true is when the current value is the minimum or maximum value. If the current value is the same as the minimum, previousValue will return undefined. Similarly, if the current value is equal to maximum, nextValue will return undefined.

19.14 Using the ProgressBar Component

LOADING 11%

The ProgressBar component allows you to quickly add progress bars to your SWF files that indicate content is loading. For example, if you use the Loader component to load in external JPEG or SWF files, you can use the ProgressBar component to display the amount of data that has been loaded.

To make the ProgressBar component display the progress of a Loader component, drag an instance of each component onto the Stage. Give the Loader component an instance name of `myLoader_ldr`, and give the ProgressBar an instance name of `myProgressBar_pb`. Using either the Property inspector or Component Inspector panel, set the `contentPath` parameter to a JPEG or SWF file. The larger the file, the easier it will be to test the progress of the file. If the file size is too small, the file will load too quickly and you will not be able to see the ProgressBar move. Click the ProgressBar instance on the Stage and set its `source` parameter to the instance name of the Loader component using the Property inspector. Test your movie, and the progress bar should gradually increment from 0% to 100%. Once the file has completely loaded, the ProgressBar component will display 100% and the Loader will display the content.

You'll notice that the ProgressBar component remains visible even after the content in the Loader has finished loading. If you want to hide the progress bar once the Loader component has displayed the content, you'll need to add some ActionScript. Click the Loader component and add the following ActionScript code using the Actions panel:

```
on (complete) {
    this._parent.myProgressBar_pb._visible = false;
}
```

Now when the Loader has completed loading the content, the ProgressBar component will be set to invisible.

If you'd rather use Timeline-based code than object-based code, you can use the following ActionScript instead:

```
var listenerObj:Object = new Object();
listenerObj.complete = function(evt) {
    evt.target._parent.myProgressBar_pb._visible = false;
};
myLoader_ldr.addEventListener("complete", listenerObj);
```

This code sets up a listener object that listens for the `complete` event to be generated by the Loader component. When the `complete` event has been generated, the inline function is triggered that will hide the ProgressBar instance on the Stage.

If you want to hide a ProgressBar component instance once the data being loaded in has fully loaded, you'll need to monitor the complete event for the Loader component. Once the content has been completely loaded, the `complete` event is triggered and can execute code that hides the Progress-Bar instance on the Stage, as described in this section.

Whenever possible, use listener objects instead of adding code directly to instances.

19.15   Using the RadioButton Component

➡ 19.9 Using the
    CheckBox
    Component

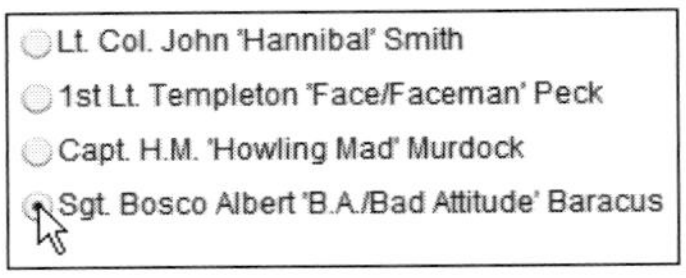

○ Lt. Col. John 'Hannibal' Smith
○ 1st Lt. Templeton 'Face/Faceman' Peck
○ Capt. H.M. 'Howling Mad' Murdock
○ Sgt. Bosco Albert 'B.A./Bad Attitude' Baracus

The RadioButton component is very similar to the CheckBox component with one important distinction: the RadioButton allows you to create groups of radio controls and allows the user to select only one item from the group.

To test whether a specific radio control is selected (or even to select a RadioButton instance using ActionScript), you need to use the selected property, as seen here:

```
trace(myRadioButton_radio.selected);
```

To get a list of all the RadioButton instances within a group, you can access the group's radioList object as seen in the code below. Note that radioGroup is the group name for the group of radio instances on the Stage:

```
for (var i in radioGroup.radioList) {
    trace(i + ": " + radioGroup.radioList[i]);
}
```

When working with groups of radio buttons, you can use ActionScript to tell you which RadioButton instance is selected on the Stage by using the selectedRadio property for the radio group. The selectedRadio returns a reference to the instance itself, which allows you to access the RadioButton instance's label, data, or other properties. The following code can be placed on the Stage or on a Button instance, although you'll need to prefix the instance name with this._parent, as shown below:

```
// displays the instance name for the selected instance.
trace(this._parent.radioGroup.selectedRadio);
// displays the data parameter for the selected instance.
trace(this._parent.radioGroup.selectedRadio.data);
// displays the label property for the selected instance.
trace(this._parent.radioGroup.selectedRadio.label);
```

If the user hasn't selected a radio button from the group of instances on the Stage, then the preceding code displays undefined for each value. Instead of using the selectedRadio property, you can also use the selection property and have the same result.

19.15   Using the RadioButton Component *(continued)*

The final property that you can use is `selectedData,` which if traced would return the data property of the currently selected item. If no item is selected, the property returns `undefined`. When using the `selectedData` property, you don't need to use `selectedRadio` or selection, as shown below:

```
// displays the data parameter for the selected instance.
trace(this._parent.radioGroup.selectedData);
```

When using the RadioButton component, make sure that you assign each radio button in a group the same groupName property.

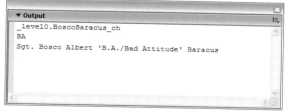

UNDERSTANDING COMPONENT MANAGERS

The component managers—the DepthManager, FocusManager, PopUpManager, and StyleManager classes—have no user interface (UI) whatsoever and manage only the components that are used in a SWF file. The component manager classes are responsible for different tasks such as managing the depths in which movie clips and instances are placed. Other component manager classes specify the tabbing order of the components on Stage so that users can logically navigate through forms or movies in Flash without necessarily using the mouse, or so they can even disable tabbing altogether. The PopUpManager class discussed is responsible for generating pop-up windows that are used in conjunction with the Alert or Window component.

Specific sections of this chapter show how to use a few of the main methods of each of the first three manager classes to perform common actions. The StyleManager component manager, which is beyond the scope of this book, is used to create named styles and colors within components. A developer would use the StyleManager to create a custom component.

19.16   Using the ScrollPane Component

If you want to be able to click and drag content instead of being forced to use the scroll-bars, make sure you set the scrollDrag property to true.

The ScrollPane component is very similar to the Loader component. However, instead of scaling the content (or component), the content is displayed along with scroll bars. This allows users to view the entire JPEG or SWF without the file being resized. This is useful if you have a limited space to display content and don't want to have Flash resize your images. By setting the scrollDrag property to true, it is possible to drag your mouse within the ScrollPane component and have the content move along with the cursor.

When loading in external content, whether you use the Loader component or ScrollPane, you can control the SWF being loaded in by using the content property. The content property is a read-only reference to the content within the movie being loaded in. For example, if you have a SWF movie with two symbols, circle_mc and square_mc, which are both on the main Timeline, you can load that movie into a holder SWF using a ScrollPane. When you add code to button symbols in your ScrollPane movie clip, it's possible to toggle visibility of the two symbols within the nested movie clip by adding the following code to a Button component:

```
on (click) {
    var btnPath:MovieClip = this._parent.myScrollPane_sp.content.circle_mc;
    btnPath._visible = !btnPath._visible;
}
```

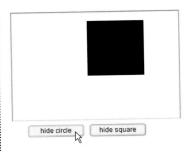

Every time the Button component is clicked within the holder movie clip, the circle_mc instance within the nested movie clip will be toggled.

The first line of code within the on (click) event handler defines a shortcut to the circle_mc instance within the nested movie clip. Notice that you refer to the myScroll-Pane_sp instance within your holder SWF and then the content property refers to the nested movie clip that is loaded into the holder movie. You can now use the shortcut, btnPath, to control the circle_mc instance in the nested movie clip. This code simply alternates the visibility of the instance between visible and invisible, but you can control the _x and _y coordinates or any other property of the movie clip as if it were directly within the movie.

19.17   Using the *DepthManager* Class

The DepthManager class allows you to manage the *depths* of movie clips and component instances on the Stage—that is, whether they render "on top of" or behind another movie clip in the SWF file. Using the DepthManager allows you to reorder the depths of existing instances or create new instances at specific depths using ActionScript. You can see an example of the DepthManager class in the following code:

```
import mx.managers.DepthManager;
circle_mc.onRelease = function() {
    this.setDepthAbove(square_mc);
};
square_mc.onRelease = function() {
    this.setDepthAbove(circle_mc);
};
```

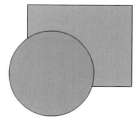

By placing the code on the Timeline and adding two movie clips to the Stage with instance names of cir-cle_mc and square_mc, you can reorder the symbols to make sure that one appears on top of the other when the instance is clicked. Before testing this code, make sure that the instances overlap slightly so you can see the layering.

The DepthManager class can be invaluable if you are adding tooltips to your Flash site and want to make sure that the tooltips always appear over other symbols, or if you have several images on the Stage and want one to appear on top of the other instances when it is clicked. In many cases, the only way you will be able to control depth in your SWF file is by using ActionScript. You might be dynamically adding new content, or using content from your Library at runtime. The DepthManager class is useful, because it can be used to dynamically control the depth of objects you are not directly adding to layers on the Stage.

You can set one instance to be on top of another instance by using the setDepthAbove() method as shown the code in this section, or you can set an instance below another instance by using the setDepthBelow() method.

➡ 16.8   Using Flash Classes

➡ 16.13 Creating Flash MX 2004 Classes

———

Another method, setDepthAt() allows you to set the depth of a specified instance to a specific depth. This can be used with the getNextHighest-Depth() method in the MovieClip class. Using these two methods together, you can always move an instance to the next highest depth, placing the instance on top of everything else on the Stage.

———

Movie clip depth can range between -16384 and 1048575.

19.18 Using the *FocusManager* Class

➡ 16.8 Using Flash Classes

➡ 16.13 Creating Flash MX 2004 Classes

Setting a default push button for a form allows the user to trigger the click event for the Button instance when they press the Enter key while filling out the form.

Using the FocusManager allows you to build more robust applications and makes filling out forms a bit easier for the users.

The FocusManager class allows you to specify tabbing order for components on the Stage. By default, each of the components already have support for the FocusManager and all you need to do is specify in what order the components will receive focus when the user presses the Tab key. The FocusManager class works by looking at the Flash movie for an object on the Stage with a tabIndex property that is higher than the current value. If there are no objects with a higher tabIndex, the tabIndex is reset to zero so the items can be tabbed through again. To set the tabIndex for an object on the Stage, simply set the object's tabIndex property, as shown here:

```
name_txt.tabIndex = 1;
email_txt.tabIndex = 2;
url_txt.tabIndex = 3;
comments_txt.tabIndex = 4;
preview_btn.tabIndex = 5;
post_btn.tabIndex = 6;
```

When the user presses the Tab key, the browser moves the focus to each element in order. Once the focus is on the last element, post_btn, pressing Tab again sets the focus to the first element, name_txt.

With the FocusManager class you can also set a default push button for an application by setting the defaultPushButton property of the FocusManager class by using the following code:

```
focusManager.defaultPushButton = post_btn;
```

Whenever a user presses the Enter key with their cursor in a TextInput field, the click event will be triggered for the post_btn Button instance.

19.19   Using the *PopUpManager* Class

The `PopUpManager` class has two methods, `createPopUp` and `deletePopUp`, which create and destroy pop-up windows. This allows you to create a pop-up window on the fly in ActionScript based on user input.

➡ 19.5 Adding Basic Event Handling

➡ 19.6 Adding Listener-Based Event Handling

If you have a form that collects data, you can launch a pop-up window if the user forgets to fill out a required field. Create a basic pop-up window using the following code:

```
mx.managers.PopUpManager.createPopUp(_root, mx.containers.Window, true);
```

Before you can test this code, you must add an instance of the Window component into your Library. To do this, drag an instance of the component onto the Stage and then delete it, leaving the component in your Library. Although not very useful at this point, the pop-up window can be customized, allowing you to add a close button, a title for the window, or content to the pop-up window by specifying the `contentPath` property.

In the following example, a pop-up window is generated when the user presses a Button instance on the Stage. A sized window (300 pixels by 200 pixels) is displayed, and the Window component displays the `error_mc` movie clip. Similar to adding an icon to a Button or other components, the `error_mc` is actually a linkage identifier value. This example also adds an event listener that listens for the close button to be clicked and then closes the pop-up window.

Select a frame on the Timeline, and type the following ActionScript into the Actions panel:

```
import mx.managers.PopUpManager;
listenerObj = new Object();
listenerObj.click = function() {
    win = PopUpManager.createPopUp(_root, mx.containers.Window, true,
{title:'Error! Error!', closeButton:true, contentPath:"error_mc", _width:300,
_height:200});
    var winObj = new Object();
    winObj.click = function(evt) {
      evt.target.deletePopUp();
    };
    win.addEventListener("click", winObj);
};
launchPopUp_btn.addEventListener("click", listenerObj);
```

The code above also illustrates the use of the `import` keyword. By using `import`, you don't have to provide the fully qualified class name in the `PopUpManager` class. In the first example, you had to refer to the PopUpManager class by its full class name, `mx.managers.Pop-UpManager`. In the second example, you imported the `mx.managers.PopUpManager` class and therefore could simply refer to the `PopUpManager` class in your code without having to use the full class name. This can often greatly reduce the amount of typing necessary as you don't have to repeatedly type in full class names.

When creating pop-up windows in Flash, it is possible to pass an object with parameters that will control the look and behavior of the Window instance. For example, by passing a `title` property, you can assign a title to the Flash window, or by setting the `close-Button` property to true, you can add a close button to the pop-up window.

When using the Pop-UpManager class to launch a window, you must make sure that you have a Window component symbol in your Library.

If you want to load content into a Window component, you must specify a `contentPath` so Flash knows what to place inside the window. The content-Path can be a SWF file, a JPEG image, or even a linkage identifier for a symbol already in your Library.

Input and Output Using Text and the Mouse

USING TEXT FIELDS TO display content is one of the most common actions in Flash. When building rich Internet applications, or even animations, you will probably use at least a little bit of text. There are several different kinds of text in Flash, and the many different ways to work with it are detailed in this chapter. In addition to getting text into and out of SWF files, you can work with mouse movements in files. Using the scroll wheel and capturing movement is also detailed in this chapter.

20.1 Understanding Browser Focus and Input Focus

➡ 20.21 Using the Selection Class

➡ 27.3 Publishing for the Web

Focusing the SWF file is incredibly important if you are building accessible SWFs conforming to Section 501 specifications for accessibility. If your SWF file is not focused, it will be difficult or impossible for a visually impaired user to click the SWF to give it focus. You should also try to focus the first Input text field for accessible SWF files if you have any forms for the user to fill out.

Focus refers to making a particular object in a browser window or file active. A SWF file can have focus in a browser window. There are several cases where you might need to focus a SWF file. For example, before a visitor can use the Tab key to tab through instances in a SWF file, the SWF itself must be in focus. Similarly, before keypress actions can be understood or recorded by the SWF file, the SWF has to have focus in the browser window.

A user must click the SWF file that's embedded in a browser to put it in focus, *or* you must make it active using JavaScript. The following JavaScript gives the SWF file focus. Place the code between the `<head>` tags in the HTML file.

```
<script language="JavaScript">
<!--
function flashFocus(){
    myMovie.focus();
}
//-->
</script>
```

Then within the opening `<body>` tag, place this function:

```
<body onLoad="flashFocus();">
```

This assumes that the SWF file's name is `myMovie` (that is, the name of your file is `myMovie.swf`). You can also find out the name of the SWF file in the `param` tag. For example, the `param` tag for this particular SWF looks like this:

```
<param name="movie" value="myMovie.swf">
```

As an alternative, in the `object` tag the name is found in `id="myMovie"`. If you use this JavaScript, the SWF file is given focus when the user opens the page. Then the SWF file can be tabbed or keypress actions from the end user can be used.

Input text fields can have focus as well, meaning that the input cursor blinks in the text field. To order four text fields, you would use code similar to the following:

```
field1.tabIndex = 1;
field2.tabIndex = 2;
field3.tabIndex = 3;
field4.tabIndex = 4;
```

To set focus on the very first text field, you could then use:

```
focusManager.setFocus(field1);
```

20.2   Understanding Text in Flash

You can use text of many different sizes, fonts, and colors in Flash. The extensive text controls enable you to add selectable text in a SWF file, which means that it can be highlighted, copied, and pasted. You can also add HTML formatting to text fields.

Text fields can be formatted with indentation, spacing, and margins, and you can justify the fields to the left, right, or center. Be careful about the size of text in a SWF, however, because very small text can become blurry on the Stage due to the anti-aliasing that is applied to make things look smoother in Flash. You can apply the alias text feature to an entire text field, but because the changes that are made to the characters are not always applied correctly, you should always look at the text fields after you publish the SWF and make sure text is legible for the particular font and size you selected. There are three main types of text within Flash, which can be chosen using the Property inspector:

Static   Static text is defined in the authoring environment and cannot be modified once the movie has been published.

Dynamic   Dynamic text fields can be changed at runtime using ActionScript and the text field's instance name; they cannot be changed by a user.

Input   Input text fields allow users to directly type text into the text field and modify its value. Input text fields are useful when you want to collect user input in a form, such as a feedback form.

➡ 2.7   Text Menu

➡ 3.11 Text Tool

➡ 5.22 Property Inspector

➡ 20.6 Setting Alias Text

➡ 20.7 Working with Static Text

You shouldn't change the width or height of text fields using the Property inspector or Info panel if you want to keep the text characters the same size. Changing the text field's dimensions this way will resize the text as well as the field.

You can create horizontal text fields and static vertical text fields.

Sometimes it is more practical to use the text-based components instead of input and Dynamic text fields. The TextInput and TextArea components have scrollbars and other controls available, which are convenient for applications that include forms or large amounts of text to display.

20.3   Setting Text Fonts

You can find and replace fonts in a FLA file by using the Find And Replace dialog: choose Edit > Find And Replace and then choose Font from the For drop-down menu.

If you want to embed all of the characters in a specific text field, type the characters into the field and then click the Character button in the Property inspector. Click the Specify Ranges radio button, then the Auto Fill button.

The more characters you embed in a SWF file, the more you will increase its file size. Only embed the characters you need to use.

If you are loading text and don't know which characters you require, embed the entire font. This is usually necessary if you are loading a lot of text or allowing users to input text into an Input text field.

Text fonts can be used to create great-looking SWF files and effects. All sorts of fonts can be found for free. Other fonts are available for a nominal cost, and most fonts can be found online for download. Once you install a font on your system, you can access it in Flash through the Property inspector. When you create a text field, set a font in the following way:

1 Select the Text tool in the Tools panel.

2 Open the Property inspector. Select a font from the Font drop-down menu.

3 Click the Text tool on the Stage and type in text.

When using static text, you do not need to embed the font using any specific process because the outlines are embedded in your SWF file automatically. Embedding adds to the size of your SWF file, but the text will look the same on anyone's computer. However, if you use a particular font in a Dynamic text field, you will need to manually embed the font for it to display correctly to all of your visitors. You can embed specific characters (using the Property inspector) if you know exactly which characters need to be displayed in the SWF files; you can embed a set of characters (for example, all numbers); or you can embed the entire font within the SWF file. You can also embed the entire font using ActionScript.

20.4　Setting Text Style and Alignment

You can set the style for text within a FLA by using the Property inspector. Text styles and attributes include:

B **Bold**　Makes the text boldface, which means each character is thicker in nature.

I **Italic**　Makes the text italicized, which means the characters slant toward the right.

■ **Text Color**　Colors the characters the color you select from the palette. Click and hold the color control in the Property inspector to select a color from the palette.

To align the text field to the right, center, or left or to justify the selected text field, click one of four buttons in the Property inspector.

Ⓐ **Align left**　Aligns the text to the left of the text field.

Ⓑ **Align center**　Centers the text field.

Ⓒ **Align right**　Aligns the text to the right of the text field.

Ⓓ **Justify**　Justifies the text field, meaning the text aligns on both the left and right sides of the text field.

➡ 2.7　Text Menu

➡ 3.11　Text Tool

➡ 5.22　Property Inspector

➡ 20.2　Understanding Text in Flash

➡ 20.3　Setting Text Fonts

➡ 20.5　Setting Text Formatting

You can find and replace font styles in a FLA file by using the Find And Replace dialog. Choose Edit > Find And Replace, then choose Font from the For drop-down menu.

20.5 Setting Text Formatting

You can also format
text using CSS and
HTML. This kind of for-
matting is added to a
FLA file using Action-
Script.

You can set the indent, line spacing, and margins for a Static, Dynamic, or Input text field by selecting the text field and choosing the Format button in the Property inspector. Indenting text moves the first line of a paragraph away from the edge of the text field by a given number of pixels. Changing line spacing affects the amount of space (measured in pixels) between each line of text. The margins are the empty space between the edge of the text field and the characters of text on every single line (measured in pixels).

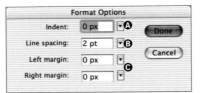

A Indent text between –720 and 720 pixels

B Space lines between –320 and 720 pixels

C Set the left and right margins between 0 and 720 pixels

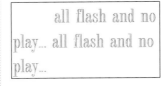

In the text field on the left, the text is indented from the edge of the text field by 50 pixels. In the center text field, the line spacing of the text is 50 pixels. The left and right margins of the text field on the right are indented by 50 pixels.

20.6   Setting Alias Text

Anti-aliasing smooths the assets in a SWF file. Many graphics are also anti-aliased in other graphics programs because it usually makes the graphic look better. When a text field has anti-aliasing applied, the edges of the characters are slightly blurred. This is fine when the text is large because it gives the characters a smoothed appearance. However, at small sizes the text can appear blurry and otherwise unclear. This has long been a problem with text in Flash and is why pixel fonts are so popular for small text sizes: they were created specifically to look clear in small sizes.

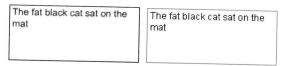

The text on the left side is anti-aliased in a SWF file, while the text on the right has alias text applied. Both fields are Arial set to 12 pts.

To remove anti-aliasing from text, select a text field on the Stage and click the Alias Text button in the Property inspector.

This helps small text sizes remain clear and legible in your SWF files for static, dynamic, and input text. Flash aligns the lines making up each character with the pixel grid, which keeps each character clear, although it will have a slightly jagged appearance. While this is fine at small sizes, large characters will be noticeably jagged. That's why this feature is best used on small fonts.

Dynamic and Input text fields can use alias text, but it is only displayed as alias in Flash Player 7. Static alias text is visible in Flash Players earlier than version 7.

If you click the Alias Text button for a field with small text, particularly 8 pts and below, you should check the legibility of the characters. Some fonts at smaller sizes (particularly those with serifs) are not very legible because of how the characters are rendered after the Alias Text button is clicked.

20.7 Working with Static Text

———

You shouldn't change the width or height of a text field using the Property inspector or Info panel if you want to keep the text characters the same size. Changing the text field's dimensions this way will resize the text as well as the field.

Static text is unchanging text that is added to the FLA file in the authoring environment. A Static text field does not have an instance name, and it cannot be modified at runtime using ActionScript. If you need to modify the text while the SWF file is playing back, use a Dynamic text field instead.

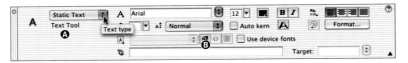

Static text fields are created by selecting the Text tool and setting the value of the Text Type drop-down menu in the Property inspector to Static Text (A). You can also make text selectable by choosing the Selectable Text button (B) in the Property inspector.

The fat black cat sat on the mat

The fat black cat sat on the mat

When you create a text field, a small handle appears in the upper-right corner of the text field's bounding box. If the handle is a circle, the field will expand horizontally while you type text into it (left). If the handle is a square, the field has a defined width, so text will wrap onto a new line when it is added to the text field (right).

You can use device fonts in Flash instead of static text. Device fonts are already on the end users' system, and because they are not embedded in the SWF file, they don't add as much file size and bandwidth as static text does. However, you don't have complete control over what the font will end up looking like. Device fonts do look sharper than regular static text, although they look a lot like alias text. To use a device font, select one of the following device fonts from the Fonts drop-down menu in the Property inspector and create the Static text field:

_sans A sans-serif font similar to Arial or Helvetica

_serif A serif font similar to Times New Roman

_typewriter A monospaced font similar to Courier

20.8   Creating Hyperlinks with Static Text Fields

Creating a hyperlink with static text is a simple task. With the Property inspector open, make sure that the information area is expanded so you can access the URL link text field.

There are two primary ways to add hyperlinks to static text instances:

- Select the text instance with the Selection tool and assign a URL that makes the entire text selection hyperlinked.

- With the Text tool, highlight only the words you want to link and then enter a value in the URL Link text field. This way of turning text into a hyperlink offers a bit more flexibility.

Either of these methods will underline the hyperlinked text in the authoring environment with a dashed line to indicate the text is linked. After the FLA is published or viewed in the testing environment, the underline will no longer be visible, so if you want the linked text to stand out, you must add some additional formatting to it.

In addition to the URL link text field, there is a Target drop-down menu that gives you four options, each of which behaves the same as the equivalent options in HTML:

_blank   Opens a brand new window

_parent   Opens in the parent frame in a frameset

_self   Opens in the current frame in a frameset

_top   Opens in the topmost frame in a frameset

You also have the option of typing in your own value in the Target menu, enabling you to use a custom frame in a frameset or an existing pop-up window.

➠ 5.22 Property Inspector

➠ 20.2 Understanding Text in Flash

➠ 20.4 Setting Text Style and Alignment

➠ 20.7 Working with Static Text

When creating hyperlinks, if you are linking to an absolute URL, you must be sure to include the `http://` before the web address.

If you want to link to an e-mail address, prefix the address with `mailto:`.

20.9   Creating Dynamic Text Fields

Flash MX 2004 shipped
without a ScrollBar
component like the one
included in Flash MX.
Therefore, if you want
to make a Dynamic or
Input text field scrolla-
ble, you'll have to cre-
ate your own scroll bar.

The Dynamic text field is very similar to the Static text field except that it can be assigned an instance name on the Stage and therefore can be modified in the SWF file during run-time. This makes it possible to do change the text on the fly in order to, for example, display a user's score in a game, or to display text that may be loaded dynamically from a web service or based on user input.

Dynamic text fields are created by using the Text tool and setting the Text Type drop-down menu to Dynamic Text. After the text field is placed on the Stage, you can assign an instance name and position the text field.

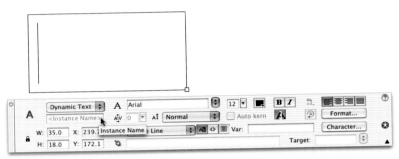

By assigning an instance name to the text field, you can control the text while the movie is playing back in the browser; you can modify its X and Y coordinates on the Stage, toggle the text's visibility, change the text based on events within the SWF, or facilitate user interaction.

20.10 Creating Input Text Fields

Input text fields collect user input from a SWF file. They are commonly used in forms and applications where users collect data such as name, phone number, or comments. Input text fields are similar to Dynamic text fields because they can be changed during playback of the SWF file. The main difference between Dynamic and Input text type fields is that Input text fields allow users to enter text into a SWF file. This input data can then be collected from the SWF and sent to a server using e-mail or other similar protocol.

There are four main types of Input text fields:

Single Line Creates a single-line input field where users can enter text.

Multiline Creates a multiline text field that automatically wraps text when it reaches the bounding box of the field.

Multiline No Wrap Wraps text only when a user presses the Enter or Return key.

Password Similar to Single Line, except that when users press a key, masks input and displays it as asterisks (*).

The TextInput component mimics the functionality of the Input text field; however, it offers you additional functionality that is not available in the Input text field on its own, such as HTML formatting and word wrapping.

➡ 5.22 Property Inspector

➡ 20.2 Understanding Text in Flash

➡ 20.9 Creating Dynamic Text Fields

➡ 20.14 Creating Text Fields Using ActionScript

One of the first things you might notice when using Dynamic and Input text fields in Flash MX 2004 is that Macromedia no longer provides a ScrollBar component as it did in Flash MX, and therefore the text isn't scrollable unless you create your own scroll bar.

20.11   Using the Label Component

If the Label component is so basic, why would you choose to use it over a Static text field? Because the Label component allows you to assign styles and HTML formatting, which helps maintain a consistent look throughout your SWF file.

The Label component is one of the simplest components you can use in Flash to display text to the user. It is a single line of text that can be formatted using HTML, but the component does not accept any focus within a SWF and will not broadcast any events.

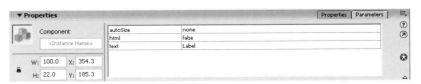

To use the Label component, drag an instance of the Label component from the Components panel onto the Stage. Select the instance on the Stage and expand the Property inspector. There are three parameters for the component in the Parameters tab: autoSize, html, and text.

The autoSize property controls how the Label component resizes and aligns the text if the text exceeds the bounds of the Label. There are four possible values for autoSize: none, left, center, and right. Selecting none will not resize the Label component at all to accommodate the text. Selecting left left-aligns the Label component and resizes the right side of the instance to fit the text. Selecting center centers the text within the Label component. If there is too much text to fit within the bounds of the label on the Stage, both the left and right sides will expand and the center of the text will remain at the horizontal center of the instance. Selecting right right-aligns text within the Label component instance and adjusts the left side of the component if there is too much text.

The html property determines how HTML-formatted text is handled within the Label component. If this value is set to true, any HTML tags will be parsed and formatted accordingly; false applies no HTML formatting, and if the label contains HTML tags they will be displayed instead of parsed.

The text property holds a default value for the Label component. If a value is defined within this field, it can be overwritten by manually setting the text property using Action-Script or by using a binding if you are using Flash MX Professional.

20.12 Using the TextInput Component

The TextInput component is similar to the Input text field because it allows users to enter text; however, TextInput is limited to a single line of text input. This component allows you to easily create forms to collect user data and integrate with web services or XML documents using Flash MX Professional 2004's Data Components.

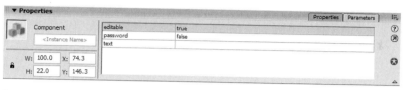

To add a TextInput component to a Flash document, drag the component from the Components panel onto the Stage. You can then set several properties using the Property inspector:

editable Controls whether or not users can modify the contents of the TextInput instance on the Stage. If you are using the component to display information to the user and do not want them to be able to modify the contents of the text field, set value to false.

password Behaves the same as the password property in the Input text field. Any characters entered by the user will be masked if this property is set to true. You will almost always want to set this value to true if users are entering passwords and you don't want other people to see the passwords on the screen.

text Sets an initial text value for the TextInput field.

If you expand the Component Inspector panel, you can modify a few additional properties as well.

maxChars Defines a maximum allowable length for strings or numbers entered into the TextInput component instance.

restrict You don't have to resort to writing ActionScript to define which characters or ranges should be permitted. If you are only allowing dates, you can set the restrict filter to 0-9-./, which would only allow digits, dashes (-), periods (.), and slashes (/).

enabled Defines whether the text field can be modified or edited. If this value is set to false, the TextInput instance appears grayed out (*dimmed*) and users cannot modify the component's contents or select the text within the component.

visible Controls whether or not the component is visible on the Stage.

Flash MX Professional 2004 allows you to bind values to parameters, the results of a web service call, or an XML document, making it possible to easily create rich Internet applications that integrate to third-party web services without you having to write much Action-Script. In fact, often you don't need to write a single line of Action-Script when you consume web services with Flash MX Professional and use data binding.

20.13   Using the TextArea Component

When using the TextArea component you always use the text property to define the value of the component, unlike the Dynamic text field, where you have to use the htmlText property if you are setting HTML formatted text.

The TextArea component is a multiline version of the TextInput component or a multiline Input text field with one dramatic difference: when the content entered exceeds the dimensions of the TextArea component instance, scroll bars will automatically appear allowing a visitor to scroll through the content.

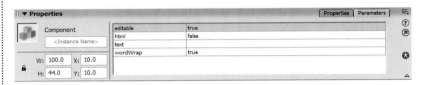

With the TextArea component instance selected on the Stage, you can modify the following properties using the Property inspector:

editable Defines whether the user can modify the contents of TextArea or whether its contents are static (unchangeable).

html A Boolean value; tells Flash whether the text contains HTML tags and formatting. Setting this value to true means that the content within the TextArea includes HTML tags such as <b> (bold) or <a> (a hyperlink) so Flash can display the content properly. If this value is set to false and the TextArea contains HTML tags, Flash displays the raw HTML code as text instead of formatting it as bold or as a hyperlink.

text Defines a value for the TextArea component. This value can be changed at any time by setting the `text` property using ActionScript.

wordWrap Controls how the text is wrapped if lines are too long to fit within the component. If `wordWrap` is set to true, Flash will wrap the lines so they fit best within the component; if `wordWrap` is set to false, the lines will only wrap when a `newline` is entered (either by pressing the Enter or Return key, or by using `\n` or `<br>` in ActionScript).

The Component Inspector panel allows you to modify several additional properties not visible in the Property inspector. Each of these properties behave exactly the same as discussed in the preceding section.

20.14   Creating Text Fields Using ActionScript

Text fields can also be created at runtime using ActionScript's `createTextField` method. The `createTextField` method takes six parameters: `instance name`, `depth`, `x position`, `y position`, `width`, and `height`. By default, the text field is set to single line, dynamic without any border, and HTML is set to false and password to false. You can modify the properties and text using ActionScript and the instance name defined when the text field was created. The default text format for the text field is left-aligned black Times New Roman font with a point size of 12. You can see an example of the `createTextField` method in the following code:

```
createTextField("myTextField_txt", 1, 100, 100, 300, 22);
```

This ActionScript creates a new text field with an instance name of `myTextField_txt`, which is set to a depth of 1 with X and Y positions of 100 pixels, a width of 300 pixels, and a height of 22 pixels. To change the value of the text in the text field, you can set either the `text` or `htmlText` property, such as:

```
myTextField_txt.text = "sample plain text";
```

Before you can set the `htmlText` property, you must enable HTML text formatting for the text instance by setting the `html` property to true:

```
myTextField_txt.html = true;
myTextField_txt.htmlText = "sample plain text";
```

To see the values and properties for the newly created text field, you can use a `for..in` loop, such as in the following code:

```
createTextField("myTextField_txt", 1, 100, 100, 300, 22);
for (i in myTextField_txt) {
  trace(i + ": " + myTextField_txt[i]);
}
```

If you want to change the text field from a Dynamic text field into an Input text field, you can use the following code:

```
myTextField_txt.type = "input";
```

➡ 20.9   Creating Dynamic Text Fields

➡ 20.10 Creating Input Text Fields

To set the `createTextField` to the next highest depth, you can use the `getNextHighestDepth` method.

FLASH WORKSPACE

AUTHORING TASKS

SCRIPTING TASKS

TESTING AND PUBLISHING TASKS

WHAT'S NEW

20.15   Restricting Input Characters

➠ 5.22 Property
         Inspector

➠ 20.10 Creating
         Input Text
         Fields

If you don't include the double backslashes before a dash, your ActionScript will not generate any errors in the authoring environment or in the testing environment. However, it also won't allow users to use the dash symbol in their input!

There are two ways to restrict user input in a text field.: you can make settings in the Property inspector or use the `restrict` property in the `TextField` class.

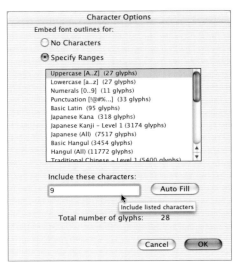

If you are using the Property inspector, you can select the characters to restrict by clicking the Character button to launch the Character Options dialog. To select which characters will be permitted, select the Specify Ranges radio button and select the characters from the list below. To select multiple options, hold the Shift or Command/Ctrl key while clicking. You can specify additional characters to accept by entering them into the text field near the bottom.

The other method of restricting characters requires you to write some ActionScript but gives a bit more control. To restrict user input to only lowercase letters, use the following ActionScript:

```
myTextField_txt.restrict = "a-z";
```

This allows the user to enter any character between a and z. If you want to allow both uppercase and lowercase letters, use the following code:

```
myTextField_txt.restrict = "a-zA-Z";
```

If you want to include only numbers, change the code to *one* of the following lines:

```
myTextField_txt.restrict = "0123456789";
myTextField_txt.restrict = "0-9";
```

You can see that in addition to using ranges using the dash (-) character, you can also specify each number or character individually. You can allow special characters (non-alphanumeric) by adding them to the end of the `restrict` string. This is useful when you want to allow special characters that might appear in a URL or e-mail address, as shown in the following snippet:

```
myTextField_txt.restrict = "a-zA-Z0-9@.";
```

20.15 Restricting Input Characters *(continued)*

This ActionScript allows any lowercase or uppercase letter, any numeric value, and the @ and . characters. If you want to exclude characters from a range and don't want to manually type in a large range of characters individually, you can use the caret (^). This allows you to specify ranges of characters (such as A-Z) except for certain characters (such as Q or X) by using the following code:

```
myTextField_txt.restrict = "A-Z^QX";
```

Because the caret (^) and dash (-) have special meanings when defining restricted characters using ActionScript, care must be taken if you want to include these values as permitted characters. In order to use the ^ or -, they must be prefixed (that is, "escaped") by a backslash (\) character; however, it is slightly more complicated than just adding that character. Because the backslash is also a special character itself, you must use a double backslash (\\) before the caret or dash, as shown in the following snippet:

```
myTextField_txt.restrict = "0-9.() \\-#";
```

This line allows any numeric values, the period (.), brackets, spaces, dashes (-), and the number sign (#). You can see that the dash is prefixed by double backslashes so the code will work.

➧ 20.12 Using the TextInput Component

➧ 20.14 Creating Text Fields Using ActionScript

USING PIXEL FONTS

Pixel fonts are still popular, even with the addition of alias text in Flash MX 2004. You might want to check out some of the commercial options available to you for pixel fonts, as quality fonts are a must-have when it comes to Flash. Pixel fonts not specifically built for Flash do not always look clear and are sometimes not very legible. Check out www.miniml.com and www.fontsforflash.com..

20.16 Accessing Text Instances Using ActionScript

___

If you use the create-TextField method in ActionScript, the instance name is assigned when you call the method, as shown in Section 20.14.

Before you can access a text field instance using ActionScript, it must have an instance name. If the text field was created using the Text tool in the Tools panel and it's a Dynamic or Input text field, you assign it an instance name using the Property inspector. It is not possible to assign an instance name to a Static text field.

Regardless of what method you use to create the instance on the Stage, the method for accessing the instance is the same. If the instance is directly on the Stage of the main SWF file, refer to it simply by its instance name and then set whatever property you're interested in. If the text instance is nested within a movie clip or other symbol in the movie, it may be necessary to use _parent and several instance names. You can also access an instance name using ActionScript by referencing the instance name you assigned to it when you created it.

To change the X or Y position of the instance on the Stage, you could use code similar to the following:

```
myTextField_txt._x = 450;
myTextField_txt._y = 380;
```

You can change the value of the text by using *either* of the following two lines. (For the *second* line to work, you must first enable HTML, either using with Property inspector or by setting the myTextField_txt.html property to true using ActionScript.)

```
myTextField_txt.text = "Hello World";
myTextField_txt.htmlText = "<b>Hello</b> <i>World</i>";
```

The first snippet sets the text property, updating the text on the Stage. If you are using HTML formatting, you set the htmlText property instead, as shown in the second snippet.

20.17 Formatting Text Fields Using CSS

Flash MX 2004 introduces the powerful feature that allows you to format text fields with Cascading Style Sheets (CSS). With CSS, you can simplify your text formatting by defining styles once and using them throughout your Flash document. This is a much better solution than using excessive font tags, as was necessary in previous versions of Flash.

CSS format and change the appearance of text, such as the color, size, font face, or alignment. CSS are frequently used to format HTML pages, in order to separate the stylistic appearance from the document's overall structure allowing greater flexibility and reuse.

In Flash, CSS offers you a way to underline, hyperlink text, and create "hover" functionality (so that when you mouse over a link, the link changes color).

There are two ways to use Cascading Style Sheets with Flash: define a style sheet within Flash or load an external style sheet file. These approaches are described in the following sections.

Although Flash has a more limited implementation of CSS than you might be used to in your other websites, it does extend the way you can format text in SWF files and is very quick and easy to implement.

20.18 Using External Style Sheets with Flash

———

Using an external style sheet has the added benefit of being able to reuse the same styles within your SWF file as you do within an HTML site. Both Flash and HTML can link to the same CSS file.

Using an external style sheet is similar to loading a remote file using `LoadVars` or an XML document. The styles are stored in an external file and loaded using the `TextField.StyleSheet` class's `load` method. Loading the style sheet into Flash is shown in the following ActionScript:

```
var styles_css = new TextField.StyleSheet();
styles_css.load("styles.css");
styles_css.onLoad = function(success) {
    if (success) {
    comment_txt.styleSheet = styles_css;
    comment_txt.text = "<p class='text'>this is a <b>sample</b> string which
includes a <a href='http://www.sybex.com'>link to Sybex</a>.</p>";
    }
};
```

This code creates a new `TextField.StyleSheet` object and loads the external CSS file, `styles.css`. After the file has completed loading, whether successfully or not, the `onLoad` callback handler is called and the `success` parameter is set, indicating whether the style sheet could be loaded by Flash. If the CSS file was successfully loaded, the style sheet is applied to the `comment_txt` TextArea component instance on the Stage and the text field is set to an HTML string with CSS formatting.

Before you can test the previous code snippet, you must also create the `styles.css` Cascading Style Sheet and save it to the same folder as the Flash document. Using any text editor, create a new document and save it as `styles.css`. In the new document, add your style definitions, such as these:

```
.text {
    color: #000000;
    font-family: Arial, Verdana, Helvetica, sans-serif;
    font-size: 12 px;
}
a:link {
    color:#FF0000;
    font-weight: bold;
}
a:hover {
    text-decoration: underline;
}
```

20.19 Using Inline Style Sheets with Flash

Creating a style sheet using ActionScript is fairly straightforward, but there is one slight glitch: the style names are slightly different if you are defining the styles using Action-Script or using an external file. An example of defining styles in ActionScript is shown in the following code:

```
var styles_css = new TextField.StyleSheet();
styles_css.setStyle(".text", {color:'#000000',
    fontFamily:"Arial, Verdana, Helvetica, sans-serif", fontSize:'12 px'});
styles_css.setStyle("a:link", {color:"#FF0000", fontWeight:"bold"});
styles_css.setStyle("a:hover", { textDecoration:"underline"});
comment_txt.styleSheet = styles_css;
comment_txt.text = "<p class='text'>this is a <b>sample</b> string which
    includes a <a href='http://www.sybex.com'>link to Sybex</a>.</p>";
```

This ActionScript example works with either a TextArea component or a Dynamic text field. The code begins by creating a new style sheet object and defining a few of styles. Each of the styles has a unique style name or uses a built-in name, such as a (for anchor tags). Every style also has a series of properties defined within a style object, which can be used to set the font, color, and several other CSS properties. Next the style sheet is bound to the comment_txt text field instance on the Stage by setting the styleSheet property for the text field. Finally, the value of the text field is set to an HTML-formatted string, which uses the defined styles.

If you are familiar with Cascading Style Sheets in HTML, you will notice that the property names are slightly different in Flash. Instead of CSS style names such as font-family, ActionScript uses fontFamily. You must be careful to use the correct name when defining styles within ActionScript.

20.20 Formatting XML with Style Sheets

Instead of using HTML-style CSS formatting with classes, you can apply style sheets to an XML-formatted document. CSS styles are included in the same way as described in the preceding sections and can be loaded from an external file or defined using ActionScript. The only difference between formatting XML with style sheets and loading CSS or applying it with ActionScript is the way the text in the TextArea component is formatted. You can use the following code to load in an external cascading style sheet and apply it to a text field instance or TextArea component on the Stage:

```
var styles_css = new TextField.StyleSheet();
styles_css.load("styles.css");
styles_css.onLoad = function(success) {
    if (success) {
    comment_txt.styleSheet = styles_css;
    comment_txt.text = "<text>this is a <b>sample</b> string which includes
        a <a href='http://www.sybex.com'>link to Sybex</a>.</text>";
    }
};
```

This code is very similar to the previous listings with one slight difference: when you are populating the TextArea component instance on the Stage, you are setting the **text** property to an XML-formatted string.

20.21 Using the *Selection* Class

The Selection class tracks when focus has changed between instances. You can use the class to set focus and to return what instance currently has focus in the SWF. The Selection class works with Dynamic and Input text fields also, so when you use a text field it traces _level0.instanceName. It does not work this way if you are tracing a component, though, because _level0.instanceName.level is reported instead.

To set a listener to alert you to when focus changes between two instances, you can use this ActionScript:

```
var selectionListener:Object = new Object();
selectionListener.onSetFocus = function(oldFocus, newFocus) {
  if (newFocus != null) {
    trace("you clicked the :'" + newFocus + "' text field.");
    trace("the previously selected text field was:'" + oldFocus + "'.");
  }
};
Selection.addListener(selectionListener);
```

In this ActionScript, a new listener object is created to report when focus changes. The first time you click an instance, the value of oldFocus is null because no instances currently have focus.

If you use Dynamic or Input text fields, they are traced as _level0.instanceName, but using a TextArea or TextInput field traces _level0.instanceName.level instead.

If an instance is not previously selected, it will report the oldFocus as "null", and likewise if you click off a component on to the Stage. oldFocus is set to whatever component was clicked last, and the newFocus is set to null

20.22   Using the Strings Panel

————

To enter a value for
the other languages,
simply double-click in
the desired cell and
enter the text directly.

————

You can view your Flash
movies in other lan-
guages by changing the
value of the Stage lan-
guage drop-down
menu at any time.

————

The choice of "Ameri-
can English" or "British
English" is a separate
setting from the Stage
language value chosen
here; this subsetting is
explained in the follow-
ing section.

The Strings panel allows you to build robust multilanguage websites using Flash.

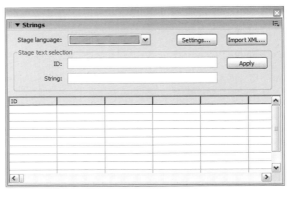

You can open the Strings panel by selecting Window > Other Panels > Strings from the main menu, or by pressing Command/Ctrl+F11. Clicking the Settings button launches the Settings panel.

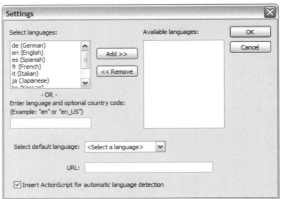

This dialog allows you to select which languages you want to add content for in your Flash document. To add a new language, select a language from the left-hand side of the dialog and click the Add button to move the selected language to the list on the right-hand side of the dialog. If the language you want to use isn't available in the left list, you can type a language and optional country code into the text field below the list. Click the Add button to add the custom language to the Available Languages list.

You can set a default language for the Flash application by selecting a language from the drop-down menu. Similar to Flash's automatic browser detection, you can have Flash automatically detect the user's language when they come to your site and display the appropriate text. After you've specified all the languages you want to support, click the OK button to return to the Strings panel. Notice that the Stage language drop-down menu has been populated with the languages you specified in the previous dialog, as well as a column for each language in the grid at the bottom portion of the panel.

The Strings panel works in conjunction with Dynamic and Input text fields on the Stage. Place a couple of text fields on the Stage and, with one of the text fields selected, enter a value in the ID field of the Strings panel. After you've entered a value for ID, enter some text in the String text field. Click the Apply button to add the ID and text string to the grid below. The string will be added to the column for the currently selected Stage language, so if your Stage language is set to en (English), the string you entered will appear under the en column in the grid.

20.23   Spell Checking Flash Documents

Before you can use Flash's built-in spell checking tool, you must configure the Spelling Setup tool by selecting Text > Spelling Setup. This launches the Spelling Setup dialog.

This dialog allows you to configure Flash's spelling tool and define which language Flash will use when it checks the spelling in your document. Flash also allows you to set various options that control whether frame labels and comments will be spell checked, or whether only text fields will be searched.

➧ 4.1   Timeline Overview

➧ 5.7   Actions Panel

➧ 20.2   Understanding Text in Flash

You can see the contents of your personal dictionary at any time by returning to the Spelling Setup dialog and clicking the Edit Personal Dictionary button. Clicking this button launches a dialog where you can edit existing words, add new words, or delete words.

There are also options to use your own personal dictionary, which might contain names or custom words that aren't used in the dictionaries that are included with Flash. After configuring the spell checker, you can run the spell check:

1   Choose Text > Check Spelling to check the spelling in the current Flash document.

2   If no spelling mistakes are found in the document, Flash rewards you with a dialog that says "Spelling check completed".

3   If there are any words that Flash doesn't recognize in the selected dictionaries, Flash displays the Check Spelling dialog, as shown in the following figure.

This dialog displays any words in your document that Flash was unable to recognize based on the options you selected in the Spelling Setup dialog. If a word is not found in the selected dictionaries, Flash gives you the option of adding the word to your personal dictionary, ignoring the single occurrence, ignoring all occurrences, changing the single occurrence, changing all occurrences, or deleting the unknown word from the string.

20.24   Embedding Font Outlines

———

Outlines for each char-
acter of each font
embedded in a SWF file
adds to file size. Use
device fonts if you need
to conserve file size.

———

To embed all of the
characters in a specific
text field, type the characters into the field and
then click the Character
button in the Property
inspector. Click the
Specify Ranges radio
button, then the Auto
Fill button.

———

The more characters
you embed in a SWF
file, the more file size
you add to the SWF.

———

If you are loading text
and don't know which
characters you require,
embed the entire font.
This is usually necessary
if you are loading a lot
of text or allowing users
to input text into an
Input text field.

Font outlines can be embedded into a SWF file so the end user can view fonts properly, as you intended for them to be seen. You do not have to embed font outlines and can instead use system fonts. However, you will not be able to ensure thwe font will display in the SWF file just as it looks on your own computer.

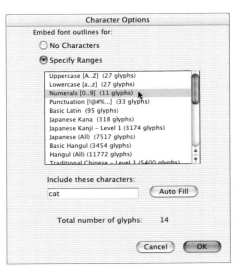

You can embed specific characters if you know exactly which characters need to be displayed in the SWF files; you can embed a set of characters (for example, all numbers); or you can embed the entire font in the SWF file.

To embed individual characters or a set of characters, follow these steps:

1 Select the Dynamic or Input text field you want to embed characters for.

2 Open the Property inspector and click the Character button.

3 Click the Specify Ranges button and select one of the character ranges from the list box. Alternatively or additionally, you can enter specific characters into the text field below the list.

You can also use ActionScript to embed an entire font into a SWF file. For example, if you were using a font called standard05_53 in a text field called `mytext_txt` and you wanted to embed that font into your SWF file, you would use the following ActionScript at the beginning of your file:

```
this.embedFonts = true;
mytext_txt.textFont = "standard05_53";
```

Then you can use that font within your Dynamic or Input text fields, and anyone who views the SWF file can see that font. If you didn't embed the standard05_53 font but still had the fields set to use it, Flash would substitute the font with the most similar font it can find or a default system font.

20.25　Using the *PrintJob* Class

The `PrintJob` class allows you to take content from a SWF file at runtime and prompt your visitor with a dialog to print the contents of the SWF. The files that you output from the SWF file are not scaled and will retain the original proportions of your SWF file's content. The `PrintJob` class allows you to print dynamic content, which means content that's pulled from the server (such as information from a web service) can be printed by the visitor.

To create a new print job, add two new pages to it, and launch the visitor's Print dialog, you could use the following ActionScript:

```
var printJob_pj:PrintJob = new PrintJob();
printJob_pj.start();
printJob_pj.addPage(news_txt);
printJob_pj.addPage(_level0);
printJob_pj.send();
delete printJob_pj;
```

After the pages are sent to the printer, you can delete the print job you created with `delete printJob_pj`, as seen at the end of the previous code snippet.

➠ 6.12 Printing and
          Sending Files

PrintJob opens the Print dialog. If the user has Acrobat or FlashPaper printer installed, they will be able to send and save the information to a file instead of printing it out.

CUSTOM CURSORS

Interesting and unique effects can be made when you have a movie clip follow the mouse cursor instead of a static image. Many sites have beautiful animations following the mouse cursor or even an animation that replaces the cursor altogether. Remember, for usability's sake, to make the cursor easy to use and not overly distracting, or you will have visitors who will not use your site to its full extent. Meaning, they'll leave the site before taking a good look around!

20.26 Using ActionScript to Find the Mouse Position

➠ 20.27 Capturing the Mouse Scroll Wheel

➠ 20.28 Creating a Custom Mouse Pointer

If you are using the default frame rate of 12 fps (frames per second), Flash executes the ActionScript in the `onEnterFrame` method 12 times every second, whether the mouse is moving or not. By using the onMouseMove method instead, you receive events only when the mouse position changes, which is much more efficient.

Using ActionScript, you can retrieve the current position of the mouse cursor within the SWF at runtime. This enables you to create custom mouse pointers and detect when the mouse is in a specific part of the Stage. One of the problems faced when tracking the mouse cursor is that you'll often want to continually know the position of the mouse cursor, not just the mouse pointer at a single point in time. There are two solutions to this problem: `onEnterFrame` or `onMouseMove`. Using `onEnterFrame` isn't the best solution because it will execute ActionScript many times a second, so it's inefficient in a SWF file.

The following code demonstrates how to create a listener in Flash that displays the mouse's position on the Stage whenever the mouse is moved. The coordinates are displayed in the Output panel in the testing environment.

```
var mouseListener = new Object();
mouseListener.onMouseMove = function() {
  trace("x:"+_level0._xmouse+", y:"+_level0._ymouse);
};
Mouse.addListener(mouseListener);
```

This ActionScript begins by creating a listener object, which you use to listen for the `onMouseMove` event. Then you create a function that is called whenever the mouse moves and simply displays the current X and Y position of the mouse on the Stage. The final line of code adds the custom listener to the mouse.

Instead of using a listener object, you can create a function similar to the previous snippet which adds the `onMouseMove` event handler to the main Timeline. The code is very similar to the previous code and is shown below:

```
this.onMouseMove = function() {
  trace("x:"+_level0._xmouse+", y:"+_level0._ymouse);
};
```

Because the ActionScript is placed directly on a frame in the main Timeline, you can use the `this` keyword to refer to the Timeline.

20.27   Capturing the Mouse Scroll Wheel

Detecting when the visitor uses their scroll wheel is a simple thing to do when you use a mouse listener. Similar to the code in the preceding section, detecting the mouse scroll wheel uses the `onMouseWheel` listener instead of `onMouseMove`:

```
var mouseListener:Object = new Object();
mouseListener.onMouseWheel = function(offset) {
  circle_mc._y -= offset;
};
Mouse.addListener(mouseListener);
```

This ActionScript moves a movie clip along the _y axis when the visitor scrolls the mouse wheel.

The `offset` parameter in the `onMouseWheel` event handler is a value that represents how fast the scroll wheel was rolled. Lower numbers indicate the mouse wheel was rolled slowly, while larger numbers indicate that the mouse was rolled faster. A typical value will be between 1 and 3, although if you scroll quickly it is possible to get values of 15 or higher.

By adding a second, optional parameter to the event handler for the `onMouseScroll` listener, you can have Flash tell you the instance name that the mouse is currently hovering over. The following example demonstrates how to pass a second parameter to `onMouseScroll` allowing you to move whichever instance the mouse is hovering over.

```
var mouseListener:Object = new Object();
mouseListener.onMouseWheel = function(offset, target) {
  if (target != undefined) {
    target._y -= offset;
  }
};
Mouse.addListener(mouseListener);
```

➠ 20.26 Using ActionScript to Find the Mouse Position

➠ 20.28 Creating a Custom Mouse Pointer

It is important to remember the offset isn't always a positive integer. The number is positive only if the mouse wheel is scrolled upward; a negative number is returned if the mouse wheel is scrolled downward.

20.28   Creating a Custom Mouse Pointer

____

If the Boolean value in startDrag is set to false or omitted altogether, the cursor still moves along with the mouse, although the cursor won't always be in the same position as the mouse.

To create your own custom mouse pointer in Flash, all you need is a movie clip symbol to use as your cursor and a couple lines of ActionScript code (although there can be one important snag that you'll deal with later on). First, you need a new movie clip symbol to use as a pointer.

1   Create a drawing (even a red circle will do), select it, and convert it into a movie clip instance.

2   After you have created the new symbol, put it on a layer at the top of your Flash movie but below any "actions" or "labels" layers.

3   Give this new movie clip an instance name: myCursor_mc.

4   Create an "actions" layer and add the following code to the first frame:

```
Mouse.hide();
myCursor_mc.startDrag(true);
```

The first line of ActionScript hides the default mouse cursor. The second line of code uses a symbol with the instance name myCursor_mc as the cursor by calling the movie clip's startDrag function. The Boolean value true in the startDrag function specifies that the movie clip is locked to the mouse position so it can be used as a pointer.

So where does the trickery come in? Well, Flash only allows one item to be draggable at a single time. If you have another movie clip that is draggable using the startDrag function, your custom cursor will stop being draggable after the startDrag function is called for the other instance. If you need to use a custom cursor and still use draggable movie clips, you could rewrite the custom cursor code to manually reposition the cursor using a mouse listener similar to the code in the preceding section. Here's a sample:

```
Mouse.hide();
var mouseListener:Object = new Object();
mouseListener.onMouseMove = function() {
  myCursor_mc._x = _level0._xmouse;
  myCursor_mc._y = _level0._ymouse;
};
Mouse.addListener(mouseListener);
```

This code is placed on a frame in the main Flash movie. Every time the mouse is moved in the SWF file, the cursor repositions to the current mouse position. Using this method allows you to drag instances around the Stage using the startDrag and stopDrag functions and yet continue to use a custom mouse cursor.

CHAPTER 21

Time and Timing

FLASH ALLOWS YOU TO USE TIME IN THREE WAYS, all of which require ActionScript. You can make use of: the time and date held by the user's computer via the `Date` class; the Flash timer (which starts from zero as soon as you start viewing Flash content and counts up in milliseconds) via the `getTimer` action; and the time-based event `setInterval`, which allows you to run code at periodic intervals.

21.1   Time Overview

Unlike HTML, Flash is not a static page-based system; it is inherently time based because of its use of frames. There is thus sometimes a need to make your code aware of time and timing. This sort of timing is typically in milliseconds.

Outside Flash's internal millisecond-based timing schemes, you have *your* time: the date and the clock time. Flash sometimes needs to be aware of this. Your time also varies depending on where *here* is in your world—the Internet is global and to get around it involves crossing time zones.

Date and Time

Flash can use two timing systems via the `Date` class, local time and UTC:

Local time   The time in your time zone. The official time in each zone is available in real time at several places on the Web, including

`http://greenwichmeantime.com/info/timezone.htm`.

UTC time   Universal Coordinated Time (or "UTC," in French phrasing) is taken to be the standard world time and it is a more accurate version of Greenwich Mean Time (GMT), which is based on astronomical time measurements. UTC is based around a precise definition of a second in terms of the atomic frequencies generated by cesium.

UTC and local time are identical (for our purposes) in the GMT 1 time zone (which includes England, Portugal, Iceland, and Morocco) except for daylight saving changes. For other time zones, UTC and the local time is different by up to plus or minus 12 hours as you traverse the globe.

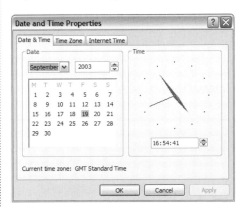 

In this Windows XP operating system, the user has set up the correct values in the Date And Time Properties window (which can be accessed by double-clicking the clock to the right of the taskbar) and has checked the option Automatically Adjust Clock For Daylight Saving Changes.

Because Flash takes UTC time from the user's computer, it is not accurate atomic clock time. It is really just an interpolation to UTC/GMT time, assuming that the user's computer has the correct local time (and details of daylight saving time) correctly defined on their operating system.

Be wary of defining a time as UTC on a website; most people don't know what it is! Consider either using GMT (which more people know about), or adding "(Universal Time)" or "(world time)" after the UTC.

21.1 Time Overview *(continued)*

In Flash, time is *always* based on the date/time on the user's computer. Flash assumes that the time on the user's computer is the correct local time and will work out the UTC time based on if it is required. This assumes a number of things:

- That the user has the correct time and date set up
- That the user has the correct time zone set up
- That the user's computer is set up to recognize daylight saving changes

To make Flash print out a time-stamp of the date/time it is currently seeing, add this code to the first frame of a new FLA:

```
trace(new Date().toString());
```

Output of the trace action

Timing

Flash is a frame-based system and runs to an internal time heartbeat: the frame rate. The frame rate is not the rate that Flash will actually run at, but it's the rate it will *try* to run at. If you set a high frame rate or have sections of processor-intensive animation, the frame rate may drop. Also, the frame rate interval is fairly arbitrary; the default frame interval of ¹⁄₁₂th of a second is not normally that useful!

The more accurate way to measure time in Flash is the Flash clock. This clock will start at 0 when Flash Player is first invoked and will count up in milliseconds. It is not affected by changes in Flash performance or loading and should be used for accurate timing rather than the frame rate. The `getTimer()` action allows you to access this value, but you cannot reset it.

If you want to periodically run code at rates other than the frame rate, you can use the `setInterval` event. You can also use it to run code after a delay by setting it to run periodically and then clearing the event at the end of its first invocation so that it will not run again. This is done via the `clearInterval()` action.

Setting the `setInterval` period to very low values (that is, interval rates that are faster than the frame rate) is possible and is a good way of achieving very smooth animation. If you do this, bear in mind that like any event-driven code, Flash can only respond to events as fast as it can handle them; if you overload Flash, you will always get slow responses.

Be very wary of giving a time and date on any website that requires the user to give sensitive information. If the user has an incorrect time set up on their computer, the time on your website will also be wrong. Some users will assume that this is because the site is broken and won't enter anything!

When you want to give the time for a global event on a website (such as a live concert or an important astronomical occurrence), many users will be confused as to whether daylight saving times are added to or ignored by the time if you specify UTC or GMT (in fact, neither refer to it). To address this, it is always a good idea to start showing a countdown close to the event, or a link to a site that explains UTC/GMT.

Unless there is a good reason to add a time readout to a website, it is a good idea not to do this—the chances of displaying the wrong time for a significant percentage of your audience is fairly high!

21.2   Retrieving and Displaying the Time of Day

The Date class allows you to create a variable holding the current time in either local time or UTC time, which can then be displayed in a text field. Every time you create a new Date, you create an instance with a *static* (that is, unchanging) date and time. Think of each instance as being a timestamp.

```
1  function addZero(digit) {
2      if (digit<10) {
3          digit = "0"+digit;
4      }
5      return digit;
6  }
7  myDate = new Date();
8  hours = myDate.getHours();
9  minutes = myDate.getMinutes();
10 seconds = myDate.getSeconds();
11 //
12 minutes = addZero(minutes);
13 seconds = addZero(seconds);
14 time = hours+"."+minutes+"  "+seconds;
15 trace(time);
16
```

```
1  function addZero(digit) {
2      if (digit<10) {
3          digit = "0"+digit;
4      }
5      return digit;
6  }
7  myDate = new Date();
8  hours = myDate.getUTCHours();
9  minutes = myDate.getUTCMinutes();
10 seconds = myDate.getUTCSeconds();
11 //
12 minutes = addZero(minutes);
13 seconds = addZero(seconds);
14 time = hours+"."+minutes+"  "+seconds;
15 trace(time);
16
```

The code on the left will create a Date instance and from it retrieve the current local time. The code on the right does the same thing for UTC time. Both these listings will create a time in the format HH.MM.SS. Note that Date.getMinutes and Date.getSeconds (plus UTC equivalents) will give a single-digit value for numbers less than 10 (for example, 7 instead of 07). The function addZero fixes this. Note the code uses string concatenation to build up the time from the individual *hours, minutes,* and *seconds* variables.

Creating an Animated Clock

To create an animated local time, you have to create a new Date instance for every new time and write it into a dynamic text field:

1   Create a new FLA. Rename the existing layer clock face. In it, add a text field and enter **hh.mm ss** to ensure it is big enough to show the time.

2   With the text selected, change its text properties via the Properties inspector so it's formatted the way you want.

3   Add a new layer above clock face called actions. In it add the following script:

If you want to add an animated clock to an existing Flash site, encapsulate the clock into a movie clip. Create a new movie clip (Insert > New Symbol) immediately after opening a new FLA in step 1 and carry out the rest of the instructions on the movie clip timeline that opens up. When you finish, drag the movie clip to where you want to show the time.

The animated clock updates the time at the frame rate, which is very processor intensive. (Flash is particularly slow in drawing text quickly because the number of curves and fills it has to redraw is high.)

```
1  function addZero(digit) {
2      if (digit<10) {
3          digit = "0"+digit;
4      }
5      return digit;
6  }
7  this.onEnterFrame = function() {
8      myDate = new Date();
9      hours = myDate.getHours();
10     minutes = myDate.getMinutes();
11     seconds = myDate.getSeconds();
12     minutes = addZero(minutes);
13     seconds = addZero(seconds);
14     time = hours+"."+minutes+"  "+seconds;
15     clock.text = time;
16 };
```

21.3   Retrieving and Displaying the Date

Retrieving and displaying the date is similar to displaying the time in the last section; simply use the methods of the Date class to pick out which parts of the time-stamp you want to display.

➡ 21.2 Retrieving and Displaying the Time of Day

Creating a Short Format Date-Stamp

```
  ⊕ ⌕ ⚲ ⊕ ✔ ▤ ⟨⊒
1 myDate = new Date();
2 month = myDate.getMonth()+1;
3 date = myDate.getDate();
4 fullYear = myDate.getFullYear();
5 dateStamp = month+"/"+date+"/"+fullYear;
6 trace(dateStamp);
7
```

To create a short format local date-stamp in U.S. order (MM/DD/YYYY), use this code.

Note that 1 is added to the month in the short-format example. This is because Flash uses 0 to 11, with January being month zero. You eliminate month+1 when using the array, given that an array is also zero-based.

To use the form MM/DD/YY, you need to change the full year value into a string and then ignore the first two characters in it. To do this, replace lines 4 and 5 with the following:

```
year = myDate.getFullYear().toString().substring(2);
dateStamp = month+"/"+date+"/"+year;
```

Creating a Long Format Date-Stamp

A short format date-stamp can be confusing to an international audience, given that the DD/MM/YY format is used in many regions. It is often safer to use a long format date-stamp, such as Jan-29-1967. To do this, you need to create an array that includes the months of the year and use the numerical month value as an index into the array:

```
  ⊕ ⌕ ⚲ ⊕ ✔ ▤ ⟨⊒
1 months = new Array("Jan", "Feb", "Mar", "Apr", "May", "Jun", "Jul", "Aug", "Sep", "Oct", "Nov", "Dec");
2 myDate = new Date();
3 month = months[myDate.getMonth()];
4 date = myDate.getDate();
5 fullYear = myDate.getFullYear();
6 dateStamp = month+"-"+date+"-"+fullYear;
7 trace(dateStamp);
8
```

FLASH WORKSPACE

AUTHORING TASKS

SCRIPTING TASKS

TESTING AND PUBLISHING TASKS

WHAT'S NEW

21.4   The Flash Timer

When you read the Flash timer value from a frame-based script, remember that getTimer() is only run at a frame boundary, so the result will only be accurate to the nearest ¹⁄₁₂th of a second (assuming the default frame rate) rather than to the nearest millisecond.

The Flash timer is a great way of testing and debugging when areas of your timeline are running slow or when you're trying to write optimized code.

When using the Flash timer, don't show the value of getTimer() until after the time trial is completed, because displaying it will significantly alter the result. The resulting constantly updating text field is one of the most processor-intensive animations in Flash and would make your readings too high.

The Flash timer is a read-only integer value that is incremented by 1 every millisecond. It is by far the most accurate way of measuring elapsed time in a Flash movie.

The Flash timer can be read via the getTimer() action. A value in seconds, such as 1.234, is usually more meaningful than the value in milliseconds, such as 1234, because seconds are the assumed measure of short time durations. To measure the elapsed time between two keyframes in seconds, you would:

1   Add the following code in the first keyframe:

```
startTime = getTimer();
```

2   At the second keyframe, add the following:

```
timer = (getTimer() - startTime) / 1000;
```

This gives you the result in seconds in the variable *timer*. To view this value, either use trace() or print it in a dynamic text field.

EXTENDING THE USEFULNESS OF DATES

As well as displaying the time to the user, the Date object has other uses. It can be used to vary the color scheme of a website (by converting the date to a color) or to create computer-generated art (by using the date as a start value for a pattern generator). You can also use it for more mundane actions such as selecting which parts of a Flash site to load, based on the current month, to give seasonal variations.

21.5 Creating a *setInterval* Timed Event

Most events are tied to either the frame rate (`onEnterFrame`) or user interaction (for example, `onRelease` and other button events). Neither frame-based nor user-interaction-based events allow you to efficiently process something that needs to be carried out after a delay, or at a periodic rate other than the frame rate. The `setInterval` event was introduced in Flash MX to fill this gap. Although it seems like a small addition to ActionScript, its effect on advanced motion graphics is profound—*all* code can now be event-driven.

⇒ 21.2 Retrieving and Displaying the Time of Day

⇒ 21.6 Clearing a setInterval Timed Event

Defining and Using a setInterval

To set up a `setInterval` event, the easiest route is to create the code you want to run in a function, then start the event countdown with

```
myInterval = setInterval(functionName, duration);
```

where *myInterval* is the name of your `setInterval`, *functionName* is the name of the function you want to run, and *duration* is how often you want it to run.

It is not obvious in the first `setInterval` example that the clock is updating only once per second. To see a more visible example, change the set-Interval duration from 1000 to 2000.

```
1  function addZero(digit) {
2      if (digit<10) {
3          digit = "0"+digit;
4      }
5      return digit;
6  }
7  this.onEnterFrame = function() {
8      myDate = new Date();
9      hours = myDate.getHours();
10     minutes = myDate.getMinutes();
11     seconds = myDate.getSeconds();
12     minutes = addZero(minutes);
13     seconds = addZero(seconds);
14     time = hours+"."+minutes+"  "+second
15     clock.text = time;
```

```
1  function addZero(digit) {
2      if (digit<10) {
3          digit = "0"+digit;
4      }
5      return digit;
6  }
7  function updateTime() {
8      myDate = new Date();
9      hours = myDate.getHours();
10     minutes = myDate.getMinutes();
11     seconds = myDate.getSeconds();
12     minutes = addZero(minutes);
13     seconds = addZero(seconds);
14     time = hours+"."+minutes+"  "+second:
15     clock.text = time;
```

The code `update-AfterEvent()` must be the last action in a function, otherwise it will not work.

The code at the left updates a clock display at the frame rate (about 12 times a second for the default rate). That's inefficient; the display only changes value every second, so 11 of 12 updates show the same text. The code at right, using `setInterval`, runs once per second, so it updates at the same rate as the content actually changes.

Using setInterval to Create Smooth Animation

Using `setInterval` when animating content at faster rates than the frame rate can make portions of the overall site move much quicker than others. However, the user won't see the extra frames because Flash will only update the screen at the start of every new frame.

In the function used to move the ball, you are not assuming a `this` path. Unlike a callback function used as an onEnterFrame movie clip event, the set-Interval function code does not scope the instance owning the event. This is because the owner of the event is not the movie clip, but the `setInterval`, *myInterval*.

```
1  smoothMover = function (moveClip) {
2      _root[moveClip]._x++;
3      updateAfterEvent();
4  };
5  myInterval = setInterval(smoothMover, 40, "ball");
6
```

To fix this, use **updateAfter-Event()**. This forces Flash to add extra frames by telling it to do a redraw at the end of each `setInterval` call.

If you place an instance called `ball` on the stage, it will move from left to right at a frame rate of approximately 24 frames per second, or as fast as Flash can manage. If you omit the **updateAfterEvent()**, you will see that it becomes jerky because Flash is updating the screen only at the frame rate, so you will miss the additional smoothing frames.

21.6   Clearing a *setInterval* Timed Event

➡ 21.5 Creating a
        setInterval
        Timed Event

If you want to run the setInterval function only once, place the clearInterval as the last line of the function.

Although Flash doesn't require you to give your setInterval a name, you should do so because you need to have a name to reference it if you want to stop it cleanly with clearInterval(). This book has therefore always named its set-Intervals in the examples.

To stop a periodic setInterval, you *must* use the clearInterval() action rather than removing the instance it is controlling. This is because a setInterval function is *not* a callback function (which is associated to the instance and so ends when the instance is removed) but is associated with setInterval itself.

Using the example from the last section, to stop the ball animation once it reaches the edge of the screen, insert the clearInterval function as follows:

```
1  smoothMover = function (moveClip) {
2      _root[moveClip]._x++;
3      if (_root[moveClip]._x>300) {
4          clearInterval(myInterval);
5      }
6      updateAfterEvent();
7  };
8  myInterval = setInterval(smoothMover, 40, "ball");
9
```

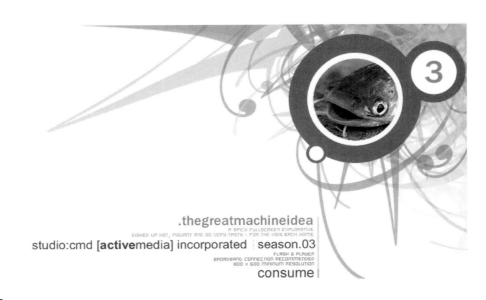

CHAPTER 22

Fundamentals of Scripted Animation

THIS CHAPTER DESCRIBES THE most common basic ActionScript building blocks used in animation.

22.1   Animating via Scripted Property Changes

➠ 18.3   Attaching
          Scripts to
          Events Using
          Functions

➠ 22.10 Changing
          Color via
          Scripts

─────

Although a button has all of the properties stated in this section, it is much harder to animate a button than a movie clip because it does not have the onEnterFrame event. Consider putting any button you want to animate inside a movie clip, then animating the movie clip.

─────

The height and width of a movie clip will change if you rotate it (because the height and width axes do not rotate with the movie clip), whereas the _xscale and _yscale do not change. Using _xscale and _yscale is therefore preferable to using _height and _width.

─────

The alpha value is stored internally as 0 to 255 steps, and the 0 percent to 100 percent value range is rounded to the nearest 0–255 value. This will almost always cause rounding errors. If you want to set alpha to either 0 percent or 100 percent, you should therefore set it explicitly (e.g., myClip._alpha = 100%) rather than relying on a counter or expression giving you exactly 100 or exactly 0.

All ActionScript-based animation works by changing properties over time, typically using the onEnterFrame event. For example, the following event handler will move a movie clip with instance name myClip_mc left to right by varying the _x property:

```
myClip_mc.onEnterFrame = function() {
  this._x = this._x+5;
};
```

The following properties can also be used to produce animation:

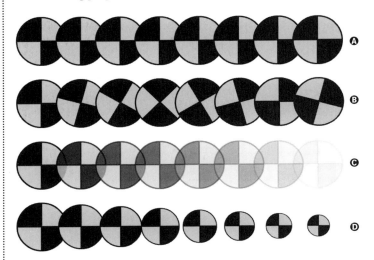

Ⓐ **Motion** By changing the _x and _y properties, you can create motion in the x (left-right) and y (up-down) directions.

Ⓑ **Rotation** By changing the _rotation property, you can rotate a movie clip, with the pivot point being the symbol's registration point. Rotation is measured in degrees.

Ⓒ **Transparency** By altering the _alpha property, a movie clip can be made to fade between opaque and transparent. The alpha property varies from 0 percent to 100 percent, with 100 being totally opaque.

Ⓓ **Size** The _xscale and _yscale properties allow you to change the size of the movie clip in percentage terms, and the _height and _width properties allow you to change size in absolute pixel values.

22.2 Attaching Events Dynamically

In complex animations, you often want your symbols to do different things at different times. The easiest way to do this is to vary the onEnterFrame script you attach to each movie clip.

The concept is best shown by example. Suppose you wanted a ball, ball_mc, to move between the left and right of the screen. You could do something like this, where you conditionally switch between two onEnterFrame scripts:

```
moveRight = function () {
  this._x += 5;
  if (this._x > 300) {
    this.onEnterFrame = moveLeft;
  }
};
moveLeft = function () {
  this._x -= 5;
  if (this._x < 100) {
    this.onEnterFrame = moveRight;
  }
};
ball_mc.onEnterFrame = moveRight;
```

Controlled by moveRight

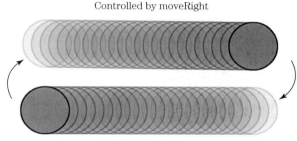

Controlled by moveLeft

The onEnterFrame handler starts off as the function moveRight, but once the x position of the ball gets beyond 300, you switch to the moveLeft function.

Dynamically Deleting Events

Sometimes you want to delete the controlling script completely. Changing the line

```
this.onEnterFrame = moveRight;
```

to the following line would do this, resulting in the ball stopping.

```
delete (this.onEnterFrame);
```

Thus, the code will

1 Run moveRight() until ball_mc has moved fully right.

2 Run moveLeft() until ball_mc has moved fully left.

3 Stop all events attached to ball_mc by deleting the current one, resulting in ball_mc stopping at the fully left position (i.e., where it started out).

➡ 18.3 Attaching Scripts to Events Using Functions

➡ 22.1 Animating via Scripted Property Changes

➡ 22.3 Attaching and Duplicating Movie Clips to the Stage

———

Although the simple example shown in this section could easily be implemented via a single event script, varying the onEnter-Frame script is much more useful for complex animations. It would, for example, be useful in a video game, where you could split the animation for a Space Invader into an information script and a dive script and switch between them using the same code structure.

———

Events are also typically attached dynamically when you duplicate or attach movie clips at runtime.

———

Using the delete action to remove an event is more desirable than equating the event to null or undefined. With null or undefined, the on-EnterFrame will still exist (although it will not do anything) whereas delete actually removes it. You can see this by looking at the debugger while trying each technique.

22.3 Attaching and Duplicating Movie Clips to the Stage

➡ 9.15 Working with Depth

➡ 18.4 Attaching Scripts to Events Using Callback Functions

The *depth* parameter of these methods defines the depth of the copy on the Flash Stage: a movie clip with a larger depth number will appear behind one with a lower one. This value should be a unique positive number between 1 and approximately 16000. If you duplicate two movie clips to the same depth, the second movie clip will overwrite the first.

The *initObject* defines the property values, event handlers, and Timeline variables you want to associate with the copy. Any changes you make to this object will be reflected in the copy.

When using ActionScript, you will often either not know how many movie clips you want on Stage (because this will be defined by user interaction), or prefer to add your movie clips dynamically (because it is more bandwidth efficient than using keyframes; the position data of dynamically attached movie clips can be calculated by your code rather than having to be downloaded as part of the SWF). You may also want to add movie clips to the Stage dynamically if you have too many of them to add manually (because you would also have to manually type in an instance name for each one!).

There are two methods for creating copies of movie clips on the Stage:

duplicateMovieClip allows you to copy instances that are already on the Stage. The advantage of this method is that it is the easier of the two to set up. Its disadvantage is that the copies and the original cannot be treated in exactly the same way: although you can remove the copies, you cannot remove the original. This invariably causes problems with your code, because you have to treat the original differently from the copies. Despite its disadvantage, duplicateMovieClip is often used in simpler effects that require lots of similar movie clips to be on Stage (such as particle effects).

attachMovie allows you to copy instances from the Library. The advantage of this method is that the copies are easier to control via code because they all behave identically, something that becomes important for more advanced effects where your code is complicated enough without worrying about the special case of the duplicateMovieClip original (e.g., in something like a Flash 3D engine). However, attachMovie is a little more complicated to set up. You must create a linkage identifier and consider export options for your movie clip. (Flash will not export a movie clip as part of a SWF unless it appears on the Timeline at *author time,* and Flash doesn't know that your ActionScript needs the movie clip.)

Duplicating Movie Clips

To duplicate a movie clip already on Stage, use the duplicateMovieClip method of the Movie Clip class. This method is also easier to set up than attachMovie: you don't need a linkage identifier, and you don't need to worry about export options. The general form of the duplicateMovieClip method is

```
originalClip.duplicateMovieClip(copyClip, depth, [initObject]);
```

The following lines will copy a movie clip named myClip_mc into a new clip named myNew-Clip and shift the copy 50 pixels to the left:

```
myClip_mc.duplicateMovieClip("myNewClip", 1);
myNewClip._x += 50;
```

When you want to change the properties, add event handlers, or define Timeline variables for the duplicated movie clips, you should use the third parameter of the method, the *init-Object* parameter.

22.3 Attaching and Duplicating Movie Clips to the Stage *(continued)*

The following code creates 100 movie clips in the center of the Stage and assigns each one the Timeline variables xSpeed and ySpeed, which are used by an event handler to move each copied clip:

```
init = new Object();
init._x = 275, init._y = 200;
init.onEnterFrame = function() {
  this._x += this.xSpeed;    this._y += this.ySpeed;  };
for (i = 0; i < 100; i++) {
  init.xSpeed = Math.random() * 2 - 1;
  init.ySpeed = Math.random() * 2 - 1;
  myClip_mc.duplicateMovieClip("copyClip" + i, i, init);  }
```

This will produce a simple explosion particle effect. The original movie clip does *not* move, which is a disadvantage of the duplicateMovieClip method.

Attaching Movie Clips

The attachMovie method is similar to duplicateMovieClip *except* that the original is copied from the Library. You do not, therefore, have to have the original on the Stage. The linkage identifier locates the original. The general form of attachMovie is

```
clipToCopyInto.attachMovie(linkageID, copyClip depth, init);
```

To define a linkage identifier:

1 Select the movie clip in the Library, then choose Linkage from the Library panels menu or right-click/⌘-click the movie clip and choose Linkage.

2 The Linkage Properties window will open. Check the options Export For ActionScript and Export In First Frame and enter a linkage identifier in the Identifier field (you can leave the second field blank).

To change the code above into code that uses attachMovie, change the last line to this:

```
this.attachMovie("ball", "copyClip" + i, i, init);
```

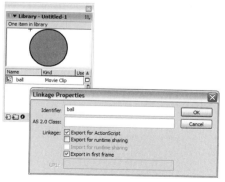

➡ 22.1 Animating via Scripted Property Changes

Notice that the code in this section uses the loop counter *i* to define a unique instance name (copyClip0 to copyClip99) and depth (0 to 99) for the copies. Duplicating or attaching large numbers of movie clips to the Stage using a loop in this way is almost standard practice.

---

attachMovie is the preferred method for attaching components to the Stage.

22.4 Simulating Random Motion

➡ 22.1 Animating via
Scripted Prop-
erty Changes

You can use random
motion on a large num-
ber of movie clips at
the same time to simu-
late particle or swarm
effects.

The Flash Stage uses
print-based coordinates,
which means that the
origin is at the top-left
corner and the positive
y direction is *down*. This
is in contrast to math-
based axes, where the
origin is in the *bottom*
left and the positive y
direction is *up*.

The following script will make a movie clip with instance name `myClip_mc` move randomly. It works by moving the movie clip one pixel from its current position in a random direction:

```
myClip_mc.onEnterFrame = function() {
  this._x += Math.round(Math.random() * 2) - 1;
  this._y += Math.round(Math.random() * 2) - 1;
};
```

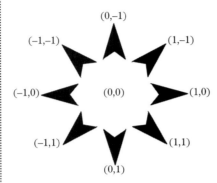

The code `Math.round(Math.random()*2)-1` gives a value of either –1, 0, or 1, so the movie clip will move in one of eight directions or stay still every frame.

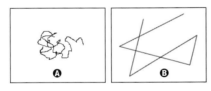

This set of results will make the movie clip jiggle on the spot (as in the left image), rather than move. More usually, you want a movie clip to move in a series of straight lines (as in the right image). This is achieved by making the movie clip move farther than 1 pixel every frame and changing direction every so often rather than every frame.

The following script re-creates the motion shown on the right:

```
myClip_mc.onEnterFrame = function() {
  if (Math.random()<0.1) {
    this.xSpeed = Math.round(Math.random() * 6) - 3;
    this.ySpeed = Math.round(Math.random() * 6) - 3;
    trace(Math.round(Math.random() * 2) - 1);
  }
  this._x += this.xSpeed;
  this._y += this.ySpeed;
};
myClip.xSpeed = 1;
myClip.ySpeed = 1;
```

The code `Math.round(Math.random() * 6) - 3` will make the movie clip move between 3 and –3 pixels every frame, and these values will only change when the `if` statement creates a random number between 0 and 1 that is less than 0.1 (i.e., once every ten frames on average).

22.5 Creating User-Triggered Motion

Rather than start animations on frame 1 of the Timeline, you may want to start (or stop) animations when certain user-generated events occur.

Suppose you want a movie clip named `ball_mc` to start animating when a user action takes place, typically a mouse click or a button click. The following code will start `ball_mc` animating as soon as the user clicks anywhere on the Stage.

```
function goBall() {
  this._x++;
}
ball_mc.onMouseUp = function() {
  this.onEnterFrame = goBall;
};
```

The `MovieClip.onMouseDown` event occurs whenever the user clicks the mouse (irrespective of whether the click occurs over the movie clip or not). This attaches the `onEnterFrame` script, which starts the animation (in this case, it makes `ball_mc` move left to right).

To make the animation start when a button is clicked, modify the script as shown:

```
function goBall() {
  this._x++;
}
start_btn.onRelease = function() {
  ball_mc.onEnterFrame = goBall;
};
```

This time, the `onEnterFrame` is attached when the button `start_btn` is click-released.

Toggling or Stopping an Animation

As well as starting an animation via user interaction, you may also want to stop it. The following modification to the `start_btn.onRelease` event handler will turn the button into a toggle; if the animation is stopped, it will restart from its last position, and if it has already started, it will be stopped:

```
start_btn.onRelease = function() {
  if (ball_mc.onEnterFrame == undefined) {
    ball_mc.onEnterFrame = goBall;
  } else {
    delete (ball_mc.onEnterFrame);
  }
};
```

➡ 18.3 Attaching Scripts to Events Using Functions

➡ 18.4 Attaching Scripts to Events Using Callback Functions

➡ 22.1 Animating via Scripted Property Changes

➡ 22.2 Attaching Events Dynamically

———

The final script in this section checks that the animation is already running by checking for the associated animating event handler (rather than actual movement). If the `ball_mc` movie clip has no `onEnterFrame` attached, then `ball_mc.onEnterFrame` will be undefined.

———

You can start and stop multiple animations by attaching or removing multiple event handlers on user events.

22.6   Simulating Target-Driven Motion

➡ 20.26 Using
ActionScript
to Find
the Mouse
Position

One of the biggest advantages of scripted animation over Timeline animation is that the former is not *fixed*—a scripted animation can change direction interactively. This is done by either changing the target position that an animated movie clip is moving toward every time the target is reached, or moving to a target position that is itself changing.

Continuously Moving to a Changing Target

The easiest form of target-driven motion is continuously following a target. This script will continually move a movie clip, `ball_mc`, toward the cursor position:

```
function goPos() {
  this._x -= (this._x - _xmouse) / 4;
  this._y -= (this._y - _ymouse) / 4;
}
ball_mc.onEnterFrame = goPos;
```

The easiest target position to illustrate is the mouse position (_xmouse, _ymouse), which is why it is used in the examples.

The examples shown also simulate inertia. The ball will slow down as it gets closer to its target position.

The animation is caused by forming a set of relationships that include the movie clip's _x and _y position properties and the cursor's corresponding _xmouse and _ymouse properties and applying them to every frame.

Conditionally Moving to a Target Position

Rather than *always* moving toward a given target, it is usually more desirable to move to a *fixed* target position and, once the movie clip has arrived there, select a *new* target position. The following script is based on the previous one but is modified to include this new functionality:

```
function catchPos() {
  this.xTarget = _xmouse;
  this.yTarget = _ymouse;
  this.onEnterFrame = goPos;
}
function goPos() {
  this._x -= (this._x-this.xTarget)/4;
  this._y -= (this._y-this.yTarget)/4;
  if (Math.abs(this._x-this.xTarget)<1) {
    if (Math.abs(this._y-this.yTarget)<1) {
      this.onEnterFrame = catchPos;
    }
  }
}
ball_mc.onEnterFrame = catchPos;
```

22.6 Simulating Target-Driven Motion *(continued)*

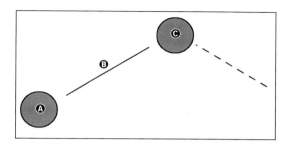

The movement consists of two portions. At (A) and (C), ball_mc uses the function catchPos() to acquire its next target position. During (B) it uses goPos() to get there. The if statement within this function checks whether or not it has reached its target (xTarget, yTarget), and if it has, the catchPos() function acquires the next target position.

A changing target position is the basis of most advanced interactivity. In the ubiquitous Space Invaders game, the scripts controlling the aliens during their dive sequence are simply trying to get to the player's ship position, but because this position is itself moving, it looks as if the aliens are responding intelligently to a changing condition. Instead, they are always *dumbly moving* toward the player's position and are reflecting the intelligent movement *introduced by the player*.

➡ 22.1 Animating via Scripted Property Changes

➡ 22.2 Attaching Events Dynamically

―――

The target position (xTarget, yTarget) is saved as a Timeline variable within the ball_mc movie clip. This means that the movie clip keeps its own independent target position, and you can use the same scripts to control other instances via additional lines such as ball2_mc = catchPos;.

USING THE DRAWING API IN PRACTICE

This chapter includes basic examples of the drawing API, but it can also be used in some very useful applications. For example, you can use the dynamic line drawing ability to create a real-time graph plotter, which could convert a constantly updated XML data stream into a chart graphic. This would be useful in a site showing business data trend charts. The basic examples in this chapter include the fundamental skills you need to create such real-time graphic displays.

22.7   Creating Drag-and-Drop Animations

➡ 20.28 Creating a
        Custom
        Mouse
        Pointer

➡ 22.8 Using
        Dynamic
        Masking

———

The code listings in this section will turn the mouse pointer to the hand pointer when you mouse over the draggable clip, which isn't the usual behavior in most operating systems. To prevent this, add a line that sets dragClip_mc.useHandCursor = false; as the last line of any of the listings.

———

You can drag only one movie clip at a time. This means you cannot use a custom mouse pointer to drag and drop a draggable movie clip.

———

If you want to center the draggable movie clip to the cursor, use an argument of true in the startDrag() method. This is illustrated in Section 22.8.

Flash allows you to quickly create drag-and-drop interfaces using the MovieClip.start-Drag method. You will most likely want to start dragging a movie clip when the user clicks it and stop dragging it when the user releases the mouse button. The following code allows this to happen for a movie clip instance dragClip_mc:

```
dragClip_mc.onPress = function() {
  this.startDrag();
};
dragClip_mc.onMouseMove = function() {
  updateAfterEvent();
};
dragClip_mc.onRelease = function() {
  this.stopDrag();
};
```

The onPress handler allows you to start the drag. The onRelease event handler stops the drag. The onMouseMove event handler forces a screen redraw every time the mouse moves and results in significantly smoother drag animations, particularly if you are using the default frame rate of 12 fps (try the script without this event handler to see the difference).

When using drag and drop in a user interface, you will usually want to do something when the movie clip is dropped on another movie clip. The following modification to the onRelease event will tell you if the movie clip dragClip_mc was dropped so that it overlaps dropClip_mc:

```
dragClip_mc.onRelease = function() {
  this.stopDrag();
  if (this.hitTest(dropClip_mc)) {
    trace("you droppped me on the drop clip!");
  }
};
```

To keep your drag-drop code simple, try to ensure that dragClip_mc is a solid shape with few gaps, because gaps may reduce the effectiveness of onPress, which will not detect a click on nonpixel areas. Also, use shapes that substantially fill their bounding boxes, like the ones shown here.

You should also consider making all draggable movie clips small. Dragging a large movie clip can be processor-intensive, especially if you are using updateAfterEvent(); other animations playing at the same time may stutter.

22.8 Using Dynamic Masking

Dynamic masking was introduced in Flash MX and allows you to define one movie clip as a mask for another. (In previous versions, masking could only be implemented within static tween animations.)

To mask a movie clip named `masked_mc` by another named `mask_mc`, use the following line of code:

```
masked_mc.setMask(mask_mc);
```

➡ 22.7 Creating Drag-and-Drop Animations

During masking, any enclosed holes within the mask movie clip will be ignored. For example, the two mask movie clips shown here would both appear as a circular mask with no hole.

The mask movie clip can contain animations, allowing you to create animated mask shapes.

Although there can only be one mask movie clip per masked movie clip, the mask can have multiple movie clips embedded on its Timeline, each of which will contribute to the overall mask shape. This allows you to create some very complex masking, such as scratch-card and video-wipe type effects.

Masking can become processor-intensive if you include large areas, so go easy!

Assuming the `masked_mc` and `mask_mc` movie clips were the square and circle shown here and you used the following code to make `mask_mc` follow the mouse and act as a mask for `masked_mc`:

```
mask_mc.startDrag(true);
masked_mc.setMask(mask_mc);
```

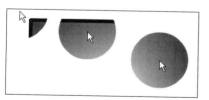

The effect would be this, with the area enclosed by the shape `mask_mc` and overlapping `masked_mc` showing.

22.9 Using Collision Detection

Rather than create a graphic and then try to write a collision detection routine for it, it is much better to design it with collision detection in mind from the start. Making sure that the graphic substantially fills its bounding box in areas where it is likely to be hit is always a good start to achieving this.

You cannot detect for a collision between two shapes directly; you can only detect for collisions between a point and a shape or between two bounding boxes. This is not a failing of Flash; there are very few quick ways of doing this in any graphics system!

There is a third collision detection type: collision between a point and a bounding box. This is almost never used; it has the disadvantages of both collision types illustrated here and none of the advantages!

Note that clip1_mc can itself include *other* movie clips, so the test can be made between a point and several movie clips. For example, a platform game could have the lifts and platforms in the same clip.

Collision detection is vital in advanced graphics and allows you a quick and easy way for two (or more) movie clips to act as if they are real objects that respond to each other when they hit each other, rather than the more usual pixel ghosts that simply pass through each other in an unrealistic manner.

Collision detection in Flash uses the MovieClip.hitTest() method. In general, you insert the hitTest test within the onEnterFrame event handler that causes the animation of one or more of your movie clips. This method will return true if it detects a collision, and it can be made to define collisions in two ways: as bounding box collisions or as shape collisions.

Bounding Box Collisions

The general form of the code that looks for a bounding box collision between two movie clips clip1_mc and clip2_mc is

```
if (clip1_mc.hitTest(clip2_mc)){
  // do something
}
```

If the bounding boxes of the two movie clips overlap, the //do something code will be executed. This works well when the two movie clips fill their bounding boxes, but it can be problematic when they do not.

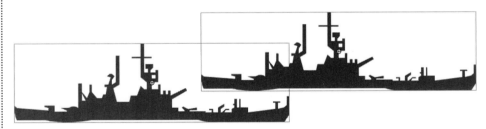

For example, the two movie clips shown here appear to be missing each other, but Flash will tell you that they are colliding because their bounding boxes overlap.

Shape Collisions

You can detect for collisions between a point and a shape using the following code:

```
If (clip1_mc.hitTest(x, y, true)){
  // do something
}
```

The //do something code will run if any part of the movie clip shape is over the point (x, y).

22.10 Changing Color via Scripts

To change the color of a movie clip, use the color class.

For the purposes of animation, the best place to create a Color instance is on the Timeline of the movie clip whose color you want to change.

Assuming you want to change the color of a movie clip named chameleon_mc, write:

```
cham_color = new Color(chameleon_mc);
```

Original   After color change

To change the chameleon to a new color, use the setRGB method of the Color class and specify the color you want to change to in hexadecimal. The following code will change the chameleon to a midgray (0xAAAAAA):

```
cham_color.setRGB(0xAAAAAA);
```

This creates a solid color change, and any color detail in the original is lost. To create a more subtle color change, you should use the setTransform method. This takes a single instance of the Object class as its argument and must have 8 properties (ra, rb, ga, gb, ba, bb, aa, and ab).

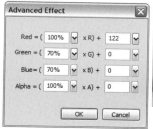

Although this method may seem initially complex, it is fairly easy to grasp once you realize it is simply a script-based version of the Advanced Effect dialog. Open this by selecting the movie clip, selecting Advanced from the Color dropdown on the Properties inspector, and then clicking the Settings button on the same panel.

To set up a color change using code:

1   Using the Advanced Effect dialog and create the color effect you are after.

2   Make a note of the eight values used (left column top to bottom, then right column top to bottom). In this case, they are 100, 122, 70, 0, 70, 0, 100, 0. Click Cancel.

3   Use the values you wrote down to define the Object instance used in setTransform. In the following listing, the Object instance is called colTrans:

```
cham_color = new Color(chameleon_mc);
colTrans = new Object();
colTrans = {ra:100, rb:122, ga:70, gb:0, ba:70, bb:0, aa:100, ab:0};
cham_color.setTransform(colTrans);
```

➥ 5.2   Color Mixer Panel

➥ 10.12 Using Motion Tween Color and Alpha Effects

The hexadecimal value of the currently selected color is always shown in the color picker and Color Mixer panel.

Creating color changes via scripting is more flexible than changing them via the Advanced Effect dialog. For example, varying the parameters of the setTransform method allows you to create subtle color changes dynamically. This effect is used as the basis of the user interface used in one of the authors' sites, www.futuremedia.org.uk.

22.11   Creating Scripted Lines

➡ 22.2   Attaching
          Events
          Dynamically

➡ 22.15 Animation
          and the
          Drawing API

───

Using updateAfter-Event() forces a screen redraw every time the mouse moves and results in a much smoother final effect.

───

The example in this section creates an empty movie clip, paper_mc, to draw into. This is common practice when using the Flash drawing methods, as it keeps your dynamically created shapes separate from other content.

───

With a little thought, it is possible to create a stack of movie clips that are drawn into, thus creating a layer-based drawing application.

To draw one or more lines in Flash:

1 Set the line thickness, color, and transparency with the `lineStyle` method.

2 Move to the start point of the line with the `moveTo` method.

3 Draw a line to the end point with the `lineTo` method.

The following code will draw a line of thickness 2 pixels, color red (0xFF0000), and 100 percent transparency, from (100, 100) to (200, 200):

```
this.lineStyle(2, 0xFF0000, 100);
this.moveTo(100, 100), this.lineTo(200, 200);
```

A Simple Doodling Application

Although fairly simplistic, the drawing features can quickly and easily create a doodling application. Add the following code to frame 1 of a new FLA, and that's it!

```
function penDown() {
  this.moveTo(_xmouse, _ymouse);
  this.onMouseMove = penDraw;
}
function penUp() {
  delete (this.onMouseMove);
}
function penDraw() {
  this.lineTo(_xmouse, _ymouse);
  updateAfterEvent();
}
this.createEmptyMovieClip("paper_mc", 1);
paper_mc.lineStyle(0, 0x606060, 100);
paper_mc.onMouseDown = penDown;
paper_mc.onMouseUp = penUp;
```

The `penDown` function occurs whenever you click the mouse and causes Flash to draw a line from the last mouse position to the current mouse position every time the mouse moves, until the user releases the mouse button. When this occurs, the event that causes the drawing (`onMouseMove`) is deleted by the function `penUp`.

If you also want the ability to clear the screen and restart, add a button instance `clear_btn` on the Stage and give it the following event handler:

```
clear_btn.onRelease = function() {
  paper_mc.clear();
  paper_mc.lineStyle(0, 0x606060, 100);
};
```

22.12 Creating Scripted Curves

Scripted curves are created in much the same way as lines except that there is one additional point that defines *curvature*.

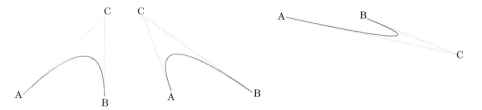

A Flash curve is created using three control points: the two end or "anchor" points of the curve (A and B) plus the curve "control point" (C). The control point defines the tangents of the curve as it goes through the two anchor points, and the distance of the control point from the curve is a measure of the curvature.

To create a curve:

1 Set the line thickness, color, and transparency with the `lineStyle` method.

2 Move to the start point of the line with the `moveTo` method.

3 Draw a curve from the start to the end point, curving toward the control point. The curve point and end point are defined as the arguments to the `curveTo` method.

The following three lines correspond to the three steps. They draw a 3-pixel-thick blue (0x0000FF) line of 100 percent alpha (totally opaque) between the points (50, 275) and (350, 300), with the control point at (200, 400):

```
this.lineStyle(3, 0x0000FF, 100);
this.moveTo(50, 275);
this.curveTo(200, 400, 350, 300);
```

The following code will produce an animated version of the above diagrams and give an indication of how to dynamically animate a curve as well as give an interactive example of how curveTo works:

```
function curve() {
  this.clear();
  this.lineStyle(0, 0xD0D0D0, 100);
  this.moveTo(100, 275);
  this.lineTo(_xmouse, _ymouse);
  this.lineTo(300, 275);
  this.lineStyle(0, 0x0, 100);
  this.moveTo(100, 275);
  this.curveTo(_xmouse, _ymouse, 300, 275);
  updateAfterEvent();
}
this.createEmptyMovieClip("paper_mc", 1);
paper_mc.onMouseMove = curve;
```

➡ 22.11 Creating Scripted Lines

➡ 22.15 Animation and the Drawing API

You can also make the event handler in the second listing shown here into an onEnter-Frame. This will result in a slower (but more performance friendly) animation.

Notice how the second listing clears the contents of the movie clip paper_mc every frame. This constant redrawing and deletion is what creates animation when using the Flash Drawing API.

22.13   Creating Scripted Filled Shapes

➡ 22.11 Creating
        Scripted
        Lines

➡ 22.12 Creating
        Scripted
        Curves

———

It is always a good idea to sketch out the sort of shape you want to create with a pencil before creating it in Flash!

To create a filled shape:

1   If you want to draw a stroke around the shape, set a line style. If you want no stroke, set a line style with a thickness of undefined.

2   Start a fill block with the beginFill method.

3   Use moveTo to move to the first line.

4   Use lineTo or curveTo to define the shape perimeter.

5   End the fill block with the endFill method.

The following code will create a green (0x00FF00) triangle with no perimeter and with corner points at (100, 50), (200, 150), and (60, 200). Note that the Flash co-ordinate system uses a print based y-axis (y axis is positive in the down direction), so that the point (0,0) is in the top left hand corner of the stage.

```
this.lineStyle(undefined, 0, 100);
this.beginFill(0x00FF00, 100);
this.moveTo(100, 50);
this.lineTo(200, 150);
this.lineTo(60, 200);
this.endFill();
```

The following code will create a yellow (0xFFFF00) leaf shape, with a 4-pixel black (0x000000) stroke and an alpha of 100 percent:

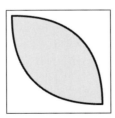

```
this.lineStyle(4, 0x000000, 100);
this.beginFill(0xFFFF00, 100);
this.moveTo(100, 100);
this.curveTo(100, 300, 300, 300);
this.curveTo(300, 100, 100, 100);
this.endFill();
```

ADVANCED GRAPHICS AND PERFORMANCE

Although the drawing API and duplicateMovieClip and attachMovie features allow you to create some compelling effects and graphic applications, be aware that the more movie clips and lines and fills you draw, the slower Flash will get. In particular, Flash becomes very slow if you draw many more than 500–600 lines. It's a good idea to delete dynamically created content once in a while.

22.14   Creating Gradient Fills

Gradients can be defined in two ways: as a simple box envelope or as a 3×3 matrix. The latter is useful for creating 3D effects (because the transformations it uses are compatible with the matrices used in 3D computations). Because matrix math is beyond the scope of this book, this section will cover only box definitions.

➡ 22.12 Creating
        Scripted
        Curves

Box gradients are defined using three arrays and one `Object` instance. The process is best shown by example. Suppose you wanted to create the leaf shape shown here with a linear gradient as its fill.

To fully define the gradient, you must:

- Define the colors, including their color values, alpha values, and positions in the gradient. These are all set within the Color Mixer panel when creating gradients manually.

- Define the orientation and size of the gradient's envelope. This is done via the Fill Transform tool in the authoring environment for manual gradient creation.

Defining the Gradient Colors

The gradient would look like this in the Color Mixer. It consists of two colors, white (0xFFFFFF) and black (0x000000) placed at the beginning and end of the gradient scale.

Programmatically, this is defined via three array objects:

```
colors = [0xFFFFFF, 0x000000];
alphas = [100, 100];
ratios = [0, 255];
```

The first array defines the two colors, and the second defines the associated alpha values. The third array defines the position (or ratio) of each color's position along the gradient scale, assuming a scale of 0–255 left to right. Because white is at the far left, and black is at the far right, the positions are simple: 0 and 255:

Continues ●

Defining the Gradient Envelope

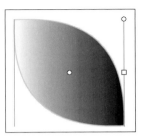

Using the Fill Transform tool, the gradient envelope looks like this.

To define this programmatically, you use an `Object` instance that must have the following properties: `matrixType`, `x`, `y`, `w`, `h`, and `r`. Here `matrixType` must be `"box"`; the remaining properties represent the (x,y) of the top-left corner of the envelope, the width and height (200), and angle (in radians) that the envelope is at (0). This gives you a "matrix" or number list that defines the envelope, and this forms the final object:

```
matrix = {matrixType:"box", x:100, y:100, w:200, h:200, r:0};
```

The `beginGradientFill` method uses the three arrays plus one `Object` instance as its arguments, plus a string value that can either be `"linear"` or `"radial"` to define which of the two gradient types you want to use. Putting it all together with some additional code (last 6 lines) to create a filled shape using our gradient, you get the following listing:

```
matrix = {matrixType:"box", x:100, y:100, w:200, h:200, r:0};
colors = [0xFFFFFF, 0x000000];
alphas = [100, 100];
ratios = [0, 255];
this.lineStyle(1, 0xCCCCCC, 100);
this.beginGradientFill("linear", colors, alphas, ratios, matrix);
this.moveTo(100, 100);
this.curveTo(100, 300, 300, 300);
this.curveTo(300, 100, 100, 100);
this.endFill();
```

If you attach this code on the first frame of a new FLA, you will see the shape illustrated at the beginning of this section.

22.15 Animation and the Drawing API

To animate using the movie clip drawing methods:

1 Create an empty movie clip to draw content into using the createEmptyMovieClip method.

2 Place your drawing code in an event handler: onEnterFrame if you are creating free-running animations, or onMouseMove to create runtime drawing tools. Attach the event handler to the created movie clip.

3 At the start of every script, erase all previously drawn content within the created movie clip with the clear method.

➠ 22.11 Creating Scripted Lines

```
function drawTriangle() {
  var i;
  for (i = 0; i < 2; i++) {
    this.x[i] += this.xSpeed[i];
    this.y[i] += this.ySpeed[i];
    if (Math.abs(this.x[i]) > 100) {
      this.xSpeed[i] = -this.xSpeed[i];
    }
    if (Math.abs(this.y[i]) > 100) {
      this.ySpeed[i] = -this.ySpeed[i];
    }
  }
  this.clear();
  this.lineStyle(0, 0x000000, 100);
  this.beginFill(0xFF0000, 100);
  this.moveTo(this.x[0], this.y[0]);
  this.lineTo(this.x[1], this.y[1]);
  this.lineTo(this.x[2], this.y[2]);
  this.endFill();
}
this.createEmptyMovieClip("paper_mc", 1);
paper_mc._x = 200;
paper_mc._y = 275;
paper_mc.x = new Array();
paper_mc.y = new Array();
paper_mc.xSpeed = new Array();
paper_mc.ySpeed = new Array();
for (i = 0; i < 2; i++) {
  paper_mc.x[i]=0, paper_mc.y[i]=0;
  paper_mc.xSpeed[i] = Math.random() * 6 - 3;
  paper_mc.ySpeed[i] = Math.random() * 6 - 3;
}
paper_mc.onEnterFrame = drawTriangle;
```

Continues ●

The code starts by creating an empty movie clip called **paper_mc**, then moving it to the center of the Stage:

```
this.createEmptyMovieClip("paper_mc", 1);
paper_mc._x = 200;
paper_mc._y = 275;
```

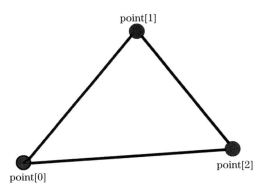

You then define four arrays **x**, **y**, **xSpeed**, and **ySpeed**. These define a set of points at position (**x**, **y**) and move with a speed and direction (i.e., velocity) defined by the lengths **xSpeed** and **ySpeed**.

Data for three such points is created via the **for** loop, each with a random position and velocity. The final line in the listing sets **drawTriangle()** as an **onEnterFrame**, meaning that it will run every frame. **drawTriangle()** moves the three sets of points every frame (by a distance and direction defined by the three velocities) and then joins the three moving points up. By erasing the triangle created in the last frame, moving the points, and then drawing a new triangle based on the new points every frame, you create the animated triangle effect.

CHAPTER 23

Interactive Sound and Video

AS WELL AS THE vector-based animation system, Flash also includes sound and video capabilities. You can use Flash to deliver dynamic content including either sound or video via the ActionScript Sound and Video classes. You can also set up live sound or video feeds using the Microphone and Camera classes.

23.1   Understanding Flash Sound and Video Classes

Flash allows you to include sound and video in your Flash content. You can use sound or video files, or use live streams that are acquired from microphone or camera equipment.

The Sound class allows direct control of sound files. The procedure to control sound is to:

1 Create an instance of the Sound class (explained in the following section).

2 Link the Sound class to a sound file (which can be in the Library, on a timeline, or at a named URL).

3 Control your sound via the sound instance.

The `Microphone` class allows you to control a live sound stream and either send it to a Flash Communications (FlashCom) equipped server (for web broadcast) or play it locally.

ActionScript control of video is generally performed via the `Movie Clip` class, and you do not need to use any other classes *unless* you want to broadcast a live video feed to the Web, control a local live video feed, or load an external Flash Video (FLV) file. When controlling live or FLV-based video, you need to use:

The `Video` class for ActionScript to be able to attach to a number of video sources.

The `Camera` class, which allows the user the same general controls for video as the `Microphone` class does for sound and can be used to create a local video source for the `Video` class, using a video camera connected to your computer as input:

The `Video` class can accept other sources via the `NetConnection` class and `NetStream` class. These classes allow you to play back video whose source is acquired over the Web (although you can also use a local FLV). They require either an external FLV (Flash video) file or a live remote stream and are not considered in this book. Learning about how to use the `Video` and `Camera` classes locally will put you in a good position to learn the two net-video classes later.

FLV files can only be created with the Professional version of Flash (using a special author time plug-in), although either version can create FLAs that use FLV content.

To broadcast live sound or video streams to the Web, you must have Flash Communications (FlashCom) server software installed, although you can play live content back locally without it. FlashCom is generally a must-have part of your online Flash presence if you intend to broadcast live content using a Macromedia-only solution.

Flash Player 7 does *not* require the FlashCom server software to play dynamically loaded video content via the FLV format. Flash Player 6 *does*. Flash MX 2004 is thus a major step forward compared to previous versions of Flash for those wishing to provide dynamic over-the-Web video content.

RUNTIME LOADING STRATEGIES FOR SOUND AND VIDEO

Sound and video files are some of the largest assets you will use in a site. It's recommended you keep your sound files as small as possible by editing them in a dedicated sound editor and loading large files at runtime (if large files are otherwise unavoidable) rather than embedding them in the SWF.

23.2   Defining a Sound Instance

Defining a sound instance is a two-part process. You first have to create the sound instance and you then must link it to a sound asset.

A "sound asset" can either be a timeline with sound attached to it, a sound file in the Library, or a sound file you want to load dynamically at runtime.

The simplest form of Flash sound is a timeline with sounds attached to its keyframes. To set up a sound instance called `timeline_sound` to control all sound attached to the Timeline `myTimeline`, use the first following line (the second line will play it once):

```
timeline_sound = new Sound(myTimeline);
timeline_sound.start(0, 1);
```

To control a sound file in the Library, you must first define a linkage identifier. Right-click/⌘-click the sound file and select Linkage from the pop-up (you can also get to this option via the Library panel's menu). This will bring up the Linkage Properties window.

Enter the linkage identifier (in this case, tune) and make sure that Export For ActionScript and Export In First Frame are both checked.

Assuming your linkage identifier is tune and you want to control it via a sound instance called `linkage_sound`, use the first two lines below (the third will play it once):

```
linkage_sound = new Sound(this);
linkage_sound.attachSound("tune");
linkage_sound.start(0, 1);
```

To control a remote MP3 sound file that will be loaded dynamically at runtime, you have to define the URL of the remote file and the sound type you want it to be handled as (streaming or event). The following code will begin loading a streaming sound file called `myMP3.mp3` (which is in the same place as the SWF), into a sound instance `dynamic_sound`. It will start playing as soon as enough of it to fill the Flash sound buffer (5s by default) has loaded:

```
dynamic_sound = new Sound(this);
dynamic_sound.loadSound("myMP3.mp3", true);
```

You are advised to start playing the sound only when you know it has loaded completely. The following code will wait until the **onLoad** event occurs, signifying that this is the case:

```
dynamic_sound = new Sound(this);
dynamic_sound.loadSound("myMP3.mp3", false);
dynamic_sound.onLoad = function() {
  dynamic_sound.start(0, 2);
};
```

➡ 10.16 Adding Sound to a Timeline

———

A timeline with sound attached to it includes any timeline that has sound instances *scoped* to it, as well as the more obvious timeline with sound attached to its keyframes (as per Section 10.16).

———

It is imperative that you always initialize a new sound instance with either new Sound(timeline) or new Sound(this); otherwise, you may get odd results when you try to use any of the Sound class's methods.

———

When loading MP3s dynamically, the second argument of the load-Sound method is true for streaming or false for event sounds.

———

Note that the linkage identifier is a string, not a variable name, which means it can have spaces in it.

———

Changing the default sound buffer is addressed in 23.8.

23.3   Starting and Stopping a Sound

➡ 23.2 Defining a
       Sound
       Instance

A common mistake is to use play() instead of start() to start a sound. If your sounds don't seem to be starting, this is the first thing to check for!

The maximum number of loops for a sound is 214,748. (No, we don't know the significance of that number.)

One of the simplest ActionScript-based sound control features is simply to start and stop a sound. Although simple, the effects of starting and stopping a sound vary depending on how you define your sound.

Starting a Sound

To start a sound instance my_sound and play it once, use:

```
my_sound.start();
```

The general form of the start() method is Sound.start(secondOffset loops), where *secondOffset* is the point (in seconds) that you want to start playing, and *loops* is the number of times you want to repeat the sound. Note that the *secondOffset* value is applied to every repeat (not just the first loop). The following line will play a sound twice, starting each at an offset of 0.5s:

```
my_sound.start(0.5, 2);
```

Stopping a Sound

To stop a sound instance my_sound with linkage identifier tune, use the following:

```
my_sound.stop("tune");
```

Note that the Linkage Identifier is never required for the Sound.start().

To stop *all* currently playing sounds, use the stop() method (with no argument) on a sound that is attached to either a linked sound or a dynamically loaded sound (i.e., the second and third sound types from the preceding section):

```
my_sound.stop();
```

If you do this to a sound that is linked to a *timeline* (i.e., the first sound type from the preceding section), the stop() will only stop sounds on that timeline.

23.4 Setting Volume for a Single Sound

Controlling sound volume is performed via the `Sound.setVolume()` method.

To set the volume for a sound at a fixed level, use `setVolume()` with an argument whose value is between 0 and 100. The following code will set the volume of sound instance `my_sound` to 50 (half full volume):

```
my_sound.setVolume(50);
```

Setting Volume Dynamically

The reason for using ActionScript-controlled sound is usually that you want to change the sound volume level *dynamically*. This is done by using a changing variable value to set the volume. The following code uses an `onEnterFrame` to fade in the sound instance `my_sound`:

```
this.onEnterFrame = function(){
  vol += 1;
  my_sound.setVolume(vol);
  if (vol == 100){
    delete(this.onEnterFrame);
  }
}
vol = 0;
```

The variable `vol` starts off as 0 and is incremented by 1 every frame until it reaches 100; it controls the volume of `my_sound`. This causes `my_sound` to fade in from zero to maximum volume.

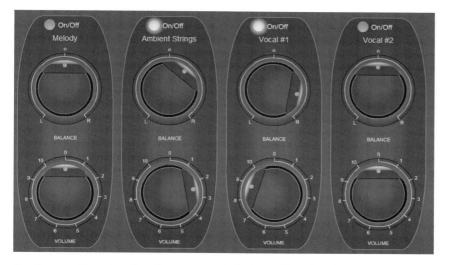

Usually, you will want to allow the user to control volume. The principle here is the same: use a variable with `setVolume()`, except this time the variable is varied via the user interface. This image shows part of an advanced Flash sound application (it's actually an interactive sound mixing board or "sound board"). The volume control knob for each channel changes a variable, which in turn is fed into a `setVolume()` to adjust the volume.

➠ 23.2 Defining a Sound Instance

➠ 23.5 Setting Volume for a Flash Site

Remember that `setVolume()` does just that—changing the volume does nothing if the sound is not playing! You won't hear the sound until you use `Sound.start()`.

For you sound experimenters, the sound volume can be set to values outside the advertised 0–100 range: values above 100 will cause sound distortion, and negative values will cause the sound to phase shift by 180 degrees.

23.5   Setting Volume for a Flash Site

➡ 15.7 Dot Notation

➡ 23.4 Setting Volume for a Single Sound

Note that the effect of applying a hierarchy of sound instances to a sound is multiplied. For example, suppose there was a sound Instance on an embedded Timeline myClip_mc (on _root) that set the volume of its Timeline to 50 percent. If site_sound was also set at 50 percent, sounds coming from myClip_mc would be at a volume of 50% × 50% = 25%.

One of the most common applications of the `Sound.setVolume()` method is to control the volume of a complete site. This is much easier to set up than it sounds (no pun intended). There are two steps involved: setting up the sound instance, and setting up the user interface to control the sound instance directly.

Setting Up the Sound Instance

To control all sound in a SWF, you must set up a sound instance that controls sound on the `_root` Timeline. This will also control all embedded timelines on `_root`, which means that *all* sound is under control of the one Sound instance. The following code will set up the sound instance `site_sound`:

```
site_sound = new Sound(_root);
```

Setting Up the Sound Control

Open Window **>** Other Panels **>** Common Libraries **>** Buttons and drag an instance of the *fader—gain* slider button from the Library panel onto the Stage.

Next, you need to wire this up to the sound instance `site_sound`. To do this:

1 Double-click the fader on the Stage to edit it.

2 Its topmost layer has actions on frame 1. Select this frame and view the script. The last two lines of this script currently read

```
sound.setVolume(level);
};
```

Change the first of these two lines to:

```
_root.site_sound.setVolume(level);
```

The slider allows the user to vary a variable *level* between 0–100. The slider control has now been changed so that this value is used in a `setVolume()` for the sound instance, `site_sound`.

424

23.6   Setting Sound Panning

The `Sound.setPan()` method allows you to control the stereo balance.

Setting Pan to a Fixed Level

To set the pan for a sound, use `setPan()` with an argument whose value is between –100 and 100, with –100 the left channel only, 0 equally balanced, and 100 the right channel only. Think of the `setPan()` method as the same as a stereo system balance control.

➡ 23.2 Defining a
        Sound
        Instance

➡ 23.4 Setting Vol-
        ume for a Sin-
        gle Sound

➡ 23.5 Setting Vol-
        ume for a
        Flash Site

`Sound.setPan()` operates the same way as `setVolume()`. The procedure to control a single sound's panning and an entire site's sound panning are much the same as volume control.

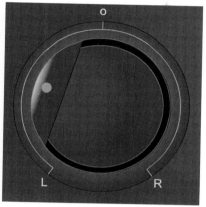

The example at left (`my_sound.setPan(0);`) is the same as a balanced control; the one on the right (`my_sound.setPan(-50);`) emulates a balance control halfway between balance and left channel only.

Setting Pan Dynamically

The reason for using ActionScript-controlled sound is usually that you want to change the sound pan level *dynamically*. This is done using a changing variable value to set the pan level. The following code uses an `onEnterFrame` to fade in the sound instance `my_sound` from the left channel only through the balanced position and to the right speaker only:

```
this.onEnterFrame = function(){
  pan += 1;
  my_sound.setPan(pan);
  if (pan == 100){
    delete(this.onEnterFrame);
  }
}
my_sound = new Sound(_root);
pan = -100;
```

The variable `pan` starts off as –100, is incremented by 1 every frame until it reaches 100, and controls the panning of `my_sound`. This causes `my_sound` to pan from the left to right channel.

23.7   Creating Sound Effects with Sound Transforms

Sound.setTransform() allows you to combine both volume and pan effects in a single control, giving you much more control over your sound.

Understanding Sound Transforms

A sound transform works as follows. Each speaker in the stereo pair has a signal associated with it, LL (left speaker) and RR (right speaker). The setVolume and setPan methods work using these two signals only, but setTransform has two other signals, RL (right channel, from left input) and LR (left channel, from right input). These are the signal values that are fed from LL into RR and vice versa. Using these four signals, you can do several things that are not possible with volume and panning alone:

- You can turn a stereo signal into a mono signal without losing any information (although you can do this with panning, you lose the signal from one or other channel).

- You can control the volume of each speaker individually (volume and pan controls treat the speakers as a linked pair).

- Implementing sound control using a *single* control rather than having to use both volume and pan controls becomes easier.

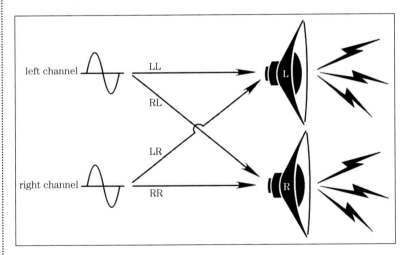

Implementing a Sound Transform

The Sound.setTransform() method requires a single object as its argument that must have four properties called ll, lr, rr, and rl, corresponding to the labels in the diagram above. The following code will set up a new object that can be used with setTransform, called soundControl:

```
soundControl = {ll:100, lr:0, rr:100, rl:0};
```

23.7   Creating Sound Effects with Sound Transforms *(continued)*

The object has been initialized with both the ll and rr signals at 100 percent, which is the default situation.

The following code will make the sound instance my_sound play in mono, whatever the signal source:

```
soundControl = {ll:50, lr:50, rr:50, rl:50};
my_sound.setTransform(soundControl);
```

This will create true mono sound whatever the source:

- If my_sound is a mono sound that uses one channel only, the transform will split the channel so that half of the signal goes into the other speaker.

- If the sound is true stereo, that is, the signal going to each channel is different, the transform will split the signal per channel so that 50 percent of it goes into the other speaker, creating a true mono sound (i.e., although two speakers are used, both of them play exactly the same signal).

A typical single sound control that can set both volume and pan at the same time would be a joystick type control, as used in many car radios and some top end stereo equipment.

LOADING MP3 FILES INTO FLASH

Flash is very picky about which types of MP3 it will load. If an MP3 file fails to load at runtime and there appears to be no problems in the code, it's probably because Flash doesn't like the MP3 format. When creating MP3 files for use in Flash, adhering to the following settings (if your encoder software allows access to them) will help:

- Set the CRC checksum, add Padding, and don't add Decoder Emphasis.

- Only use "Preferred" bit rates. MP3 has no real standard rates, but these are as close as it gets for common web design compression rates: 20, 24, 32, 40, 48, 56, 64, 80, and 96 Kbps, with 20 being the most compressed (lowest quality).

In general, a useful rule to find out whether Flash Player will load an MP3 is if the Flash authoring environment refuses to import an MP3 file, Flash Player is unlikely to load it at runtime.

23.8   Working with Dynamically Loaded Sound

➡ 23.10 Retrieving
MP3 Sound
Meta Tags

Flash is very particular about which MP3 sounds is will import, and it is important that you confirm that your MP3 files are suitable. Generally, if the Flash authoring application allows import of an MP3, the runtime Flash Player will load it as well.

A streaming sound will start playing as soon as it begins to load, although you have to reload it every time you want to play it. It is useful for loading long sound files that will only be played once (such as songs on a video jukebox).

An event sound will become available for playing when it has fully loaded, and requests to play it before that time will be ignored. An event sound can be re-used once its loaded and is useful for short, often-used sounds such as incidental noises (button clicks, for example), jingles, or sound loops.

Flash allows you to load an MP3 file during runtime as either streaming or event sounds. (See the definition of these two types in the margin.)

Runtime sound loading is handled via the `Sound.loadSound(filename, isStreaming)` method. This will load a sound file *filename* as either a streaming sound (`isStreaming = true`) or an event sound (`isStreaming = false`).

Loading Streaming Sounds

Assuming you want to load a streaming MP3 file `my.mp3` into a sound instance `my_sound`, the code would be:

```
my_sound = new Sound (this);
target.loadSound ("my.mp3", true);
```

The sound will start playing as soon as the sound buffer has loaded enough content to begin (5 seconds of sound, by default).

You can change the buffer size by assigning an integer value to the property `_soundbuftime`. The following code will increase the sound buffer time to 10s:

```
_soundbuftime = 10;
```

Setting the sound buffer to low values is undesirable; reducing the buffer size may mean that the buffer empties, causing periods of no sound as the buffer fills up again.

Loading Event Sounds

Event sounds are slightly more complicated than streaming sounds, as any attempt to play them will fail until the sound has loaded in completely. To allow for this, use the `Sound.onLoad` method as shown below:

```
my_sound = new Sound(this);
my_sound.loadSound("my.mp3", false);
my_sound.onLoad = function() {
  my_sound.start();
};
```

Protecting Your Sound Files

You should note that dynamically loaded sounds will appear in the user's browser cache and therefore become available to the user directly. If you wish to prevent this from happening, you are advised to use load levels or shared libraries instead, both of which make the sound files less accessible to the casual user because they are embedded in a SWF file. This issue applies mostly to streaming soundtracks (where the full song would appear in the cache as an MP3). If you cannot do this, a good workaround to avoid the user finding MP3s is to rename the MP3 files with a common web design file extension other than .mp3 (such as .jpg).

23.9 Creating Sequenced Sound

Playing a single sound is fine for playback of prerecorded soundtracks or single button click and other user interface sounds, but more advanced sound schemes require the use of *sequenced sound*.

Sequencing is when sound samples are played one after another in quick succession to form a seamless and continuous soundtrack or other more specialized sound (such as digital speech, where you would sequence allophones, or small speech sections) to make up sentences.

Sequencing should be performed only with event sounds with linkage identifiers. Other sound types (especially streaming sounds) are incompatible with the close timings needed.

The *onSoundComplete* Event

The secret of creating sequenced sound in Flash is accurately knowing when the current sound has ended. The following code will trace a message "finished" when the current sound attached to instance `loop_sound` has completed:

```
loop_sound = new Sound(this);
loop_sound.attachSound("loop");
loop_sound.start()
loop_sound.onSoundComplete = function() {
  trace("finished");
};
```

Mixing Loops

The way to extend the preceding code is to quickly start a *new* sound as soon as the last one has completed. This is best done by attaching a different sound to the sound instance and then restarting it. Replacing the onSoundComplete event code as follows achieves this:

```
loop_sound.onSoundComplete = function() {
  loop_sound.attachSound("loop2");
  loop_sound.start();
};
```

The code to create interactive soundtracks and interactive mixing desks (or "sound boards") is not much more than the code seen here, the only difference being that you are constantly changing the loop to be played and several sound loops are playing at the same time.

Sequenced sound relies on sound loops—any sound that can be seamlessly repeated. To create sequenced soundtracks is slightly more complicated because your loops must have the ability to be seamlessly spliced to *each other* as well as to themselves. In the example in this section, loop1 must be seamlessly spliceable to loop2.

Sequenced sound can be used to create interactive soundtracks. At the end of each sound loop, the sequencing code will look at one or more triggers to decide on what the next loop should be. Typical triggers include the page the site is currently at (stored in a variable) or a Boolean that is true if the user has interacted with the user interface in the last five seconds.

Like all event code, onSoundComplete is very accurate (it is usually good to 1/10th of the frame rate) *unless* you are loading Flash Player so heavily that it cannot quickly respond to new events. Don't be surprised when interactive soundtracks break up if you also have intensive animation going on at the same time.

23.10 Retrieving MP3 Sound Meta Tags

The MP3 format can include meta tags containing descriptive text about the sound file. These tags are only available for sounds that are loaded at runtime via `Sound.loadSound()`.

MP3 tags are created as part of the conversion process when you convert raw sound sample files (such as WAV) into MP3. Your conversion software will typically have an MP3 meta data entry window such as the one shown here, which allows you to enter the tag values.

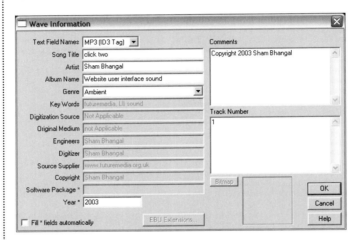

The id3 format has two revisions, 1.0 and 2.0. Although Flash recognizes both types of tags, the 1.0 tags are the most useful and are sufficient for most Flash applications (such as online MP3 jukeboxes or when you want to add meta data for web design sounds). The ActionScript properties that relate to the 1.0 tags are these:

SOUND PROPERTY	NOTES
Sound.id3.title	Limit to 30 characters for maximum compliance to the spec
Sound.id3.artist	As above
Sound.id3.album	As above
Sound.id3.comment	As above
Sound.id3.genre	Up to 3-digit integer number
Sound.id3.year	4-digit number

The most common genre values you will typically use for sounds created specifically for web design (and their associated integer numbers) are "sound clip (37)" for all button clicks and other user interface sounds, and "soundtrack (24)" for custom music you have created as a backing track for the site. The genre property contains many specialized song types from "Christian rap" all the way to "porn groove", but the most common broad ones you may want to use (other than soundtrack) are "ambient (26)", "alternative(20)", "classical(32)", "dance(3)", "game(36)", "rock(17)".

Although the Macromedia documentation uses Sound.ID3, this doesn't work in ActionScript 2, which is case-sensitive. You should instead use Sound.id3.

23.10   Retrieving MP3 Sound Meta Tags *(continued)*

Retrieving id3 information

The Sound.id3 property contains all available id3 data found in a loaded sound, and the Sound.onID3 event will trigger when this data has been loaded. The following code will retrieve the album property of a dynamically loaded event sound my.mp3, which is attached to a new sound instance my_sound:

```
my_sound = new Sound(this);
my_sound.loadSound("my.mp3", true);
my_sound.onID3 = function() {
  trace(my_sound.id3.album);
};
```

The following code will list *all* available meta data via a for..in loop that cycles through and outputs all defined id3 properties:

```
my_sound = new Sound(this);
my_sound.loadSound("my.mp3", true);
my_sound.onID3 = function() {
  for (var prop in my_sound.id3) {
  trace(prop+" : "+my_sound.id3
  }
};
```

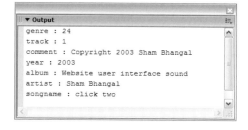

```
▼ Output
genre : 24
track : 1
comment : Copyright 2003 Sham Bhangal
year : 2003
album : Website user interface sound
artist : Sham Bhangal
songname : click two
```

When testing the use of MP3 id3, your operating system may display the id3 tags as part of the file properties. For example, you can see the id3 properties of an MP3 file in Windows XP by right-clicking it, selecting Properties, and looking at the Summary tab of the Properties window that appears.

Any meta data contained in MP3 files imported into the authoring environment is lost (because Flash always converts imported sound data to its own internal format), so it cannot be accessed.

23.11 Understanding the Flash Player Privacy Settings

➡ 23.13 Reading Microphone Properties and Permissions

➡ 23.15 Reading Video Properties and Permissions

A well-built Flash site that uses either the local microphone or camera should be able to cope with the user denying access to these resources without hanging. This is discussed in the sections listed above.

Although Flash allows any user to broadcast the current video and/or microphone streams being produced by their local machine (a fairly powerful ability which turns your computer into a desktop-based broadcast channel!), you may need to give the user control of this via privacy settings.

Right-clicking/⌘-clicking a running SWF file and selecting Settings from the contextual menu will bring up the Macromedia Flash Player Settings.

Click the Privacy icon 🔒 to allow or deny Flash Player access to any attached microphone or web cam, and click the microphone 🎤 and web cam 📷 icons to select and configure your input devices.

If a SWF tries to access your local microphone and web cam, you will usually see this window appear within the SWF.

CHECKING MICROPHONE AND VIDEO HARDWARE COMPATIBILITY WITH FLASH

You can tell whether your microphone and/or camera hardware is being picked up by the Flash Player by

1 Opening a new FLA and immediately testing it.

2 Right-clicking/⌘-clicking the running SWF and choosing Settings, then looking at the Camera 📷 and Microphone 🎤 tabs. If no hardware resource is found by Flash Player, you will see a message similar to this:

Note that Flash looks for a sound card that is *capable of hosting* a microphone rather than a microphone that is *actually connected*; Flash will show the "no microphone found" message for very few computers, given that all modern desktop computers have a sound card with a microphone-in socket.

23.12 Playing Back Captured Sound with the *Microphone* Class

➡ 23.13 Reading Microphone Properties and Permissions

➡ 23.14 Playing Back Captured Video with the Camera Class

The `Microphone` class allows Flash Player to capture sound from the locally attached microphone and either play it back to the local speakers, or broadcast it to the Web via Flash Communications (FlashCom) server software. This book will look at the former option.

Given that there is only one active microphone that Flash can refer to at any time, the `Microphone` class is *static* (i.e., there is only one of them and you don't have to define it with `new` to use it—much like the `Camera` class). Instead, you refer the captured stream from the microphone to a variable. The following code assigns the captured microphone stream to a variable `myAudio`:

```
myAudio = Microphone.get();
```

Following this line, you refer to the stream via the variable name, `myAudio`. To be able to hear the captured audio, you also have to assign the stream `myAudio` to a timeline. This sets the Timeline up to accept the captured stream. The following line will allow the current Timeline to accept the stream:

```
this.attachAudio(myAudio);
```

Following these two lines, the Microphone channel is ready for use. You can check this by speaking into the microphone; you should hear a slightly delayed version of your captured voice from your computer's speakers.

You will also see the sound level of the captured sound appearing as an animated bar if you right-click/⌘-click the running SWF, select Settings, and click the tab with the microphone icon on it:

You can now capture both the captured sound level and the gain setting (defined by the user via the slider in the Microphone Settings tab) with the properties `activityLevel` and `gain`. If you place a movie clip consisting of a filled square and instance name `square_mc` on the Stage, the following code will animate it in tune with your voice:

```
function animation() {
  level = myAudio.activityLevel*100/myAudio.gain;
  square_mc._xscale = level;
  square_mc._rotation = level*3.6;
}
myAudio = Microphone.get();
this.attachAudio(myAudio);
square_mc.onEnterFrame = animation;
```

The `onEnterFrame` script creates a variable *level* that is derived from the activity level (input volume) and gain of the captured sound signal and rotates and scales the `square_mc` instance based on it. Scream to make it dance.

The `get()` and `attachAudio()` methods must be used in that order, or the sound channel will not be set up correctly.

___

If your microphone doesn't seem to work, you should check the microphone input level setting. Many sound card drivers set the microphone input to mute or zero by default, and you may have to override or change these hardware properties manually.

___

Although you can assign the microphone stream to more than one variable, there is usually little need to do so; there is only one physical microphone device, so all the streams will be of the same signal.

___

The `Microphone` class is almost identical to the Camera class when used with local camera equipment.

23.13   Reading Microphone Properties and Permissions

➡ 23.12 Playing Back Captured Sound with the Microphone Class

In general, you should allow the user to make microphone gain and echo suppression settings. What makes *your* local microphone work better may make another user's setup sound worse, so let them decide the best settings! The only time it's recommended you set them is when you are creating a custom Microphone interface that replicates the Settings windows gain and suppression controls.

Note that the Microphone.muted property will be false *unless* the user has previously allowed access and saved this setting or has seen the Flash "Allow local to access your camera and microphone?" message and clicked Allow. If you check this property before they have done the latter, you will get true (denied), so it is a good idea to hold off the check until well after the Microphone.get().

Although there is an event handler that will fire when the user changes the microphone permissions (Microphone.onStatus), this event will *never* run if the user has checked Remember in the Privacy settings (given they will not change per session and all events run on change).

Several properties and status events can be read or acted on, the most important being the microphone permission settings (A), echo suppression (B), and microphone gain (C). All these features are also available to the user via the Settings window during a running SWF: right-click/⌘-click the SWF and click the Privacy and Microphone icons.

Echo suppression does just that: suppresses echo effects in the microphone signal. Although it can be set by the user, you can also set it using ActionScript via `setEchoSuppression()`. The following lines set up a Microphone channel for use and then set the echo suppression to true (enabled). Set it to false to disable.

```
myAudio = Microphone.get();
this.attachAudio(myAudio);
myAudio.setEchSuppression(true);
```

Permission settings can be set using the `muted` property. If it is true, microphone access has *not* been granted; it *has* been granted if it is false. Adding the following code to the end of the last listing will trace an appropriate message if the user has elected to deny access to the local microphone:

```
if (myAudio.muted == true) {
   trace("You dont know what you're missing!");
}
```

The gain of the microphone sets the amplification that Flash Player will apply to the input microphone signal. It can vary from 0 percent to 100 percent, and is set at 50 percent by default. Adding the following line to the end of the example code so far will set the gain to 60 percent:

```
myAudio.gain=60;
```

23.14 Playing Back Captured Video with the *Camera* Class

Flash allows you to access several types of video streams and play them back in Flash Player. This section discusses locally acquired video—i.e., video that is captured from a camera connected to your computer.

To view a local video stream, you need two things: a reference to the `Camera` class to acquire the local video stream and a `Video` class instance to view the stream in.

Given that there is only one active video camera that Flash can refer to at any time, the `Camera` class is static (i.e., there is only one of them, and you don't have to define it with `new` to use it—much like the `Microphone` class). Instead, you refer the captured stream from the `Camera` class to a variable. The following code assigns the captured video camera stream to a variable `my_cam`:

```
my_cam = Camera.get();
```

Following this line, you refer to the stream via the variable name `my_cam`. To view the captured video, you also have to assign the stream `my_cam` to an instance of the `Video` class. To create a video instance:

1 In the Library panel, click the Panel Menu icon 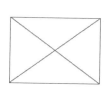 at the top left to bring up the Panel Options menu. Select New Video. A new Embedded Video symbol will appear as shown. Note that there is no preview of this symbol; the video is a blank video that you will fill at runtime with `my_cam`. Drag an instance of this symbol onto the Stage. You will see a box with an "X" inside it, as shown. This will be the same color as the layer color you have placed it in.

2 Select the video instance and resize it as required.

3 Using the Properties inspector, give it an instance name. For the purpose of example, call it `my_video`.

➡ 23.12 Playing Back Captured Sound with the `Microphone` Class

Even if you play back a largish video stream, the bandwidth profiler gives a very low reading. This is a big advantage of using nonembedded video streams; the video is streamed in *after* the main SWF has loaded and is not a part of it.

Flash can intermittently ignore inputs from certain camera equipment (although the operating system may still recognize the signal perfectly). If this happens, rebooting the computer seems to clear the problem.

Continues

➠ 23.15 Reading
Video Prop-
erties and
Permissions

Although discussing
only the Camera class
may seem rather limit-
ing to some readers, it
is a big step to moving
forward and using the
more flexible remote
web-based video classes
NetStream and Net-
Connection, which
allow you to use the
video instance with
either a remote prere-
corded FLV (Flash
video) file or a remote
live stream using a
Flash Communications
equipped server.

The Camera class is
almost identical to the
Microphone class
when used with local
camera equipment.

23.14   Playing Back Captured Video with the *Camera* Class *(continued)*

Now that you have a video instance on the Stage, you can direct your Camera stream, my_cam, into it with the following line:

```
my_video.attachVideo(my_cam);
```

Following these two code lines, the Video channel is ready for use, and you can check this by running the SWF when your camera equipment is on; you should see a slightly delayed version of your captured video, filling the previously empty instance my_video.

23.15 Reading Video Properties and Permissions

Several video properties and status events can be read or acted on, the most important being the microphone permission settings (which the user also has access to via the Flash Player Settings) and the height, width, and frame rate of the displayed video.

Permission settings can be found using the `muted` property. If it is set to true, Camera access has *not* been granted; it *has* been granted if it is false:

Assuming a camera stream `my_cam` (see the last section if you are unsure on how to set this up), the following code will trace an appropriate message if the user denies use of the local camera to Flash Player:

```
if (my_cam.muted == true) {
  trace("You dont know what you're missing!");
}
```

The height, width, and frame rate of the video can be changed via the `Camera.setMode()` method. This has the following general form:

```
myCameraVar.setMode(height, width, fps, favorSize);
```

The *height* and *width* parameters set the height and width of the video, and the *fps* value defines the frame rate. The *favorSize* value allows you to decide what you want Flash to do if the camera equipment can't meet the specified dimensions and rate. Setting this to true makes Flash drop the frame rate (i.e., it favors the height and width values); setting it to false means that Flash will try to maintain the fps, making the video smaller if it has to.

The following line will set the camera stream, `my_cam`, to 200×150, 10 fps with *favorSize* set to true:

```
my_cam.setMode(200, 120, 15, true);
```

The default `setMode` values used are 160×120, 15 fps, and *favorSize* true.

The `Camera.muted` property will be false *unless* the user has previously allowed access and saved this setting or has seen the Flash "Allow local to access your camera and microphone?" message and clicked Allow. If you check the `muted` property before they have allowed access, you will get true (denied), so it is a good idea to hold off the check until well after the `Camera.get()`.

Although there is an event handler that will fire when the user changes the camera permissions (`Camera.onStatus`), this event will *never* execute if the user has checked Remember in the Privacy settings (given the camera permissions will not change per session).

CHAPTER 24

Runtime Content Delivery

THERE ARE MANY DIFFERENT ways to organize and deliver a SWF file online. You might want to load all of your content into a shell of a SWF file and then organize the data using ActionScript. You might create all of your text fields and movie clips using ActionScript, organize your content into XML files on the server and, when the information is requested by your visitors, load it into the SWF. Or, you might take a simpler approach and create all of the assets in the SWF file and load much less content at runtime.

What approach you use depends largely on the kind of site you are constructing, the size of it, and the level of complexity you use when you create the file. Time and money are usually very real factors as well! This chapter shows you some of the different techniques you might use when creating your Flash files for delivery online.

24.1   Understanding Content Delivery Strategies

___

When loading video content into a SWF file, you should consider buffering the content. You can set a buffer time using the `set-BufferTime` method of the `NetStream` class.

There are many different styles and approaches to delivering Flash content online. A SWF file might be a "rich Internet application," an animation, a front-end for a CD-ROM, an advertisement, video playback, a streaming web cam application, a simple website, and so forth. You might create a complex SWF file that connects to a database and also uses a socket server so visitors can interact with each other. Or you might create a linear SWF file that is a cartoon animation. All of these kinds of SWF file require different strategies for execution.

The main thing to consider for your content delivery strategy is what method you will use to load content, if any at all. How you structure your data is a major concern, because it will affect how you build a large part of your FLA. If you use XML data, you must write ActionScript that can understand and extract that information from the XML document. If you interact with a web service, you must create the service and then either bind data to parts of your SWF or write ActionScript that can request and interpret the data that returns to the SWF.

When you create SWF files for the Web, there are several reasons why you should try to dynamically load content into a SWF file, whether the content is video, text, images, XML, variables, or other forms of data. A dynamic site is one in which any form of data loads into the SWF file at runtime. Dynamic sites allow you to

- Minimize file size of the main application.

- Make your documents more versatile.

- Easily update your documents (because you won't need to manually enter new data into a FLA file or create complex schemes to display data).

- Update photos without having to replace old versions in a FLA file (simply replace the JPEG on the server and the new version loads).

- Help your visitors load only content that they request, saving bandwidth for you and the visitor.

- Easily integrate with other technologies.

- Build dynamic sites easily using `LoadVars` and the Data components.

24.2 Creating Load Targets and Load Levels

There are several ways to load variables to Flash from external files, using functions such as LoadVariables and LoadVariablesNum or the LoadVars class. (See the following section for LoadVars.) The following shows you how to load variables from a text file into a movie clip using loadVariables:

```
this.createEmptyMovieClip("variables_mc", this.getNextHighestDepth());
loadVariables("variables.txt", variables_mc);
function checkLoaded() {
  var isLoaded:Boolean = variables_mc.hasLoaded != undefined;
  if (isLoaded) {
    trace("loaded");
    clearInterval(loadedInterval);
  }
  return isLoaded;
}
var loadedInterval = setInterval(checkLoaded, 100);
```

The first line creates a movie clip with an instance name of variables_mc at runtime. Then the loadVariables function loads the contents of a text file into the movie clip. The rest of the ActionScript defines a function called checkLoaded, which tests if the contents of the remote file have finished loading. If a variable called isloaded is defined within the movie clip instance, then the external file has finished loading, so a trace statement is sent to the Output panel.

The final line of code is a little bit tricky. It calls the setInterval function that then calls the checkLoaded function repeatedly approximately every 100 milliseconds. Why continually call checkLoaded? Because Flash is asynchronous: it doesn't wait for the contents of the file to be completely loaded before continuing to process the next line of code. That means that if you load variables from your external file and immediately try to access the values—before ensuring that the file has been completely loaded—you will probably encounter lots of errors and unexpected behaviors.

In ActionScript, the clearInterval function clears the interval after the variables have completely finished loading. To test this example, make sure you first have a file called variables.txt that has some variables defined, like this one:

```
&name=Nate+W.&position=mentor&hasLoaded=1
```

Similar to the formatting of URL variables in a web browser, the values are passed as key/value pairs, delimited by ampersands (&). Each pair consists of the "name" of the variable (which will be loaded into a movie clip in Flash), an equal sign, and the variable value. The final key/value pair, hasLoaded=1, is a flag that tests if all variables have been loaded into Flash. The earlier example used the checkLoaded function to test if variables_mc.hasLoaded was defined or not. By always testing the last value in the text file,

———

The checkLoaded function returns a Boolean (true or false) value that indicates whether or not the content has finished loading.

Because you are calling the checkLoaded function continually every 100 milliseconds, it can cause the SWF to slow down; this hurts older or slower machines. Exercise caution: don't overuse intervals and clear them when they're no longer needed to reduce load on the end user's resources.

———

You aren't limited to loading static text files. You can also load variables based on the results of a ColdFusion, PHP, ASP, or CGI server side template.

Continues ●

24.2   Creating Load Targets and Load Levels

Because the amper-
sand is a string delim-
iter, take special care
when loading external
data using the load-
Variables function. It
might be truncated if
the string has an
ampersand in the
name/value pair. This
taints the data that is
being loaded. Any
ampersands appearing
within the loaded con-
tent (that aren't sepa-
rating name/value
pairs) must be con-
verted to a URL-safe
value such as %26,
which you can find by
placing the following
ActionScript code
within the SWF:
trace(escape
("&"));.

The GET method sends
the values along the
URL, where the length
of data that can be sent
is very limited, because
you should limit a URL
string to 256 characters.
POST sends the values
as form variables and
encodes them in the
HTTP header, allowing
you to send much
larger amounts of data.

(continued)

you can make sure that all variables have been completely loaded before trying to access their values.

A variation on `loadVariables` allows you to set values in a movie clip instance and then send those values to the remote server-side template. This allows you to build dynamic SWF files. The following is an example of this technique:

```
this.createEmptyMovieClip("variables_mc", this.getNextHighestDepth());
variables_mc.message = "this is just a test.";
variables_mc.loadVariables("http://localhost:8500/loadVariables.cfm", "POST");
// …
```

The first line is the same as the previous example, creating a movie clip at runtime that will send and receive the variables between Flash and a remote script. The second line sets a parameter called `message` in the movie clip instance. The third line uses the `loadVariables` method of the `MovieClip` class to send the values within the movie clip to the remote ColdFusion page. The second parameter in `loadVariables` refers to how the variables will be sent and must be either GET or POST. The rest of the ActionScript (defining the function and calling `setInterval`) is exactly the same as the previous example.

24.3 Loading Variables into a Timeline

The LoadVars class allows you to load variables and text from remote files without having to resort to using the setInterval and clearInterval functions to repeatedly check for variables. The LoadVars class has two event handlers: onData and onLoad. These handlers allow you easily execute code when certain events are triggered.

```
var variables_lv:LoadVars = new LoadVars();
variables_lv.load("variables.txt");
variables_lv.onLoad = function(success) {
  if (success) {
  trace("name:"+this.name);
  } else {
  trace("error!");
  }
};
```

This ActionScript creates a new LoadVars object that can send and load variables into the SWF file at runtime. After creating a variables_lv object, you can call the load method and pass a relative or absolute URL to load the content from. This example uses the onLoad event handler. The difference between the onLoad and onData event handlers is that onData is called after the contents have been loaded, but before the name/value pairs have been parsed. The onLoad event handler is called after the load or sendAndLoad methods have completed and the name/value pairs have been parsed.

When you use the onLoad event handler, one parameter is passed to the function, which indicates whether the load operation was completed successfully. If the file cannot be loaded, an error is thrown and the value of the success parameter is set to false. If the file loads successfully, one of the values from the remote file is displayed in the Output panel in the testing environment. If not, an error message is displayed in the Output panel. The keyword this within the onLoad event handler refers to the current LoadVars object where all the variables were loaded to.

You can use the onData event handler instead of the onLoad event handler if you want to load a bunch of text from a text file instead of loading variables. Using onDate means that you don't have to worry about escaping any ampersands (&) within the external file. You can see an example of onData in the following snippet:

```
var variables_lv:LoadVars = new LoadVars();
variables_lv.load("variables.txt");
variables_lv.onData = function(data) {
  trace(data);
};
```

➡ 24.2 Creating Load Targets and Load Levels

➡ 24.6 Dynamically Loading Images

➡ 24.7 Dynamically Loading Video

The process of using FlashVars is fairly straightforward, but you must be careful to modify both the object and embed tags because some tags allow Flash to load the appropriate SWF files; whereas different sets of tags allow Netscape and other browsers to also load the SWF files. Therefore, all changes that you complete for one set of browsers must also be duplicated for the other set of browsers.

Continues ●

24.3   Loading Variables into a Timeline *(continued)*

_____

Because FlashVars also relies on the ampersand (&) to split up name/value pairs, you must take special precautions if your content being loaded also contains characters that are special to Flash. Any ampersand characters in the external file must be converted to %26 or the values will not import properly.

In this ActionScript, the complete contents of the file are passed into the data parameter within the function. This is different from the onLoad event handler, which receives a parameter that indicates whether the file was successfully loaded or not.

One other means of loading variables into Flash is using the FlashVars property within the HTML page you embed the SWF file into. Using FlashVars means the variables are immediately available to the SWF file, and you don't need to use any special event handlers or continually check whether or not the variables are available within your SWF. FlashVars is an excellent choice for passing simple values into Flash without having to resort to loading external files. Using FlashVars requires that you modify the object and embed tags that render the SWF file in the user's browser. Open the HTML file that is generated by Flash when you publish your FLA. Add the following tag beside the existing param tags:

```
<param name="FlashVars" value="name=Nate+W.&position=mentor" />
```

Next, within the existing embed tag, add the following value:

```
FlashVars="name=Nate+W.&position=mentor"
```

Now you can access these two values in the SWF file by tracing _level0.name or _level0.position.

LOADING VARIABLES USING *LOADVARIABLESNUM*

Another way of loading external variables into Flash is loadVariablesNum. As you can probably imagine, this function is fairly similar to loadVariables, with one small difference. Instead of loading the variables into a movie clip on the Stage, the loadVariablesNum function loads variables into different *levels*. The following code demonstrates how to use this function:

```
loadVariablesNum("variables.txt", 2);
function checkLoaded() {
  var isLoaded:Boolean = _level2.hasLoaded != undefined;
  if (isLoaded) {
    for (var i in _level2) {
      trace(i + ": " + _level2[i]);
    }
    clearInterval(loadedInterval);
  }
  return isLoaded;
}
var loadedInterval = setInterval(checkLoaded, 100);
```

24.4 Creating Font Symbols

When using a font that most visitors do not have installed on their computers, it might be necessary to embed the font symbol in your Library. This means the font outlines will be available when you publish the SWF and upload the file to a web server. The font is embedded right inside the SWF file so you can use the font outlines and have the characters display correctly.

1   In a Flash document, open the Library by pressing F11.

2   Click the Options menu and select New Font from the drop-down menu. Flash displays the Font Symbol Properties dialog, allowing you to set the desired font, styles, size, and font name.

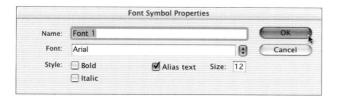

3   Once you have set up the font, click the OK button to close the dialog and return to the Stage and Library panel. The new font symbol and the unique name you assigned to it are visible in the Library.

After you create a new font symbol, that font can be used in your SWF. For example, you can embed the font symbol or you can create a font library that can be shared between many SWF files on a server. Those fonts can be imported at runtime by following a few very simple steps, described in the next section.

Fonts can have large file sizes, and some may be quite limited in characters. However, embedding an entire font means that you can use the font in a dynamic text field and have all of the characters in that particular font available for use.

EASE VS. FILE SIZE

Using components to load content is an extremely easy way to build a FLA file. All you have to do is drag, drop, and enter a URL that points to what you want to load into that component. The Streaming Media components and Loader component in particular make it very easy to load content. However, you might notice that V2 components introduce some significant file size of their own, sometimes exceeding 30K just to load your content in. Therefore, you should only use these components on their own for prototype applications, SWF files where file size doesn't matter, or when you are already using many other components. When you already have several other components in your SWF file, the architecture is already contained in the SWF, so only a small amount of file size is added to the file if you include a progress bar.

24.5   Using Shared Fonts

___

Carefully watch the file
size of the fonts that
you import into a SWF
file. Many fonts can be
extremely large files,
which is a lot of data
to transfer on the Web.
Check file sizes and
make sure that your
audience has sufficient
Internet connections
to handle loading
large fonts.

Create a new font symbol using the steps outlined in the preceding section. When you
have a font, or several fonts, in the Library, save the FLA file and publish it to a SWF file.
This SWF file is a font library of sorts, and in this example is called `myFonts.swf`.

1   Create a new FLA file and choose File > Import > Open External Library. The Open As
    Library dialog opens.

2   Select the FLA you created containing font symbols that you want to share, which in
    this case would be `myFonts.fla`. The Library from that document opens in Flash.

3   Drag the font symbol you want to share between the documents into your current FLA
    file's Library or onto the Stage.

4   Right-click the new font symbol in the Library of the SWF you are loading the font
    into. The Linkage dialog opens.

5   Deselect the checked boxes in the Linkage dialog and then select the Import For Run-
    time Sharing check box.

6   Type the name of the SWF file that you saved the fonts in.

7   Create a dynamic text field, and in the Property inspector select the name of the shared
    font in the Font drop-down menu. It will have a small asterisk next to the name of the font.

8   Save and publish the FLA file.

Upload both the SWF that's importing the fonts and the one that contains the library of
fonts onto the Web. These two files will share fonts. The SWF loading the font loads it
from the other SWF that contains the symbol.

TRACKING PROGRESS

There are many components available that can track the progress of your content as it
loads into a SWF file. These components are usually called progress bar or preloader
components. A progress bar component is included with Flash MX 2004 and can load
all sorts of kinds of content in a SWF file. There are many other progress bar
components available online for download.

24.6 Dynamically Loading Images

There are several different ways that you can load images into Flash, although there are quite a few restrictions on loading those images. The only image file type that can be loaded into a SWF at runtime is a JPEG. A JPEG can be saved as optimized at any quality level you choose, but the JPEG image must *not* be saved as progressive if you want to load it into a SWF. Perhaps the easiest way to load an image into Flash is to create a movie clip instance on the Stage and assign a behavior.

1 Create a movie clip instance and place it on the Stage. You can create a movie clip from within the Library and drag it onto the Stage, or convert a symbol on the Stage into a movie clip by selecting it with the Selection tool and pressing F8.

2 Assign the movie clip instance on the Stage an instance name. Make sure the Stage is selected instead of the instance.

3 With the Stage selected, open the Behaviors panel and choose the Movieclip > Load Graphic behavior.

4 In the text field at the top of the Load Graphic dialog, enter an absolute or relative URL to a JPEG image and select the movie clip instance in the tree control at the bottom.

5 After the movie clip instance is selected and you've entered the proper URL to the JPEG, click OK to generate the appropriate ActionScript code on the main Timeline.

If you want to write ActionScript yourself without resorting to using a premade behavior, you could use an existing movie clip on the Stage, or you can create the movie clip at runtime using ActionScript and load the JPEG image into the new movie clip. You can see an example of the latter in the following code:

```
this.createEmptyMovieClip("photo_mc", this.getNextHighestDepth());
photo_mc.loadMovie("whatididlastsummer.jpg");
```

By calling the movie clip's `loadMovie` method, you are able to load an external movie clip at runtime. When this code is placed on the main Timeline of the FLA, the `this` keyword refers to the Stage. The `getNextHighestDepth` method makes sure the movie clip is created on the next highest depth so it doesn't appear below other symbols in the SWF.

Whenever possible, use relative addressing when referring to instances within the FLA. Relative addressing makes the SWF file more portable and won't cause headaches when you load the SWF into other SWF files.

Even though there are several limitations on what images can be dynamically loaded into a SWF, almost every image type can be imported into Flash in the authoring environment and saved in the Library.

24.7 Dynamically Loading Video

———

In earlier versions of
Flash, you had to use
the Flash Communica-
tion Server to load FLV
files at runtime.

———

You can publish to
Flash Player 6 using
ActionScript 1.0 if you
want and still dynami-
cally load FLV files. You
will need to make sure
you write your Action-
Script using version 1
practices.

There are two ways you can play back dynamically loaded videos using Flash MX 2004.
The first way requires Flash MX Professional 2004, because it uses the Streaming Media
components to load an FLV file at runtime and stream it in a SWF file. The second way
can be used in both Flash MX and Flash MX Professional because it involves streaming an
FLV at runtime using the NetConnection and NetStream classes.

To load FLV files manually using ActionScript, add the following code to a frame in the
main Timeline:

```
var mediaPlay:mx.controls.MediaPlayback;
mediaPlay.setMedia("video1.flv", "FLV");
mediaPlay.play(0);
```

Before you can test this ActionScript, you need to make sure that you have a MediaPlayback component on the Stage with an instance name of mediaPlay (of course, you could
also replace any references of mediaPlay in the preceding snippet with the instance name
of your existing Media component). Then the ActionScript assumes you have an FLV file
called video1.flv in the same directory as the Flash document. Using the setMedia
method allows you to define the contentPath and mediaType for the streaming file.
Finally, you begin to play back the MediaPlayback component instance by calling the play
method and setting the starting point to the beginning of the file (zero seconds).

Another way you can stream FLVs is by using the NetConnection and NetStream classes in
Flash MX or Flash MX Professional. They take a bit more effort and bit more ActionScript;
however, it can still be done in as few as seven lines of code. The following ActionScript is
all you need to load an external FLV into a SWF at runtime, although you need to add an
item to your Library and Stage before the code will work.

```
var holiday_video:Video;
var netCon_nc:NetConnection = new NetConnection();
netCon_nc.connect(null);
var netStr_ns:NetStream = new NetStream(netCon_nc);
holiday_video.attachVideo(netStr_ns);
netStr_ns.setBufferTime(3);
netStr_ns.play("video1.flv");
```

Before publishing the file, open the Library and follow these steps:

1 Click the options menu button in the upper-right corner of the Library panel and select
   New Video to add an Embedded Video symbol to the FLA.

2 Select the video symbol in the Library and drag it onto the Stage.

3 Give this instance an instance name using the Property inspector and resize the video
   symbol on the Stage to the same dimensions as the FLV. The preceding code uses an
   instance name of holiday_video and assumes an FLV name of video1.flv.

4 Make sure the ActionScript is in the FLA and then publish your file.

24.8   Using Components to Load External Content

Loading content into Flash using components is a fairly straightforward task, thanks to the aptly named Loader component. The Loader component can be used to load SWF files or JPEG images into Flash at runtime. The Loader component has a couple other benefits, including events that are generated by Flash when the content has finished loading. This makes adding progress bars to the Loader very easy. The Loader component even has the option to resize the component instance if the content is too large, which means your content will not be scaled.

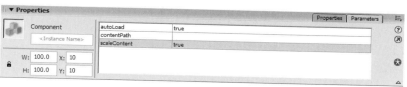

To use the Loader component, expand the Components panel and drag a copy of the component onto the Stage. With the component still selected on the Stage, open the Property inspector.

The Loader component has three parameters that can be modified using the Property inspector: `autoLoad`, `contentPath`, and `scaleContent`.

autoLoad Boolean value that indicates whether or not the content should be loaded automatically (`true`) or whether the component's load method needs to be called explicitly (`false`).

contentPath The absolute or relative URL to the SWF or JPEG image to load into the component.

scaleContent Boolean value indicating whether the content being loaded in should resize itself to fit the component (`true`) or whether the component should not scale at all (`false`).

The Loader component's methods and properties can be accessed by ActionScript to load images at runtime. The following code loads a JPEG image into a Loader component two different ways at runtime using ActionScript:

```
// -- method one --
myLdr.load("images/image1.jpg");
// -- method two --
myLdr.contentPath = "images/image1.jpg";
myLdr.load();
```

You can also use other components to load SWFs or JPEGs. For example, you can use the Window component or ScrollPane to load remote content by setting their respective `contentPath` parameters.

If you are building a presentation using the screens-based authoring environment, then you can set the contentPath for a screen to an external SWF or JPEG as well.

Alias text might become fuzzy in a SWF file that is scaled in the Loader component.

Progressive JPEG files cannot be loaded into a SWF file, even using the Loader component.

24.9   Handling the Loading Process

When you are loading data across domains, you must either use a cross-domain policy file or make sure you are loading from exactly the same domain. This means you must even have the same virtual domain and ensure it is included in the address. For example, www .mysite.com is not considered to be the same as mysite.com.

There are many different ways you can load data and images into a SWF file, and sometimes the order in which data is loaded has to be handled in a specific way. You can load variables into a SWF using `loadVariables` or `LoadVars`; you can load complex data using Flash Remoting, web services, or the Flash Communication Server. You can even load data from XML, text, or HTML files. MP3, FLV, and non-progressive JPEG files can be dynamically loaded into a SWF at runtime. But how you load data into a file is fairly important.

If you try to access something before it loads, then your attempt will fail because the data or content is not completely loaded. For example, if you want to load an image and then "do something" in the SWF after it has completely loaded, you need to check that the image is completely loaded before you do something else in the file. This is seen in the following ActionScript:

```
myProgress = function (img) {
  var bytesLoaded = img.getBytesLoaded();
  var bytesTotal = img.getBytesTotal();
  var percentLoaded = Math.floor(bytesLoaded/bytesTotal*100);
  trace("%"+percentLoaded+" loaded.");
  if (percentLoaded == 100) {
    clearInterval(polling);
    trace ("do something");
  }
};
myclip.loadMovie("cat.jpg");
var polling = setInterval(myProgress, 1000, myclip);
```

This code loads an image and uses an interval to check the progress of the loading. `get-BytesLoaded` and `getBytesTotal` check whether the image is fully loaded before the interval is deleted and something else is done in the SWF.

There are many different ways that you can handle loading of data. Although you might want to make sure the content is loaded before manipulating it (as in the previous code), you might want to manipulate the loading of data in different ways. For example, you could use an array and load data sequentially. You could hold the URLs of content (perhaps SWFs or JPEGs) in an array and then load one of them into the SWF after an event is called. You could use a timer to call an event every five seconds (using `setInterval`) and then load the next file into the SWF.

24.10 Using the *MovieClipLoader* Class

Working with the `MovieClipLoader` class is similar to loading movie clips using Action-Script, except this class has a few very useful events. These events notify you when the content has fully loaded, when the content has started loading, and even as the content loads, allowing you to build a fairly robust progress bar for your external movie clips and JPEG images. In its most basic form, the `MovieClipLoader` class can load an external image, as shown in the following code:

```
var movieLoader_mcl:MovieClipLoader = new MovieClipLoader();
movieLoader_mcl.loadClip("images/socksthecat.jpeg", myImage_mc);
```

The `myImage_mc` instance is an existing movie clip on the Stage, although you could have just as easily created the movie clip using the `createEmptyMovieClip` method. The real power of the `MovieClipLoader` class comes from taking advantage of the various listeners, so you can use the `MovieClipLoader` in conjunction with the ProgressBar component or your own custom progress bar. Here's an example of loading a JPEG and using the listeners:

```
var mclListener:Object = new Object();
mclListener.onLoadComplete = function(target) {
  trace(target + " has completed loading.");
};
mclListener.onLoadProgress =
  function(target, numBytesLoaded, numBytesTotal) {
    trace(target + " is " +
        int(numBytesLoaded/numBytesTotal*100)+"% loaded");
  };
var movieLoader_mcl:MovieClipLoader = new MovieClipLoader();
movieLoader_mcl.addListener(mclListener);
movieLoader_mcl.loadClip("thepizzaguy.jpg", myImage_mc);
```

The first line of code defines a listener object that holds the required ActionScript for the listeners. The next line defines a block of code that executes when the `onLoadComplete` listener is invoked. The listener is called when the image has fully loaded, which is useful if you are using a progress bar on the image and want to hide the progress bar after the content finishes loading. The other listener you're using is the `onLoadProgress` listener, which monitors the progress of the download. While the content loads into the `Movie-ClipLoader`, it invokes the listener every time content is written to the disk when it's being loaded. The `onLoadProgress` receives three parameters: the target movie clip defined in the `loadClip` method and the final two parameters that report the current number of bytes loaded and the total number of bytes being loaded in using `loadClip`.

The example in this section divides the number of bytes currently loaded by the total number of bytes and then converts the number to an integer value using the `int` function to create a percentage between 0 and 100.

24.11   Using Runtime Shared Libraries

Just as with shared font libraries, you have to be careful about how much information in the shared library you are loading into your SWF and whether your audience can handle the amount of data that's loaded.

Shared libraries can be a very easy and efficient way of sharing data across many SWF files. They are particularly useful when you are building hybrid HTML and Flash websites.

Using a runtime shared library involves two main steps:

- Building the source shared library file and providing a URL where the SWF file will be uploaded to on the Internet.

- Creating the destination file that relies on assets in the source document. It is available at a specific URL.

You can reuse assets throughout a site across multiple SWF documents when you use runtime shared libraries. If you happen to modify the shared asset in the source file, the changes are reflected in each of the files loading that asset. This makes development much simpler because you don't have to modify the asset in each file individually.

1 The first step is to create a new Flash document that serves as the shared library. Create a new symbol you want to share with other SWF files in this document.

   a Create a movie clip or graphic symbol and draw a shape. After you finish drawing, right-click the symbol in your Library and select Linkage from the contextual menu.

   b In the Linkage Properties dialog, check the Export For Runtime Sharing check box and type in the URL of the SWF file where the shared asset document will be uploaded to. Publish, save, and close the Flash document.

2 The second step is to create a new document that loads your shared asset created in the first step.

   a Add a new symbol to the Library in the second Flash document. This symbol will be a placeholder that you can position on the Stage. It will be replaced at runtime by the shared asset.

   b Right-click the placeholder symbol in the Library panel and select Linkage from the contextual menu.

   c When the Linkage Properties dialog opens, select the Import For Runtime Sharing check box and give the symbol the same identifier as the shared asset created in step 1.

   d Enter the URL of the shared library SWF in the URL text field and close the dialog.

Publish both the Flash documents and upload the SWF files to the proper location. View the Flash document created in the second step that calls the shared asset created in step 1. You will notice your placeholder symbol is replaced by the one from the shared library.

CHAPTER 25

Web Services and XML

COMPONENTS ALLOWING YOU TO connect to web services, and other assorted Data Connection components, are new features in Flash MX Professional 2004 and allow you to easily work with sources of data that are loaded into a SWF file at runtime. The WebServiceConnector component allows you to consume remote web services easily, usually without having to write a single line of ActionScript. Web services are available on a remote server that can be used (or *consumed*) by other applications such as a SWF movie. While you can still use Flash MX Remoting to do the same thing, the new style of consuming web services in Flash is much easier and, because of this, quite a bit faster to work with.

All the features described in this chapter are available only in Flash MX Professional 2004.

25.1   Defining Web Services

Web Services panel
⌘ Shift F10
Ctrl Shift F10

If you are using ColdFusion MX and have a ColdFusion Component (CFC), you can access the component's functions by appending ?WSDL on to the end of the URL. For example, if you have a CFC named blog.cfc in the root of your website, you can access that CFC as a web service by entering the URL http://www.yoursite.com/blog.cfc?WSDL, but you will only be able to access functions where the access has been set to remote.

Web services are defined in the Web Services panel (Window > Development Panels > Web Services; Flash MX Professional 2004 only). There are three ways to define a new web service:

- Click the Define Web Services button in the upper left of the Web Services panel.
- Right-click within the Web Services panel and select Define Web Services from the contextual menu.
- Click the Options menu within the Web Services panel and select Define Web Services from the contextual menu.

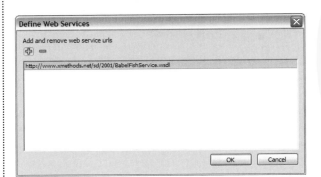

When the Define Web Services dialog opens, you can add a Web Service URL by clicking the Add Web Service button (the plus sign). A new item will be added to the Web Service URL list, where you can type the URL that targets the web service.

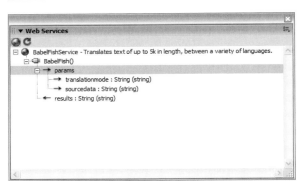

To modify an existing web service URL, double-click the URL and update the entry. If you want to remove a web service from the list, click the entry in the list and then click the Remove Web Service button (the minus sign) at the top of the Define Web Services dialog. When you are finished adding and removing web services, click the OK button to return to the Web Services panel.

Any new web services you defined should now appear within the Web Services panel. If the web service isn't visible in the panel, double-check its URL in your browser and make sure you can properly connect to the service. Now you can expand each of the web services and view their methods and parameters. You can also right-click/Control-click an existing web service and select View WSDL from the contextual menu to view that web service's WSDL (Web Services Description Language) file.

If for any reason the web service changes, refresh the list of defined web services and their respective methods and properties by clicking the Refresh Web Services button at the top left of the window.

25.2 Adding Method Calls to the Flash Document

Adding a method call embeds a WebServiceConnector component within the document. It also fills out both the WSDLURL of the web service and the operation parameter, which is the name of the method. This is entered into the Property inspector or Component Inspector panel (in Flash MX Professional 2004 only).

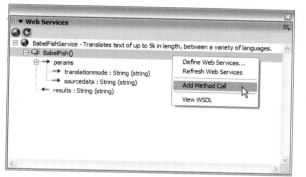

To add a method call to your Flash document, open the Web Services panel. Expand the web service you want to use by clicking the + icon next to its name, then right-click/Control-click the method you want to invoke. Select Add Method Call from the contextual menu.

Flash automatically places an instance of the WebServiceConnector component on the Stage. Open the Property inspector or Component Inspector panel to confirm that both the WSDLURL and operation fields are filled in for you.

This is usually a good time to type in an instance name for the WebServiceConnector instance on the Stage using the Property inspector. You will not be able to add any bindings until an instance name has been provided for the component.

Web Services panel
⌘ Shift F10
Ctrl Shift F10

Property inspector
Ctrl F3
⌘ F3

Component Inspector panel
Alt F7
Option F7

FLASH WORKSPACE

AUTHORING TASKS

SCRIPTING TASKS

TESTING AND PUBLISHING TASKS

WHAT'S NEW

25.3   Creating Bindings

25.12 Formatting
Results
Using the
Bindings
Tab

**Component
Inspector panel**
[Alt] [F7]
[Option] [F7]

A binding creates a connection between components. For example, you might be connecting one of the data components (providing a source of data) to a component that's used to display or use that data. To add a binding between the web service and your Flash document (in Flash MX Professional 2004 only), follow these steps:

1   Click the WebServiceConnector component instance on the Stage, and then select the Bindings tab in the Component Inspector panel.

2   In the Bindings tab, click the Add Binding button near the top of the tab. Or you can click the Options menu in the Component Inspector panel and choose Add Binding from the drop-down menu.

3   At this point, if you haven't yet given the instance on the Stage an instance name, a dialog appears telling you that you need to name the instance before you can use the object as a target. Click the Rename button to give your component an instance name and press OK to continue to the Add Binding dialog.

4   From this dialog, choose which parameter you want to add a binding to. Select a field or property and click OK. You will now see a new binding in the Bindings tab.

If you now click the binding in the Bindings tab, you will see that you can set which instance on the Stage the binding is bound to by double-clicking the value column beside Bound To. The Bound To dialog now appears.

25.3 Creating Bindings *(continued)*

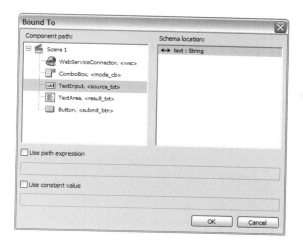

To bind the values to the web service, first add a binding using the preceding method, then choose the desired component to bind the value to, and finally choose an option from the Schema Location column. Click OK when you are finished.

If the web service returns an array, you can bind the array to the dataProvider schema and the List or ComboBox instance will be populated by the results of the web service call.

You can bind a schema item that's not in the schema tree by checking the Use Path Expression check box and typing in a path expression. The formatting required depends on the kind of data that is being bound.

Depending on which component you are trying to bind the value to, you will see different results in the Schema Location box. The Label component only has a text : String option, meaning that the component will only allow you to bind simple values such as Booleans, strings, numbers, etc. If you are binding the value to a ComboBox component, you are able to set the value : String, dataProvider : Array, selectedIndex : Number, or selectedItem : Object. Binding to a List component lets you set the dataProvider : Array, selectedIndex : Number, selectedIndices : Array, selectedItem : Object or selectedItems : Array.

USING WEB SERVICES WITHOUT THE WEBSERVICECONNECTOR COMPONENT
You can use web services without the use of the WebServiceConnector component by adding the class to the library. You can find the WebServiceClasses in the Classes common library (Window > Other Panels > Common Libraries). ActionScript is then used to interact with the web services instead of using the Component Inspector panel.

25.4   Invoking Web Services Using Behaviors

Invoking a web service means you are *calling* the web service so you can start using a method or function of that service in your SWF file (a feature of Flash MX Professional 2004 only). This is as simple as adding an instance of the Button component to the Stage and adding a behavior. After the button instance is on the Stage, make sure the button is selected and expand the Behaviors panel by pressing Shift+F3, or by choosing Windows > Development Panels > Behaviors. Add a behavior to the button by pressing the Add Behavior (+) button in the top left of the Behaviors panel. From the drop-down menu, choose Data > Trigger Data Source.

When the Trigger Data Source dialog opens, select the WebServiceConnector component instance from the Select Data Source Component area that's now available.

After you are finished, click OK to close the dialog. Test the SWF file; now when you click the Button component instance, the values that are bound to the component instances are sent to the web service. If the web service returns a value, it is automatically bound to whatever bindings were defined using the Bindings tab. The components on the Stage are updated based on whatever bindings have been made. For example, if you have a TextArea instance on the Stage and a value is bound to it, the text string will be visible in the TextArea.

25.5 Loading XML Documents Using the XMLConnector

The XMLConnector component (available only in Flash MX Professional 2004) shares many similarities with the WebServiceConnector component. The primary difference is that the WebServiceConnector uses WSDL to describe the data, whereas the XMLConnector uses XML. This makes it easier than ever to load an XML document into Flash and display the data without the need for writing large amounts of ActionScript.

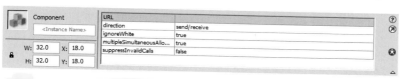

Expand the Components panel and drag an instance of the XMLConnector component onto the Stage. Enter the URL of the XML file that you need to load into the SWF file. You can do this by selecting the XMLConnector instance on the Stage and entering the URL to the XML file in the URL text field in the Property inspector or within the Parameters tab of the Component Inspector panel.

Now you need to set the *direction*:

Send Allows you to send an XML packet from Flash to a specific URL (which can be a ColdFusion template, PHP template, ASP.NET, Java, and so on) where it can be processed or the data can be further manipulated.

Receive Loads an external XML file from an existing URL where you can manipulate it in your Flash movie.

Send/Receive A combination of the two previous settings where you are sending an XML packet to a specific URL and getting an XML packet back from the server.

Components panel
Ctrl F7
⌘ F7

Property inspector
Ctrl F3
⌘ F3

Component Inspector panel
Alt F7
Option F7

25.6 Importing Schemas

Component Inspector panel
Alt F7
Option F7

A schema is a list of the data within the XML file or web service that you are loading into the SWF (available in Flash MX Professional 2004 only). Adding fields and properties to the schema is an important step because it will help you create bindings while you are building the current application. There are two ways to define the schema in your application: either you can define the schema manually by adding component properties and fields using the buttons in the Schema tab in the Component Inspector panel, or you can import an existing schema from an XML file.

Importing a schema is an easy process. Find the Schema tab in the Component Inspector panel, click the results item in the schema list, and click the Import A Schema From A Sample XML File button on the far right of the tab.

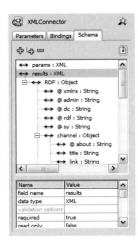

A file browser then opens where you can select an XML file to use as your schema. If you are trying to load an XML file from your site, locate the file using the file browser, click the filename, and click the Open button. If you are trying to load an XML file from an external site (such as an XML feed for a blog or news system) the easiest way is to save a local copy of the XML file to your hard drive and then import the schema using the previously outlined steps. After importing the schema, you will see new fields and properties in the schema, as shown here.

25.7 Triggering XML Calls

One of the best features of web services and XML in Flash MX Professional 2004 is that you can use them without having to write a lot of ActionScript. For example, you might have seen how easy it was to invoke a web service using a behavior in Section 25.4.

If you simply drag an instance of the XMLConnector component onto the Stage and then import a schema and add your bindings, you will notice that the values in your other components never seem to be populating. In order to actually invoke the XML call, you need to call the XMLConnector's `trigger()` function. This can be done by adding a single line of ActionScript to the Timeline (or screen) within your movie.

If you want to add the code to your Timeline, you need to add the ActionScript like the following on a frame on the Timeline, where `myXMLConnector` is the instance name of your XMLConnector component:

```
myXMLConnector.trigger();
```

If you are using screens, use the following code instead:

```
on (reveal) { myXMLConnector.trigger(); }
```

Actions panel
`F9`

Components panel
`Ctrl` `F7`
`⌘` `F7`

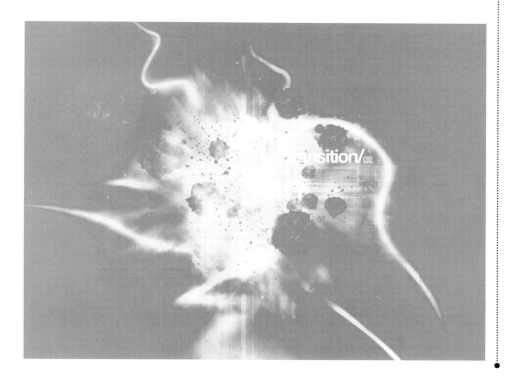

25.8   Loading Content from Different Domains

If you want to load content from different domains, or if you have your own web service that you wish to let other people consume in Flash, you will need to understand cross-domain policy files and a SWF file's security sandbox. Policy files are new in Flash MX Professional 2004, and they allow you to define which other domains are able to access your SWFs, XML, and web services. These policy files are written in XML and must be called `crossdomain.xml` and reside in the root folder for your domain name. For example, if you have a domain named `somedomain.com`, your policy file would have to be located at `http://www.somedomain.com/crossdomain.xml`.

A basic `crossdomain.xml` policy file would be:

```
<!-- http://www.somedomain.com/crossdomain.xml -->
<cross-domain-policy>
  <allow-access-from domain="www.otherdomain.com" />
</cross-domain-policy>
```

The preceding policy file allows any requests that originate from `www.otherdomain.com` to load Flash content from your website. You can have as many `<allow-access-from>` XML nodes as you want, and you can allow access to only certain IP addresses instead of having to use a domain name. You can also go one step further and use a wildcard (*) in a domain name, which will allow any domains that match the wildcard to load Flash content from your site:

```
<!-- http://www.somedomain.com/crossdomain.xml -->
<cross-domain-policy>
  <allow-access-from domain="www.otherdomain.com" />
  <allow-access-from domain="216.239.33.100" />
  <allow-access-from domain="*.thirddomain.com" />
</cross-domain-policy>
```

The last domain listed, `*.thirddomain.com`, allows any SWF file with a domain ending in `.thirddomain.com` to load Flash content, including `www.thirddomain.com`, `my.thirddomain.com`, and even `thirddomain.com`. If you want to allow all domains and IP addresses to be able to access your Flash content, you could have a basic XML policy file such as the following:

```
<!-- http://www.somedomain.com/crossdomain.xml -->
<cross-domain-policy>
  <allow-access-from domain="*" />
</cross-domain-policy>
```

25.8 Loading Content from Different Domains

(continued)

The preceding policy file allows all domains and all IP addresses to access your Flash content. One limitation of the policy file and wildcards is that you cannot use wildcards within an IP addresses.

When testing your SWF files in the authoring environment, the policy files and sandbox security rules don't apply and you are able to freely access remote web services. The same rule seems to apply if you test your SWF files from your local hard drive in a web browser or from the standalone Flash Player or testing environment. When you upload your SWF files to the Internet and then try to access them from a web browser, the security rules apply. When you try to view the SWF you see a Security Sandbox Violation message in the Flash Player Debug Console, which shows a message similar to the following:

`*** Security Sandbox Violation ***`

`Connection to <URL to Web Service WSDL or XML> halted - not permitted from <URL to your SWF>`

To work around the following error you have to write your own web service in a server-side programming language (for example: ColdFusion, ASP.NET, PHP, JSP, etc.) residing in the same domain as the SWF, consume the remote web service, and return the result to the SWF file. Alternatively, you could find out if the remote server has a `crossdomain.xml` policy file on the root folder of the server that allows access from your server.

➡ 25.5 Loading XML Documents Using the XML-Connector

➡ 25.13 Debugging Web Service and XML Documents

Remember when you are using wildcards within a domain name, the wildcard must be at the beginning of the domain name and must be followed by a dot and a suffix. You cannot use a wildcard such as `*oogle.com` and have it match `www.google.com`.

COMPARING WEB SERVICES AND FLASH REMOTING

Flash Remoting typically uses a lot less bandwidth than SOAP-based communication such as that used with the WebServiceConnector component. For a very detailed breakdown of bandwidth and speed, check out the benchmark tests that are outlined at `http://www.flashorb.com/articles/soap_vs_flash_remoting_benchmark.shtml`.

Despite the bandwidth and speed, it is usually a lot easier, faster, and, depending on its size and the traffic your site gets, cheaper to use the new methodology that Flash MX 2004 introduces. You will have to assess your own situation and then choose which way is best for you.

25.9   Using the DataHolder Component

Components panel
Ctrl F7
⌘ F7

Actions panel
F9

The DataHolder component is available only in Flash MX Professional 2004 and is used for storing data so it can be bound to components in the SWF file. This is useful if you are using the WebServiceConnector to connect to a remote web service and the service returns an XML object. Using only a few lines of ActionScript, you can assign the results of the web service to the DataHolder component so the XML is automatically parsed. Then it can be bound to a text field.

If you are consuming a web service returning XML data, you can set an event handler to store the XML result into the DataHolder component so you can bind the data to other components on the Stage. This can be accomplished by using the following code:

```
var listenerObj:Object = new Object();
listenerObj.result = function () {
  datahandler.data = new XML(wsconn.results);
}
wsconn.addEventListener("result", listenerObj);
```

This ActionScript creates a listener that waits for the **wsconn** WebServiceConnector instance to return a result from the server. When a result is received, the listener object's function is executed and the results from the web service are copied into the DataHandler instance. Now you are able to add bindings from the DataHandler instance on the Stage to other components within the Flash document.

25.10   Calling Web Services Using ActionScript

If you are familiar with Flash Remoting, you might be interested in knowing that you can also invoke web services using ActionScript instead of resorting to the Bindings tab in the Component Inspector panel and setting the WebServiceConnector parameter values in the Property inspector or Component Inspector panel. The easiest way to add the Web-ServiceConnector to a SWF file is to drag a copy of the component onto the Stage and delete it, which leaves the copy in the library. Then you can add the following Action-Script to a frame on the Timeline:

```
import mx.services.WebService;
var WebServiceURL:String =
  "http://services.xmethods.net/soap/urn:xmethods-DomainChecker.wsdl";
var myWS = new WebService(WebServiceURL);
var callback = myWS.checkDomain("macromedia.com");
callback.onResult = function(result) {
  trace(result);
};
```

The first thing that happens in the preceding code is the external `mx.services.WebService` class is imported into the SWF. By importing the class, you avoid having to give a fully qualified class name in the constructor, as seen in the following code:

```
var myWS = new mx.services.WebService(WebServiceURL);
```

Next, the code creates an alias to the web service itself and invokes the `checkDomain` method within the web service. When a result is returned from the server, the `onResult` function is triggered and the result is displayed in the Output panel. If an error occurs while attempting to consume the web service, Flash tries to trigger the `onFault` function, if it exists.

➠ 15.5   Entering Code in the Actions Panel

➠ 25.3   Creating Bindings

➠ 25.8   Loading Content from Different Domains

➠ 25.9   Using the DataHolder Component

➠ 25.11   Calling Web Services Using Flash Remoting

➠ 25.12   Formatting Results Using the Bindings Tab

➠ 25.13   Debugging Web Service and XML Documents

Actions panel
`F9`

Components panel
`Ctrl` `F7`
`⌘` `F7`

Property inspector
`Ctrl` `F3`
`⌘` `F3`

Component Inspector panel
`Alt` `F7`
`Option` `F7`

Even though you're creating the connection to the web service manually using ActionScript, you still need to have a copy of the WebService-Connector component in your library.

25.11   Calling Web Services Using Flash Remoting

Actions panel
[F9]

Property inspector
[Ctrl] [F3]
[⌘] [F3]

Component Inspector panel
[Alt] [F7]
[Option] [F7]

_____

You must install the free Flash Remoting components (available from Macromedia) before you can work with Flash Remoting. These components install libraries that you include into your SWF files when you publish them.

Although no new functionality has been added to Flash Remoting in Flash MX 2004 at the time of writing, you still have a choice between using the newer way of data connection with web services and the older method of Flash Remoting. Before you can take advantage of Flash Remoting, you need to install the Flash Remoting Installer (available for Windows and Macintosh) so you can use the proper code libraries that are added to the Flash directories. These .AS files are then compiled with the SWF file when you publish the FLA.

The example in Section 25.10 can be rewritten for Flash Remoting as follows:

```
#include "NetServices.as"
var callback = new Object();
callback.onResult = function(result) {
  trace(result);
};
var WebServiceURL =
  "http://services.xmethods.net/soap/urn:xmethods-DomainChecker.wsdl";
var gatewayURL = "http://localhost:8500/flashservices/gateway/";
var ws_conn = NetServices.createGatewayConnection(gatewayURL);
var myWS = ws_conn.getService(WebServiceURL, callback);
myWS.checkDomain("macromedia.com");
```

If an error occurs while attempting to consume the web service, a SWF file then tries to trigger the `callback.onStatus` function, if it exists.

More information and examples for Flash Remoting MX can be found at

```
http://www.macromedia.com/software/flashremoting/
```

If you've installed Updater 3 for ColdFusion MX or have ColdFusion MX 6.1 (also known as Red Sky) installed, you might have to enable Flash Remoting support in the XML configuration files. More information can be found at this URL (broken here to fit in print, but keep it all on one line):

```
http://www.macromedia.com/support/coldfusion/j2ee/
  cfmxj2ee_enabling.html#enablefr
```

Flash Remoting comes included with ColdFusion MX. It is available for purchase if you're using ASP.NET and Java. There is even a group of people who created a version of Flash Remoting that's able to work with PHP, called AMFPHP. AMFPHP is free to download and install.

25.12　Formatting Results Using the Bindings Tab

If you're using the WebServiceConnector or XMLConnector components in Flash MX Professional 2004 and want to format your data before binding it to a ComboBox, List, or other component, you're in luck. Use the Bindings tab in the Component Inspector panel and click the binding you want to format. With the binding selected, change the value for formatter from none to one of the following: Boolean, Compose String, Custom Formatter, Date, Rearrange Fields, or Number Formatter.

For example, if you were consuming a web service or XML document that contained an array of items (a blog, for example) you can set the List component's dataProvider property to the array of items in the blog. This ultimately leads to a list of all the columns being displayed in the List component. In order to format the value, select Rearrange Fields for the formatter, and then double-click the Value column beside the formatter options to open up the Rearrange Fields dialog. In the Fields Definitions input box, type label=title, where *title* is the name of one of the values in the blog object. Click OK to close the dialog and return to the Stage and test the movie. You will now see the List component's label set to the title of the blog entry.

If you want to bind multiple values to the label, you can modify the formatter option value to label='<title> (<creator>)'. Note that now the values are enclosed in angle brackets (< >), and the blog creator's name appears in parentheses.

Setting the label parameter for the List component

➡ 25.3 Creating
Bindings

**Component Inspector
panel**
Alt F7
Option F7

25.13 Debugging Web Service and XML Documents

Actions panel
F9

Output panel
F2

If you experience problems with your web services and XML, Macromedia has included a method to output some events to a log that is displayed in the Output panel. This helps you debug the SWF file, which helps pinpoint any errors that may be occurring and allow you to fix the problems. To enable the logging feature, simply enter the following snippet into your Flash document as a frame action:

```
_global.__dataLogger = new mx.data.binding.Log();
```

To disable the log, set the logger to null, like so:

```
_global.__dataLogger = null;
```

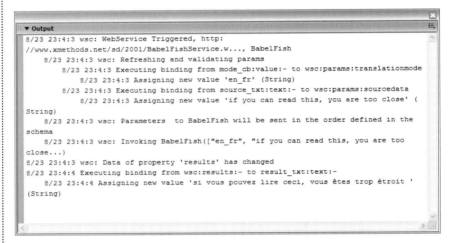

When you test your Flash document, Flash displays a detailed log of events in the Output panel, as shown here. This helps you determine the cause of problems if your applications are behaving unexpectedly. The events which appear in the Output panel include:

■ Executing bindings

■ Calling web service methods

■ Loading XML documents

■ Web service and XML events for status and result

■ Events for validated data fields

TESTING AND PUBLISHNG TASKS

PANEL

EYES
HAIR
MAKE-UP
MOUTH
SKIN

Hair Styles

CHAPTER 26

Testing and Debugging the Movie

THERE ARE TWO AREAS where you need to confirm for any Flash content you create: that the content will load smoothly and in a timely fashion when viewed on the Web, and that your ActionScript works as expected.

The first issue is handled via the Bandwidth Profiler, and the second uses both the Output and Debugger panels.

- 26.1 **Using the test environment**
- 26.2 **Using the Bandwidth Profiler**
- 26.3 **Debugging with the Output panel**
- 26.4 **Using the Debugger panel**
- 26.5 **Using breakpoints**

26.1   Using the Test Environment

Flash allows you to test your Flash content within the authoring environment via the Test Movie, Test Scene, and Debug Movie options.

Testing a Movie

Although you create the FLA file in the authoring environment, the final content is created by running the SWF file via the Flash Player. You can compile the FLA into the SWF and view it within the Flash authoring tool with the Control > Test Movie menu option.

The test environment may not give an accurate representation of the final Flash presentation. In particular, it may not use the same version of the Flash Player that is installed in your browser, and it does not read the HTML/XHTML file that Flash creates when you publish for the Web. You are strongly advised to publish your Flash content and view it through the browser at regular intervals.

The test environment is fundamental to producing Flash content, and you should use it often to constantly confirm that your most recent additions to the FLA work as expected.

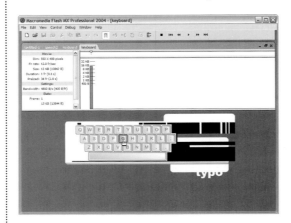

The following additional options are available:

- You can limit the test to compile only the current Timeline (either the current scene or the current movie clip, depending on which you have open) with Control > Test Scene.

- You can test a movie in debug mode by selecting Control > Debug Movie. This will open a new window showing the playing SWF; for simplicity, this is called the test environment in this book.

- You can compile an entire project with Control > Test Project. This option only appears in the Professional version of Flash, and is grayed out unless you have a project currently open in the Project panel.

Differences between Testing and Publishing

The test environment has features that you will not find when viewing a SWF via the standalone Flash Player or through a browser:

- Error windows will pop up during execution if any errors are found.

- Trace commands will cause information to appear in the Output panel by default.

- Debugging information is available via the Debugger panel if you are in debug mode.

- Bandwidth information is available via the Bandwidth Profiler (select View > Bandwidth Profiler when you are in the test environment).

26.2   Using the Bandwidth Profiler

When you view Flash content from your local machine, it loads almost instantaneously. Once deployed on the Web, content loading is limited by bandwidth, and your SWF will no longer load immediately. The Bandwidth Profiler allows you to see (and fix) the impact of this effect.

Using the Bandwidth Profiler to Simulate Web Delivery

The Bandwidth Profiler tests the ability of a SWF to stream and investigates the timings involved in playing back the SWF over a limited bandwidth connection.

To compile the current FLA into a SWF and test it for playback over a limited bandwidth connection:

1 Choose Control > Test Movie to enter the test environment. If the Bandwidth Profiler is not present, select View > Bandwidth Profiler (in the test environment). Also, select View > Streaming Graph (in the test environment) if it is not already checked.

2 Choose View > Simulate Download from the authoring environment to simulate download of the SWF over a limited-bandwidth web connection. You can select the speed of the connection you want to simulate via the test environment's View > Download Settings submenu.

The SWF will simulate the running of the SWF on the Web and will only be able to play frames as they are loaded (or *streamed*) in. Playback will include any pauses caused by limited bandwidth.

The Bandwidth Profiler shows this graphically at the top of its graph; the solid bar (B) shows the frames that have already loaded and are available to be played. The playhead (A) is the current frame being played. If the playhead ever catches up with the end of the bar—i.e., if (A) is ever at the same frame as (B)—it will have to stop until additional frames are loaded.

The cause of the pause can be investigated further by looking at the profiler graph itself.

The bars (C) represent the loading process in kilobytes, and the thick line (D) shows the bandwidth limit. If this line is crossed, as in (E), then a pause will occur. The height of the peak tells you the amount of content that has to be loaded before the playhead can begin playing again.

Several options will fix this effect, thus allowing streaming to occur without pauses:

Add additional frames before the peak. By adding new frames before the peak, you allow more time for content to stream in. The simplest way to do this is to lengthen the duration of animations before the peak *without* adding any new assets.

FLASH WORKSPACE

AUTHORING TASKS

SCRIPTING TASKS

TESTING AND PUBLISHING TASKS

WHAT'S NEW

Bandwidth Profiler (toggle)
[Ctrl] [B]
[⌘] [B]

Streaming graph
[Ctrl] [G]
[⌘] [G]

Clicking any bar in the Bandwidth Profiler graph will make the SWF jump to that frame.

The Flash MX 2004 Bandwidth Profiler addresses SWF compression. Previous versions of Flash do not and will give incorrect results (the profiles will show values for an uncompressed SWF only).

Frame by frame graph
[Ctrl] [F]
[⌘] [F]

———

For a detailed hardcopy of file size data, select File > Publish Settings, go to the Flash tab, and check Generate Size Report. When you click Publish at the bottom of the window, a text report will appear in the Output panel.

———

The Bandwidth Profiler only simulates download over the Web for the current SWF. If this SWF loads in additional SWFs or other media (such as sound, video, or text files) these will not be bandwidth limited.

Simplify your assets. By optimizing your symbols and media (sound and video), which reduces preceding file size, you can reduce the peak.

Preload some (or all) of your assets. By stopping (or pausing) your Timeline until a significant amount (or even all) of it has loaded, you prevent pauses once it starts playing.

Using the Bandwidth Profiler to Investigate Per-Frame File Sizes

As well as investigating streaming, the Bandwidth Profiler can be configured to show the file size associated with each frame. This allows you to identify the frames that require the most bandwidth.

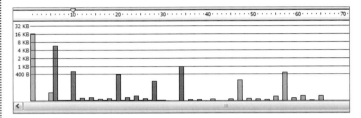

To change to this view, select View > Frame By Frame Graph. Occasionally, you will find that the largest peak shown in the streaming graph is not the same as the one in the frame by frame graph. If the biggest frame in the frame by frame graph comes before the peak in the streaming graph, the former frame is probably the real problem in your streaming strategy.

Bandwidth and ActionScript

There are a number of common issues that the Bandwidth Profiler will throw up in ActionScript-heavy sites. The following points will help you deal with them:

- If you find that an ActionScript gotoAndPlay() or gotoAndStop() doesn't seem to be going to the right frame, use the Bandwidth Profiler to make sure that the frame you are jumping to has streamed in. If it hasn't, Flash will jump to the last frame currently loaded.

- Component class definitions will load in at frame 1 by default. This can be undesirable because the user will see a blank screen for a few moments. To fix this, specify another frame. Select File > Publish Settings > Flash tab, then click the Settings button next to the ActionScript Version drop-down. In the ActionScript Settings window, change the Export Frame For Classes from 1 to Frame 2.. Changing the export frame to frame 2 allows you to at least add a site loading message at frame 1 rather than showing that blank screen!

- You should *never* change the load order from Bottom Up on the Flash tab of the Publish Settings if you follow the usual convention of placing all actions on the top-most layer of each Timeline. Doing so would mean that symbols appear *after* the controlling ActionScript, giving Flash nothing to attach event scripts to. This may cause nonexecution of much of your event driven code.

26.3   Debugging with the Output Panel

Using the `trace()` action allows you to send debug information to the Output panel during testing. The trace window will pop up automatically as soon as your script encounters a trace action. You can force it to appear manually in the Test Environment by choosing Window > Output.

You would typically use the `trace()` action when you want to

- View the changing state of a variable.

- Check program flow proceeds as expected by tracing messages (such as "function is now executing") at critical points in your code

- Tracing timing information to see how fast parts of your code are executing (this is much better than showing values in a text field, as text field update is one of the things that really slows Flash down, and would make your timing results inaccurate).

Using the trace() Action with Variables

The `trace()` action will send its argument to the Output panel every time a trace action is encountered during code execution. For example, the line `trace("hello");` would produce the output shown here.

Usually, you want to know the value of a variable. If you have a variable x and want to know its value following a calculation, you use `trace(x);`.

Although the `trace()` action takes one argument, you can use string concatenation to form a string. The following code includes a `trace()` action that allows you to see the values of both variables i and j as the loop increments:

```
for (i = 0; i < 6; i = i + 2) {
  j = 2 * i;
  trace("i: "+i+"\nj: "+j+"\n");
}
```

Debug Movie
Ctrl Shift Enter
⌘ Shift Enter

———

Flash recognizes any character preceded with a backslash (\) as a control code. The \n control code is commonly used with `trace()` and represents a newline.

———

If you try to trace a variable that has not been defined yet (or has been equated to an expression or call that gives no value), you will see a value of `undefined`.

Stop debugging
F11

Debugger panel
Shift F4

Although Flash 5 introduced the Debugger panel, many Action-Script users still prefer the Output panel because it allows you to create more precise debugging information (the Debugger panel can get a little crowded, especially in Action-Script-heavy FLAs that use components.

Rather than deleting `trace()` actions following testing, consider commenting them out by changing them to `//trace()`. This allows you to reinstate them easily if you feel the need for detailed debugging later.

You can tell Flash to ignore `trace()` actions when publishing via File > Publish Settings > Flash tab > Omit Trace Actions.

Using the trace() Action with Instances

When you are working with instances, you can trace each property with `for..in`. The following code will trace all properties of an object instance `myObj`:

```
myObj = {x:45, y:true, z:"sheepdip"};
for (prop in myObj) {
  trace("property " + prop + " of myObj is " + myObj[prop]);
}
```

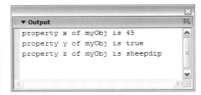

```
▼ Output
property x of myObj is 45
property y of myObj is true
property z of myObj is sheepdip
```

TESTING KEYBOARD INPUTS

The Flash authoring environment will listen for keypresses at all times (so that it can respond to keyboard shortcuts), and this may mask them from any SWF you are testing. This may be important if you are building forms or other advanced text-entry applications. To stop Flash from masking keypresses, select Control > Disable Keyboard Shortcuts when you are in the test environment.

26.4   Using the Debugger Panel

The Debugger panel gives you a real-time view of all data on any timeline within the running SWF. You can also manually change any value you see.

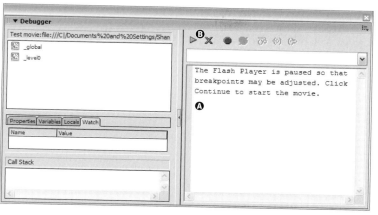

To start a debugging session, select Control > Debug Movie. If your FLA contains ActionScript, you will see a message as shown (A). Click the button (B) to start the SWF and debugger.

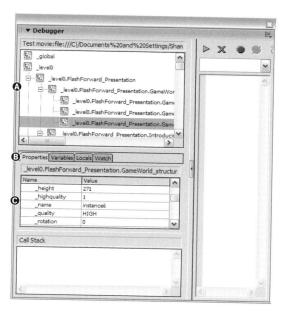

The Display List pane (A) shows the Timeline hierarchy. Clicking any movie clip in this hierarchy allows you to view the clip's properties and other data associated with its Timeline. This information is accessed via the tabbed area (B) and will appear in the pane (C).

Continues

26.4 Using the Debugger Panel *(continued)*

Viewing Movie Clip Properties

To view or change any movie clip property, select the movie clip you want to examine from the top pane, then select the Properties tab. This will show you all properties associated with the movie clip and their values.

To change any property, double-click the value. It will become a text entry area, allowing you to enter a new value. As soon as you press the Return or Enter keys, the movie clip will change its Stage appearance to reflect the new value.

Viewing Data

To view all data currently within a timeline (or "scoped to the timeline"), select any movie clip in the top pane as before and then click the Variables tab.

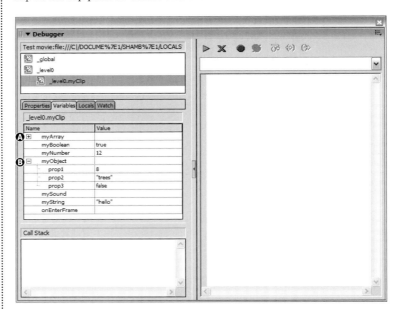

Any complex data type (such as an array or object) will be shown with a little + against it (A). Clicking the + will show a tree diagram of the data type's properties (B). Notice that event handlers are also included as "data"; this is a good way of confirming that your event handlers are attached to the correct movie clip if they don't seem to be working.

26.4 Using the Debugger Panel *(continued)*

You can change a variable or property as per the last section—simply double-click the value and enter a new one.

The Watch List

You will often find that your SWF contains a lot of data, particularly if it contains components, screens, or slides (because the classes associated with them create a lot of data!). In these cases, you will want to ignore all data except a few select variables. The Watch list allows you to set up a custom list of variables to address this situation..

To watch a variable, you must first add it to the Watch list. You can do *either* of the following:

- Right-click/⌘-click the variable in the Variables tab and select Watch. This will be grayed out if your selected data is not capable of being watched. A little icon ● will appear next to your chosen data. Click the Watch tab to see it in the Watch list.

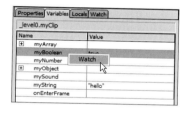

- From the Watch tab, right-click/⌘-click the lower pane in the Watch tab and select Watch (A). A blank entry will appear with <undefined> in the Name column (B). Double-click/⌘-click in the column and enter the *full absolute* path to the data (C). A full path to the variable `myBoolean` in the movie clip `myClip` (which is on the main Timeline) would be `_level0.myClip.myBoolean`.

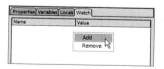 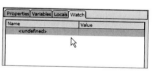 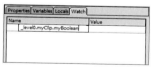

You can add as many items to the Watch list as you need, but be aware that the Watch list is *not* saved with the FLA.

➡ 26.5 Using Break-
     points

If real-time debugger operation is too fast for you to see what is happening, select Modify > Document to temporarily drop the frame rate before testing. A frame rate of 1–5 is usually much less confusing!

The debugger will only show instances or variables that exist on the current frame. If a variable suddenly disappears, it is either because the Timeline the variable exists on has been deleted, or the variable has been deleted by ActionScript.

Unless you enter the test environment with Control > Debug Movie, the Debugger panel will remain inactive. If you close and then reopen the panel, it will also become inactive.

26.5   Using Breakpoints

➡ 26.4 Using the
        Debugger
        Panel

Continue
[F10]

Stop debugging
[F11]

———

You should add break-
points only to lines that
contain instructions
that will be compiled. If
you do add breakpoints
to other lines (such as
lines containing com-
ments or a } brace
only), Flash will raise an
error when it attempts
to create the SWF to
perform a test movie.

Although real-time debugging is useful for seeing how values change over time, it is sometimes difficult to debug the scripts that cause the value changes in the first place. To
debug a script, you need to be able to temporarily stop the script at critical lines where
you think there might be a problem and note the value changes the line has caused. Once
you are happy with your changes, you should typically restart the script and continue to
the next critical line. Such a stop point is called a *breakpoint*.

There are two stages in working with breakpoints: setting breakpoints in the Actions
panel and testing them in the Debugger panel.

Setting Breakpoints

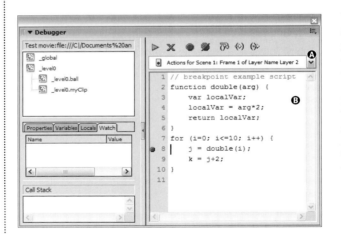

To set a breakpoint or clear an existing one in the authoring environment, click in the gray margin to the left of the
line you want to add a breakpoint in the Actions panel
script pane. A red dot will appear against the line to signify a breakpoint.

You also have the option to
set (or modify) breakpoints
just before starting the
debugger in test mode. Select
Control **>** Debug Movie, then
select a script from the top-
right drop-down menu (A).
Your chosen script will appear
in the pane below it (B). The
same features just noted can
be used to set or reset your
breakpoints.

Note that when you add breakpoints using the second method, the breakpoints will only
exist for the current test; when you come out of the test, the breakpoints will disappear
(i.e., they are *temporary* breakpoints). If you use the first method, they will still be there.

26.5   Using Breakpoints *(continued)*

Testing with Breakpoints

To test your script using breakpoints, test using the Debugger panel via Control > Debug Movie, then click the Continue icon ▷ at the top of the Debugger panel to start debugging. As soon as the Flash Player hits the first breakpoint, it will pause execution, and you will see the following in the right debugger pane.

You can view or set any variable or property values (as noted in the last section) while the SWF is paused. Once you are ready to move on, you can use the Breakpoint menu in the debugger.

This consists of two halves. The first half (A) allows you to decide what to do next with respect to breakpoints. The second half (B) allows you to move line by line within the current script so you can see what is happening at lines around the breakpoint.

To move between breakpoints and/or edit them, use the first set of icons. Once program execution has stopped at a breakpoint, you can:

- Click the Continue icon ▷ again. Normal execution will resume until the next time a breakpoint is seen. If your breakpoint is in a loop, program execution will halt at the same point because the loop takes program execution back to the same breakpoint.

- Click the Stop Debugging icon ✕ . This will exit debugging, and the Debugger panel will become disabled. SWF execution will continue with no breaks.

- Click the Toggle Breakpoint icon ⬤ to remove or add a breakpoint at the current line.

- Click the Remove All Breakpoints icon ⬤ to ignore all breakpoints. The test will proceed without stopping at any further breakpoints, and the debugger will stay active. The breakpoints that you added will still be there when you exit the test.

To switch to moving between individual lines of your code, you can use the second set of icons. When you move between lines, the last line executed is denoted by the arrow icon ⮕. At the end of each line, you can look at or change any data using the facilities noted in the bulleted list above. When the program execution jumps to a function or other program block that includes local variables, they are shown in the Locals tab. Also, when program execution jumps to a function, the function name is listed in the Call stack.

- Click the Step In icon ⬇ to execute the next line and stop. If the next line is within a function, then the debugger will step in to the function and debug that as well.

- Click the Step Over icon ⬆ to execute all lines in the current block. Use this icon when (for example) you are in a loop and don't want to stop at each line of every loop iteration.

- Click the Step Out icon ⬆ to execute the next line in the listing. If the next line is within a function, then the debugger will step out of the function by running all lines of it and jumping back to the calling script. This means that you do not see program execution inside the function.

Step in
F6

Step over
F7

Step out
F8

A local variable is one that has been defined within a block (such as a function or loop) using the var keyword.

You will typically use the Step In icon to confirm that all the function calls you are making go to the function you expect. Once you have confirmed this, you can use Step Out to skip debugging the function code because you have already confirmed it works.

CHAPTER **27**

FLASH WORKSPACE

AUTHORING TASKS

SCRIPTING TASKS

TESTING AND PUBLISHING TASKS

WHAT'S NEW

Publishing and Deploying Flash Content

IT'S IMPORTANT TO GET a good handle on publishing Flash files for the Web or other media. A Flash document must be published before it can be viewed in the Flash Player. You can also publish a FLA into other formats, such as image or QuickTime movies. Executable files can be created that have the Flash Player included right within the EXE. This means that the file can be distributed on a CD-ROM and you do not have to worry whether the user has the correct version of the Flash Player installed or not. With the flexibility Flash offers, as well as a wealth of options, you have a lot of control over the files you publish.

- 27.1   **Understanding the files created by Flash**
- 27.2   **Choosing publishing options**
- 27.3   **Publishing for the Web**
- 27.4   **Publishing for the desktop**
- 27.5   **Publishing bitmap formats**
- 27.6   **Publishing QuickTime movies**
- 27.7   **Creating sites**
- 27.8   **Detecting Flash Player**
- 27.9   **Creating projects**
- 27.10 **Publishing projects**

27.1   Understanding the Files Created by Flash

Publish Settings

Ctrl Shift F12
⌘ Shift F12

———

Create publish profiles
in the Publish Settings
dialog. Click the Create
New Profile button and
choose a name for the
profile before making
your selections.

———

In order to use the
same publish profile
with multiple Flash
documents, you need
to first create the pro-
file, export the profile,
and then import it into
any other files where
you want to use the
same settings.

By default, Flash creates two files when you publish your Flash movie, a SWF and an HTML template. The SWF file contains all the animation or web services you built in your FLA. The HTML that's created is a bare-bones template that embeds the SWF into a web page so it can be seen in a web browser. There are several other options available when you publish a FLA file, such as what version of ActionScript will be used in the SWF file, or what quality the audio and JPEG images will be in the application.

The Publish Settings dialog also allows you to specify other files that are generated by Flash when publishing your files. Options include SWF files and HTML files as mentioned earlier, but you can also have Flash generate GIF, JPEG, and PNG images of your Flash movies, as well as Windows- and Mac-compatible Projector files (files that include your Flash movie and an integrated standalone Flash Player), or you can even generate a QuickTime movie of your Flash application.

FLASH APPLICATIONS ON A LARGE SCALE

If you are creating a large Flash application, it's always advisable that you draft out your project first in a program such as Visio. Programs like Visio help you organize flowcharts and other visual documents. Particularly when you are working with a team of designers and developers, it's very important to establish a clear direction to take the project in. Then Flash helps you out further by its Project and Site creation tools.

27.2   Choosing Publishing Options

Publish settings can be customized by using the Publish Settings dialog. You can launch the dialog by selecting File **>** Publish Settings from the main menu. The Publish Settings dialog allows you to choose which files will be created or replaced each time you publish the FLA file, and you can customize the settings for every file that Flash creates.

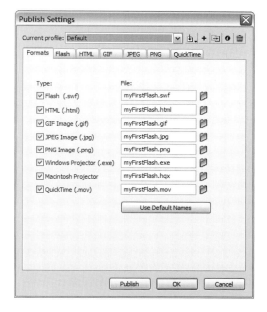

You can see in the graphic that every one of the file formats has been selected, and that most of the formats appear as tabs near the top of the dialog. When you click each of these tabs, you can customize the publish settings for each format. To add or remove format types, simply select or deselect the check box under the Type label in the Formats tab. You can also rename the file for each of the formats being published. By default, Flash uses the same name as the FLA document and only changes the extension. However, if you want Flash to generate `index.html`, for example, instead of the default file name, you only need to change the value in the File column for that specific format type.

Flash MX 2004 introduces publish profiles, which allow you to specify different publish settings for your FLA files. This means you can use the exact same settings for multiple files so the audio quality and other settings are consistent throughout a site. Publish profiles can be imported or exported as XML files, which allows you to share the publish settings among different FLA files; you can even distribute the XML publish profile file to other employees.

➧ 6.11 Publish Settings

➧ 7.13 Exporting Movies

➧ 27.3 Publishing for the Web

➧ 27.4 Publishing for the Desktop

➧ 27.5 Publishing Bitmap Formats

➧ 27.6 Publishing QuickTime Movies

Publish Settings
Ctrl Shift F12
⌘ Shift F12

When publishing files, you must make sure you don't overwrite a document that you have edited elsewhere. For example, if you edit the HTML file associated with the FLA you're working on, you will overwrite the HTML when you publish the file. If you deselect HTML in the Format tab of the Publish Settings dialog, then the file will not be overwritten.

27.3 Publishing for the Web

The HTML tab includes several options for aligning Flash content in an HTML page. You can also change the size of the SWF and control basic playback as well as access the version detection settings from the HTML tab.

Pressing the Set button next to Audio Stream or Audio Event opens the Sound Settings dialog and allows you to modify the quality settings for each sound file.

At the time of writing, there are major changes expected for embedding SWF files in an HTML document. Refer to www.macromedia.com /devnet/activecontent for the latest information and links.

Click the Flash tab near the top of the Publish Settings dialog to display the following graphic.

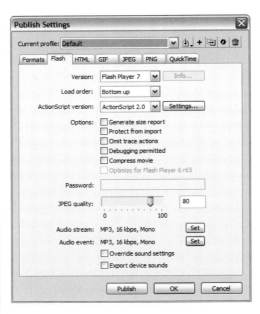

You can change all the settings revolving around SWF files, JPEG, and sound quality, as well as which version of Flash and ActionScript you are targeting. If you are creating a very basic SWF, you should set Version to as low a Flash Player version as possible in order to be compatible with the greatest number of visitors possible. The values in the Version drop-down menu range from Flash Player 1 all the way up to Flash Player 7. The ActionScript Version combo box has two options: ActionScript 1.0 and ActionScript 2.0. If you're using ActionScript 2.0 content in your FLA and are using classes, you can click the Settings button next to the drop-down menu to launch the ActionScript Settings dialog. This dialog allows you to specify any additional class paths to your class files as well as to set which frame the classes will be exported on.

The six check boxes can control everything from preventing other people from importing your SWF file into other files to choosing whether you want to let people debug the Flash movie remotely or password-protect the ability to perform remote debugging.

Generate Size Report Displays a report of all the symbols, frames, scenes, fonts, and bitmaps within your FLA and how big each item is within the SWF file. This can help you debug your file and see if you need to compress images further or reuse fonts to help reduce the overall file size of the SWF. The report is displayed in the Output panel within Flash as well as in an external text file in the same directory as your FLA.

Protect From Import Makes it more difficult for users to import your SWF file into a new Flash document. Selecting this option requires you to specify a password in the Password text field below, which means those importing your file must enter a password before they can import the file. Note that selecting the Protect From Import does not make it impossible to import the files. There are tools out there that can remove this setting from a SWF file, thus disabling any sort of protection.

Omit Trace Actions Causes Flash to ignore trace statements in the current SWF file. This is a good option to select before uploading files to a production environment. Even though trace statements are displayed in the Output panel in the test environment, omitting them from the SWF file will result in a slight performance increase.

Debugging Permitted Allows you to enable or disable remote debugging of your SWF documents. Enabling this option password-protects the ability to debug the SWF file by entering a password in the Password text field below. Selecting this option and publishing the SWF creates an SWD in the same directory as your SWF. This allows you to remotely debug the Flash movie within the Flash debugger.

Compress Movie Only available when publishing for Flash Player version 6 or later (and not available when publishing for Flash Lite 1). This option reduces the overall file size of the SWF file that you publish.

Optimize For Flash Player 6 r65 Disabled unless you select Flash Player 6 from the Version drop-down menu at the top of the dialog. Users must have Flash Player 6 r65 or higher to take advantage of increased performance.

Password Enabled only if you select the Protect From Import option or Debugging Permitted option from the check boxes above. Enabling either of these options and specifying a password means that users must enter the correct password before they can import the SWF movie or view the movie's debugging information.

JPEG Quality slider Allows you to set the amount of compression that's applied to images within the SWF movie. The lower the number, the more information is compressed and ultimately the lower the quality of the image. Setting the JPEG quality at 100 means images will not be compressed and your files will be larger. You can override this setting for specific images in the FLA file by modifying the image's properties in the Library. Make sure the Compression drop-down is set to Photo (JPEG) and deselect the Use Document Default quality. This enables you to have different compression settings for each image in your Library.

➥ 27.8 Detecting Flash Player

Publish Settings
Ctrl Shift F12
⌘ Shift F12

———

If you're using Flash MX Professional, you will have an additional version listed in the Version drop-down menu called Flash Lite 1.0, which is a profile you can use when you're developing for NTT DoCoMo handheld devices.

———

Load order refers to which order the layers will be loaded into the SWF movie. By default the load order is "bottom up," meaning that the bottom layers are loaded first and the top layers are loaded last. The other option for load order is "top down," where the top layer is loaded first and the bottom layers are loaded last.

27.4   Publishing for the Desktop

Publish Settings

⌈Ctrl⌉ ⌈Shift⌉ ⌈F12⌉
⌈⌘⌉ ⌈Shift⌉ ⌈F12⌉

———

Publishing projector files
can lead to some very
large files. Publishing a
blank movie with no
instances on the Stage or
symbols in the Library,
the Windows Projector is
approximately 965 KB.
The same file as a Mac-
intosh Projector (an HQX
file) is about 1,770 KB.
In comparison, the SWF
file generated is a mere
1 KB.

Flash allows you to publish files, called projectors, which are designed to be used as standalone applications. This means that the users don't need to have the latest Flash Player, or even a Flash Player at all. The SWF and Flash Player are bundled together in a single EXE file, which launches the standalone Flash Player when the user runs the file.

To create a projector, you need to open the Publish Settings dialog and select either Windows Projector (`.exe`) or Macintosh Projector (`.hqx`) from the Formats tab. You can see that selecting either one of these check boxes doesn't add any new tabs in the dialog. The file will be published into the same directory as the FLA you are working on.

There are many utilities that work hand-in-hand with Flash projectors. Third-party programs have been created to help you develop solutions that integrate tightly with an operating system such as Windows. For example, this software enables you to create desktop applications, copy files to the hard drive, and more. Check out `www.northcode.com/swfstudio` and `www.flashjester.com` for examples of software tying in with projectors.

27.5 Publishing Bitmap Formats

Flash supports publishing to three bitmap image formats: GIF (`.gif`), JPEG (`.jpg`), or PNG (`.png`). These options can be selected in the Formats tab of the Publish Settings dialog. Each option adds a new tab at the top of the dialog below the Current Profile drop-down menu where you can customize the settings for each format. The GIF tab allows you to publish the movie as either a static or animated GIF as well as set looping options.

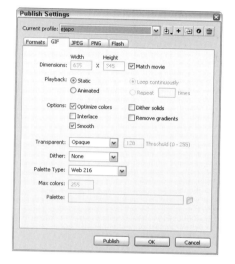

Dimensions Change the image's dimensions by changing the values. Change the width and height to create a thumbnail image of your Flash movie without having to open up another program such as Fireworks or Photoshop. If you check Match Movie, Flash matches the size of the GIF to the dimensions of the Stage.

Options Allows you to choose the quality and appearance of the image. Optimizing, interlacing, or smoothing the image results in output of varying quality and appearance.

Transparent Specifies whether the background of the GIF is completely transparent or alpha (a partial transparency). If alpha is chosen, you set the amount of threshold.

Dither Specifies the kind of dither used for the GIF. Dither alters pixels to try to approximate colors that are not available in the color palette. Dithering can increase file size but improve the way the image looks. Diffusion is the better quality (but higher file size) of the two options that are available.

Palette Type Tells Flash which type of palette it should use to manage colors, such as Web 216 (the 216 web-safe color palette), Adaptive, Web Snap Adaptive, or a custom palette. Selecting Custom enables the Palette text field below where you can either enter a path to a palette location, or browse for a palette location by clicking the folder icon and launching the Open dialog, where you can select a custom palette file such as a Color Table (`.act`) file.

➥ 6.11 Publish Settings

Publish Settings
Ctrl Shift F12
⌘ Shift F12

By setting a value in the Filter Options drop-down menu, it is possible to compress the PNG files further and reduce file sizes in most cases.

Custom palettes are useful if you have a series of SWF files that you want to share the same color palette so you won't have any minor color differences in your company logo or other symbols in your Flash file.

FLASH WORKSPACE

AUTHORING TASKS

SCRIPTING TASKS

TESTING AND PUBLISHING TASKS

WHAT'S NEW

Continues ●

27.5   Publishing Bitmap Formats *(continued)*

You can export a range of GIF files to publish by specifying a range of frames on the Timeline. Place the labels of #first and #last on a new layer to tell Flash where to begin and stop exporting.

By default, publishing a Flash movie as a JPEG or PNG will export only the first frame. You can specify a different frame to publish by creating a frame label named #Static.

PNG files are a cross-platform bitmap that is the native format of Macromedia Fireworks. With support for transparent images much better than a GIF, PNGs have their own separate alpha channel.

You cannot load progressive JPEG files into Flash.

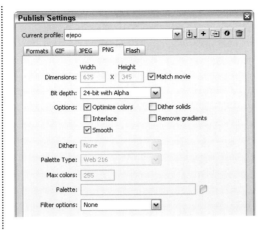

The PNG tab is very similar to the GIF settings. It allows you to customize the published image's dimensions similar to the other two bitmap formats. You can specify one of three values for Bit Depth: 8-bit (256 color image), 24-bit (thousands of colors), or 24-bit With Alpha (thousands of colors with an alpha channel). The higher the bit depth, the higher the file size will be. The Optimize Colors check box helps reduce file sizes slightly by making sure unused colors are not included in the image's color table. An interlaced PNG will incrementally display in a web browser as it loads instead of displaying after it has completely loaded. Smoothing a PNG can improve its quality somewhat and make text look a little crisper, but it can also cause the image to look jagged similar to aliased text if you aren't using a solid color for the image background. Dither, Palette Type, Max Colors, and Palette are all disabled unless you are set the Bit Depth drop-down menu to 8-bit.

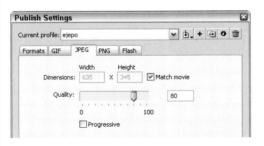

The JPEG tab is much simpler than the GIF tab because it has only three options. This publishing option allows you to create 24-bit bitmap images.

Dimensions Similar to the GIF tab, you can set the dimensions of the image to be published or use the Match Movie check box.

Quality Setting the quality to a low number produces smaller files with less quality. You can use a high quality, which means larger file sizes as a result.

Progressive Controls whether the JPEG image will be progressive and load incrementally in a web browser, making it appear to load faster on slower Internet connections.

27.6 Publishing QuickTime Movies

Flash allows you to publish your Flash documents as QuickTime movie files. This allows you to work with the QuickTime player (and editing tools) to integrate SWF content with other media files. It also enables you to create media that's intended for broadcast or integrate a SWF layer with video content.

You should remember that the latest version of SWF (for Flash Player 7) is not supported in the QuickTime player. Flash Player 6 isn't supported either. You have to publish your SWFs as version 5 or earlier for them to work properly, and you can't include any elements that are specific to version 6 or greater. You also need the QuickTime player installed on your system. Select the Flash tab and select Flash Player 5 from the Version drop-down menu before selecting Publish.

THE INTERNET EXPLORER HASSLE

Around the time of writing, much discussion was rippling among developers about possible changes that are being made to Internet Explorer. It is not clear at this time (due to court appeals) whether changes will be made to the browser and the code you use to embed SWF files. Solutions to help developers cope with possible changes are being developed, including some by Macromedia. Visit www.microsoft.com and www.macromedia.com for the latest information.

Publish Settings
[Ctrl] [Shift] [F12]
[⌘] [Shift] [F12]

If you forget to change the version of your Flash file, you will be alerted to the fact that QuickTime does not have a handler for this kind of movie.

In addition to exporting QuickTime files, you can import them into Flash as well. Quick-Time is also used to facilitate the importing of various kinds of media, from static images to sound.

When you publish your files as QuickTime files, you might lose some of your scripting when the MOV file is played in a player. Make sure that you test your published MOV files thoroughly in the QuickTime player.

27.7   Creating Sites

Project panel
[Shift] [F8]

———

Sites are created in
order to be used in
projects and with ver-
sion control systems.

Flash MX 2004 supports editing sites from remote computers using FTP or a local or network path or by supplying connection info for a version control system. You can create
and edit sites to work with the version control features built into Flash. To define a site:

1 Select File > Edit Sites from the main menu. The Edit Sites dialog opens and allows
   you to create a new site, edit existing sites, and duplicate and remove existing sites.

2 Click the New button to open the Site Definition dialog. You can assign your site a name
   and local folder, as well as the e-mail address and name of the user modifying the files.

3 Use the Connection drop-down menu to choose None, Local/Network, FTP, and
   SourceSafe Database. Choose where you would like to locate your files.

4 After making this selection, fill in the forms that appear with the appropriate information. For example, if you choose FTP you will need to enter information on connecting
   to the server. If you choose to use Local/Network, you need to specify the location of
   the files. If you choose SourceSafe Database, you need to click the Settings button
   before making your settings.

5 Click OK to exit the dialog.

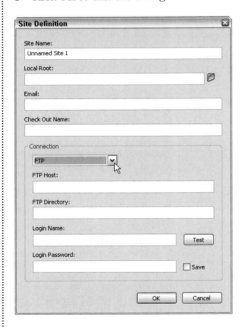

After you create a new site, you can start working with the sites you define in Projects.
Open a new site by choosing File > Open From Site. You can overwrite files on your system using files that are located remotely. Flash will alert you if this option is available
(namely, you have the file on your system to overwrite). This helps you work with the latest version of a file and then upload it when you're finished.

27.8   Detecting Flash Player

You can detect the Flash Player using a new version detection system that is built right into Flash. The Flash Player detection allows you to set the names of the files that are created as part of the system. All you need to do is upload the files that are generated in the following process to the server, and a Flash player detection system is automatically put in place for you.

1 Open the Publish Settings dialog and select the HTML check box under the Formats tab.

2 Select the HTML tab, and then select the Detect Flash Player check box. Click the Settings button.

3 In the Settings dialog, enter file names for your main HTML page and the detection and redirect pages, or use the default names Flash provides. Optionally, you can enter a minor revision of the player to detect for and click OK when you are finished.

When you publish the document, several HTML pages, a GIF file, and a SWF are generated in the directory with your FLA. The files that are generated are as follows:

- **Detection File** The first file your visitor arrives at, which contains the version detection. You pass out or link this URL for your potential visitors.

- **Content File** The file that contains the SWF you publish. Modify the HTML on this page if you want to embed the SWF in a more interesting page.

- **Alternate File** The page containing information about going to download the current Flash Player. Visitors are redirected to this page if they do not have the required Flash Player to view your content.

Continues

27.8 Detecting Flash Player *(continued)*

Publish Settings
[Ctrl][Shift][F12]
[⌘][Shift][F12]

——

You can work with
Flash Player detection
only if you are detect-
ing for Flash Player 4 or
greater. You cannot use
this system to detect for
earlier versions of the
player.

——

You can enter in your
own file names for the
HTML documents that
the detection system
generates. You can also
specify a file on your
hard drive as the alter-
nate content page.

——

If visitors do not have a
Flash Player, or need to
update the player, they
are redirected to a page
that notifies them they
need to visit Macrome-
dia to grab the latest
player.

You can upload the published files to the Web, or you can test the detection on your own computer. Double-click the Detection File (`yourMovie.html`), which will then direct you either to the HTML file containing your SWF or to the alternate document if the correct player is not installed.

27.9   Creating Projects

Available only in Flash Professional, Flash project files group several files together to manage larger projects. A Flash project file has an `.flp` extension and is simply an XML file containing a list of all the files within the project. Unlike a FLA file, a project file is automatically updated by Flash and doesn't need to be saved manually.

1   Create a new project in Flash. There are two ways to create a new Flash project file: you can use the Project panel to create a new project, or you can choose File > New and select a Flash Project from the New Document dialog.

2   After you name your FLP file, if you already have an open project, Flash will prompt you and ask you if you want to close the current project and open the new one.

3   Click OK to open the new project file. Notice the name of the project is now located in both the title of the Project panel and within the root folder of the project.

To associate a project with an existing site, click the Project button  at the top of the Project panel and select Settings from the contextual menu. The Project Settings dialog opens and you can select a predefined site from the Site drop-down menu. If you need to edit or add a new site, you can access the sites by clicking the Version Control button and selecting Edit Sites from the contextual menu. This opens the Site Definition dialog, where you can modify the connection info and site information as needed.

Adding files to your Flash project is accomplished by either clicking the Add File(s) To Project button in the lower right-hand corner of the Project panel or by clicking the Project pop-up menu and selecting Add File from the contextual menu. The Add Files To Project dialog opens, where you can select files to add to your FLP.

➡ 27.7   Creating Sites

➡ 27.10   Publishing Projects

Project panel
Shift F8

———

Version control is built into the project architecture to make sure that those working on projects do not overwrite their teammates' work. It also helps ensure that the most current files, not older versions, are used.

———

Only one project can be open in Flash at a single time.

———

Projects are available only in Flash MX Professional.

27.10   Publishing Projects

➡ 6.11 Publish
          Settings

➡ 27.7 Creating Sites

➡ 27.9 Creating
          Projects

Project panel
[Shift] [F8]

To test a project, choose Test Project from the Project drop-down menu. You must have a default document and either an FLA or an HTML document within the project in order to test it. If you don't have at least one of those, an error message is shown.

The default publish settings are used unless you specify otherwise using publish profiles.

Projects are available only in Flash MX Professional, and only one project can be open in Flash at any given time.

To publish a project, select either Publish Project or Test Project from the Project pop-up menu in the Project panel. If a default document has not been defined for the current document, Flash prompts you to select one from a list of documents that opens. You might need to set particular publish profiles for the FLA files that are within the project you are going to publish. To set a publish profile for a project, follow these steps:

1   Click the Project button in the Project panel and select Settings from the drop-down menu. The Project Settings dialog opens.

2   Select the FLA file you want to set the profile for.

3   Select a publish profile from the Profile drop-down menu at the bottom of the dialog. It displays the profiles that are available for that particular FLA file.

4   Click OK when you are finished.

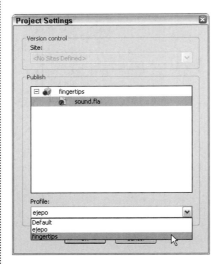

To publish the entire project, all you need to do is select Publish Project from the Project button in the Project panel. After you choose to publish your project, you will see a couple Publishing dialogs appear momentarily while the project is creating the published files.

WHAT'S NEW

APPENDIX

**What's New in
Flash MX 2004**

499

Appendix: What's New in Flash MX 2004

The following table gives an overview of the new features offered by Flash MX 2004 and Flash MX Professional 2004. It includes cross-references to the book sections covering new features, allowing Flash MX users to quickly review new features and workflows.

Flash MX 2004 and Flash MX Professional 2004 have certain differences. Such differences are marked in the tables as follows:

* Feature is supported in Flash MX Professional 2004 only.

** There are differences in support for this feature, typically:

- Partial support in Flash MX 2004 and full support in Flash MX Professional 2004.

- More options are available in Flash MX Professional 2004.

Interface Enhancements

FEATURE	DESCRIPTION	WHERE TO LEARN MORE
Accessibility enhancements Dialog	Keyboard options for all common tasks.	6.8 Keyboard Shortcuts
Menu rationalization	Re-ordering of menu elements, particularly the Insert and Modify menus.	2.4 View Menu 2.5 Insert Menu
Start page	New panel at application start.	7.2 The Start Page
Help panel	Revised Help system.	2.12 Help Menu 5.23 Help Panel
History panel	Advanced undo/redo functionality plus ability to make portions of the history into a new command.	5.15 History Panel
Strings panel	Support for multilanguage site authoring.	5.17 Strings Panel 20.22 Using the Strings Panel
Project panel*	Management of multifile sites using a dedicated project (FLP) file and panel.	5.19 Project Panel 7.6 Starting Flash Projects 27.9 Creating and Managing Projects
Web Services panel*	Allows you to define the web service resources that your site will interact with.	5.13 Web Services Panel 25.1 Defining Web Services
Third-party extensions	JSAPI (JavaScript Advanced Programming Interface) allows third-party extensions to the authoring interface.	14.5 Installing and Uninstalling Commands and Behaviors
AS file editor*	Full-screen ActionScript editor becomes available when you create a new AS (ActionScript) file.	7.5 Starting ActionScript, Communication, or Flash JavaScript Files 15.12 Using External Scripts with #include
Save And Compact	Optimization of saved FLA to remove unused information.	2.2 File Menu
Site management	Macromedia Dreamweaver–style site management.	27.9 Creating and Managing Sites

Design Features

ENHANCEMENT	DESCRIPTION	WHERE TO LEARN MORE
Behaviors	Drag-and-drop ActionScript modules.	5.8 Behaviors Panel 11.2 Understanding Behaviors 14.5 Installing and Uninstalling Commands and Behaviors 25.4 Invoking Web Services Using Behaviors
Timeline effects	Create animated transitions via pre-built effects.	10.17 Understanding Timeline Effects
Screens	Create slide/form based content without the need for timelines.	10.27 Setting Screen Properties and Parameters 10.28 Building Slide Presentations 10.29 Building Form Applications 10.30 Controlling Screens and Adding Transitions
V2 components	Precompiled component "packages."	19.1 Introducing v2 Components
Revised templates**	New templates for mobile devices and other areas.	7.7 Opening from Templates
Spell checker	FLA document spell-checking facilities.	20.23 Spell Checking Flash Documents
New video encoder and Video Import Wizard**	Better video encoder. Import wizard invoked when importing video content to the authoring environment.	13.5 Importing Video 13.9 Optimizing Video
Streaming Flash video**	Streaming video facilities available without the need for a FlashCom server.	14.6 Installing the FLV Exporter and Understanding Codecs
New/enhanced import options	Authoring environment supports import of Adobe PDF and Adobe Illustrator 10 files.	13.12 Importing Illustrator Files 13.13 Importing PDF Files
Text enhancements	Better support for small text.	20.6 Setting Alias Text
HTML/CSS	Enhanced support for HTML tags, including images loaded into HTML text. Support for a subset of the Cascading Style Sheet standard within Flash text.	20.9 Creating Dynamic Text Fields 20.17 Formatting Text Fields Using CSS

New and Enhanced ActionScript Features and Classes

ENHANCEMENT	DESCRIPTION	WHERE TO LEARN MORE
ActionScript 2 class-based coding**	Java-like class structures and compile time strong typing.	16.12 Understanding Flash MX 2004 Class-Based File structures 16.13 Creating Flash MX 2004 Classes
New `PrintJob` class	ActionScript support for runtime printing.	20.25 Using the `PrintJob` Class
New `MovieClipLoader` class	Support for runtime SWF loading.	24.10 Using the `MovieClipLoader` Class
Mouse class enhancements	New mouse wheel support.	20.27 Capturing the Mouse Scroll Wheel
Live sound and video	Real-time sound and video facilities via newly documented classes.	23.12 Playing Back Captured Sound with the `Microphone` Class 23.14 Playing Back Captured Video with the Camera Class

New and Enhanced ActionScript Features and Classes (continued)

ENHANCEMENT	DESCRIPTION	WHERE TO LEARN MORE
Enhancements to the Sound class	Support for MP3 meta tags and runtime MP3 loading.	23.8 Working with Dynamically Loaded Sound 23.10 Retrieving MP3 Sound Meta Tags
Runtime exception handling	Support for JavaScript exceptions.	17.9 The try, catch, and finally Keywords

v2 Components and ActionScript

ENHANCEMENT	DESCRIPTION	WHERE TO LEARN MORE
New v2 components**	Large number of new components.	19.12 Using the Loader Component 19.13 Using the NumericStepper Component 19.14 Using the ProgressBar Component 20.11 Using the Label Component 24.8 Using Components for Loading External Content 25.9 Using the DataHolder Component
New v2 component classes	New classes to deal with depth, focus, and pop-ups.	19.17 Using the DepthManager Class 19.18 Using the FocusManager Class 19.19 Using the PopUpManager Class
Components and dynamic data*	New features for integrating components within applications.	25.3 Creating Bindings 25.6 Importing Schemas

Index

Note to the Reader: Throughout this index boldfaced page numbers indicate primary discussions of a topic.

D

data event handlers, 326
data structures, 314
DataHolder component, **464**
Date class, 392, 394
date-stamps, 395
dates
    retrieving and displaying, 395
    usefulness of, 396
Debug menu, 29
Debug Movie command, 27
Debugger in Windows, 8
Debugger panel, 80, **477–478**
debugging. *See* testing and debugging
Debugging Permitted option, 487
defaultPushButton property, 358
defaults
    palettes, 156
    for scripts, 99
    for sound, 247
Define Web Services dialog, 454
defining
    classes, 306
    web services, 454
delay for code hints, 99
Delete Swatch command, 60
deleting
    color from gradients, 154–155
    components, 339
    events, **401**
    frames and keyframes, **170**
    layers, 171
    primitive parts, **144**
    selection elements, 128
    symbols, 132, 233, 239
    Timeline effects, **184**
delivery, content. *See* content delivery
deploying. *See* publishing and deploying
depth
    instances in, 331
    managing, 357
    preferences for, 97
    in shapes, 151–152
    splitting animation for, 165
DepthManager class, 357
Deselect All command, 20
deselecting selections, 128
Design Panels command, 30
desktop, publishing for, **488**

Detect Accessibility command, 26
detecting
    collision, **410**
    Flash Player, **493–494**
detection files, 493–494
Development Panels command, 30
device fonts, 368
dialogs, 18
dimensions
    for bitmap formats, 489–490
    for Stage, 122
direction
    of curves, **146**
    for XML documents, 459
direction boxes for Timeline effects, 184
Disable Keyboard Shortcuts command, 28
Distort option for Free Transform tool, 51
Distort tool for faux perspectives, **141**
Dither option, 489
do..while statements, **319–320**
docked panel areas, 7–8
Document command, 24
Document Properties dialog, 122
documents. *See* files and documents
domains, loading content from, **462–463**
Don't Close Gaps option, 54
dot notation
    in scripts, **284**
    for variables, **297**
Download Settings command, 22
drag-and-drop animations, 408
dragging marquees, 126
dragOut event handler, 325
dragOver event handler, 325
drawing, **133**
    API for, 407, **417–418**
    external tools for, 136
    options for, 96
    shapes for. *See* shapes
drawTriangle method, 418
Duplicate command, 20
Duplicate Swatch command, 60
Duplicate Symbol dialog, 232
duplicateMovieClip method, 402–403
duplicating. *See* copying
dynamic actions
    attaching events, **401**
    loading
        images, 447

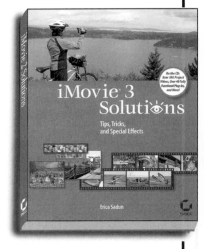
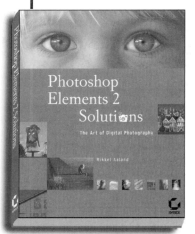